Microsoft® Windows®
2000 Professional

INSTALLATION AND CONFIGURATION
HANDBOOK

Microsoft® Windows® 2000 Professional

INSTALLATION AND CONFIGURATION HANDBOOK

Jim Boyce

Microsoft® Windows® 2000 Professional Installation and Configuration

Copyright© 2000 by Que®

International Standard Book Number: 0-7897-2133-3

Library of Congress Catalog Card Number: 99-65437

Printed in the United States of America

First Printing: January 2000

02   01   00   4   3   2

Trademarks

Warning and Disclaimer

ASSOCIATE PUBLISHER
Jim Minatel

SENIOR ACQUISITIONS EDITOR
Jenny L. Watson

DEVELOPMENT EDITORS
Lorna Gentry
Rick Kughen

MANAGING EDITOR
Lisa Wilson

PROJECT EDITOR
Natalie Harris

COPY EDITORS
Kelly Talbot
Pamela Woolf

INDEXER
Tina Trettin

PROOFREADERS
Mona Brown
Billy Fields
Bob LaRoche

TECHNICAL EDITORS
Mark Reddin
Mark Hall

TEAM COORDINATOR
Vicki Harding

SOFTWARE DEVELOPMENT SPECIALIST
Aaron Price

COVER AND INTERIOR DESIGN
Anne Jones

LAYOUT TECHNICIANS
Tim Osborn
Gloria Schurick

PRODUCTION CONTROL
Dan Harris
George Poole

Contents at a Glance

VI | Appendixes

Table of Contents

IV The Administrative Tools

14 System Backup and Disaster Recovery 259

15 Certificate Manager 281

16 Component Services Explorer 295

About the Author

Jim Boyce is a former Contributing Editor and monthly columnist for *WINDOWS Magazine*. Jim has authored and co-authored over 40 books about computer software and hardware. He has been involved with computers since the late 1970s as a programmer and systems manager in a variety of capacities. He has a wide range of experience in DOS, Windows, Windows NT, and UNIX environments. In addition to having a full-time writing career, Jim is a founding partner and vice president of Minnesota Webworks, a Midwest-based Web development firm (http://www.mnww.com).

Jeff Durham is a consultant and trainer for Mercury Communications. An associate professor for Indiana University/Purdue University of Indianapolis, he has been recently published in Windows NT Systems magazine, and has contributed to many book topics ranging from Visual Basic 6.0 to Windows 2000.

Karen Ellington is a Microsoft Certified Trainer and Systems Engineer with eight years of experience in Microsoft operating systems. She is also a Compaq Accredited Systems Engineer and IBM Professional Server Expert and Instructor. She has spent the last two years training and doing migration consulting for the release of Windows 2000. A dedicated gamer, she is excited about the release of Windows 2000 Professional and can be reached through e-mail at karen@cyberjag.com or her website www.cyberjag.com.

Gerry O'Brien. I have 12 plus years experience working with IBM compatible personal computers. I own a small company that sells computer hardware, software and services on a part time basis, and I integrate computer solutions for a medical clinic through this company. My company also develops custom software applications with our current project aimed at the tourism industry. I am expereienced in dealing with Windows NT domains using client software such as Windows 3.x, Windows 95/98 and NT Workstation. I administer a Windows NT Domain for The Hardman Group Ltd. at four field offices using ADSL technology, Virtual Private Networks, Proxy Server and Exchange Server. I also provide technical support on hardware and software as well as providing training for their employees on their productivity software. I am a Microsoft Certified Professional in Windows NT Server 4.0 and NT Workstation 4.0, and I am steering my certification towards the MCSE Windows 2000 track. I also have started on acquiring my MCSD credential as well. I have just completed beta testing on Microsoft's Windows 2000 Professional, Server and Advanced Server operating systems. I have also completed beta testing for Microsoft's DirectX 7.0 and 7.0a technology, and I will be beta testing the upcoming DirectX 8.0.

Blair Rampling is an information technology consultant from Delta, British Columbia. He specializes in bringing large, unruly networks into neat running order. Optimizing servers and reducing administrative overhead are his main focii, along with Microsoft Exchange administration. He also works extensively with Linux and OpenVMS.

Acknowledgments

Writing a book about any beta software is a challenge, but writing about a beta operating system is particularly so. The help of several people has made the task much easier. I offer my sincere appreciation to the following people for their assistance in making the completion of this book a possibility:

Jenny Watson, for the difficult task of putting together the team and keeping everyone on task.

Lorna Gentry, for her typical outstanding job of molding the material into shape.

Rick Kughen and Beverly Scherf, for the direction they provided that helped put the book's content on target.

Mark Reddin, for providing a detailed and on-target technical review and picking up pieces here and there.

Tell Us What You Think!

As the reader of this book, *you* are our most important critic and commentator. We value your opinion and want to know what we're doing right, what we could do better, what areas you'd like to see us publish in, and any other words of wisdom you're willing to pass our way.

As an Associate Publisher for Que, I welcome your comments. You can fax, email, or write me directly to let me know what you did or didn't like about this book—as well as what we can do to make our books stronger.

Please note that I cannot help you with technical problems related to the topic of this book, and that due to the high volume of mail I receive, I might not be able to reply to every message.

When you write, please be sure to include this book's title and author as well as your name and phone or fax number. I will carefully review your comments and share them with the author and editors who worked on the book.

Fax: 317.581.4666

Email: opsys@mcp.com

Mail: Publisher
        Que
        201 West 103rd Street
        Indianapolis, IN 46290 USA

Introduction

About This Handbook

The Microsoft Windows 2000 Professional Installation and Configuration Handbook is designed for intermediate and advanced users who need a concise guide to deploying and configuring Windows 2000. This book covers all aspects of Windows 2000 installation and deployment, including distributed or push deployment in a LAN or enterprise environment. Whether you are installing Windows 2000 on a single computer or hundreds, you'll find the answers to your installation and configuration questions.

In addition to covering installation topics such as basic, custom, and automated setup, *The Microsoft Windows 2000 Professional Installation and Configuration Handbook* covers all aspects of Windows 2000 configuration. Topics covered include hardware installation and removal, system administration, management tools, and installation/configuration of optional components such as Internet Information Services, Index Server, and Message Queuing Service, to name a few.

New Windows 2000 Features and Functions

Windows 2000 Professional represents a significant change in appearance and functionality over Windows NT 4.0. Under Windows 2000 Professional's hood are a range of core changes that improve reliability, interoperability, networking, application support, hardware support, performance, and much more.

In addition, Windows 2000 Server includes additional new features and changes that have an impact on clients running Windows 2000 Professional for networking, interoperability, application support, and other areas. This introduction examines the new features in Windows 2000 Professional and also describes features in Windows 2000 Server that have the most impact on Windows 2000 Professional users.

NOTE This book covers the majority of feature and interface changes in Windows 2000 Professional. It does not cover all new features and changes for the Windows 2000 Server family of operating systems but instead focuses primarily on issues related specifically to Windows 2000 Professional. For a more complete description of Windows 2000 Server topics, refer to *Special Edition Using Microsoft Windows 2000 Server,* from Que. ■

User Interface

The Windows 2000 interface borrows from the Windows 98 interface, adding new elements and changing some existing elements to create an interface that will be both familiar and foreign to Windows NT 4.0 users.

Control Panel Changes The new Control Panel in Windows 2000 becomes the locus for configuration, control, and setting changes. In effect, the Control Panel becomes your command-and-control center to a much higher degree than in Windows NT.

New objects in the Windows 2000 Control Panel include the following:

- *Add/Remove Hardware.* Use to add, remove, or troubleshoot hardware devices. Opening this folder starts the Add/Remove Hardware Wizard, with which you can scan the system for new hardware, troubleshoot a device, and uninstall or unplug a device.

- *Administrative Tools.* The Administrative Tools folder provides quick access to several management tools for configuring the system and applications, working with the event logs, and tracking performance, among other administration tasks. Each of the objects in the Administrative Tools folder functions as a Microsoft Management Console (MMC) snap-in. The Administrative Tools folder brings most system management functions within a handful of MMC console snap-ins, centralizing system management functions.

▶ **See** "The Administrative Tools," **p. 257**

- *Fax.* Windows 2000 includes a fax service that enables you to send and receive faxes from your workstation. Use the Fax object in the Control Panel to configure the Fax service.

▶ **See** "Fax," **p. 167**

- *Folder Options.* The Folder Options object in the Control Panel enables you to define global options that determine the way folders display their contents. You also can access the Folder Options property sheet from the Tools menu of most folders. With the Folder Options property sheet you can enable and configure web content on the desktop, enable single-click to open, specify a range of folder view options, view and modify file associations, and configure offline files.

▶ **See** "Setting Folder Options," **p. 168**

- *Power Options.* This object enables you to configure power management functions for your computer. Windows 2000 includes support for Advanced Power Management (APM) and Advanced Configuration and Power Interface (ACPI), which is essentially an extension of Plug and Play. Both standards enable Windows 2000 to take advantage of power-saving features such as automatically shutting down hardware when not in use and putting the system into hibernation (storing the entire contents of RAM to the hard disk, enabling the system to return to its previous state when it "wakes up").

▶ **See** "Setting Power Options," **p. 183**

- *Scanners and Cameras.* This object enables you to add, configure, remove, and troubleshoot scanners and digital cameras.

▶ **See** "Setting Scanners and Cameras," **p. 187**

- *Scheduled Tasks.* The Scheduled Tasks folder in the Control Panel contains tasks that you have scheduled for execution and enables you to add and remove scheduled tasks. The Scheduled Task Wizard in the Scheduled Tasks folder steps you through the process of scheduling an application to execute at specified times including daily, weekly, monthly, one time only, when the computer starts, or at logon. For a finer degree of control over scheduling tasks, use the At command from the command console.

▶ **See** "Scheduling Tasks," **p. 187**

■ *Users and Passwords.* This object (see Figure I.1) enables you to add, configure, and remove user accounts for the local computer, taking on some of the functions formerly found in the Windows NT 4.0 User Manager and User Manager for Domains. Advanced options in the Users and Passwords object enable you to configure digital certificates, configure logon, and open the Local User Manager, which enables you to manage local groups as well as user accounts.

▶ **See** "Setting Users and Passwords Options," **p. 190**

▶ **See** Chapter 12, "Managing User Accounts and Groups" **p. 217**

FIGURE I.1

The Users and Passwords property sheet.

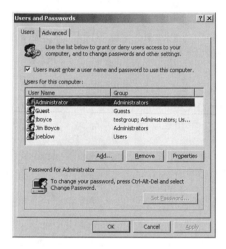

Some objects in the Control Panel have changed slightly to reflect new features or changes in function. These objects include the following:

■ *Network and Dial-up Connections.* Windows 2000 integrates all network connections, both physical and dial-up, in the Network and Dial-up Connections object in the Control Panel (see Figure I.2). The consolidation of network settings in the Network and Dial-up Connections object actually makes it more difficult to configure network settings as it buries physical network settings an additional level deep.

FIGURE I.2

The Network and Dial-up Connections folder.

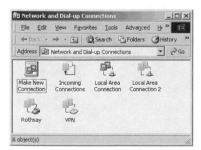

■ *Phone and Modem.* The Phone and Modem object integrates telephony and modem properties and settings into a single property sheet. This enables you to configure modems, dialing rules, and other telephony properties through a single set of controls.

Printers and Scheduled Tasks   The Printers and Scheduled Tasks folders have been removed from My Computer and placed instead in the Control Panel to further centralize system management in the Control Panel.

▶ **See** "Printing," **p. 15**

▶ **See** "Scheduling Tasks," **p. 187**

Start Menu Options   Microsoft has overhauled the Start menu in Windows 2000 to simplify the interface for inexperienced users and make it easier for you to locate your documents and various system resources.

Personalized Menus   Personalized Menus is a new element of the Start menu that keeps track of the frequency with which you open programs and folders, hiding lesser-used items and making it easier for you to quickly access those items you use most often. Note that personalized menus don't include all of the items, but instead hide those that haven't been used recently.

My Documents   The Documents item on the Start menu contains the My Documents folder, which can make it easier to open documents you keep in the My Documents subdirectory. You can configure the Start menu to expand the My Documents folder right from the Start menu, enabling you to quickly browse through My Documents to locate a file. Figure I.3 shows My Documents configured for expansion. With this feature turned off, clicking My Documents on the Start menu opens the My Documents folder rather than expanding its contents on the Start menu.

Other Start Menu Changes   Start Menu Options, which you can access through the taskbar properties, enables you to configure additional options for the Start menu. You can turn on or off display of certain items such as Favorites, Administrative Tools, etc. Particularly useful is the ability to expand the Control Panel, Printers, and other folders from the Start menu.

My Network Places   The Network Neighborhood folder in Windows NT 4.0 has been renamed My Network Places in Windows 2000 and its contents have been changed in an effort to simplify access to network objects by inexperienced users. Rather than containing a list of the computers and network printers in your workgroup or domain as the Network Neighborhood does, My Network Places includes an icon named Computers Near Me where these computers are listed, moving these objects a layer deeper in the interface (not really an improvement, in this author's opinion). As in the Network Neighborhood, the Entire Network object enables you to browse for network resources located in other workgroups or domains.

FIGURE I.3
My Documents
expanded on the
Start menu.

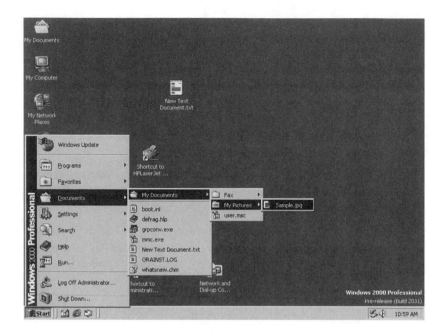

System File Protection   Windows 98 protects the files in the Windows folder by hiding the files when you browse to that folder. Windows 2000 does much the same thing, hiding files in the system root folder and subfolders. The folder includes a link named Show Files that when clicked, unhides the files in the folder.

In addition, the Folder Options properties include a setting named Hide Protected Operating System Files. When this option is enabled, certain system files such as BOOT.INI, NLDR, and others are hidden regardless of their location. Hiding these files prevents their accidental deletion and potential corruption of the system. Turning off this option makes these files visible.

Hardware and Reliability

Several changes and new features in Windows 2000 improve on Windows NT's reliability and expand hardware support and ease of configuration.

Plug and Play   Windows 2000 supports Plug and Play (PnP) to simplify hardware installation and configuration. On systems containing a PnP BIOS, Windows 2000 can automatically detect, configure, and install support for PnP-compliant devices. This capability significantly eases hardware installation and configuration by enabling Windows 2000 to configure the device so it does not conflict with other hardware in the system. PnP also simplifies hardware installation by automating processes that previously required more extensive user intervention in Windows NT.

On systems that do not contain a PnP BIOS, PnP features in Windows 2000 still simplify device installation and configuration by enabling Windows 2000 to scan for legacy devices and install drivers based on that hardware detection. Manual installation is still required for some non-PnP devices, however.

Device Manager   The Device Manager, like its cousin in Windows 95/98, serves as a sort of control center for your system's hardware. The Device Manager is implemented as an MMC snap-in (see Figure I.4). As with the Device Manager in Windows 9x, the Windows 2000 Device Manager lets you view device settings and resource assignments, configure devices, remove devices, update drivers, and troubleshoot devices.

FIGURE I.4
The Device Manager.

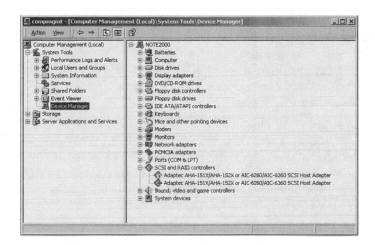

Configuration Changes Without Restart   Microsoft has redesigned many aspects of Windows 2000 to make it possible to implement hardware changes without requiring a system restart. Although some hardware configuration changes still require the system to restart, most can be accomplished dynamically.

Digitally Signed Drivers   In an effort to improve driver support and make the Windows 2000 system more reliable, Microsoft has implemented support for digitally signed drivers. As the Microsoft Windows Hardware Quality Lab (WHQL) tests and certifies device drivers, it issues encrypted digital signatures to the manufacturer for inclusion in the driver. When you install a device driver, Windows 2000 automatically checks for the driver signature. If no signature is found (indicating the driver has not been certified by the WHQL), Windows 2000 displays a dialog giving you the option of halting the driver installation process if you choose.

Safe Mode Boot   A welcome addition to Windows 2000 that Windows 9x users have enjoyed is Safe mode, which enables you to boot the system with a minimal set of standard drivers, potentially bypassing driver or configuration problems that otherwise would prevent the system from booting normally. Once the system is booted in Safe mode you can reconfigure settings and change drivers in an attempt to overcome whatever problems the system is experiencing.

Repair Command Console   The Repair Command Console is in some ways similar to the Windows 9x Command-Prompt Only boot option. Booting the system with the Repair Command Console option gives you a console environment (command prompt) in which you can run diagnostic utilities, perform certain configuration and repair functions, and if necessary, perform recovery operations. The Repair Command Console supports all the file systems supported by Windows 2000, enabling you to read NTFS as well as FAT and FAT32 partitions from the boot console.

The Repair Command Console includes several built-in commands that you can use to view and manipulate the file system; view, enable, and disable services; start repair operations; and manage partitions.

▶ **See** "System Repair and Recovery," **p. 276**

APM and ACPI   Windows 2000 includes support for Advanced Power Management (APM) and Advanced Configuration and Power Interface (ACPI), which is essentially an extension of Plug and Play. Both standards enable Windows 2000 to take advantage of power-saving features such as automatically shutting down hardware when not in use and putting the system into hibernation.

Mobile Support   In addition to supporting APM and ACPI, as well as file synchronization features discussed elsewhere in this chapter, Windows 2000 expands support for mobile systems by expanding support for PC cards, including hotswapping. Other mobile system features in Windows 98 that have been migrated to the Windows 2000 operating system include support for docking stations and docking/undocking the system. Windows NT systems required third-party drivers to accomplish these tasks.

Memory Addressing   Windows 2000 Professional and Windows 2000 Server can address up to 4GB of RAM. Windows 2000 Advanced Server and Windows 2000 Data Center support up to 64GB of RAM through the Enterprise Memory Architecture. In addition, Windows 2000 improves kernel-mode write protection, enabling the system to mark occupied memory pages and prevent other processes from writing to them. This helps prevent drivers or parts of the operating system from writing to in-use memory, thereby crashing the system.

Networking and Security

Windows 2000 sports several changes and additions to networking features and its security models. The following sections examine these changes and additions.

DNS   Domain Name Service (DNS) support in Windows 2000 is enhanced to improve performance. DNS supports dynamic updates (RFC 2136), which enables a Windows 2000 Professional client to register updates to the DNS Server when address events such as a new address assignment or address renewal occur. Clients assigned addresses through DHCP submit a request to the DHCP Server to register a PTR (pointer) record on their behalf when the address event takes place. The client registers its A record by itself, although the DHCP Server service can be configured to register both records, if desired. Clients with statically assigned IP addresses register both the A and PTR records themselves.

In addition to dynamic updates, the DNS cache is enhanced in Windows 2000. You now can manipulate the DNS Client service (which handles DNS caching) for troubleshooting, which allows you to start, stop, and pause the service as necessary. Several Registry entries enable you to configure the DNS cache. One noteworthy feature of the DNS cache is its support for *negative caching*. When the response to a query to a DNS server is negative, the DNS cache will cache the negative response; subsequent queries for the same name will be returned as negative from the cache until the negative cache timeout expires. Increased control over caching can enable you to optimize system performance.

DHCP The DHCP client in Windows 2000 has been improved in several ways. One of the most significant changes is the DHCP client's capability to automatically assign an IP address to the system at startup when no DHCP server is present. This is particularly useful in small, private networks (not connected to the Internet) with no dedicated server to dynamically assign addresses. The DHCP client continues to search for a DHCP server every five minutes. If one is found, the client releases its current address and accepts the address and subnet mask offered by the DHCP server.

▶ **See** "Understanding the Domain Name System (DNS)," **p. 402**

 TIP The DHCP client assigns addresses using the Microsoft-reserved Class B network 169.254.0.0 with the subnet mask 255.255.0.0.

IPSec Windows 2000 adds support for IP Security (IPSec). IPSec uses cryptography-based security to provide access control, connectionless integrity, data origin authentication, protection against replays, confidentiality, and limited traffic flow confidentiality. IPSec enables the system to process each IP datagram against a set of filters defined by the administrator for a computer, user, group, or entire domain. IPSec services process the datagram according to the filters. In effect, IPSec support lets you implement firewall services in a very broad way across the enterprise, allowing or denying traffic between specific IP addresses, types of traffic, port, and so on, based on the respective computers, users, groups, or domain.

IPSec configuration and implementation is relatively complicated and requires a good understanding of TCP/IP and authentication mechanisms. You configure IPSec filters and settings through group policies. Configure a Windows 2000 Professional system to use IPSec through the computer's TCP/IP properties.

▶ **See** "Understanding TCP/IP," **p. 397**
▶ **See** "Configuring IPSec," **p. 412**

 TIP In addition to IPSec, you also can use TCP/IP filtering to define (on a less-defined scale) which IP traffic is allowed or denied for TCP ports, UDP ports, and IP protocols. Configure TCP/IP filtering through the computer's TCP/IP settings.

SmartCard Support Windows 2000 adds support for SmartCard readers and the ability to authenticate (log on) using credentials stored on a SmartCard. This feature helps improve security because not only would a user have to have a valid account on the system, he also would have to have the SmartCard to go along with it.

Internet Connection Sharing (Proxy)   Windows 2000 incorporates a new feature called *Internet Connection Sharing* that enables a single Internet connection to be shared by multiple users across the LAN (see Figure I.5).

Internet Connection Sharing brings two primary advantages. It enables multiple computers to share a single dial-up connection to the Internet, which decreases costs associated with Internet access in fewer modems, phone lines, and dial-up connection charges. And, because Internet Connection Sharing acts as a proxy server, it hides your LAN (with the exception of the computer acting as the proxy server) from the Internet, thereby adding a layer of security to your LAN. Internet Connection Sharing doesn't provide the same level of protection as a firewall, but it does make it more difficult for outsiders to access your systems.

NetBIOS Elimination   Windows 2000 uses NetBIOS to communicate with Windows 9x, Windows NT, and other clients requiring NetBIOS support. Windows 2000 uses DNS for name resolution, however, in Windows 2000 environments. By default, the Workstation, Server, Browser, Messenger, and NetLogon services all use DNS and NetBIOS in parallel when establishing a new connection. The first method that succeeds in any given connection attempt is the one used.

Because Windows 2000 clients do not need NetBIOS for name resolution, you can reduce or eliminate NetBIOS traffic, particularly in pure Windows 2000 environments. You can disable NetBIOS altogether if it isn't needed, eliminating the network traffic it otherwise would generate. NetBIOS is enabled and disabled through the WINS tab in the system's TCP/IP properties.

FIGURE I.5
Internet Connection
Sharing.

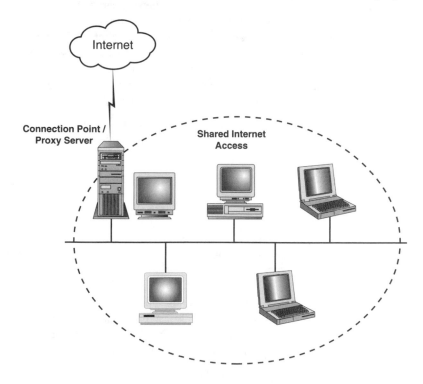

▶ **See** "Managing Protocols," **p. 52**

PPTP/L2TP Support

Windows 2000 offers several capabilities that make it a solid remote network client. Included in these features are support for Point-to-Point Tunneling Protocol (PPTP) and the more secure Level 2 Tunneling Protocol (L2TP). Both protocols enable a Windows 2000 computer to establish a secure, private connection to a computer or LAN via a public pipeline such as the Internet. This capability enables remote Windows 2000 clients to access resources on remote systems through inexpensive, public access points, eliminating in many cases the expense and management overhead of a dedicated remote access point to the needed computer or LAN.

▶ **See** "VPN Connections Through ICS," **p. 423**

Kerberos and Single Sign On (SSO) Authentication

Windows 2000 adds support for Kerberos authentication, enabling Single Sign On (SSO) authentication. Kerberos is a standard security mechanism that relies on *tickets*, which are encrypted data packets issued by a Key Distribution Center (KDC) to authenticate a user's identity and other information. SSO means that a user can authenticate a single time and access network resources across the enterprise without authenticating again. This enables the user to access resources on a variety of servers running various operating systems without multiple log ons.

Internet/Intranet Services

Windows 2000 adds several new features and improves on existing Windows NT features in the areas of Internet and intranet services. The following sections explain the major changes and improvements.

Internet Explorer 5.0

Windows 2000 incorporates Internet Explorer 5.0, which offers additions and improvements over Internet Explorer 4.x, such as expanded and improved support for Dynamic HTML (DHTML), performance improvements, and several enhancements to support improved site and content development.

Internet Information Services (IIS)

Windows 2000 Professional includes Internet Information Services (IIS), which enables you to configure a computer running Windows 2000 Professional as a web and FTP server. You might, for example, create an intranet server for a department or small business using a Windows 2000 Professional workstation.

While IIS on a Windows 2000 Professional computer isn't appropriate for an Internet server because Windows 2000 Professional is limited to 10 concurrent connections, it does make a good departmental or small business server. For support of more than 10 concurrent connections (such as for an Internet server), consider IIS and one of the Windows 2000 Server family of operating systems.

▶ **See** "A Quick Review of IIS Features," **p. 42**

File System

Windows 2000 incorporates some significant additions and improvements to file system-related services and features. These changes mean enhanced control over disk utilization, greater flexibility for file system design, and improved management.

NTFS Changes   The NTFS file system has been changed for Windows 2000 over Windows NT 4.0 to support several new features for performance and flexibility. Windows NTFS version 5, which is included in Windows 2000, maintains compatibility with NTFS version 4 in Windows NT 4.0, but because the physical disk structure is different for version 5, it requires that you upgrade your existing NTFS volumes to version 5 to take advantage of these new features. Several of the following sections highlight the major changes in NTFS and other file system services that affect performance or that make possible new features in Windows 2000.

Dynamic File System (DFS)   The Dynamic File System (DFS) provides a new disk structure over the current partition-based structure in which a physical disk can contain no more than four partitions. Through an extended DOS partition, these types of drives can contain multiple logical drives.

DFS makes it possible to create disks containing essentially an unlimited number of volumes. Volumes on a dynamic disk can be formatted to any of the file systems supported by Windows 2000. DFS also enables other benefits such as the capability to dynamically resize volumes. Basic disks (those created using the standard partition format) can be upgraded to dynamic disks without any loss of data. Reverting a dynamic disk back to a basic disk requires deletion of the volumes on the disk, which destroys the data on the disk and therefore requires a backup.

▶ **See** "Support for Dynamic Volumes," **p. 343**

Disk Quotas   Changes in NTFS add the capability to define and enforce disk quotas in Windows 2000. With quotas you can limit folder size on a per-user basis, giving you a high degree of control over system-wide storage (see Figure I.6). Imposing quotas helps you optimize storage space by forcing users to delete unnecessary files and reduce wasted storage space while still offering the flexibility to give each user an adequate amount of space. Disk quotas also help you manage storage growth more effectively by enabling you to parcel out storage space on an as-needed basis. Quotas can be implemented on a group basis using policies or on an individual basis.

FIGURE I.6
Using disk quotas to
allocate storage space.

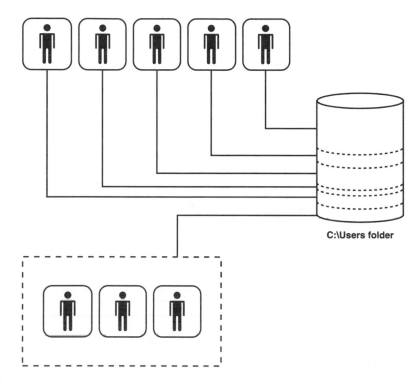

Distributed Link Tracking   Distributed Link Tracking (DLT) is another new feature in NTFS version 5. DLT adds a volume-wide indexed ID for each file, enabling DLT to track files and preserve shortcuts and OLE links even if a file is renamed or moved, including to another computer.

Reparse Points and File System Filters   *Reparse points* are another new feature added in NTFS version 5. Reparse points are NTFS objects that carry special attribute tags and are used to trigger additional functionality in the file system. These tags work in conjunction with file system filters to extend the capability of the NTFS file system, enabling features and functions to be added to the file system (including by third parties) without the need to redesign or restructure the file system. Several new features in Windows 2000's file system are implemented using reparse points and file system filters:

- NTFS Directory Junctions
- NTFS Mount Points
- Remote Storage Service
- Native Structured Storage
- Encrypting File System

Directory Junctions and Mountable Folders   Directory Junction Points, a new element in NTFS version 5, enables the creation of mountable folders. A *mounted folder* is a physical volume that is mapped to an empty NTFS folder on the same or different disk (see Figure I.7). In effect, the mounted volume appears to be a part of the physical disk structure where the volume is mounted. A good example of the use of mountable volumes is extending the apparent free space on a disk. Rather than replace a nearly full disk, you could add another disk and mount it as a folder on the existing volume.

FIGURE I.7
A mounted volume.

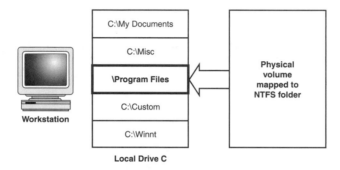

C:\My Documents

C:\Misc

\Program Files

C:\Custom

C:\Winnt

Workstation

Local Drive C

Physical volume mapped to NTFS folder

▶ **See** "Working with Mounted Volumes," **p. 355**

Hierarchical Storage Management and Remote Storage Services   Hierarchical Storage Management (HSM) and Remote Storage Services (RSS) work together to enable seldom-used files to be archived to slower, less expensive data storage devices, such as from the hard drive of a network file server to an optical disk or tape. Windows 2000 maintains the directory and property information, enabling it to move the data back when it is requested by a user.

RSS, developed by Seagate (maker of Backup Exec and other storage solutions), monitors the target file system and when available storage space drops below a specified point, automatically archives the data.

Encrypting File System (EFS)   Although NTFS offers a high level of security, the capability to remove a storage device and mount it on another system makes it possible for someone to take ownership of and view the data, bypassing security altogether. Windows 2000 adds the capability to encrypt files and folders to offer an additional layer of protection for the data. This can be particularly useful for mobile computers such as notebooks that are more susceptible to theft. The domestic (U.S./Canada) version of Windows 2000 supports 128-bit encryption, whereas the international versions support 40-bit encryption.

Sparse File Support   Large data files can sometimes include large areas of *non-meaningful data*, or large strings of zeros. The meaningful data is stored as ones. Windows 2000's NTFS version 5 adds support for *sparse files*, in which an attribute of the file is marked to indicate to the I/O subsystem to treat the file as a sparse file. When Windows 2000 stores the file, it allocates the meaningful data on the storage medium and stores the range information for the non-meaningful data rather than the zeros that otherwise would be used as placeholders (see Figure I.8). When the file is accessed, Windows 2000 reads the range information and automatically returns the correct number of zero bits. In a file containing a large amount of non-meaningful data, the storage space decrease can be significant.

FIGURE I.8
NTFS v.5 supports
sparse files.

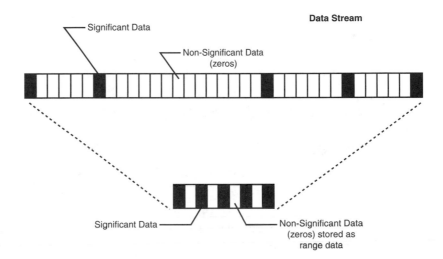

FAT32 Windows 95 OSR2 and Windows 98 both support FAT32 volumes, a 32-bit implementation of the FAT file system that originated with DOS. FAT32 offers increased performance, larger volumes, and more efficient disk storage. Previously, reading and writing to FAT32 volumes under Windows NT required a third-party utility. Windows 2000 now provides native support for FAT32 volumes. This support is particularly beneficial for systems that multiboot between Windows 9x and Windows 2000, enabling both operating systems to see and modify the FAT32 volumes. Support for FAT32 also provides a better option than FAT on systems where NTFS is not desired.

 TIP To add support for FAT32 volumes for Windows NT, check out FAT32 for Windows NT, from Winternals Software, which you can locate on the web at http://www.winternals.com.

Printing

Windows 2000 provides a handful of printing improvements that expand printer support and enhance print quality and ease-of-use. These improvements include the following:

- *Printer Drivers and Support.* Windows 2000 builds on the large number of printers supported by previous versions to cover more than 2,500 printers. The new UniDrive5 print driver provides improved color and printing performance. UniDrive5 also supports OEM customization, enabling developers to more easily integrate custom printing features.

- *Publishing Printers in the Active Directory.* You can publish printers in the Windows 2000 Active Directory, organizing them by purpose rather than location. This lets users browse for printers based on functions such as color capability, paper size, and so on, or by physical location (specific floor or department, for example) rather than by network connection. This change makes it easier for users (particularly inexperienced users) to locate printer resources.

- *Improved Color Management.* The Image Color Management API in Windows 2000 improves color document printing performance and reliability.

- *Internet Printing.* The Internet Printing Protocol (IPP) enables you to print to a printer designated by a URL on the intranet or Internet. You also can view print queue status through a web browser and download install print drivers across the Internet.

In addition, Windows 2000 Advanced Server and Data Center Server offer print server clustering to provide redundant print capability when a print server fails.

Application Support

Windows 2000 offers several improvements for application support, including local applications and client/server applications:

- *COM+.* Component Object Model enables developers to create component-based and integrated web applications. COM+ extends COM to simplify development and improve reliability, flexibility, and scalability.

- *Microsoft Transaction Services.* MTS is a Windows 2000 server-side component that works with COM+ and is targeted at the creation of distributed client/server applications.

- *Microsoft Message Queuing Service.* MSMQ is another development-related service that enhances the ability to create and deploy reliable client/server applications. MSMQ provides reliable network communication capabilities between application components.

Windows Installer

The Windows Installer Service is a new application installation service included with Windows 2000 (and which will be made available as service packs for Windows 95 and Windows 98). In addition to other functions, the Windows Installer is designed to eliminate application installation problems such as incorrect DLL substitution and missing components. Windows Installer also provides support for on-demand installation, enabling applications and application components to install automatically from CD or network drives when the user requires it. Applications must be written specifically to take advantage of the Windows Installer features.

File Synchronization

Windows 2000 improves on the file synchronization features in the Windows 9x and Windows NT 4.0 Briefcase with a new feature called Offline Folders. Windows 2000 gives you the ability to make network resources available offline, enabling you to continue to work with those network resources when not connected to the network. In essence, Offline Folders creates a sync copy of the network resource on your local computer. Directory structure and security settings are maintained, making the folders and their contents easy to locate and use without compromising security. You can synchronize Offline Folders manually or allow Windows 2000 to synchronize them automatically when you reconnect to the network.

Administration

Windows 2000 represents a radical departure from Windows NT 4.0 in terms of administration and management tools:

- *Administrative Tools.* Standalone administrative applications in Windows NT 4.0 are largely replaced by Microsoft Management Console (MMC) snap-ins. This change enables you to customize your management tools and also offers better flexibility for managing computers and resources both locally and remotely.

▶ **See** "Administrative Tools," **p. 257**

- S*ervice Pack Structure.* Windows 2000 improves service pack installation significantly by no longer requiring that service packs be reapplied after base software or hardware changes. Windows 2000 monitors selected system files to prevent them from being overwritten by older versions and also helps automate restoration of files if replacement does occur. Windows 2000 also supports *slipstreaming*, enabling service packs to be added to installation shares and eliminating the need for users to apply service packs after installing the operating system from an installation share.

Group Policies

Windows 2000 expands on Windows NT's policies to enable system administrators to define and manage computers and users. The Group Policy snap-in for the MMC enables you to define nearly every setting affecting user profile configuration, computer settings, resource access, and security. The following are the key functions that group policies provide:

- *Manage and Enforce User and Computer Settings.* User profile settings in the group policy define the user's working environment and privileges/restrictions and in part define the HKEY_CURRENT_USER hive. Computer settings in the policy define the local machine Registry hive (HKEY_LOCAL_MACHINE) and define the computer's configuration.

- *Redirect Folders.* You can use group policy settings to redirect local folders to network shares.

- *Assign Scripts.* Group policies enable you to assign scripts on a computer- or user-basis for such events as startup, shutdown, logon, or logoff.

- *Manage Applications.* The software installation extension to group policies enables you to assign, update, publish, and repair applications.

- *Set Security Options.* You can use various security settings in a group policy to enforce restrictions and control access on a computer- or user-basis.

Server-Side Technologies

A handful of major changes in the Windows 2000 Server family of products have a major impact on Windows 2000 Professional in the enterprise. Although these features are not part of Windows 2000 Professional and therefore fall outside the scope of this book, they bear a mention here.

Active Directory   The Active Directory (AD) is one of the most significant server-side changes in Windows 2000. The AD forms a hierarchical name space in which objects in the enterprise (or a single server) can be named and tracked. These include such objects as users, groups, printers, files, and so on. The AD maintains information about each object and simplifies the process of locating objects. For example, you can integrate printers into the AD and make it much easier to locate printers based on function rather than by physical location or server attachment.

Intellimirror   Intellimirror is another server-side addition to Windows 2000 that simplifies application distribution and support, desktop configuration management, remote operating system installation, and roaming user profiles. A primary application of Intellimirror is to enable applications to be installed automatically when a user requires it. For example, you might click an icon to start an application, and when Windows 2000 discovers that the application is not installed locally, it automatically installs the program. In addition, if certain components of the application are not yet installed (you've never used the thesaurus, for example), Intellimirror will automatically install it when you try to use it for the first time.

In effect, Intellimirror can distribute any software, including the Windows 2000 operating system and settings. This makes Intellimirror a great tool for supporting roaming users who log in from different places across the enterprise. Intellimirror makes it possible for these users to automatically have the same operating system settings, desktop configuration, documents, and applications regardless of where they log on.

Conventions Used in This Book

In Windows 2000 you can use either the mouse or keyboard to activate commands and choose options. You can press a command's or menu's hotkey, use the function keys, or click items with the mouse to make your selections. In this book, command and menu hotkeys are underlined and bold as in the following example:

Choose **F**ile, **O**pen to display the Open dialog box.

In this book, key combinations are joined by a plus (+) sign. For example, Ctrl+C means to hold down the Ctrl key, press C, and then release both keys. The following example shows a typical command:

Choose **E**dit, **C**opy, or press Ctrl+C.

Occasionally, you might need to press a key, release it, and then press another key. If you need to press Alt, F, and then O, for example, the command would be similar to the following:

Press Alt, F, O to display the Open dialog box.

Names of dialog boxes and dialog box options are written as they appear on your display. Messages that appear at the command prompt are displayed `in a special font`. New terms are introduced in *italic* type. Text that you type is shown in **boldface**. If you see an instruction to "Enter **some text**," it means to type the text **some text**, and then press Enter. If the instruction tells you to "Type **some text**," it means to type the text but not press Enter.

 N O T E   Notes provide additional information that might help you avoid problems. They offer advice or general information related to the current topic. ■

 TIP   Tips provide extra information that supplements the current topic. Often, tips offer shortcuts or alternative methods for accomplishing a task.

CAUTION

Cautions warn you if a procedure or description in the topic could lead to unexpected results or even data loss or damage to your system. If you see a caution, proceed carefully.

TROUBLESHOOTING

Margin cross-references direct you to related information in other parts of the book. Right-facing triangles indicate later chapters, and left-facing triangles point you to information earlier in the book.

▶ **See** "The FAT and FAT32 File Systems," **p. 72**

▶ **See** "Managing User Accounts and Groups," **p. 217**

Internet references such as the following point you to sites on the Internet where you can find additional information about a topic being discussed:

 ### MICROSOFT'S WEB SITE

`http://www.microsoft.com`

Installing Windows 2000 Professional

Pre-Installation Planning

In this chapter

Overview

Although running Setup to install Windows 2000 is easy, the entire installation process can be complicated. With complex security and compatibility issues to consider, getting all aspects of the installation right the first time can be a challenge and requires careful thought and planning. This chapter gives you the background information you need to begin the installation process.

If you are an experienced Windows NT administrator, most if not all the information in this chapter should be familiar to you. If you're relatively new to Windows NT/Windows 2000, however, the following sections will be indispensable for helping you plan and carry out the installation.

Exploring Compatibility Issues

When planning a Windows 2000 installation, you need to consider a number of compatibility issues that will determine how (and if) your existing programs will run, whether you'll be able to access your existing files, and so on. The following sections explore these compatibility issues.

Application Compatibility

Out of necessity to support a large installed application base and to enhance its appeal, Windows 2000 supports DOS and 16-bit Windows (Win16) programs in addition to Win32 applications. (Support for OS/2 applications was dropped with Windows NT 4.0.)

In general, Windows 2000 can run DOS programs and Win16 programs written for Windows 3.x. Many Win16 programs run equally well under Windows 2000 or Windows 3.x. Some Win16 programs, such as those that require private virtual device drivers (VxDs), do not run under Windows 2000.

Programs that conform to the Windows 9x compatibility logo requirements also run under Windows 2000, so most Windows 9x programs will run fine under Windows 2000. Microsoft allows for exceptions in compatibility, however, so the Windows 9x logo on a program is a good indicator but does not guarantee compatibility with Windows 2000.

If you're upgrading your system to Windows 2000, or you intend to dual-boot between DOS or Windows 9x and Windows 2000, verify your programs' compatibility. Check with the software publisher's technical support staff to determine if the version of the program you're using will run successfully under Windows 2000.

 TIP Many Windows NT/2000 programs are optimized to take advantage of such features as multithreading for improved performance. Consider upgrading to the Windows 2000 version of an application even if your current version is compatible to take advantage of that optimization.

Integrating with Other Operating Systems

Because of its support for a wide variety of network protocols, Windows 2000 integrates easily with various other operating systems. Through its included TCP/IP protocol, Telnet, FTP, and third-party support for NFS, X Window, and other utilities, you can easily connect Windows 2000 systems to UNIX systems. Windows 2000's NetWare-related services and NetWare clients make it easy to connect Windows NT systems to NetWare servers and also to emulate or replace NetWare servers using Windows 2000 servers.

Naturally, Windows 2000 also integrates well with Microsoft's other operating systems and environments, including Windows for Workgroups and Windows 9x.

Understanding File System Issues

One key compatibility issue you need to consider is your file system(s). You must decide whether to upgrade your file system to NTFS (NT File System). Compatibility with HPFS and FAT/FAT32 also are factors. These and other file compatibility issues are explored in the following sections.

▶ **See** "The FAT and FAT32 File Systems," **p. 72**
▶ **See** "The NTFS File System," **p. 74**

The FAT and FAT32 File Systems The FAT file system originated with DOS. FAT32 came along as an add-on to Windows 95 and is included with Windows 98. FAT32 offers several performance improvements over FAT, though neither provides the high level of security or redundancy offered by NTFS. FAT and FAT32 are quite adequate in environments that don't require extensive security and actually can offer better performance than NTFS because of the added overhead caused by NTFS.

▶ **See** "The FAT and FAT32 File Systems," **p. 72**

Windows 2000 fully supports the FAT and FAT32 file systems. Unlike Windows NT, which requires a third-party driver to read and write FAT32 volumes, Windows 2000 provides native support for FAT32. If you choose not to convert your existing FAT/FAT32 partition(s) to NTFS, Windows 2000 will be capable of reading and writing to the file system without any problems. For best performance, however, consider converting any existing FAT volumes to FAT32 on your system after you upgrade to Windows 2000.

NTFS The NT File System, or NTFS, provides many advantages over the FAT and FAT32 file systems. These advantages include recoverability, fault tolerance, security, and more. In short, NTFS is an ideal option in most cases.

You can convert your existing partition(s) to NTFS without any problems, if you will be using Windows 2000 as your only operating system. Like DOS and other operating systems, Windows 2000 isolates the file system from your programs so they will have no trouble accessing files.

NTFS might not be a workable solution if you plan to use other operating systems on your computer. This is because DOS, OS/2, and Windows 9x don't support NTFS. If you have one or more of these operating systems on your computer in addition to Windows 2000, and you convert your file system to NTFS, these other operating systems will no longer be capable of reading the files in the NTFS volume. If these other operating systems are contained in that volume, they will no longer load.

One solution to this problem is to leave the existing file system intact and create a new partition for NTFS. You'll enjoy the benefits of NTFS for Windows 2000 without losing accessibility to your existing files for your other operating system(s). Unfortunately, creating a new partition for NTFS generally will mean resizing your existing partition, which requires deleting and re-creating the partition. You'll first have to back up your entire existing file system and restore it after the repartitioning (assuming all the files will still fit in the reduced partition).

N O T E   These compatibility limitations apply only on the local computer. A Windows 9x computer, for example, can access an NTFS volume on a Windows 2000 computer across the network because file access then becomes a function of the network redirector, not the file system itself. ▨

HPFS   Early versions of Windows NT supported OS/2's High Performance File System (HPFS). Windows NT 4.0, however, dropped HPFS support, and support has not been resurrected in Windows 2000. A Windows 2000 computer can't read or otherwise access an HPFS volume on a local drive. If your system contains an HPFS volume and you have to access its files in Windows 2000, you must convert the HPFS to FAT, FAT32, or NTFS. The only way to achieve this is to copy the files using OS/2 from the HPFS volume to a FAT volume, which then can be accessed by Windows 2000 or converted to an NTFS volume.

Disk Compression   Disk compression has been common in PCs for many years and became popular with the introduction of DoubleSpace and DriveSpace in DOS and third-party solutions such as Stacker. Windows NT, however, has been slow to support disk compression outside the NTFS.

Under Windows 2000 you can compress and decompress individual files or directories. The compression process is not automatic—you must manually initiate the compression. Windows 2000 does, however, decompress the files automatically when you use them. Also, Windows 2000 automatically compresses new files created in any folder with the compression attributed set. So, you only have to compress a folder once, and all new files created in the folder will be compressed. You therefore enjoy the benefits of disk compression without the same level of performance drop occasioned by DriveSpace and similar compression utilities.

Because it doesn't support DriveSpace compressed volumes, you will have to reconfigure your system if you intend to use Windows 2000 on a system that also contains DOS or Windows 9x and compressed DriveSpace volumes. You'll be able to access the DriveSpace volumes while running DOS, Windows 3.x, and Windows 9x, but not while running Windows 2000. To access the files in the DriveSpace volume under Windows 2000, you must copy the files to a noncompressed FAT volume outside of Windows 2000 or move the files to a network server.

Understanding Security Issues

If you're moving from an operating system such as DOS or Windows 9x to Windows 2000, you might not be familiar with many of the security issues surrounding Windows 2000. On Windows for Workgroups and Windows 9x systems, a user can create an account and password on-the-fly by entering a new account name and password in the Logon dialog box. Under Windows 2000, each user must have a preexisting account created by an administrator on the computer or in its domain in order to log on and gain access to the computer's and network's resources. This provides a much higher degree of control over access to the computer and network.

> **CAUTION**
>
> Enabling users to dual-boot their systems between DOS or Windows 9x and Windows 2000 is a potential security risk. You should not leave DOS or Windows 9x on the system or allow the user to boot to either of these operating systems if the computer's local resources must be secure. Because of the lower level of security of these operating systems compared with Windows 2000, it's possible for an unauthorized user to access restricted information on the system and possibly the network. Windows 2000 plugs that security gap by requiring every user to have a valid account and password.

Windows 2000 includes a default set of standard user groups, each with specific levels of access privileges. The one you should be most interested in at this point is the Administrators group. Users in this group have access to all resources on the system. Administrators can create user accounts and groups, assign permissions to resources, control sharing of resources, and shut down the system.

N O T E   Administrator access does not guarantee full access to all directories or files. A user can create a directory or file but not grant access to it by administrators. Administrators can, however, take ownership of the directory or file to gain access to it, if needed. ■

Groups and permissions are explored in more detail in Chapter 11, "Understanding System Administration and Security." For now, understand that you must be prepared to create an Administrator account when you install Windows 2000 on individual workstations. After installation, you can create additional accounts and apply appropriate group status and permissions to those accounts.

> **CAUTION**
>
> Make sure you remember the password you assign to the Administrator account when you install Windows 2000. Without the password, you won't be able to log on after installation.

Also begin planning what level of access each user will need to each local workstation and to network resources. For even greater control over security and configuration issues, consider using group policies.

▶ **See** "Managing Group Policies," **p. 225**

Preparing for Installation

Now that you have an understanding of the issues that will affect installation, you're ready to begin planning the setup and deployment. The following sections will help you get started.

N O T E Before you begin installing Windows 2000, examine your system to verify that all components are functioning and it's ready and configured for a trouble-free installation. ■

Following is a hit list of tasks to include in the planning process (covered in more detail in following sections):

■ Verify hardware compatibility

■ Acquire compatible drivers and software

■ Determine and record network/ATM settings

■ Verify firmware version (Alpha systems only)

■ Disconnect the UPS

■ Detect/disable FPU error

■ Back up critical files

■ Create a repair disk

■ Plan network options

Checking Hardware Compatibility

As Windows NT's market share has expanded, so has support for a wide variety of hardware, which carries into Windows 2000. Windows 2000 directly supports a variety of systems and peripherals through drivers included with Windows 2000.

N O T E Support for your computer's CD-ROM drive and associated host adapter is particularly important because Windows 2000 installs from the CD (unless you're installing across the LAN). Windows 2000 supports a variety of SCSI and non-SCSI CD-ROM drives. ■

Avoid potential problems by ensuring that your hardware is compatible to the degree you require under Windows 2000 before starting installation. This is particularly important if you're buying a new system for Windows 2000.

You can use Microsoft's Hardware Compatibility List (HCL) to verify hardware compatibility with Windows 2000. The HCL lists the hardware that has been tested and certified as compatible with Windows 2000, and it includes footnotes for specific items detailing special driver requirements or limitations to compatibility. You can access the HCL through Microsoft's Internet site. You'll also find the HCL on the Windows 2000 CD in the Support folder.

Microsoft's Web Site

```
http://www.microsoft.com/ntserver/nts/techdetails/default.asp
```

```
http://www.microsoft.com/hcl
```

A hardware item might still be compatible even if it isn't listed in the HCL. Some devices emulate more common devices. For example, many sound cards emulate Sound Blaster cards, which are supported by Windows 2000. Check with the manufacturer if your hardware isn't listed to determine whether the hardware is supported directly by Windows 2000 or if the manufacturer offers a Windows 2000 driver for the device.

Retaining Network/ATM Settings

Before you install a new copy of Windows 2000 in a LAN environment you need to determine what network settings the PC will use. The information you need is described in Table 1.1. Chapter 3, "Networking Installation and Configuration," also explains these items in greater detail.

Table 1.1   Network Settings for Installation

Item	Description
Adapter type	Adapter manufacturer/model in case Windows 2000 is incapable or incorrectly detects NIC.
Topology	10baseT, Thinnet, etc. in case Windows 2000 is incapable or incorrectly detects topology.
Adapter settings	IRQ, I/O base address, RAM settings as applicable.
Domain or workgroup	Name of domain or workgroup in which computer will belong.
Computer name	Unique name by which computer will be known on network.
Protocol(s)	Network protocols such as TCP/IP, NetBEUI, IPX/SPX, etc., and associated settings (IP and DNS addresses, etc.).
Optional services	Network print services, Internet Information Server (IIS), etc.

Before you update an existing Windows NT or Windows 9x installation to Windows 2000, you should determine and record the computer's existing network settings as described in

Table 1.1. You also should record protocol settings, particularly for protocols with several settings such as TCP/IP. Although Windows 2000 will usually perform the update without losing the settings, you should have them on hand as a safeguard.

One case in which you must record the settings is if you're using asynchronous transfer mode (ATM). Windows NT 4.0 uses a monolithic driver with integrated modules for local area network (LAN) Emulation Client service, ATM User to Network Interface (UNI) signaling, and the ATM hardware interface.

The ATM UNI signaling component and LAN Emulation Client services are now integrated in Windows 2000, but the ATM hardware interface is provided by a miniport driver rather than a monolithic driver. Setup detects the ATM adapter card and installs the updated miniport driver and other Windows ATM service components. Because of the change in driver structure, however, Windows 2000 doesn't retain the previous ATM configuration settings. Follow these steps to preserve ATM settings:

1. Boot the system and record all parameters configured for the monolithic ATM driver.
2. Use the LECS interface at the ATM switch to configure the E-LAN names and all associated parameters (media type, LES/BUS ATM addresses, and maximum packet size).
3. Perform the installation/upgrade, and then review Chapter 3 to configure the new ATM driver with the previous driver's settings.

Disconnect the UPS

During installation, Windows 2000 Setup attempts to detect devices connected to the system's serial ports. This can cause problems with systems connected by serial cable to a UPS. Disconnect the serial connection to the UPS before starting the installation process.

Detecting and Disabling FPU Division Error

During Windows 2000 installation, Setup checks the CPU in your system for the floating-point division error that exists in early Pentium chips. If the error is detected, it prompts you to disable the FPU (floating-point unit). If you want to continue the installation process, however, you can do so. If you later decide to disable the FPU, you can use a utility called PENTNT that is included with Windows 2000.

To use PENTNT, locate the file \i386\PENTNT.EX_ on your Windows NT CD. Open a command prompt, and then issue the following command to expand the file to your hard disk:

```
expand d:\i386\pentnt.ex_ c:pentnt.exe
```

Substitute the appropriate source drive letter, and a different location on the hard disk for the expanded file if you want. Next, open a console and enter the PENTNT command.

TIP You might want to check your system's FPU prior to starting the Windows 2000 installation process to determine whether your Pentium CPU contains the FPU bug. If it does, you can install a newer chip without the bug. Use the directions described previously to expand and run the PENTNT utility. If your CPU doesn't contain the FPU bug, PENTNT will inform you of that fact.

Backing Up Critical Files

Another necessary step in installing Windows 2000 is to back up your system's critical files. Backing up the entire file system is the best option, because it ensures that all your files are backed up. If you want to back up only some of your files, you'll find the following sections helpful for various types of systems. In addition, the sections discuss general backup strategies.

Choosing a Backup Method

The method you use to back up your system's files depends on the operating system you're currently using, whether your system is connected to a network, and the type of local backup hardware available to you (floppy, tape, CD-R/RW). The following sections cover a variety of possibilities.

N O T E   *CD-R* refers to CD-Recordable and *CD-RW* refers to CD-Rewritable, but CD-ROM refers to read-only CDs. ▨

Local Backup Hardware   Simply copying files to floppy disk is a good option if you have few document or other files to back up. If your system contains a tape drive, CD-R, Zip drive, or other backup hardware, you might prefer to back up your data files to this type of device. First, verify that the device is supported under Windows NT 2000. Also, verify that the backup software you will be using will run under Windows NT 2000. You can import media created with Windows NT Backup with Windows 2000's Backup program.

If the backup software runs only on your old operating system (such as DOS, Windows 3.x, or Windows 9x), you'll have to retain the old operating system and create a dual-boot configuration. This will enable you to boot the old operating system, restore the files, and then boot Windows 2000 to use them.

Network Backup   Another option is to back up your files to a network server. If you're considering this option, consult your network administrator to determine whether space is available on a server and for help in backing up the files. The administrator probably will help you schedule the backup at a time when the increased network traffic from the backup won't have a major impact on other users.

As with a local backup, make sure the backup program you use to back up the files to the server will run under Windows 2000. If not, you'll have to create a dual-boot system.

DOS Systems

On DOS systems, back up your existing CONFIG.SYS and AUTOEXEC.BAT files. If you're using a network, back up the network files, such as PROTOCOL.INI and any other network configuration files specific to your network type. Back up all important document files as a precaution.

Windows 3.x Systems

On Windows 3.x systems, you should back up your CONFIG.SYS and AUTOEXEC.BAT files. In addition, back up the SYSTEM.INI and WIN.INI files from your Windows directory, as well as PROGRAM.INI, WINFILE.INI, CONTROL.INI, and PROTOCOL.INI. In fact, you should consider backing up all the INI files in the Windows directory—this will give you backups of all your Windows system initialization files and your application INI files.

Windows 9x Systems

You should back up your Windows Registry, initialization files, and system files. These include the following:

CONFIG.SYS
AUTOEXEC.BAT
WIN.INI
SYSTEM.INI
PROTOCOL.INI
USER.DAT
SYSTEM.DAT
IO.SYS
MSDOS.SYS
COMMAND.COM

 TIP You have four configuration files to back up if your system is a dual-boot system (DOS and Windows 9x). If you perform the backup from DOS, the files are CONFIG.SYS, AUTOEXEC.BAT, CONFIG.W40, and AUTOEXEC.W40. If you perform the backup from Windows 95, the four files are CONFIG.SYS, AUTOEXEC.BAT, CONFIG.DOS, and AUTOEXEC.DOS.

Windows NT Systems

If you are upgrading your existing Windows NT system to Windows 2000, you should first back up the Registry. You also should consider backing up BOOT.INI, NTDETECT.COM, and NTLDR from the root directory of the hard disk to a floppy disk. These three files control the Windows NT boot process.

Creating and Updating a Repair Disk   In addition to backing up the files described in the previous section, you should have a Windows NT repair disk for your current Windows NT installation. If you don't have a current repair disk, create one before you upgrade to Windows 2000. If you do have a repair disk, you should take the time to update it before upgrading.

N O T E During the installation of Windows 2000, you have the option of creating a repair disk for
2000. You should allow Setup to create the repair disk for you. However, you should have
a repair disk for your current version prior to upgrading, because the two will not be compatible. ■

To create a repair disk for NT prior to the upgrade, execute the program RDISK.EXE
(Emergency Repair Disk utility, or ERD) in the \WINNT\SYSTEM32 directory to create a
repair disk. ERD lets you create a repair disk and update an existing repair disk.

Click the Create Repair Disk button and follow the prompts to create the disk. To update your
existing repair disk, insert the repair disk in drive A and choose the Update Repair Info button. Follow the prompts to complete the update.

Evaluating and Planning the File System

After you back up your important files, analyze your existing file system and determine what
changes you need to make to run Windows 2000. The following sections provide an overview
of the issues you need to consider.

N O T E For a more in-depth discussion of FAT, FAT32, NTFS, and other file system issues, see
Chapter 5, "Optimizing the File System." The following sections offer quick pre-installation
tips on what to do for specific file systems. ■

FAT/FAT32 Versus NTFS   Windows 2000 is fully compatible with the FAT file system used on
DOS and Windows 95 systems, as well as FAT32 found on Windows 98 and the OEM/SR2
version of Windows 95. You can continue to use the FAT and FAT32 file systems if you want.
As mentioned previously, however, NTFS offers much better security and fault tolerance.

Unfortunately, DOS and Windows 9x don't support NTFS; therefore, they can't read NTFS
volumes. If you currently use only Windows 2000 or plan to use only Windows 2000 after you
upgrade, you can convert your existing FAT volume to NTFS. Setup will give you the option
of doing so when you install or upgrade to Windows 2000. There is nothing you need to do
before the installation process to prepare for the conversion (unless you want to back up your
file system first).

If you will be using DOS or Windows 9x on the system in addition to Windows 2000 (dual-
boot configuration) and you want to use NTFS, remember that DOS and Windows 9x cannot
read any of the files in the NTFS volume. You have to repartition the hard disk to add an
NTFS volume. To repartition the hard disk, follow these steps:

1. Back up the entire file system.
2. Create a bootable disk for your DOS or Windows 9x operating systems to use if you
    have problems with the installation.
3. Delete the existing partition.

4. Using FDISK, create a new partition for the FAT volume, leaving space on the disk for the NTFS partition.

5. Format the FAT partition with FORMAT.

6. Reinstall the previous operating system.

7. Restore the files to the FAT volume from the backup set.

8. Run Windows NT Setup to create the NTFS partition.

NOTE Adding an NTFS partition is a cumbersome process. Converting an existing FAT partition to NTFS is simple, however, and Setup can perform that task for you. You don't lose any of your existing files in the conversion. Because it is such a lengthy and involved process to add an NTFS partition to a fully partitioned disk, you should only retain the FAT file system if you must continue to also use DOS or Windows 9x on the system; otherwise, let Setup convert the FAT volume to NTFS. ▪

Converting from HPFS Microsoft dropped support for the HPFS file system in Windows NT 4.0. If your system contains an HPFS partition and you want to continue to access it under Windows 2000, you have to convert the HPFS partition to an NTFS partition. To do so, you need the following utilities:

- ▪ *CONVERT.EXE*. This Windows NT utility converts a FAT or HPFS volume to NTFS. It is included with Windows NT.

- ▪ *BACKACC.EXE*. This OS/2 utility (which runs under OS/2) copies the HPFS access control lists to a file. After converting the volume to NTFS, use the ACLCONV.EXE utility to incorporate the access control lists into the new NTFS volume.

- ▪ *ACLCONV.EXE*. This Windows NT utility incorporates the access control lists created by BACKACC.EXE into the converted NTFS volume.

CAUTION

The ACLCONV.EXE utility is included with versions of Windows NT prior to 4.0, but is not included with Windows NT 4.0 or Windows 2000. Make sure you have a copy of ACLCONV.EXE prior to starting the conversion process.

To convert the HPFS volume to NTFS, follow these steps:

1. Boot the system to OS/2 and run the BACKACC.EXE utility to copy the access control lists to a file. Give the file a short name and place it in a directory (or on a floppy disk) that Windows NT can access.

2. Boot the system to your current version of Windows NT.

3. Run the CONVERT.EXE utility to convert the HPFS volume to NTFS, using the following example as a guide:

```
CONVERT C: /FS:NTFS
```

In this example, `c:` specifies the volume to be converted, and the `/FS:NTFS` switch specifies that the volume be converted to NTFS.

4. After converting the volume to NTFS, run the utility ACLCONV.EXE to restore the old HPFS security settings to the NTFS volume. The following is an example:

```
ACLCONV backupfile /LOG:logfile
```

In this example, you should replace *backupfile* with the name of the ACL backup you created under OS/2 in step 1. Replace *logfile* with the name of a log file in which you want ACLCONV to log error and status messages.

Integrating Compressed Volumes   As explained previously in this chapter, Windows 2000 doesn't support DriveSpace volumes, and Microsoft has no plans at this time to support DriveSpace beyond Windows 9x. You have to uncompress those volumes to make the data visible to Windows 2000. If you still need to take advantage of compression, you can compress the files under Windows 2000 using Explorer.

If you're running DOS, you must use the DRVSPACE utility included with DOS to uncompress the drive. If you're using Windows 9x, choose Start, Programs, Accessories, System Tools, and DriveSpace to start the DriveSpace program.

N O T E   You need enough free space on the host drive to contain the uncompressed files; unfortunately, you might not have enough. Check with the system administrator about backing up your compressed volumes to a network server if your system is connected to a network. After the compressed volumes are safely backed up, you can delete them from your system. Then, install Windows NT 2000, convert the file system to NTFS, and copy the files to the NTFS volume from the network server. █

Planning Network Options

After you plan how to incorporate your existing file system under Windows 2000, you need to consider your options for networking. During installation, Setup prompts you to specify whether you want your system to become part of a workgroup or a domain.

N O T E   This chapter provides only an overview of workgroups and domains to enable you to decide which applies to your installation. For a detailed discussion of domains, domain management, and workgroups, see Chapter 11, "Understanding System Administration and Security." █

▶ **See** "Understanding the Windows 2000 Security Model," **p. 199**

▶ **See** "Managing Domains and Workgroups," **p. 197**

The choice you make depends on your LAN structure, the presence of domain controllers, and how your workstation will participate on the network and access resources. If you're not sure which model to use, consult your network administrator.

In addition to determining what role your computer will play in the network, before running Setup you need to decide which network protocols, clients, and services you need to use. The protocols and clients you choose depend to a large extent on the other computers and servers on your network. If you're installing Windows 2000 on a NetWare network, for example, you should probably use the IPX/SPX protocol and NetWare client, which will enable you to access resources on NetWare servers.

The following sections offer an overview of options, protocols, clients, and services for various network environments.

Choosing a Protocol   Windows 2000 provides built-in support for the following network protocols:

- *NetBEUI*. Well-suited to small networks, but can't be routed. For this reason, NetBEUI is not a good choice for large networks, but the ease with which you can configure it makes it ideal for small networks that do not require routing.

- *NWLink (IPX/SPX)*.   Microsoft developed NWLink to be compatible with Novell NetWare's IPX/SPX protocols. NWLink offers the advantages of NetWare compatibility, routability, and ease-of-configuration. It is a good choice for networks of all sizes.

- *TCP/IP*. One of the oldest protocols but still provides excellent performance, reliability, and routability. TCP/IP works well in any size network and is a necessity for connecting to the Internet. The only disadvantage to TCP/IP is that it requires considerably more configuration than NetBEUI and IPX/SPX. Through DHCP, however, you can greatly simplify TCP/IP configuration and management.

▶ **See** "Using Dynamic Host Configuration Protocol (DHCP) for Dynamic Address Assignment," **p. 401**

- *DLC*.   The Data Link Control (DLC) protocol is included to enable you to connect Windows NT computers to IBM mainframes and access printers connected directly to the network, rather than to a server. It is not intended as a primary network protocol.

- *AppleTalk*. Enables Windows 2000 Systems to communicate with Apple computers; usually applicable only for servers running Services for Macintosh.

Unless you are connecting your computer in a mixed environment, you only need one network protocol. Any of the three primary protocols (NetBEUI, IPX/SPX, and TCP/IP) will work well, depending on the size of your network.

You can use multiple protocols, which makes sense in many situations. For example, if you connect to computers on your LAN through a wired connection but connect to the Internet through a dial-up connection, you might consider using TCP/IP in combination with IPX/SPX or NetBEUI. TCP/IP will serve as the protocol for your Internet connection, while your other protocol will handle LAN traffic.

Before installing Windows 2000, decide what protocol is best for you based on your network environment. If you choose NetBEUI or IPX/SPX, you should not have to determine any settings prior to installation. If you choose TCP/IP, however, you must decide whether you will assign a specific IP address to your computer or use DHCP to retrieve an IP address from a DHCP server. For detailed information on setting up TCP/IP, see Chapter 22, "Internet and Intranet Connections."

▶ **See** "Understanding TCP/IP," **p. 398**

You can add other network protocols and services after you install Windows 2000. It's a good idea to limit the protocols and services you install during setup to a minimum, enabling you to test the network before you begin adding other protocols and services.

Part

I

Ch

1

An Overview of Setup

The process for installing Windows 2000 is straightforward and is explained in detail in Chapter 2. This section of this chapter gives you a brief overview of Setup so you'll know what to expect and can begin planning the installation.

Installing Windows 2000 on New Systems

You can install Windows 2000 on a new system that contains no previous operating system. Windows 2000 Setup detects and installs support for the system's CD-ROM controller and drive, enabling Setup to install from the CD. Setup also partitions and formats the disk according to your specifications. On systems that support booting from CD, you can boot the system with the Windows 2000 CD to start the Setup process.

Upgrading from Windows NT and Windows 9x

You can easily upgrade an existing Windows NT 3.5x, 4.x or Windows 9x installation to Windows 2000. Setup takes care of migrating applications and settings to the new environment. To upgrade, you must have either local or network access to the Windows 2000 file set (local CD or network distribution share).

Windows 2000 will not upgrade Windows NT 3.x and Windows 3.x systems. You must install to a new folder on these systems and reinstall applications.

Creating Multiboot Systems

To retain your existing operating system (DOS, Windows 3.x, Windows 9x, or Windows NT), you can install Windows 2000 to a new directory. After installation, you'll be able to boot either Windows 2000 or your other operating system, as desired. At startup, the system presents a character-based menu enabling you to select which operating system you want to boot. If your previous operating system included multiboot configuration files, you'll still have the ability to select that operating system's boot options, just as you did before installing Windows 2000.

Setup will not migrate your current user settings or applications to the new Windows 2000 installation when you install Windows 2000 to a new directory to create a multiboot system. You have to customize the settings after installation and reinstall many of your applications in order to use them under Windows 2000. This is primarily because the applications' DLLs and other support files must be copied to a location where Windows 2000 can locate them. The programs' Registry settings must also be incorporated into the new Windows 2000 Registry.

Many programs, however, will work without reinstallation. Before you reinstall a program, try to run it. If the program doesn't use Registry settings or require its DLLs to be in a specific location, it's likely you'll be able to run the program without reinstalling it.

If you have to reinstall an application, you don't have to place it in a new folder. Back up any program support files you have customized (such as templates); then under Windows 2000, reinstall the program in its current directory. After completing the installation, restore your customized files. The program should run under Windows 2000 just as it does under your other operating system(s).

2

Windows 2000 Professional Installation

Overview

Installing Windows 2000 is a relatively simple task if you've done the necessary planning (see Chapter 1, "Pre-Installation Planning). The steps you take during installation depend on the type of system and installation you want to achieve (multiprocessor, multiple operating systems, cross-network installation, etc.). This chapter offers tips and procedures for installing Windows 2000 Professional in a variety of situations.

> **N O T E** This chapter focuses on installing Windows 2000 on a single computer. See Chapter 6, "Automated and Push Deployment," for tips and techniques on installing Windows 2000 on multiple systems. ▨

Installation Quick Start

After you perform the installation pre-planning, you have two options: Upgrade an existing operating system or perform a clean installation of Windows 2000 (install Windows 2000 as a new operating system in a new folder).

Upgrading to Windows 2000

You can upgrade Windows 95, Windows 98, and Windows NT Workstation versions 3.51 and 4.0 to Windows 2000 Professional. (Windows 3.x systems require a clean installation.) Setup takes care of migrating registry and program settings and you can use your existing programs without modification (in most cases) or reinstallation. Setup gives you the option of providing upgrade packs for applications (provided by the application developer) during the Setup process to update them for use with Windows 2000. Use the following steps to upgrade to Windows 2000:

1. Boot your current operating system and insert the Windows 2000 CD.

 TIP You can start your system with the Windows 2000 CD inserted if your system can boot from the CD. Setup boots from the CD and starts the Setup process automatically.

2. Windows 2000 Setup starts automatically if your CD drive is configured to autoplay (not applicable to Windows NT 3.51) and asks if you want to upgrade to Windows 2000. Click **Y**es to start the upgrade.

   Or, if Windows 2000 Setup doesn't start automatically, execute the file \I386\WINNT32.EXE on the Windows 2000 CD.

3. The Setup Wizard prompts for information about your computer, network, and desired settings (as described later in this chapter in the section "Information Requested by Setup"). Follow the prompts to provide the information. When you've supplied the necessary information, Setup copies files and completes the installation process.

N O T E Keep track of the password you supply during Setup for the Administrator account. You won't be able to administer the system (or even log on if no other accounts already exist) without the administrator password. ▪

Windows 2000 as a New Installation

You can perform a clean installation of Windows 2000 on any system, but clean installs are particularly targeted to the following situations:

▪ The system is new and has no operating system, or the hard disk is blank.

▪ Your current operating system doesn't support upgrade to Windows 2000 (DOS, Windows 3.1, OS/2, UNIX/Linux).

▪ You don't want to retain existing application, dial-up, or other custom settings, but instead want to start from scratch with a fresh OS (operating system) installation.

▪ You want to retain your existing OS and be able to boot the existing OS or Windows 2000 as your needs dictate.

After performing your pre-installation planning, follow these steps to perform a clean installation of Windows 2000:

1. If your existing OS uses the folder name you want to use for Windows 2000, rename the existing OS's folder.

2. Choose one of the following methods to start Setup:

   Windows 95/98/NT: Run \I386\WINNT32.EXE or let Autoplay execute it when you insert the CD.

   Windows 3.1: Run \I386\WINNT.EXE.

   Systems with bootable CD: Insert the Windows 2000 CD and restart the system.

   Non-compatible OS or no OS: Insert the first Setup diskette in drive A and restart the system.

N O T E Your system might be capable of booting from CD if it is relatively new, but probably needs to be configured in the BIOS to do so if it currently doesn't boot from the Windows 2000 CD. ▪

3. If prompted by Windows 2000 to choose between an upgrade or install of a new copy, choose the option to install a new copy.

4. Follow the Setup prompts to specify settings for the installation (as described later in this chapter in "Information Requested by Setup") and when prompted for the location for Windows 2000, be sure to specify an empty folder.

Part
I

Ch
2

CAUTION

Keep track of the password you supply during Setup for the Administrator account. You won't be able to administer the system (or even log on if no other accounts already exist) without the administrator password.

Post Installation

After Setup finishes, it restarts the system a final time. If you directed Setup to configure the system for multiple users, you will need to log on (otherwise you'll be logged on automatically). Press Ctrl+Alt+Del to access the Logon dialog. Log on with the Administrator account and password you provided during Setup, or in the case of a Windows NT upgrade, any existing user account.

 If your system automatically logs you on but you prefer to require a standard logon, you can configure that option through the Users and Passwords object in the Control Panel. Open Users and Passwords, and then click the Advanced tab and select the option Require users to press Ctrl+Alt+Delete before logging on.

 Windows 95 and Windows 98 upgrades: Unlike Windows 95/98, you must have a valid user account to log on to a Windows 2000 system.

Right-click My Computer and choose Manage; then create user accounts as desired with Local Users and Groups in the Computer Management console.

▶ **See** "Creating Local Accounts," **p. 218**

 You should avoid using the Administrator account as your daily working account because it poses security risks, particularly if you spend a lot of time on the Internet. A malicious site could potentially compromise your system or data if you are logged on as Administrator when you access the site. Create a standard local user or domain user account and use it as your daily working account. You will, however, need to use the Administrator account for certain configuration tasks. If you receive an Access Denied or similar message when trying to install software or configure the system, log off and log back on as Administrator.

Basic Installation Options and Procedures

The previous section served as a quick-start guide to installing Windows 2000. This section examines Setup in a little more detail, describing the information you'll need to provide and options you'll have when installing Windows 2000. Additional Setup tasks such as creating a Setup diskette set also are covered.

Information Requested by Setup

Part

I

Ch

2

The Setup wizard can request several items of information during Windows 2000 installation that vary according to the type of installation you perform and selections you make within the wizard. The following list explains these items:

- *Licensing Agreement.* You must agree to the Licensing Agreement to proceed with the installation.

- *Upgrading to the Windows 2000 File System (NTFS).* You can upgrade the disk on which you install Windows 2000 to NTFS from FAT/FAT32 during Setup. If you prefer, you can convert to NTFS at a later time, instead.

▶ **See** "Evaluating and Planning the File System," **p. 33**

▶ **See** "Converting a FAT Volume to NTFS," **p. 357**

- *Select Special Options.* Customize Windows 2000 Setup, language, and accessibility settings. You can use multiple languages and regional settings.

- *Regional Settings.* Change system and user locale settings for different regions and languages.

- *Personalize Your Software.* Name and organization to whom this copy of Windows 2000 is licensed.

- *Computer Name and Administrator Password.* Specify unique computer name different from other computer, workgroup, or domain names on the network. Change the name Setup suggests if desired. Setup automatically creates an Administrator account during the installation but you must specify a password for the account (unless upgrading from Windows NT 3.51/4.0). Always assign an Administrator password for security. Note that you can configure whether Windows 2000 automatically logs you on at startup through the Users and Passwords object in the Control Panel.

- *Date and Time Settings.* Date and time for your region, time zone, and whether you want Windows 2000 to automatically adjust for daylight savings time.

■ *Networking Settings.* Typical settings option performs automatic configuration with basic network settings. Use Custom settings option to manually configure network clients, services, and protocols.

■ *Workgroup or Computer Domain.* Specify either a domain or workgroup to join during Setup.

■ *Provide Upgrade Packs.* During upgrade from Windows 95/98 you have the option of providing upgrade packs during Setup that modify your existing software. Upgrade packs are available from the appropriate software vendors. Setup prompts for the upgrade pack(s) at the appropriate time.

Installing Across the Network

There are no special steps to take to install or upgrade to Windows 2000 from a network share. However, you need to make sure your network connection remains accessible during the file copy process. Simply connect to the network share containing the Windows 2000 source files and execute the WINNT.EXE or WINNT32.EXE programs, as appropriate.

Creating a Setup Diskette Set

In previous versions of NT you could use a command-line switch with the WINNT.EXE and WINNT32.EXE Setup tools to create a set of boot diskettes for installing Windows NT. Windows 2000 takes a different route, providing a separate application to create the Setup disk set.

 TIP You can save yourself the trouble of creating a Setup boot disk set if your system can boot from its CD drive. Just insert the CD in the drive and reboot to restart the system. Setup will start automatically.

N O T E Your copy of Windows 2000 probably came with a set of Setup boot disks, but you might need to create a new set if the originals are lost, damaged, or unavailable. ■

Have four blank, formatted, high-density diskettes on hand and follow these steps to create the Setup boot disk set:

1. Boot your system and open a command console.
2. Change directory to the \Bootdisk folder on the Windows 2000 CD.
3. Execute the program MAKEBOOT.EXE (16-bit version for DOS/Windows 3.x) or MAKEBT32.EXE (32-bit version for Windows 95/98/NT).
4. Follow the prompts provided by the program to create the disk set.

Winnt and Winnt32 Command Switches

The Winnt.exe and Winnt32.exe programs, which set up Windows 2000, provide several command-line switches you can use to control the way the programs function. Following is the syntax for the Winnt command. Table 2.1 lists Winnt command-line options.

```
WINNT [/s[:sourcepath]] [/t[:tempdrive]] [/u[:answer file]] [/udf:id[,UDF_file]]
➥[/r:folder] [/r[x]:folder] [/e:command] [/a]
```

Table 2.1   Winnt Command-Line Options

Option	Function
/s[:sourcepath]	Location of Windows 2000 source files; must be full local or UNC pathname.
/t[:tempdrive]	Location for temporary Setup files and installation partition.
/u:[answer file]	Perform unattended Setup using specified answer file; requires /s option.
/udf:id[,UDF file]	Specify unique ID and use Unique Database File (UDF) to modify answer file for unattended Setup. ID determines which answers in UDF file are used.
/r[:folder]	Create optional folder that remains after installation; specify folder name as *folder*.
/rx[:folder]	Copy folder during Setup but delete after installation.
/e	Specify command to be executed after GUI-mode Setup completes.
/a	Enable accessibility options.

Following is the syntax for Winnt32. Table 2.2 lists Winnt32 command-line options.

```
winnt32 [/s:sourcepath] [/tempdrive:drive_letter] [/unattend[num]:[answer_file]]
➥[/copydir:folder_name] [/copysource:folder_name] [/cmd:command_line]
➥[/debug[level]:[filename]] [/udf:id[,UDF_file]] [/syspart:drive_letter]
➥ [/checkupgradeonly] [/cmdcons] [/m:folder_name] [/makelocalsource]
➥[/noreboot]
```

Table 2.2   Winnt32 Command-Line Options

Option	Function
/s:sourcepath	Location of Windows 2000 source files; you can specify multiple sources with multiple /s switches.
/tempdrive:drive_letter	Location for temporary Setup files and Windows 2000 installation partition.
/unattend	Upgrade previous version of Windows 2000 in unattended Setup mode; implies acceptance of EULA.

continues

Table 2.2 Continued

Option	Function
/unattend[*num*]:[*answer_file*]	Fresh install in unattended mode; *num* is number of seconds between file copy and system restart and *answer_file* is answer file for Setup options.
/copydir:*folder_name*	Copy optional folder specified by *folder* to the system root folder during Setup; use multiple switches to copy multiple folders. Folder remains after Setup completes.
/copysource:*folder_name*	Copy optional folder specified by *folder* to the system root folder during Setup; use multiple switches to copy multiple folders. Folder(s) deleted after Setup completes.
/cmd:*command_line*	Execute specified command after Setup but before final system restart.
/debug[*level*]:[*filename*]	Log information to specified file; levels are 1-errors, 2-warnings, 3-information, 4-detailed.
/udf:id[,*UDF file*]	Specify unique ID and use Unique Database File (UDF) to modify answer file for unattended Setup. ID determines which answers in UDF file are used.
/syspart:*drive_letter*	Copy Setup startup files to drive, mark drive active for install in another computer, which continues Setup on boot. Requires /tempdrive switch. Not available for Windows 9x.
/checkupgradeonly	Analyze system for upgrade compatibility but don't install; creates Upgrade.txt (Windows 9x) or Winnt32.log (Windows NT) log file in current OS system root folder.
/cmdcons	Install Recovery Console during Setup.
/m:*folder_name*	Copy files from specified folder if exist rather than default source location.
/makelocalsource	Copy all installation source files to local hard disk; for cases where CD not available after Setup starts.
/noreboot	Don't restart system after final Setup phase.

See Chapter 6, "Automated and Push Deployment," for more detailed explanation of unattended and advanced Setup options.

Multiple Processor Systems

Generally, Setup correctly detects a multiprocessor system and installs the correct HAL (Hardware Abstraction Layer) to support the multiprocessor system. Correct detection and SMP support involves two things: the system's BIOS and the HAL selected during Setup. If the BIOS doesn't correctly report the proper system type, Setup might automatically select the wrong HAL to install, resulting in single processor support on an SMP system, or high CPU utilization for one of the CPUs in an SMP system when the system is idle.

Make sure your system's BIOS is up to date if you experience problems with SMP support after installation. To specify which HAL gets installed, press F5 during the first part of text-mode Setup to access a menu with which you can select the HAL for installation.

Part

I

Ch

2

Installing Multiple Operating Systems

In most cases you'll install Windows 2000 as the only OS on your system(s). In some situations, however, you might want to install multiple operating systems, selecting the needed OS at system startup. For example, you might need to retain Windows 9x to run applications not supported by Windows 2000, or run UNIX or Linux in addition to Windows 2000.

Windows 3.x, Windows 9x, Windows NT, and Windows 2000 can all share a single partition. Install the other operating systems first, and then perform a clean install of Windows 2000 to the same partition. Make sure to install Windows 2000 in a new folder. When you boot the system, the Windows 2000 boot loader gives you a menu showing the other operating systems. Select the one you want to use.

 If you don't mind having to use Fdisk to activate a partition to boot, consider placing Windows 2000 in a separate partition. If you later have problems with any installed operating system, having them in separate partitions can simplify reinstallation, because you can remove and re-create the partition to clean out the old OS.

 You can edit the BOOT.INI file to specify which OS boots by default and the timeout value to wait for menu selection. You also can use the System object in the Control Panel to accomplish the same thing.

UNIX and Linux must be installed in a separate partition from Windows 2000. You can install either operating system first, because they'll reside in different partitions.

To boot the other OS, use Disk Management in the Computer Management console to activate the partition containing the desired OS:

1. Open the Computer Management console in the MMC and click Disk Management.
2. Right-click on the partition you want to make active, then click **M**ark Partition Active.
3. Exit Computer Management and reboot the system.

When you want to reboot in Windows 2000, use Fdisk or the appropriate command to mark the Windows 2000 partition as active, then restart the system.

 TIP See the *Microsoft Windows 2000 Professional Installation and Configuration Handbook* CD for a copy of PartitionMagic that will help you create, convert, and manage your disk partitions.

## CHAPTER 3

Networking Installation and Configuration

Overview of Windows 2000 Networking

Windows 2000 includes built-in networking, including support for a wide range of Network Interface Cards (NICs, or network *adapters*), network *clients*, network *protocols*, and network *services*. The NIC connects the computer physically to the network. Protocols serve as a communications language of sorts for the network traffic. For two systems to communicate over the network, both require the same protocol. TCP/IP, NetBEUI, and IPX/SPX are common network protocols supported by Windows 2000.

A *network client* serves as a network agent, handling network authentication and resource access. A *network service* provides special services such as file and printer sharing.

You can install and configure network adapters, protocols, and services when you install Windows 2000. You can also modify them at any time after setup. Either process is essentially the same.

N O T E   This chapter focuses on common network adapters, client, protocol, and service tasks and settings. See Chapter 22, "Internet and Intranet Connections," for detailed information on configuring and using dial-up connections. Several chapters in Part V explain how to install and configure optional networking components such as Internet Information Server (IIS), Index Server, and others. ■

Managing Adapters

Although you will probably install your network adapters when you first install Windows 2000, you can install and manage adapters at any time. The Network and Dial-Up Connections icon in the Control Panel enables you to manage network-related objects and services. The Add/Remove Hardware wizard enables you to add and remove network adapters. The following sections explain how to manage NICs under Windows 2000.

 The Network and Dial-Up Connections folder shows an icon for each network connection. You'll see a separate icon for each adapter if your system contains more than one. When managing network connections, make sure that you select the correct one. Systems with multiple NICs are called *multi-homed*.

Adding and Removing NICs

You use the Add/Remove Hardware object in the Control Panel to add and remove NICs. To add a NIC, install the network hardware, then boot the system, log on, and run the Add/Remove Hardware wizard. The wizard searches for Plug and Play–compatible devices and will locate the NIC if it supports PnP. If not, you can select Add a New Device and then allow the wizard to attempt to detect the device or choose the NIC from a list, just as you would when installing any other type of device.

To remove a NIC, run the Add/Remove Hardware wizard and choose Uninstall/Unplug a Device and follow the wizard's prompts to select and remove the NIC.

Setting NIC Properties

In addition to adding and removing network adapters, you can set the properties of installed adapters. These properties typically include the NIC's resources (IRQ and base address), transceiver type, and other options.

To set an adapter's properties, follow these steps:

1. Open the Network and Dial-Up Connections folder from the Settings menu.
2. Right-click the connection you want to modify and choose Properties from the pop-up menu to access the properties for the selected device (see Figure 3.1).

FIGURE 3.1
Manage adapter and other properties through the connection's properties.

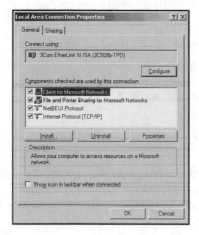

3. Verify that the correct adapter is listed in Connect Using (to make sure you're modifying the right adapter in a multihomed system), and then click Configure to access the adapter's properties. Figure 3.1 shows a typical NIC's properties.
4. In the adapter's Properties sheet, use the properties on the Advanced, Driver, and Resource tabs to configure the NIC's settings.
5. After making your selections, click OK to apply the settings and close the adapter's Properties sheet.

N O T E The Sharing tab enables you to share a connection with other users (such as sharing a dial-up Internet connection with other users on your LAN). See Chapter 22 for more information on connection sharing. ▪

▶ **See** "Internet Connection Sharing," **p. 420**

▶ **See** "Viewing and Managing Devices," **p. 118**

Part

I

Ch

3

Managing Protocols

You must have at least one network protocol installed to access network resources and share local resources. The General tab of the connection's Properties sheet shows currently installed protocols and enables you to add, configure, and remove network protocols.

N O T E You must be logged on as a member of the Administrator group to make changes to the system's configuration. ■

Adding Protocols

Follow these steps to add a protocol:

1. Open the General tab of the connection's Properties sheet and click Install. Windows 2000 displays the Select Network Component Type dialog.

2. Click Protocol and then click Add.

3. Choose the protocol you want to install from the Network Protocol list and click OK.

After you choose OK, Windows 2000 adds the protocol to your system, but you might still need to configure the protocol's settings. (Later sections in this chapter explain how to configure specific protocols; in most cases, you do not need to restart the system for the change to take effect.)

Removing a Protocol

To remove a network protocol, open the Properties sheet for the connection, select the protocol from the list of installed components, and click Uninstall. This removes the protocol for all adapters and services. You need to restart the system for the change to take effect.

Disabling a Protocol Without Removing It

Instead of removing a protocol from your system, you might want to disable the protocol from a specific adapter. For example, in a multihomed system, you might want to disable TCP/IP from your LAN connection but not from the WAN connection, using NetBEUI locally to prevent security breaches or denial-of-service attacks to local systems while still allowing Internet access through the WAN port.

To disable a protocol from a connection, simply open the Properties sheet for the connection and deselect the check box beside the protocol. This *unbinds* the protocol from the connection. Click OK and then restart the system.

N O T E Unbinding a protocol was previously accomplished in Windows NT through the Bindings tab. ■

► For more information about Bindings in Windows 2000, **see** "Advanced Settings and Bindings Options," **p. 56**

Configuring Specific Protocols

Some protocols, such as NetBEUI, do not offer any configurable options. Others, however, do enable you to configure various options that determine how the protocol functions on your system. To configure a protocol, open the connection's Properties sheet, click the protocol in the Installed Components list, and then click Properties.

Of the five default protocols included with Windows 2000, only the AppleTalk, IPX/SPX, and TCP/IP protocols are configurable. Because of its relative complexity, TCP/IP is covered as a separate topic in Chapter 23. The following sections explain how to configure the IPX/SPX and AppleTalk protocols.

Part
I

Ch
3

Configuring IPX/SPX

You can configure a handful of options for the IPX/SPX protocol. To do so, open the Properties sheet for the connection, click the NWLink IPX/SPX protocol, and click Properties. Windows 2000 displays the NWLink IPX/SPX properties shown in Figure 3.2. Specify settings according to the settings described in Figure 3.2.

IPX node address of computer.
Leave at zero unless using IPX
routing or File and Print
Services for NetWare.

FIGURE 3.2
The Network number field is dimmed if only one NIC/frame type is present.

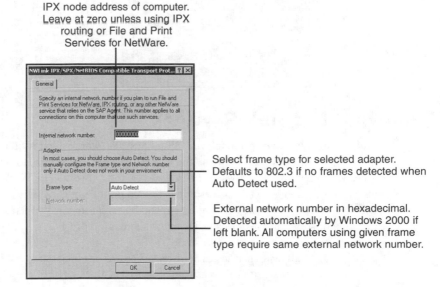

Select frame type for selected adapter.
Defaults to 802.3 if no frames detected when
Auto Detect used.

External network number in hexadecimal.
Detected automatically by Windows 2000 if
left blank. All computers using given frame
type require same external network number.

N O T E   Unless you intend to run File and Print Services for NetWare on your computer or use IPX routing, you should not have to configure the IPX/SPX protocol on your computer. The default settings should work properly. ■

Configuring AppleTalk

AppleTalk offers only two Protocol Properties options you can modify. Click AppleTalk in the General tab of the Connections Properties sheet, and then click P**r**operties to access the AppleTalk properties shown in Figure 3.3.

N O T E   AppleTalk *zones* provide a means of organizing AppleTalk networks. Each physical LocalTalk network is assigned a unique zone name. In essence, AppleTalk zones function much like Windows 2000 workgroups or domains in that they enable users to quickly locate often-used resources. ▪

Check to enable inbound connections.
Deselect to prevent connections to
your computer.

FIGURE 3.3
The zone list is empty until you physically connect to the AppleTalk network.

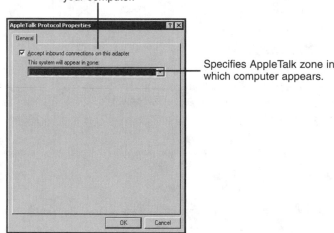

Specifies AppleTalk zone in which computer appears.

Managing Network Services

In addition to at least one protocol, your Windows 2000 workstation requires various services to enable specific network functions. The Computer Browser service, for example, enables your computer to browse for resources on the network. The Workstation service enables your computer to access resources shared on the network. The number and type of services you use on your workstation depend on the protocols you use, whether you use RAS, and a host of other factors specific to each situation.

N O T E   RAS stands for Remote Access Services. RAS enables the computer to dial out and connect to other systems as well as function as a dial-up server. ▪

During Windows 2000 installation, Setup installs a basic set of services that enable your computer to access the network. In Windows NT, these services appeared in the Network Properties sheet. In Windows 2000, you manage them under the Services and Applications branch of the Computer Management MMC console. Right-click My Computer and choose Manage to open the Computer Management console.

To manage network services in Windows 2000, click the connections icon in the Network and Dial-Up Connections folder to open the connection's Properties sheet. The Components Checked Are Used by This Connection list shows installed services.

To add a network service, follow these steps:

1. Click Install to display the Select Network Component dialog.
2. Click Service and then Add. Scroll through the Network Service list to locate and select the service to install, or click the Have Disk button if you want to install a third-party network service.
3. Choose OK; Windows 2000 installs the service and, depending on the selected service, might prompt you for additional configuration information.

To remove a network service, open the properties for the connection, select the service, and then click Uninstall. Windows 2000 removes the service and, if necessary, prompts you to restart the system.

Modifying Identification Settings

Each computer has a name associated with it that identifies the computer within its domain or workgroup. You might want to rename a computer to more accurately reflect its use, location, primary user, and so on, or to eliminate a conflict with another computer having the same name.

You modify network ID settings through the System Properties sheet, which you can access in either of two ways: Right-click My Computer and choose Properties, or choose Advanced, Network Identification in the Network and Dial-Up Connections folder.

The Network Identification tab in the System Properties sheet provides two methods for changing network ID. Click Network ID to run a wizard that steps you through the process of specifying a computer name and choosing a domain or workgroup. The wizard also helps you create an account in the domain if you don't already have one. Doing so, however, requires that you specify an account and password with Administrator privileges in the domain.

To simply change settings without the wizard, click Properties on the Network Identification tab to access the Identification Changes dialog shown in Figure 3.4.

Part

I

Ch

3

FIGURE 3.4
The Network ID wizard automates assigning unique computer name and domain or work-group membership, but you can click Properties to make manual changes.

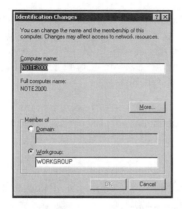

You also can change the DNS suffix and NetBIOS name for the system. By default, Windows 2000 takes the DNS suffix from the group policies applicable to the computer. The local setting (which you're setting here) is used when the group policy is disabled or the DNS suffix is not specified in the group policy. To make DNS suffix or NetBIOS name changes, click **M**ore on the Identification Changes dialog to access the DNS Suffix and NetBIOS Computer Name dialog. In the **P**rimary DNS suffix box, type the desired domain suffix in the form *domain.suf* (such as mydomain.com). The domain suffix is appended to the computer name to create a Fully Qualified Domain Name, or FQDN. Use the **N**etBIOS computer name box to specify the NetBIOS name for your computer. In most cases, the NetBIOS computer name is the same as the computer name specified in the Identification Changes sheet.

Advanced Settings and Binding Options

The Network and Dial-Up Connections folder provides a tabbed Advanced Settings sheet you can use to set advanced options. This sheet includes the protocols that are bound to specific services and the priority order of network providers. To access these settings, open the Network and Dial-Up Connections folder and choose Adva**n**ced, Advanced **S**ettings (see Figure 3.5).

Changing Bindings

When you select a protocol's check box in the connections' properties, you bind the protocol to all services (as applicable) in the connection. In some cases, you'll want to unbind a protocol for specific services. For example, you should consider unbinding the TCP/IP protocol from the File and Printer Sharing service for computers connected to the Internet to reduce the possibility of unauthorized access to the systems. With TCP/IP bound to this service, it's a fairly simply matter for a hacker to browse—if not gain access to—your system.

FIGURE 3.5

Use Advanced Settings to control protocol binding for services and provider order.

To unbind a protocol from a specific service, open the Adapters and Bindings tab in the Advanced Settings sheet. In the Connections list, select the connection you want to modify. In the Bindings for Local Area Connection list, locate the service and deselect the protocol where it is listed under the service. You can later reselect the protocol to rebind it to the service.

N O T E Disabling a protocol, service, or adapter is not the same as removing it. Disabling it simply turns it off; removing it deletes the object from the system. If you think you might need the network object later, you should disable it. It's easier to re-enable an object than to reinstall it. ■

Changing Provider Order

Windows 2000 can access network resources using more than one network provider. You can control the priority of network providers, defining which one is used first. Changing the priority can improve performance by targeting a specific provider that might offer better performance or that you want to use most often.

To control provider order, open Advanced Settings and click the Provider Order tab (see Figure 3.6). Click the provider you want to move, then click either the up or down arrow button on the dialog to move the provider up or down in the list.

Part

I

Ch

3

FIGURE 3.6
Change processing priority for network and print providers through the Provider Order page.

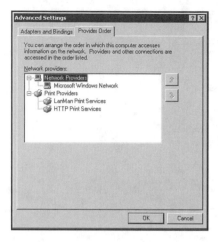

Networking Without a NIC

Windows 95 introduced a feature called Direct Cable Connection that enabled you to network two computers using the parallel or serial ports and a special cable rather than a NIC. Windows 2000 expands on this capability by supporting infrared as well as serial and parallel ports. This section explains how to configure this type of network connection (referred to here as a *direct connection*).

▶ For more information about configuring Windows 2000 as a dial-up server and enabling modem connections to your computer, **see** "Configuring a Dial-Up Server," **p. 423**

A computer can act as a host or guest in a direct connection. As a host, the computer shares its local resources with the other computer, subject to applicable security restrictions, permissions, and rights on the host. As a guest, your computer accesses shared resources on the other computer, subject to the other computer's security settings.

You configure host and guest connections separately because a computer will typically function as one or the other, but not as both. However, there is no reason you couldn't use the computer in either capacity, depending on the situation and your needs. You can configure a separate guest connection for each available port. For host connections, all ports are combined into a single connection, but you can selectively enable and disable ports for the connection. A host connection can support multiple connections, such as concurrent connections, through both the serial and parallel ports.

You can buy cables to implement a direct connection. If you're not sure whether the cable you have is correct or if you want to make your own cables, you can use Figures 3.7 and 3.8 as a guide to testing or making a cable. For testing, use a volt-ohm meter or inexpensive continuity tester to check continuity (resistance) between pins on each end of the cable to verify the correct hookup.

FIGURE 3.7

Cable pinouts for a
serial network cable.

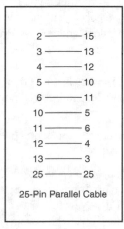

2 ——— 3	2 ——— 3
3 ——— 2	3 ——— 2
4 ——— 6	4 ——— 5
5 ——— 5	5 ——— 4
6 ——— 4	6 ——— 20
7 ——— 8	7 ——— 7
8 ——— 7	8 ——— 20

9-Pin Serial
Null-Modem Cable

25-Pin Serial
Null-Modem Cable

FIGURE 3.8

Cable pinouts for a
parallel network cable.

| 2 ——— 15 |
| 3 ——— 13 |
| 4 ——— 12 |
| 5 ——— 10 |
| 6 ——— 11 |
| 10 ——— 5 |
| 11 ——— 6 |
| 12 ——— 4 |
| 13 ——— 3 |
| 25 ——— 25 |

25-Pin Parallel Cable

Part

I

Ch

3

Configuring the Connection

You use the Make New Connection wizard in the Network and Dial-Up Connections folder to configure a direct connection:

1. Open the Network and Dial-Up Connections folder and start the Make New Connection wizard. Click **N**ext after the wizard starts.

2. Choose the option **C**onnect Directly to Another Computer, and then click **N**ext.

3. Choose either **H**ost or **G**uest depending on the role you want your computer to play in the connection, and then click **N**ext.

4. Select the port for the connection (serial, infrared, or parallel), and then click **N**ext.

5. Select the users you want to allow to connect to your system (host mode only) or whether you want the connection available to other users who log on to your system (guest mode only). Click **N**ext.

6. For guest connections, specify the name for the connection to appear in the Network and Dial-Up Connections folder. Host connections default to the name Incoming Connections and can't be changed. Click Finish.

Setting Incoming Connection Properties

After you configure a connection for incoming access, you can modify its settings to control which ports it uses, who can access the system, and which network components are bound to the connection. Open the Network and Dial-Up Connections folder, right-click Incoming Connections, and choose Properties to access the properties for the connection.

Enabling/Disabling Specific Ports   The General tab enables you to specify which ports are enabled for incoming access and their settings. Also, although you can configure the Incoming Connections settings to support multiple ports, you might want to disable one or more ports. To do so, right-click Incoming Connections and choose Properties. Select and deselect ports in the Devices list as desired, and then click OK.

To set properties for a port, click the port in the Devices list, and then click Properties. You can configure only the serial port and modem; parallel and infrared ports offer no settings to change.

▶ For more information about port properties settings, **see** "Setting Phone and Modem Options," **p. 180**

Controlling User Access   The Users tab enables you to specify which user accounts on your system are allowed remote access through Incoming Connections. Select and deselect users in the Users Allowed to Connect list as needed. Click New to create a new user account, Delete to delete the selected account, or Properties to view the properties for the selected account.

Two options on the Users tab offer additional control:

■ *Require*. Require all users to secure their passwords and data. This requires client to select Require Data Encryption on Security tab of connection, enabling encryption for connection.

■ *Always*. Always allow directly connected devices such as palmtop computers to connect without providing a password. Allow devices connected physically to computer to connect without password.

Specifying Allowed Protocols, Clients, and Services   Use the Networking tab of the Incoming Connection properties to specify which clients, services, and protocols are bound to the direct connection. As with LAN properties, simply select/deselect components as desired. Click a component and click Properties to set properties for the component.

## CHAPTER 4

Configuring Interface and Systems Options

Customizing the Windows 2000 Professional Interface

There are several ways to customize the interface to affect the way Windows 2000 appears and functions. You can customize the desktop by changing video drivers, applying a screen saver, changing fonts and colors for screen elements, and so on. Other customization options enable you to control performance properties such as the size of the swap file (virtual memory), default boot option, and other startup and operational options.

N O T E This chapter focuses on desktop configuration options and performance/startup options to help you optimize performance. The chapter does not cover customization issues such as sound schemes that are primarily preference settings with little effect on performance or usability. For coverage of those topics, refer to *Special Edition Using Microsoft Windows 2000 Professional* from Que. ▪

▶ **See** Chapter 10, "Exploring the Control Panel," and Chapter 7, "Managing Hardware," to learn how to configure display adapter settings and change display drivers.

Using the Active Desktop

The Active Desktop in Windows 2000 combines the Windows desktop with the Internet Explorer 5.x browser to provide a common way to access information from your local hard disk, corporate network, or the Internet. You can use the same techniques to access applications, folders, files, and Internet URLs that designate Web sites.

The Active Desktop enables you to do the following:

- Use HTML pages or graphics as desktop wallpaper, Active Desktop items, or channel screen savers.
- Customize the appearance of explorer bars in the browser window.
- Create and customize toolbars.
- Customize the Start, Programs, and Favorites menus.

N O T E Internet addresses, such as http://www.microsoft.com, are referred to as Uniform Resource Locators (URLs) ▪

The following sections detail each element of the Active Desktop.

Configuring the Taskbar and Toolbars

You can simplify your access to URLs, folders and files by configuring the Windows 2000 taskbar and toolbars by doing the following:

- Adding new toolbars to the taskbar
- Adding floating toolbars to the Active Desktop
- Customizing the Quick Launch toolbar

To add a toolbar to the taskbar or to customize the Quick Launch toolbar, follow these steps:

1. Right-click the taskbar and choose **T**oolbars.
2. Click the following toolbars to add to the taskbar:

- *Address*. Enables you to open a URL, local resource name (such as a folder), or remote resource name (such as a network share) from the taskbar (see Figure 4.1).

- *Links*. Contains shortcuts to often-used resources. Modify the contents of the Links toolbar by adding and removing shortcuts from the \Documents and Settings*user*\Favorites\Links folder, where *user* is your user logon name. Alternatively, simply drag items to the toolbar.

- *Desktop*. Gives quick access to folders, shortcuts, and other objects on the desktop.

- *Quick Launch*. Gives quick access to most often-used applications, documents, and other resources. Add objects to the Quick Launch by adding shortcuts to the \Documents and Settings*user*\Application Data\Microsoft\Internet Explorer\Quick Launch folder. Alternatively, simply drag items to the toolbar.

- *New Toolbar*. Enables you to specify name of a folder or Internet URL to create new toolbar.

Part

I

Ch

4

FIGURE 4.1
Provide quick access to often-used applications or other objects by placing additional toolbars on the taskbar and desktop.

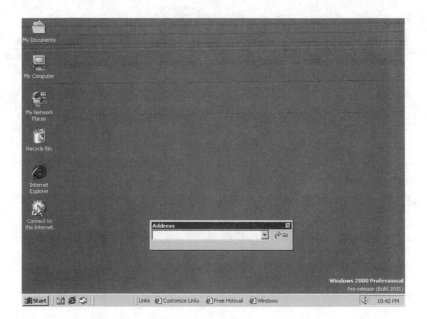

3. Repeat the preceding steps to add additional toolbars to the taskbar.

To add a floating toolbar to the Active Desktop, simply click and drag the toolbar to the desktop.

 TIP   Left-drag the toolbar's title bar to the taskbar to move it back to the taskbar.

Configuring Explorer Bars

Explorer bars in My Computer, Windows Explorer, and the Internet Explorer browser offer a method of browsing through a list of links while the pages that those links point to are opened in the right side of the window.

The four explorer bars are the following:

- *Search*. Displays a list of services that offer search capabilities.
- *Favorites*. Displays the list of URLs that have been added via the **A**dd to Favorites option in the Internet Explorer browser.
- *History*. Displays a list of folders that contain links to URLs that you have accessed, organized by the days and weeks that you last accessed them.
- *All Folders*. Displays list of all network and local folders.

To view or hide Explorer Bars, click **V**iew, **E**xplorer Bar and then select the desired option.

Using Web Content as Wallpaper

You can display an HTML page as the wallpaper on the Active Desktop. The HTML page must be on your local computer or on a network drive and must be referenced by a filename, not an Internet URL.

To use an HTML page as wallpaper, follow these steps:

1. Right-click the desktop and click P**r**operties.
2. On the Web tab, select Show **W**eb Content on my Active Desktop.
3. On the Background tab, browse to (or specify the path to) the desired HTML page.

Adding Live Content to the Desktop

You can add a live Web object to the desktop, which can be a Web page or smaller component such as a stock or news ticker:

1. Right-click the desktop and click P**r**operties.
2. On the Web tab, select Show **W**eb content on my Active Desktop.

3. Click **N**ew to access the New Active Desktop Item dialog.

4. Enter the URL in the **L**ocation box and click OK.

5. On the Web tab, select the URL you just added and click P**r**operties.

6. Use the object's property sheet to schedule updates and specify other options for the object.

NOTE Live Web content on the desktop works best with a live (continuous) Internet connection, but you also can use live content with a dial-up Internet connection. ■

Customizing Folders

Chapter 10, "Exploring the Control Panel," explains how to set global options that define how all folders appear and function. This section explains how to customize individual folders to add a background, modify filename appearance, add a folder comment, or apply an HTML template to the folder.

Windows 2000 provides a wizard to help you customize folders. Open the folder you want to customize and choose **V**iew, **C**ustomize This Folder to start the wizard. Figure 4.2 describes the dialog that appears after you click **N**ext. The wizard raises additional dialogs depending on your selections here.

Choose to customize
current folder

FIGURE 4.2
You can restore default settings as well as customize a folder using the wizard.

Apply background image to folder and change filename text foreground/ background color

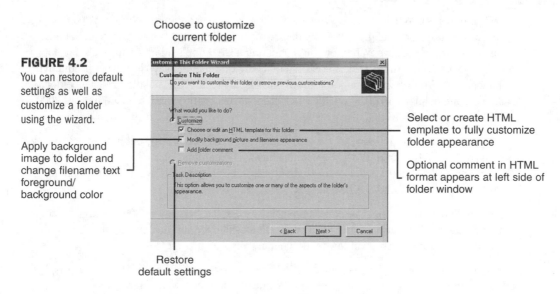

Select or create HTML template to fully customize folder appearance

Optional comment in HTML format appears at left side of folder window

Restore
default settings

The option Modify Background **P**icture and Filename Appearance enables you to assign an image file in BMP, JPG, or GIF format as the background for the folder, which can provide a visual cue to help you quickly pick out the folder on a crowded desktop. You also can change the foreground and background color for filename text under the icons, which also serves as a good visual cue.

The Add **F**older Comment option enables you to assign HTML code to affect the appearance of the left folder pane. Using this option requires an understanding of HTML. The wizard raises a dialog in which you can enter the HTML code if you select this option.

The Choose or Edit an **H**TML Template for This Folder option enables you to choose an existing HTML template or modify a template to create a new one. Windows 2000 provides five predefined templates to choose from. By default, the HTML templates are stored in *systemroot*\Web. Create additional templates in that folder as desired.

N O T E   This section is intended to show experienced HTML users the options available to them to customize folders. Creating or modifying HTML documents falls outside the scope of this book. For an in-depth look at HTML programming, refer to *Special Edition Using HTML 4, Sixth Edition*, by Molly Holzschlag, published by Que. ■

Using Multiple Displays

Like Windows NT, Windows 2000 supports multiple displays, although Windows 2000 makes it easier to set up and configure multiple displays. Several types of applications can benefit from two or more displays. Whether you're running a CAD application, doing Web development, or just wanting more desktop real estate, using multiple displays is a great productivity enhancement. You can move windows from one display to another, position reference documents on one display and place your work documents on another, and so on. Windows 2000 supports up to ten individual displays.

Each adapter must be AGP or PCI (or a combination of the two types), but it does not have to be the same model or from the same manufacturer. The computer's BIOS detects the adapters according to slot order or, in some systems, based on a BIOS setting that enables you to specify the default VGA device.

After installation, one adapter serves as the primary display. Windows 2000 displays the logon dialog on the primary display, and most applications will open on the primary display. You can then move the application's window to a secondary display.

Configuring multiple displays is very easy in Windows 2000. After you verify that the display adapters you are using are compatible with Windows 2000 (check the Hardware Compatibility List), follow these steps to configure the adapters:

1. Shut down the computer and install the additional adapters.

2. Boot the system. Windows 2000 will detect the new adapters and install the appropriate drivers for them or install a standard VGA driver if it is unable to adequately detect the adapter type.

3. Right-click the desktop, choose Properties to access the display properties, and then click the Settings tab. Figure 4.3 shows the Settings tab with two displays installed.

4. Click one of the numbered monitor icons or select an adapter from the Display list, and then adjust the screen resolution and color depth for the selected display. Repeat the process for the other display.

5. Click and drag the numbered monitor icons to arrange the displays according to your physical monitor layout.

6. Refer to Figure 4.3 for additional options, and then click OK or Apply to apply the settings.

▶ For detailed information on setting other display properties and changing display drivers, **see** "Controlling the Display," **p. 162**

FIGURE 4.3
Click Identify to visually identify the selected display.

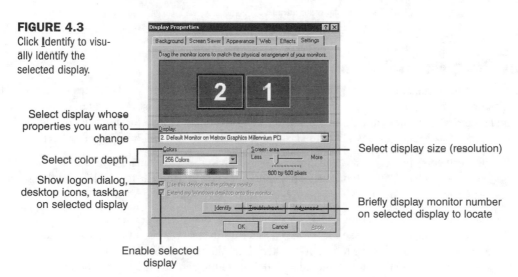

Select display whose properties you want to change

Select color depth

Show logon dialog, desktop icons, taskbar on selected display

Select display size (resolution)

Briefly display monitor number on selected display to locate

Enable selected display

Part

I

Ch

4

Customizing the Start Menu and Taskbar

Windows 2000 provides several options you can use to control the appearance and function of the Start menu and taskbar. For example, like Windows NT and Windows 9x, you can drag the taskbar to any of the four edges of the display or from one display to another (multiple displays in use).

Setting Taskbar Options

To set taskbar options, right-click the taskbar and choose Properties to access the Taskbar property tab. Figure 4.4 explains the available options.

FIGURE 4.4
You can drag the taskbar to a new location as well as specify properties to control its appearance.

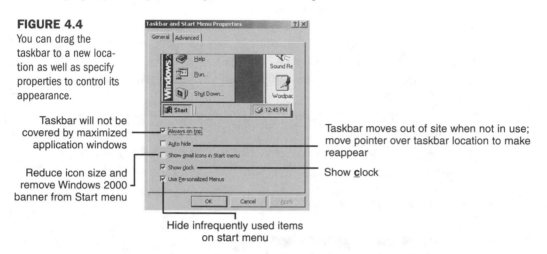

Taskbar will not be covered by maximized application windows

Reduce icon size and remove Windows 2000 banner from Start menu

Taskbar moves out of site when not in use; move pointer over taskbar location to make reappear

Show clock

Hide infrequently used items on start menu

Setting Start Menu Options

You can easily customize the position of menu items on the Programs and Favorites menus with drag and drop to reorder them according to your preferences. Just click and drag a menu item where you want it on the menu. You can restore the default locations, if desired, using the Start Menu Options tab of the taskbar properties (which will be explained shortly).

You also can copy, move, or create a shortcut to an item in the Programs, Favorites, or Settings menu. Just right-click on the item and drag it to the desktop or to a folder, and then choose Copy Here, Move Here, or Create Shortcut(s) Here from the context menu.

To customize Start menu settings, right-click the taskbar, choose Properties, and then click the Start Menu Options tab (see Figure 4.5). Click Add to start a wizard that helps you add to the Start menu. Click Remove to remove an item from the menu. Click Advanced to open an Explorer window in your Start Menu folder and then add or remove shortcuts to or from the folder as desired.

 TIP Your Start Menu folder is located in \Documents and Settings*user*\Start Menu, where *user* is your Windows 2000 logon name.

Use Re-sort to rearrange the items on the Start menu into their default locations if you have relocated menu items, and use Clear to remove from the Start menu references to recently used documents, programs, and Web sites.

FIGURE 4.5

Control the Start menu and some cascading menus (such as Programs) from the Start Menu Options tab.

The Start Menu Settings list on the Start Menu Options tab offers several settings to further customize the Start menu:

- *Display Administrative Tools.* Include Administrative Tools folder on the **P**rograms menu. Turn off if you seldom use the Administrative Tools or usually access them from the Control Panel.

- *Display Favorites.* Include Favorites folder on Start menu. Turn off if you seldom or never use Favorites folder.

- *Display Logoff.* Show Logoff command on Start menu. Turn off if you want to force users to use Shutdown or Ctrl+Alt+Del to log off.

- *Expand Control Panel.* Expand Control Panel as cascading menu when clicked rather than opening Control Panel folder. Figure 4.6 shows the Control Panel expanded.

- *Expand My Documents.* Expand My Documents folder to show contents as a cascading menu off the Start menu instead of opening the folder.

- *Expand Network and Dial-Up Connections.* Expand Network and Dial-Up Connections folder to show contents as a cascading menu off Start menu instead of opening the folder.

- *Expand Printers.* Expand Printers folder to show printers as cascading menu off Start menu instead of opening Printers folder.

- *Scroll the Programs Menu.* Display **P**rograms menu as scrolling list rather multiple columns.

- *Use Personalized Menus.* Hide infrequently used items in **P**rograms menu to simplify the menu. Use scroll buttons on menu to view hidden items. Turn off to show all items immediately when menu opened.

Part

I

Ch

4

FIGURE 4.6
You can expand the
Control Panel and sev-
eral other objects on
the Start menu.

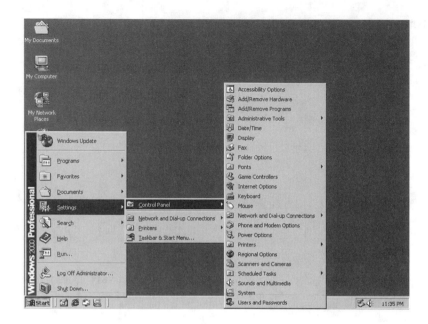

## CHAPTER 5

Optimizing the File System

Overview of Windows 2000 File Systems

File systems define the way in which operating systems organize, store, and retrieve data from physical disks and their respective partitions. Different file systems are supported under different operating systems and have advantages and disadvantages, depending on the requirements of the system and user. Some features are supported exclusively by some file systems and not others.

Microsoft has made major changes to the Windows 2000 supported file systems and their respective features. Most notable of these changes are the addition of FAT32 support and enhancements to NTFS (New Technology File System). Each file system has advantages and disadvantages, depending on the functionality, required disk and volume size, security concerns, and types of hardware in place at a given Windows 2000 installation.

This chapter focuses on how to get the most from the Windows 2000 supported file systems, enhanced features of NTFS, and file system optimization. The chapter also discusses each of the FAT file systems (FAT12, FAT16, and FAT32) because they continue to be needed in some configurations.

N O T E Windows 2000 also supports CDFS (Compact Disk File System) and UDF (Universal Disk Format) for CDs and DVDs—systems used solely to support read-only media. Because these systems aren't configurable, I don't discuss them in this chapter. ▪

The FAT and FAT32 File Systems

There are three FAT (File Allocation Table) file systems supported in Windows 2000: FAT12, FAT16, and FAT32. FAT12 is generally reserved for very small media (such as floppy disks), and Windows 2000 will only format to FAT12 on volumes smaller than about 16MB, depending on disk geometry. Because of its limitations, FAT12 doesn't deserve much discussion here. In general, however, FAT file systems perform best on smaller volumes and might be ideal for these because of their low file system overhead.

Under Windows 2000, FAT file systems support long filenames—up to 255 characters, including spaces and multiple periods. Names preserve case but are not case-sensitive. FAT file systems offer no support for local file security or other NTFS enhancements.

The FAT16 File System

FAT16 is probably the most universally supported of the FAT file systems because it can be read from any Microsoft and many non-Microsoft operating systems. As such, FAT16 is required on systems that will be multibooting operating systems other than Windows 9X and Windows 2000—a requirement you need to keep in mind when planning a dual installation.

Planned volume size is also important because FAT16 continues to be limited to 4GB volumes in Windows 2000. In addition, if a volume less than 2GB in size is formatted for the FAT file system, Windows 2000 automatically formats it FAT16.

> **CAUTION**
>
> Windows 2000 does not have the capability to convert from a FAT16 volume to a FAT32 volume. This should be considered when installing on small partitions or upgrading systems with existing FAT16 partitions.

The FAT32 File System

FAT32 is the file system enhancement introduced with Windows 95 OSR2, supported by Windows 98, and now included in Windows 2000. It provides for much larger volume sizes and much more efficient use of disk space as a result of smaller cluster sizes. Use of FAT32 can also lead to performance increases due to decreased fragmentation of data and applications.

FAT32 systems create and can use a backup copy of the File Allocation Table and any critical data structures. As a result, FAT32 volumes are more immune to file system failures than FAT16 volumes.

Windows 2000 can format drives up to 32GB as FAT32 and will do so automatically for drives larger than 2GB when FAT is the selected file system. Although Windows 2000 cannot create drives larger than 32GB, the operating system has the capability to access these larger drives if they have been created by other operating systems.

> **N O T E** If you require FAT32 volumes larger than 32GB on a Windows 2000 system, be sure to create the volumes prior to upgrading to or installing Windows 2000. Otherwise, you'll need a Windows 98 multiboot system to create the volumes. ■

FAT Considerations

During setup, there are several issues to consider when formatting a drive as FAT. First, if the drive is less than 2GB, Windows 2000 automatically formats it as FAT16; if the drive is over 2GB, it's formatted as FAT32. In addition, if you are upgrading or performing a multiboot installation on a system where Windows 9x is already installed on a FAT partition, the default setting for Windows 2000 Professional is to leave the file system intact. You can choose to upgrade the file system to NTFS, but dual-boot capability will be lost. Finally, if you choose FAT during installation and later decide to convert to NTFS, there will be MFT (Master File Table) fragmentation issues to deal with as a result of the conversion.

▶ **See** "Disk Defragmenter," **p. 336**

Part

I

Ch

5

NOTE One argument for using FAT volumes on earlier versions of NT was for simplified recovery in the event the system did not start due to issues such as corrupt drivers.

The addition of the Recovery Console in Windows 2000 provides administrative access to NTFS partitions for recovery purposes and eliminates any advantages of FAT in these scenarios. The Recovery Console is covered in Appendix B, "Windows 2000 Professional Troubleshooting Guide." ▪

To summarize, use FAT16 for the following occasions:

- Multibooting with OSs other than Windows 9x.
- Partition size is small, and local file security is not an issue.

Use FAT32 for the following occasions:

- Multibooting with Windows 9x.
- Partition size is larger than 2GB, and local file security is not an issue.

There are disadvantages to the FAT file systems, mostly in their inability to take advantage of features native to Windows 2000. Although FAT running under Windows 2000 will support functionality such as long filenames, it does not provide for disk quotas, compression, encryption, local file security, and other features exclusive to NTFS.

The NT File System (NTFS)

NTFS (New Technology File System) is supported only in Windows NT and Windows 2000. Although NTFS has been the native file system for Windows NT since its original release, Windows 2000 has a new version, NTFS 5.0. As a result, you might encounter problems if your system dual boots older versions of Windows NT and Windows 2000.

CAUTION

The issues—and problems—involved in systems that dual boot NT and Windows 2000 are likely to remain moving targets for some time. In general, your best bet is to use this configuration for a brief time only—for example, during testing and migration.

NOTE The NTFS driver provided in the NT 4.0 Service Pack 4 and higher allows NTFS 5.0 drives to be mounted under NT 4.0 on multiboot systems. This driver (NTFS.sys) disables many of the features of NTFS 5.0, and this configuration is recommended only in migration or evaluation scenarios.

To multiboot systems with both NT 4.0 and Windows 2000 where both need access to NTFS 5.0 volumes, copy the NTFS.sys driver from the Service Pack over the existing system driver on the NT 4.0 installation. Again, this is not recommended as a long-term solution. ▪

Unlike FAT, NTFS can support extremely large partitions; however, it also carries a higher file overhead. The theoretical maximum for both files and partitions is 16EB, but functionally, partitions are limited to 2TB due to hardware limitations. NTFS is not recommended on partitions smaller than 50MB due to file system overhead considerations, and you cannot use NTFS to format small media such as floppy disks.

Probably the best way to discuss NTFS is through its basic features and Windows 2000–specific enhancements. Some of the basic features of NTFS include the following:

- *Long filenames* were introduced with Windows 95 and are supported on all file systems under Windows 2000. Names of up to 255 characters are supported, including spaces, periods, and case. Filenames are not case-sensitive but do support case sensitivity for POSIX (Portable Operating System Interface for UNIX) compliance.

- *Local file and folder security* is probably the single most important reason to select NTFS. This feature allows permissions to be applied on the file and folder level to limit access levels for groups and users.

- *Separate recycle bins* are maintained for each local user. This provides continued security access control until deleted files and folders are completely removed from the system.

- *Recoverability* of the file system is provided through two features of NTFS: *transaction logging*, which allows NT to handle I/O operations as individual transactions, and *sector sparing*, which allows NT to remap data to good clusters and mark bad clusters as unusable.

- *File, folder, and volume compression* is supported to preserve disk space. (NTFS compression is covered in detail in the next section.)

These basic features alone should provide enough reason to use NTFS as the file system of choice on systems where FAT is not required. In addition, under Windows 2000, NTFS 5.0 offers many new enhancements that improve usability, security, and control for the system. Some of the new features are the following:

- *Distributed Link Tracking.* This allows shortcuts and application links on NTFS volumes to remain accurate even if the target location of the link is moved.

- *Disk Quotas.* These enable administrators to track or limit user disk utilization on a per volume basis.

- *Extension of Volumes without a Reboot.* This provides for additional free disk space to be added to existing volumes on-the-fly without the need to restart the system.

- *Encryption.* Encrypting files and folders allows for additional security on systems (such as laptops) where physical security might be an issue. NTFS 5.0 uses a public key-based method for encryption and provides a policy-based option for creating a separate agent key for recoverability purposes.

Part
I

Ch
5

■ *Volume Mount Points*. These enable volumes to be "added" to another volume by tying them to an empty folder in the existing structure. This feature provides for the use of fewer drive letters as well as a single local access point for users.

NTFS volumes can be created in several ways. During installation or upgrade there are options for formatting or converting the file systems on existing or new partitions to NTFS. The default option in Windows 2000 Professional is to not convert the file system to NTFS for existing FAT volumes, but conversion can be selected. Windows 2000 will automatically convert all existing NTFS 4.0 volumes to NTFS 5.0 upon installation or upgrade.

> **CAUTION**
>
> Converting FAT or NTFS 4.0 volumes to NTFS 5.0 is a nondata-destructive process, but converting *from* NTFS to another file system is a data-destructive process. To convert an NTFS volume to another file system, you have to back up all the data, format the volume, and then restore the data.

If you don't convert or create NTFS volumes during the installation process, you can do so afterward with no loss of data by using the convert.exe command-line utility.

convert.exe

convert.exe can be used at any time and does not require a reboot unless there are files currently open on the volume to be converted (page files are a common example). In the event there are open files on the volume, conversion will occur on the next reboot.

The syntax for convert.exe is as follows:

```
C:\convert.exe X: /fs:ntfs [/v]
```

X is the volume to be converted and /v is an optional parameter to run the conversion in verbose mode (all information displayed). Figure 5.1 shows the command prompt for the convert.exe command.

FIGURE 5.1
convert.exe on drive with open files.

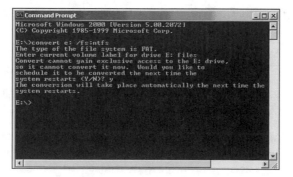

Compression and Encryption

NTFS in Windows 2000 allows volumes, folders, and files to be compressed to conserve disk space. It is very useful on systems where disk space is at a premium, such as laptops.

Compressing Volumes

The procedure for compressing an entire NTFS volume under Windows 2000 is very straightforward and can be applied to any volume, with the exception of the Windows NT Boot Loader (NTLDR) file on the system partition. Compressing heavily accessed volumes on lower or minimum resource systems, however, might reduce system performance because there is some degree of overhead involved in compression.

> **CAUTION**
>
> For performance purposes, Windows 2000 limits compression on drives with large clusters. Compression cannot be used on drives where the cluster size is greater than 4KB.

To compress a volume on Windows 2000, follow these steps:

1. Open either Windows Explorer or My Computer and locate the volume you want to compress.

2. Right-click the volume to be compressed.

3. Select the Properties command from the context menu.

4. On the General tab of the Properties dialog box, check the Compress Drive to Save Disk Space check box.

5. Choose Apply.

6. The Confirm Attribute Changes dialog box appears (see Figure 5.2). To compress the entire drive, select the Apply Changes to This Folder, Subfolders, and Files radio button.

7. Click OK twice to exit both dialogs.

Part

I

Ch

5

FIGURE 5.2
Use the Confirm Attribute Changes dialog box to apply the new compress attributes to the entire drive or the volume root only.

Compressing Files and Folders

The method for compressing folders and individual files is almost identical to that of volume compression, with the exception of one additional step. You must first right-click to view a volume's Properties sheet and then open the General tab, as shown in Figure 5.3. Click the Advanced button on the General tab to access the options to enable compression and encryption attributes.

FIGURE 5.3

The Advanced button on the General tab of the Folder Properties dialog box gives you access to the compression and encryption attributes.

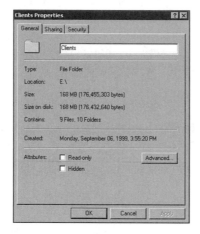

The directory listing in Windows 2000 does not automatically display compressed files and folders in an alternative color from uncompressed objects by default. You can check the file or folder properties to determine whether the compression attribute is selected. Because compressed objects function just like uncompressed objects and because faster systems have minimized the performance impact of compression, this makes perfect sense: Compression is transparent to the user.

If you need to provide a visual cue to indicate which objects have been compressed, you can set a new color for those objects as an option (although the default color cannot be changed). To view compressed objects in a different color (blue) from uncompressed objects, do the following:

1. Open the folder containing the compressed object in Windows Explorer or My Computer.

2. Click Tools, Folder Options to open the Folder Options dialog box.

3. Select the View tab in the Folder Options dialog box (shown in Figure 5.4). In the Advanced Settings section, check the Display Compressed Files and Folders with Alternate Color option check box.

4. If you want to have this option in effect for all your files and folders, click the Like Current Folder button in the Folder views section of the dialog box. Otherwise, click OK.

When you've completed the above procedure, compressed objects appear in blue in the right pane of the Explorer window and the main pane of the My Computer window.

FIGURE 5.4
The View tab of Folder Options dialog box enables you to apply a different color to one or all compressed objects on your system.

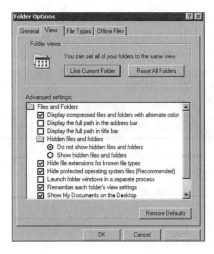

Copying and Moving

When you move files and folders to new locations, they take on the compression attribute of the target location, with two exceptions:

- If the target location is on the same NTFS volume as the original location, the object retains its original compression attribute.
- If the target location is a FAT volume, the file is decompressed because the NTFS compression attribute is not supported on other file systems.

compact.exe

Windows 2000 also provides a command-line utility called compact.exe. This utility enables all the same functionality of the GUI interface with some additional granularity of control through switches and the capability to force compression if it was interrupted for any reason. If used with no switches, compact.exe displays the compression status of the files and folder in the current location.

Switches for compact.exe are demonstrated in Table 5.1.

Table 5.1   compact.exe

<Switch>	<Function>
</c>	<Compresses the specified file or folder>
</u>	<Decompresses the specified file or folder>

continues

Part

I

Ch

5

Table 5.1   Continued

<Switch>	<Function>
</f>	<Forces compression on objects where the compression attribute might already be set but compression is not complete>
</i>	<Continues the operation if errors are encountered>
</a>	<Allows operation to be performed on system and hidden files by causing them to be displayed>
</q>	<Reports "quick" summary information only>
</s>	<Used with the /c or /u, specifies application to all subfolders>

Encryption

The encrypting file system (EFS) driver in Windows 2000 provides an additional level of security on NTFS volumes by making the files unreadable to users who do not have an appropriate "key" to decrypt the file. This is useful on systems that are not physically secure (such as laptops) or for sensitive information.

You can encrypt individual files or entire folders, but in most circumstances, you should encrypt at the folder level. Encrypting at this level provides additional security when you use applications that create temporary copies of files because the copies will also be encrypted. Managing encryption is also simplified by working with whole folders rather than individual files. If you decide to encrypt only a single file in an unencrypted folder, Windows 2000 generates a detailed warning dialog box, as shown in Figure 5.5.

FIGURE 5.5
When you encrypt a single file rather than the entire folder, this warning box reminds you that the file can be decrypted when it is modified—unless you opt to encrypt the parent folder.

Encrypting files and folders is almost identical to compressing files and folders. To implement encryption, do the following:

1. In My Computer or Windows Explorer, right-click the file or folder to be encrypted. The context menu is displayed.

2. Select Properties from the context menu. The General tab of the object Properties dialog box is displayed.

3. In the Attributes section of the General tab, click the Advanced button. The Advanced Attributes dialog box opens.

4. Select the Encrypt Contents to Secure Data check box.

5. Click OK twice to exit all dialogs. Note that, as with compression, there might be a slight delay if you are encrypting a large folder.

NOTE You cannot encrypt and compress the same object. These are mutually exclusive operations and selecting one will deselect the other. ▪

Windows 2000 file encryption uses a public key/private key method for user access where two keys are generated for the user. The *public key* is used to encrypt and is available to the system for use. The private key can decrypt and can only be used by the owner.

This method encrypts the selected object with an individual file encryption key, which is then encrypted with the owner's public key. The owner's private key is used for decryption. The system administrator can create a separate recovery agent key through a group policy for security against the loss of the owner's access to the encrypted data.

Encrypted objects remain encrypted when you move or copy them on NTFS partitions and during backup operations. Windows 2000 automatically encrypts files moved into encrypted folders.

When you use encryption or compression, you need to be certain to balance your need for security or saved disk space against the possibility of lost performance. Optimizing the performance of the file systems is a key consideration in the installation and configuration of Windows 2000 and the topic of our next section.

Optimizing File System Performance

Although there are some general best practices for file systems under Windows 2000, file system optimization remains a series of trade-offs between system performance and implementation needs and requirements. Some of the primary areas to be considered are discussed in the following sections.

System Considerations

System requirements vary widely. Pure Windows 2000 Intel computers are able to use any of the available file systems, but other operating systems have special requirements to function:

■ *Multiboot systems (non-NT)* require the use of either FAT16 (any OS) or FAT32 (Win98x only) for the system partition. NTFS partitions cannot be accessed when booting under other OSs.

■ *Multiboot systems (NT)* require the NTFS.sys driver from NT 4.0 SP 4 or higher for NT 4.0 to be able to access NTFS 5.0 drives.

Part

I

Ch

5

Cluster and Volume Size

Smaller cluster sizes provide for more efficient use of disk space. Larger cluster sizes might reduce fragmentation in some cases, but they leave more unused space. Volume size is the primary factor in determining which version of FAT is used for formatting. NTFS is generally the best choice on Windows 2000 systems, but there are some issues to consider because it is limited on small volumes due to file system overhead:

- FAT12 is used automatically on floppy disks and volumes less than 16MB in size.
- FAT16 is used automatically on drives less than 2GB in size (when formatted FAT) and becomes inefficient on drives larger than about 500MB.
- FAT32 is used automatically on drives larger than 2GB in size (when formatted FAT), but Windows 2000 cannot create FAT32 partitions larger than 32GB (although it can mount them).
- FAT32 and NTFS are more efficient in their use of disk space (smaller cluster sizes) than FAT16.
- NTFS is the most efficient file system for larger drives and for accessing files in large folders.
- NTFS is inefficient on drives smaller than 50MB due to file system overhead.

Fragmentation

Fragmentation occurs when contiguous clusters are not available and portions of a file must be stored in different locations on the volume. Drives that are heavily fragmented are less efficient because they require multiple drive locations to be accessed. If the system requirements can support the NTFS format at installation, this is the preferred format. Converting to NTFS later causes fragmentation in the NTFS MFT (Master File Table) and might affect file system performance.

▶ **See** "Disk Defragmenter," **p. 336**

Encryption

The *encrypting file system (EFS)* is a new feature of Windows 2000 and NTFS 5.0. Encryption and decryption are transparent to the user, but the process does create some system overhead. When you are deciding whether to implement encryption, you must weigh your need for security against the performance loss.

N O T E The performance loss your system will suffer as a result of encryption depends on your system's unique resources and configuration. ▪

Compression

Optimizing NTFS using file, folder, or volume compression is simply a matter of balancing the need for lower disk space utilization against the performance hit that might occur with compression (primarily with large or heavily accessed files). Additionally, compression might be more efficient with certain types of data because those types achieve a better compression ratio. Perhaps the best way to determine the functional impact of compression is to use the Properties tab of the object to check the object size before and after compression.

Part

I

Ch

5

Automated and Push Deployment

Automating and Customizing the Setup Process

An automated or custom setup is designed to offer the network administrator or OEM (*original equipment manufacturer*) an efficient way to install the Windows 2000 operating system with minimal or no user intervention. Automating the setup process is a tremendous time-saver for the Network Administrator who must install the OS onto several computers within an organization.

To automate setup, the network administrator creates and edits files that the setup process will use to answer the questions—such as usernames, network identification, and so on—that setup asks during the GUI phase of the installation.

Another option for automating the setup process is to use a *push* installation. A push installation is one that uses a software application such as Systems Management Server (SMS) to distribute the necessary files and components onto other computers automatically, avoiding the need for individual user setups.

N O T E   Although most of the installation procedures are identical for both the OEM and Administrator, OEMs are offered some customization options relating to splash screens and customer support information. I don't delve too deeply into these special requirements as they are directly related to OEMs. (OEMs get all kinds of support files and user guides and programs to help them with these features.) This chapter concentrates on the deployment of Windows 2000 for the Network Administrator. ▓

Automated installations are performed on what are known as *target computers*. Target computers might have an existing operating system, or they might be new systems with no partitioning on the hard disk drives.

To automate or customize setup, you employ what is called a *distributed setup*. Distributed setup is described in detail in later sections of this chapter, as are the tools and techniques for deploying.

Understanding Setup

Before you move into a lengthy description of automating and customizing techniques, it's important to understand some basic principles of the setup process. The Windows 2000 setup process is responsible for gathering information about the hardware on the computer and then preparing the operating system to work with that hardware. Setup solicits responses from the installer in relation to user information.

How the setup process proceeds depends on the way in which you initiate it. You can set up Windows 2000 as an upgrade from Windows 95 or Windows NT 4.0, you can install Windows 2000 from scratch on a computer that contains no operating system at all, or you can perform customized, unattended installations.

▶ **See** Chapter 1, "Pre-Installation Planning," **p. 23**

▶ **See** Chapter 2, "Windows 2000 Professional Installation," **p. 39**

N O T E Windows 2000 will not upgrade versions of Windows NT earlier than 3.51 or Windows 3.x versions. ▪

During an installation onto a computer that contains no operating system files yet, a character-based portion of setup installs temporary files to the hard drive so that the GUI portion of setup can be run at a later time. These temporary files are actually a small installation of Windows 2000 that provides the necessary software to perform the installation. This arrangement enables the setup routine to actually use multiple threads of execution if necessary to install the operating system. When setup is complete, Windows 2000 removes the temporary files.

When setup enters the GUI portion, the user is then required to make decisions on certain customizations. For example, Windows 2000 offers several options for regional settings and languages. Users are also asked to determine where installation files are stored. If users choose a location other than the default, they see an Advanced Option screen, such as the one shown in Figure 6.1.

FIGURE 6.1
The Advanced Options screen is where you determine the location of the installation files and the destination directory if you choose not to accept the defaults.

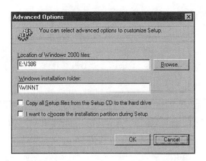

Setup also prompts the user for identification pertaining to the user and company name, Administrator password, date and time settings, network settings, and whether the computer will participate in a workgroup or domain environment. The user must also choose which file system to use for this installation (FAT or NTFS).

▶ **See** "Understanding File System Issues," **p. 25**

When the user has selected the options offered by the wizard, the setup routine begins to configure the necessary components and install the required files. During the setup process, Windows 2000 will take quite some time identifying the hardware that is installed on the user's computer. Windows 2000 does a thorough job at this and will even list hardware components for which it has no drivers.

When all hardware devices have been detected and the necessary files are installed, Windows 2000 restarts the computer and then starts the operating system.

Key Setup Control Files

To automate the setup process, you use several key files that control the setup process in an unattended manner. These files provide the necessary configuration and identification information that the setup process needs.

To customize the setup process, you need to be familiar with five files:

- Unattend.txt
- Uniqueness Database File (UDF)
- $$Rename.txt
- Cmdlines.txt
- Txtsetup.oem

Take a look at each in turn and see an example of what each looks like.

The Unattend.txt File   The Unattend.txt file is known as the *answer file* and is used to provide the necessary information required by setup to complete the installation without user intervention.

Unattend.txt is simply an ASCII text file that contains information pertaining to questions for which the setup process prompts the user to supply answers. You can automate setup to run unattended by making the necessary entries in this file because the setup process pulls the information needed from the file.

The answer file is broken into sections. Each section contains information relating to hardware categories—for example, storage devices, video card and monitors, keyboards, and so on. These sections list the necessary driver information or hardware configuration parameters.

The Unattend.txt file is in the i386 directory on the Windows 2000 CD-ROM.

To understand what the file is all about, look at each section one at a time.

The first section is labeled [Unattend]. In this section you see four entries.

UnattendMode=FullUnattended simply tells setup that this is to be a completely unattended setup and that all information is provided within this answer file necessary to complete the setup. If the information is not present in the answer file, an error is generated.

This key can have the following values:

- GUIAttended. Requires the end user to answer all questions presented during the GUI portion of setup.
- ProvideDefault. This is used to indicate that the answers in the answer file are defaults. The user is required to change any answers during the setup that are different from the defaults displayed.

■ DefaultHide. The same as ProvideDefault, only the user is not shown the answers or given the option to change them.

■ ReadOnly. The same as the DefaultHide option. However, it offers the end-user the option of entering a new value instead of changing one. This can be used to enforce some answers to defaults but not all.

OEMPreinstall = No is used to indicate whether setup should copy all the OEM folders from the distribution computer to the target computer.

TargetPath = WINNT is used to indicate where setup will install the Windows 2000 operating system. This can be any folder of your own choice, and it does not have to exist on the target computer.

Filesystem = LeaveAlone is used to tell setup what to do if it is installing onto a computer that already contains a formatted partition. The available options are LeaveAlone and ConvertNTFS. Setup will either leave the existing format intact or will convert it to the NTFS file system. Your partition must be larger than 512MB in order to use NTFS.

Other entries that are available for this section are the following:

■ ComputerType. Contains information on the HAL. It is only used if the OEMPreinstall option is set to Yes. It also takes two parameters, Retail and OEM. Retail tells setup that the HAL is a part of Windows 2000, whereas OEM indicates that a custom HAL will be provided.

■ InstallFilesPath. This option uses a string to indicate the path to the location of installation files that are required for the mini-setup during an OEM installation. This option is only valid when you use the Sysprep tool to create the Sysprep.inf file.

■ KeepPageFile. A Boolean option with valid values of 0 or 1, the default being 0. This option also is used in the Sysprep.inf file to indicate whether the pagefile should be resized automatically on the target computer.

■ KeyboardLayout. Uses a layout description that can be found in the [Keyboard Layout] section of the Textsetup.sif file and determines the keyboard layout to install as default.

■ NTUpgrade. A Boolean Yes/No value that indicates whether to upgrade an existing version of Windows 2000. It can only be used with the Winnt32.exe command. If you have the OEMPreinstall = Yes option on, this option must be No.

■ OEMFilesPath. This entry directs setup to the OEM folder if it was not placed in the \i386 folder on the distribution share.

■ OEMPnPDriversPath. Indicates the path where the Plug and Play drivers are located. This entry is used for driver files that are not included with Windows 2000, such as third-party drivers that were released after Windows 2000's debut.

Part
I

Ch
6

■ OEMSkipEula. This is another Boolean Yes/No option that is used to indicate whether the EULA (End User License Agreement) should be displayed for the end-user to either accept or reject it. If you are an OEM and you are preinstalling Windows 2000, you must set this option to No, as a requirement of the Microsoft OEM agreement.

■ OverwriteOemFilesOnUpgrade. If you are performing an upgrade and you have files that were provided by an OEM during an earlier install of Windows 2000, this option will overwrite those files with any of the same name that are included with the version of Windows 2000 you are installing. This is a Yes/No value option as well.

■ Repartition. This option takes a Yes/No value, and it is actually a dangerous setting to use. This option, when set to Yes, causes setup to delete any existing partitions on the hard drive and then to repartition and format the hard drive using the NTFS files system. Use this option only if you are performing an unattended installation from the Windows 2000 CD-ROM because it will erase any files that are copied to the drive.

■ Win9xUpgrade. You specify either Yes or No to perform an upgrade of an existing Windows 9x installation. This key is only valid in the Winnt32.exe command-line installation.

The next section, [UserData], deals with information specific to the user that will be identified on the target computer.

FullName = "Your User Name" corresponds to the entry that requires a user's name for the target computer. Enter the name of the user who will be using the target computer here. You must provide this value for a completely unattended installation.

OrgName = "Your Organization Name" is used to identify your company or organization. You must provide this value for a completely unattended installation.

ComputerName = "COMPUTER_NAME" gives the computer a NetBIOS name that is used to identify it on the network. Users are prompted for the name unless you use an asterisk as the value.

The next section, [GuiUnattended], contains options and settings that are asked during the GUI portion of setup.

TimeZone = "004" as indicated sets the time zone to Pacific Northwest. For a complete list of time zone values, see the Windows 2000 Resource Kit.

AdminPassword = * sets the administrator's password to NULL, meaning that there is none at this moment. Enter the password that you would like to use here.

AutoLogon = Yes tells setup to perform an automatic logon. This option cannot be used on an upgrade.

`AutoLogonCount` = 1 allows the computer to perform one automatic logon using the Administrator user account and password. After this one autologon, you will need to log on manually.

There are other entries that can be included in this section. These are listed and briefly explained as follows:

- `Arguments`. Uses a string value and is used by custom programs that accompany setup.
- `AutoLogonAccountCreation`. A Boolean value used for Windows 2000 Professional only. This is mostly used by OEMs who will choose the YES option. This allows the home or end user to agree to the EULA (End User License Agreement) and enter the product ID and identification information and then has the computer log on automatically.

N O T E OEMs are required to run setup a certain way that causes the EULA to be displayed. They cannot perform a complete, unattended install due to this restriction. It is designed to provide the end-user with the option of accepting or declining the license agreement. ■

- `DetachedProgram`. A string value that indicates the path to a program that runs concurrently with setup.
- `OEMSkipRegional`. Takes either a 0 or a 1 for a value (Boolean), which is used mostly by OEMs in the event that they might not know where the computer is destined for and therefore should not enter any regional settings. It is used only on Windows 2000 Professional.
- `ProfilesDir`. Contains a path to the Windows 2000 profiles folder. This option is only valid on clean installs.

The next section of the `Unattend.txt` file is the `[GuiRunOnce]` section. This is used to indicate any programs or applications that you want to run when the first login is completed. The commands necessary to run the programs are required to be in quotes. You must also have the appropriate rights to run the commands, or an error is generated.

The `[Display]` section is responsible for setting the display resolution and color depth. You need to know the available settings for the hardware that you will be installing. This section contains the following values:

- `BitsPerPel`. Specifies the bits per pixel of the video adapter being installed. It accepts values such as 8 or 16, which indicate 256 or 65,536 colors respectively.
- `Vrefresh`. Indicates the vertical refresh rate of the video hardware being installed.
- `Xresolution`. Is used to indicate a valid horizontal resolution.
- `Yresolution`. Indicates a valid vertical resolution.

Part

I

Ch

6

You use the [Networking] section to specify which networking components are to be installed. This section accepts three options:

- BuildNumber. This takes an integer value that indicates the build number that Windows 2000 or NT contains when performing an upgrade.

- InstallDefaultComponents. Takes a Yes/No value to indicate that setup should install default networking components. These default components are network adapters, the TCP/IP protocol, File and Print Sharing for Microsoft networks, and Client for Microsoft Networks.

- UpgradeFromProduct. Defines the name of the product that you are upgrading from. The valid entries are the following:

    - WindowsNTWorkstation

    - WindowsNTServer

    - WindowsNTSBServer

    - Windows95

The last section of the file is [Identification]. This section is used to provide your computer with an identification on the network. It can contain the following values:

- DomainAdmin. Is used to specify a user account that exists on the domain and has the right to create computer accounts in the domain.

- DomainAdminPassword. Specifies the password for the preceding account.

- JoinDomain. If you are installing this computer in a domain, you use this value to indicate the name of the domain that the computer will be a member of.

- JoinWorkgroup. Use this when the computer will not be a part of a domain.

- MachineObjectOU. You use this to specify the Organizational Unit that this computer will belong to. It accepts the value indicating this using the full LDAP pathname.

CAUTION

Take extreme caution with the DomainAdminPassword value. That value is written in the Unattend.txt file as text only and therefore can cause a security risk.

You have now walked through each portion of the Unattend.txt file. Using the information you've learned here, you can create as many of these files, for as many different configurations, as you need.

The UDF (Uniqueness Database File)   The Unattend.txt, or answer file, can work in conjunction with a Uniqueness Database File (UDF).

Network Administrators use a UDF file to perform customization of an unattended install for individual users. They set up the defaults for every computer in the Unattend.txt file and use the UDF file to specify unique answers to questions during the GUI portion of setup that customizes the install for each individual computer.

You can apply a UDF file by specifying it in the setup command line with the /udf:id[,UDF_file] command-line parameter. The id and UDF_file portions indicate the specific user ID section in a specified UDF file.

The UDF file format is displayed in Listing 6.1.

Listing 6.1 UDF File Format

```
[UniqueIds]

fransmith = UserData, Unattended
 joeuser = UserData, GUIUnattended
```

In this example, when you specify the user ID corresponding to fransmith, the information is merged into the UserData field in the answer file. Any data presented here will override any entry in the answer file.

The $$Rename.txt File   Another file used by the setup process is the $$Rename.txt file. You need to concern yourself with this file only if you will be copying files during the setup process that need to be renamed using long filenames. This file is seldom used in most installations.

For each folder that contains files that need to be renamed, you must provide a $$Rename.txt for that folder. Listing 6.2 shows the format for the Rename.txt file.

Listing 6.2   Rename.txt File Format

```
[section_name_x]

short_name_1 = "long_name_1" short_name_2 = "long_name_2"
 short_name_3 = "long_name_3"
```

As you can see, this file is fairly straightforward. You simply list the short name and the corresponding long name. Setup will copy the file over and rename it using the long name.

The section_name_x parameter should be replaced with the correct pathname to the folder that has the files that need to be renamed.

The Cmdlines.txt File   The Cmdlines.txt file is similar to a batch file. It is responsible for specifying any commands that the System Administrator wants to run after the setup process completes.

Part

I

Ch

6

For example, you might set a command to run the name and location of a setup.exe file for the purposes of installing an application. If you are installing Windows 2000 along with Microsoft Office 2000, you could specify the location and command line of the setup files for the Office 2000 setup application; in that situation, that suite of applications would then be installed at the end of the Windows 2000 setup process.

Like the $$Rename.txt file, the format for this file is relatively simple, as shown in Listing 6.3.

Listing 6.3 *Cmdlines.txt* File Format

```
[Commands]

"<command_1>" "<command_2>"
```

Setup will run each command in the order that it is presented in this file. Note that you must surround the commands with quotation marks.

CAUTION

You need to be very careful what user account you are logged in to when running the Cmdlines.txt file. If the command runs an application that modifies the Registry under the user data, those settings are applied only for the user that is currently logged on.

The *Txtsetup.oem* File The Txtsetup.oem file should be created and provided by third-party hardware vendors. It is used to describe the necessary files and settings to install and configure any hardware devices that you are adding and are not a part of the Windows 2000 setup CD-ROM.

In most situations, this file only concerns OEMs because most users will ensure that their hardware is on the HCL. If it is, Windows 2000 setup will install the necessary drivers for it during the setup process.

You can create this file yourself, but you should be very familiar with the hardware that you are installing.

Customizing Setup

You can customize the setup process by modifying the previously mentioned files and using one of the following methods of automating setup:

- Sysprep
- Syspart

■ SMS

■ Bootable CD-ROM

■ Remote Installation

Customization of the setup process involves modifying the default set of configuration files. Using the knowledge that you have gained in the explanations of the key setup files, you should have little or no trouble performing a customized installation of Windows 2000.

To start the setup process, the user or administrator needs to connect to the network share. This can be done by using a system that is connected to the network already using an existing OS. Alternatively, you can create a network setup disk that allows a brand new computer containing no OS to boot from the diskette and connect to the network share.

To run setup, you need to execute one of two files, depending on what operating system you are using. If you are using NT 3.51, 4.0, or Windows 95/98, you start setup by running Winnt32.exe; if you are using DOS, you need to run Winnt.exe.

You can use the necessary command-line options and switches, as indicated below. The syntax for the command is as follows:

```
Winnt [/a][/s:sourcepath][/t:tempdrive][/i:inffile]
[/f][/o][/l][/unattend:answerfile][/r:folder][/rx:folder]
[/udf:id[,UDF_File]]
```

Note that not all parameters are used for both Winnt.exe and Winnt32.exe. The following lists display each command's available options.

These are the Winnt.exe command-line parameters:

/a. Is used to enable the accessibility options.

/s:*sourcepath*. Is used to indicate where the Windows 2000 install files are located. You must specify the full path or UNC name.

/t:*tempdrive*. Is used to specify the location where setup will copy the temporary setup files. If you omit this option, setup will copy these files to the partition or drive that contains the largest free space.

/i:*inf_file*. Specifies the location of the setup information file. You do not specify a path—just the filename. The default setup file is Dosnet.inf.

/l. Creates an error log file that setup will use to record errors that were encountered during the file copy phase. It is named $Winnt.log.

/unattend:*answer file*. Is the name and location of the file that contains the answers to the question posed during the setup phase.

/r:*folder*. Indicates an optional folder to be installed. You can use the /r switch multiple times for more than one folder.

/rx:*folder*. The same as the /r switch with the exception that setup will delete this folder upon completion.

/udf:*id[,UDF_file]*. Is used to indicate which identifier is to be used for this particular installation. The UDF file will be explained later, but it contains certain settings that will override sections in the answer file.

The syntax for the Winnt32.exe command is as follows:

```
Winnt32 [/s:sourcepath][/syspart:drive_letter]
[/tempdrive:drive_letter][/copydir:folder_name]
[/copysource:folder_name][/cdm:command_line]
[/debug [level][:filename]][/I:inf_file][/x]
[/unattend][/unattend[num]:answer_file]
[/r:directory][/e:command][/udf:id[,UDF_file]]]
```

These are the Winnt32.exe command-line parameters:

/s:*sourcepath*. Is used to indicate the source of the installation files. One difference between the /s: switch in Winnt and Winn32 is the fact that with Winnt32, you can use multiple /s: switches to specify multiple servers to use simultaneously. This can reduce network load on one server. The setup files must be located on all servers specified, and they must use the same folder hierarchy.

/syspart:*drive_letter*. Is useful for performing a partial installation onto a hard drive, marking that partition as active, and then installing the drive into another computer. When you boot the new computer, setup continues with the next phase. You must use the /tempdrive parameter with this option.

/tempdrive:*drive_letter*. Tells setup where to store the temporary files and to install Windows 2000 there.

/copydir:*folder_name*. Can be used to replace the /r: option. Essentially, it enables you to specify a folder name that will be created under the Windows 2000 installation folder. You can create multiple folders with this option as well.

/copysource:*folder_name*. Creates a folder under the Windows 2000 installation folder as well, but it is used to place files in that are used for the setup process. These can include custom files specific to your organization. Although the /copydir: option does the same thing, the folders created using this option are deleted upon setup's completion.

/cmd:*command_line*. Using this option, you can run a command, such as a batch file, before setup completes the final phase.

/debug[*level*][:*filename*]. Is used to create a log file, specified by *filename*, that contains the debug information at the level specified by *level*. By default, a file called Winnt32.log is created at a level of 2 and can be found under the C:\ root.

/i:*inf_file*. Has the same use as that of the Winnt.exe command-line option. It specifies the location of the information file to be used by setup. It also has a default of Dosnet.inf.

/x. Use this option to prevent the creation of the four boot floppies. You would use this if you already have the diskettes or are installing from a bootable CD-ROM.

/unattend. This option should only be used if you already have an existing Windows NT installation that you are going to upgrade. This will provide an unattended installation because it will take the user and other settings from the existing installation.

/unattend[*num*]:[*answer_file*]. Use this option to perform an unattended installation using information found in the answer file under specified. Use the *num* field to indicate a time delay, in seconds, that setup waits for after it finishes copying files and when it should restart.

/r:*directory*. Installs subfolders under the Windows 2000 installation directory.

/e:*command*. Is used to execute the command specified after setup has completed.

/udf:*id*[,*UDF_file*]. This option enables you to customize the answer file by specifying a Uniqueness Database File and the section ID of that file that will override certain settings in the answer file.

Deploying a Distributed Setup

Distributed setup can be a complex undertaking, depending on your company's or organization's setup and number of computers. Essentially, to perform a distributed setup, you first create a distribution directory or *Distribution Folder.* Then, you place the distribution folders on one or more servers in the network and run automated installs on the workstations. As you can imagine, deploying a distributed setup requires some planning. The following sections of this chapter walk you through the planning and deployment process.

Creating the Distribution Directory

To perform an automated or push installation of Windows 2000, you must set up a distribution directory and share that directory on a network server or computer that is connected to a network. This distribution directory contains the necessary files that are required to install Windows 2000 over the network. The diagram in Figure 6.2 outlines the Distribution Folder and its contents.

N O T E With the introduction of Windows 95, Microsoft replaced the term "directory," with the term "folder." Though the term has changed, the meaning remains the same, and the terms continue to be used interchangeably. ▪

Part
I

Ch
6

FIGURE 6.2
This structure is the recommended layout for the Distribution Folder for use in automated and customized setups. You must create this folder as it is displayed for the setup process to function correctly.

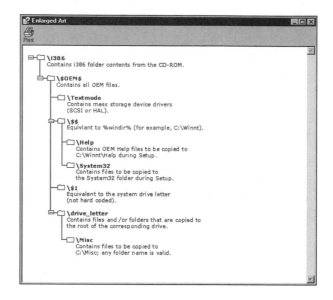

i386 Folder   As you can see from the diagram, the parent folder of the distribution directory is the i386 folder.

NOTE   The Alpha platform is that of the Digital Equipment CPU that has been used for some time on mini- and some microcomputer hardware. Alpha is actually a faster chip, when compared to the clock speed of the Intel CPU, because it uses a different internal architecture. Microsoft does not support the Alpha for this release of Windows. ■

On the Windows 2000 CD-ROM, you will find the \i386. Copy the entire contents of this folder to the appropriate folder on the network share.

The \$OEM$ Folder   The first subfolder within the i386 folder is the \$OEM$ folder. This folder contains all the remaining subfolders and any files or folders that you copy into it for the setup process. You can include tools in this folder that are used for the automated setup process.

Also included in the OEM subfolder is a file called Cmdlines.txt. This file is a simple ASCII text file that is read by the setup process to determine whether any special commands or programs need to be run during the GUI setup process. You can also use it to install applications after the initial setup of the OS.

The *textmode* Folder   The next subfolder is the textmode folder. If any folder is going to cause you headaches, it is this folder. You need to copy all *hardware abstraction layers (HALs)* and device drivers into this folder that might be needed by any hardware devices installed on the target computers. If you fail to verify that the OS supports the installed hardware, users will have trouble getting the devices to work properly.

Within this folder you need to find or create a `Txtsetup.oem` ASCII text file. This file provides necessary information about the hardware that is referenced in the `[OEMBootFiles]` section of the `Unattend.txt` file.

The \$$ Folder   The next OEM subfolder is the `\$$` folder. This folder is actually intended to be a mirror of the NT root folder and its subfolders when installed on the target computer. As you saw in Figure 6.1, the two subfolders `\Help` and `\System32` normally are found under the `\WINNT` folder on the hard disk drive.

When Windows 2000 is installed on the target computer, the directory structure starts with a top-level folder. If you leave the defaults that Setup uses, your Windows 2000 installation resides under the `\WINNT` folder. All other folders are subfolders of this one.

The contents of the `\$$` folder—including all subfolders—are copied into this `\WINNT` directory during the setup process.

The \$1 Folder   The `\$OEM$\$1` folder is used to indicate the drive on which Windows 2000 is to be installed.

Operating systems, such as MS-DOS and Windows 98, require their boot files and system files to reside on the first primary partition of the first hard disk in the computer. Windows 2000 only requires the boot files (files such as `ntldr`, `ntdetect` and `boot.ini`) to be installed there. The remaining system files can reside on any valid primary or extended partition on any other hard disk in the computer. ▪

N O T E

If you have any drivers that are not included as a part of Windows 2000 and they need to be installed during setup, you need to create one more subfolder under the `\$1` subfolder called `\Drivers`. You can rename this folder anything you choose, as long as you reference it with the given name in all setup key files. This folder will replace the `\Display` and `\Net` folders used in the Windows 2000 setup.

The *drive_letter* Folder   Next, you can see the `\drive_letter` subfolder. This folder corresponds to the root drive on the target computer and contains files that will be copied to that root drive during setup. An example of this subfolder's use would be `\$OEM$\C`, where C is the root drive of the target computer.

You can also create subfolders on the target computer by specifying them within this subfolder such as `\$OEM$\C\Temp`. Any files that are placed into this folder can be renamed during the copy process. They must be specified in the `$$Rename.txt` file (discussed earlier in this chapter) and they must contain short names.

Deployment Tools

One of the recommended tools to use in a push deployment of Windows 2000 is Systems Management Server (SMS). SMS uses a package to distribute the software installation to the various computers. SMS requires that you have the necessary files arranged in the directory structure discussed earlier.

SMS version 2.0 comes with predefined packages for Windows 2000 in the Server and Professional editions.

One of the unfortunate aspects of using SMS is the fact that it cannot be used to perform an installation of Windows 2000 on a new computer. The SMS client software must exist on the target computer. You can, however, perform a clean install into another directory or partition on the target computer, or you can perform a push installation for the purposes of upgrading.

SMS can help you perform many of the tasks required to deploy Windows 2000 in your organization. You should have someone on site that is familiar with SMS. Although you can perform some tasks without understanding SMS, it is a good idea to have someone who can configure SMS correctly.

Here are some ways in which SMS helps you deploy Windows 2000:

- *Distributing Source Files to Sites.* SMS uses what are known as *senders,* which are used to send the necessary files over the network. They can do this using various protocols and limiting themselves to a narrow portion of the bandwidth to reduce network burden.

- *Monitoring the Distribution.* Using status messages, SMS monitors the completion of each step.

- *Selecting Computers.* SMS is very good at maintaining an inventory of computers on your network and enables you to choose the computers that follow the minimum hardware requirements for Windows 2000 prior to deciding on a deployment to that computer.

- *Operating System Rights.* With a push deployment, one of the major concerns is, of course, security. You must provide certain rights to the computer or user to complete the installation. SMS can provide these necessary rights without allowing users to gain access to areas of the system that they do not understand.

- *Start the Installation Automatically.* This ability makes the installation easier to perform by not requiring the user to do much of anything. It also allows the user to specify a time to initiate the installation procedure based on when the computer will be not be in use.

- *Status Reports.* SMS generates reports on the progress of the installation and can be used to verify the various tasks performed.

 TIP A complete discussion of SMS and its use is beyond the scope of this book. To gain a real understanding of how to best employ SMS in your system environment, read through the SMS documentation, obtain a copy of *Using SMS 2.0, Special Edition*, by Que, or work with someone who is familiar with SMS.

The SIDWalker Tool   Another tool that is included in the Windows 2000 Resource Kit for deployment purposes is SIDWalker. SIDWalker is a set of security administration tools that enable an Administrator to perform domain Security Identifier (SID) migration. This might be necessary if you are changing your domain completely from a Windows NT 3.51/4.0 to Windows 2000.

The use of SIDWalker is designed to function in three steps, or phases:

1. *Planning.* It is always a good idea to plan any changes or migrations concerning user and user rights before you actually implement those changes.

2. *Account Mapping.* This enables the Administrator to map existing accounts to determine whether the current access levels are adequate or need to be changed in some way.

3. *Conversion of ACLs.* ACLs—*access control lists*— are a part of every user account under NT. When user accounts have been mapped and decisions made as to any changes, those changes will require an update of the ACLs to ensure that the updated accounts have access to the correct resources.

This particular procedure can easily take up a day or more per phase. Once again, planning is the best defense against mistakes during the deployment process.

SIDWalker itself actually consists of three separate programs:

- *Showaccs* is a command-line tool that is used to examine the access control list entries.

- *Sidwalk* (note that this is spelled "sidwalk" and not "sidewalk") is also a command-line tool that is used to edit the access control list and replace old SID occurrences with the new SID.

- *Security Migration Editor* is a snap-in for the Microsoft Management Console (MMC). You use this tool for editing the mappings between old and new SIDs.

Each of these tools is described in detail in the SIDWalker section of the Windows 2000 Resource Kit.

The Sysprep Tool   Sysprep tool is another tool that many Administrators or OEMs will appreciate.

Sysprep can be used to create a disk image ready for duplication on other computers. One of the reasons that Sysprep is an excellent deployment tool is that it enables you to install on one "Master Computer" the operating system and applications you want to reside on all client computers.

When you run Sysprep, it actually uses a third-party disk-imaging process that will transfer the necessary configuration to the target computers.

> **CAUTION**
>
> When using Sysprep to deploy from a Master Computer, remember that the configuration of all target computers must be identical to that of the Master Computer. If you fail to ensure identical configurations on all computers, you are likely to experience hardware identification problems.

Part
I

Ch
6

To build a Master Computer, follow these major steps in using Sysprep:

1. Install Windows 2000 Professional on your Master Computer. Ensure that the hardware configuration is identical to the target computers. Do not join the Master Computer to a domain and leave the Administrator password blank.

2. After you install Windows 2000, perform the necessary configurations and install any applications that will be a part of the target computers.

3. Verify that the image you created is correct by performing a client audit.

4. When you have verified that the image is acceptable, run Sysprep with the `Sysprep.inf` option to prepare the image for distribution.

5. When you have completed the preceding steps, you are ready to duplicate the disk using your third-party duplication software.

These files are used by Sysprep:

- `Sysprep.exe`. The executable file that runs the Sysprep tool. There are four options that can be used with Sysprep:

    `-quiet`. When you specify this option, Sysprep will not display any messages on the screen.

    `-nosidgen`. If you are installing a domain controller, you can specify this option, and Sysprep will not generate a SID.

    `-reboot`. Causes the computer to reboot automatically.

    `-noreboot`. This will perform all modifications to the Registry as necessary but will not reboot the computer.

- `Sysprep.inf`. This file is identical to the `Unattend.txt` answer file used by setup, but `sysprep.inf` provides answers for the cloning process. The following sample of this file is taken from the Windows 2000 Resource Kit:

```
[Unattended]
OemSkipEula=No
OemPreinstall=Yes
TargetPath=\WINNT

[GuiUnattended]
AdminPassword=*
TimeZone=20
OemSkipWelcome=1

[UserData]
FullName = "User Name"OrgName = "Organization Name"ComputerName
➥ = OEM_Computer

[SetupMgr]
DistFolder=C:\sysprep
DistShare=win2000dist
```

```
[Identification]
JoinWorkgroup=WORKGROUP

[Networking]
InstallDefaultComponents=Yes
```

■ Setupcl.exe. This utility actually performs four different functions:

Modifies the SID on the local computer so that you don't have duplicate problems in the domain.

Indicates that this computer was cloned by writing a value into the Registry.

Reads through the Sysprep.inf file. This is necessary for ensuring that the proper user pages are displayed during the mini-setup phase.

Runs the mini-setup wizard.

N O T E Be aware that Sysprep and Setupcl take the place of the rollback.exe utility that was used in NT 4.0. ■

When these processes are complete and the computer is restarted for the first time, the mini-setup wizard will run and display the necessary user pages such as the EULA, Regional Settings, and so on.

For more information on Sysprep, see the Windows 2000 Resource Kit documentation.

Other Deployment Tools   The Resource Kit offers an assortment of other deployment tools worthy of mention here. These tools include the following:

■ *ApiMon.* Times and counts API calls. APIs are application programming interfaces that are used by application developers to access the underlying functionality of an operating system or component.

■ *ClonePrincipal.* Performs a domain migration that clones user accounts without deleting the original account.

■ *Clustcfg.* Is used when you are setting up the Windows Clustering Service.

■ *Dependency Walker.* Assists in the automatic repair of applications written specifically for Windows 2000; this tool monitors all of the dependent files for a given application and detects when those files have been damaged or deleted.

■ *Microsoft License Server.* Monitors and tracks licenses for Terminal Services (Windows 2000 Server comes with Terminal Server Services as a part of the operating system).

■ *MoveTree.* Windows 2000 uses Active Directory as its way of organizing domains. Each "domain" is actually known as a forest and contains trees. The MoveTree tool allows for moving users, computers, and organizational units between domains in a single forest.

▶ **See** "New Windows 2000 Features and Functions," **p. 2**

Part

I

Ch

6

N O T E   The Active Directory is an important component of Windows 2000. To gain a better understanding of Active Directory, see the Windows 2000 documentation or Help files or read Que's *Practical Windows 2000 Professional*, by Ed Bott. ■

■ *Netdom*. Enables you to manage domain migrations and trust relationships from the command line.

■ *Setup Manager*. You can use this tool to create your unattended script files using a wizard-based interface.

■ *Terminal Services Client Creator*. As the name suggests, this tool creates the necessary diskettes to install the Terminal Server Client software on a client computer. These clients can be Windows for Workgroups, Windows 9x, or Windows NT.

■ *Terminal Services Configuration*. Enables you to configure and manage your Terminal Services.

■ *Terminal Services Manager*. Enables the Administrator to monitor and control Terminal Services on all Windows 2000 Servers within the domain.

Planning a Deployment

One of the first steps involved in planning a deployment is to ensure that you are familiar with the features and enhancements that are a part of the Windows 2000 family of products. When you are familiar with the features that are available in Windows 2000 Professional, you need to map these features to your business goals.

N O T E   This book provides information necessary for the deployment of Windows 2000 Professional, but you also should become familiar with the Windows 2000 Server version because it will likely be used to replace or upgrade your existing server software. ■

During the first phase of deployment planning, it is important to set goals for the deployment process. During the goal-setting phase of deployment planning, you need to answer many questions. Though those questions are unique to each organization, they might include the following:

■ Should you change over all computers in the organization at once, or should you make the change gradually?

■ What are you prepared to do about training?

■ Do you have the necessary staff to perform the deployment?

■ Will your existing hardware handle the upgrade?

■ What operating system are you going to deploy?

After you define your goals, you can begin the process of assigning tasks to your deployment team. This team should be made up of members of your IS organization who have a good understanding of your present network setup and are also familiar with the Windows 2000 product. During this phase of the deployment planning process, you might need to provide or arrange for training of these staff members.

Now that you have your team in place, it is a good idea to sit down and document your plans for deployment. The areas that you should be concerned with, of course, will vary based on your own organization's needs, but there should be a baseline or default set of documents that you create regardless of any differences. Some of the information you need to document includes the following:

- *Current Environment*. Documenting the software and hardware currently present in your organization can help you determine where any upgrades are necessary to meet the hardware requirements. You also need to be concerned with legacy or proprietary software and whether it will function correctly under Windows 2000.
- *Deployment Phases*. By providing a roadmap of how you intend to deploy Windows 2000, you can keep the project on track and on time. This can be a major concern for budgeting purposes as well.
- *Staff Requirements*. Most companies will need to know what is required in regards to staff when it comes to performing the deployment and whether any additional staff will be required afterwards. Your organization might not be prepared to hire extra IS staff during or after the rollout. Document this carefully.
- *Risk Assessment*. Likely the one document that can prove to be a lifesaver. You should record any potential risks that can delay or prevent the deployment from completing. Issues such as staff changes or perhaps even corporate takeovers could certainly put a monkey wrench in the works.
- *Pilot Testing Plan*. You will want to set up a test environment prior to going corporatewide with the new operating system. Even though this is obviously more important in a larger corporation, it is still important in a small 10-user office environment, nonetheless.

Although certainly not a complete deployment planning guide, the information outlined here can provide you with a good starting point. If you are the one responsible for deploying Windows 2000 in your organization, research your needs carefully and acquire the Windows 2000 Resource Kit. The tools and documentation can make your life a lot easier.

Deploying Windows 2000 Professional

When you have all your documentation completed and reviewed, you are ready to begin the deployment of Windows 2000 Professional.

The method that you choose for deployment depends on whether you want to do a push installation or you intend to perform the setup at each computer separately.

If you are going to perform the setup from each individual computer, ensure that you have created the necessary distribution directory structure and copied the required files over as described earlier in the chapter. Make all necessary modifications to the answer file and any UDF files that you intend to use.

If your computers already contain an operating system and are connected to the network, simply locate the \i386 directory and run Winnt.exe or Winnt32.exe with the unattend option to start the unattended installation on your workstations.

If you have a larger organization and the concept of setting up Windows 2000 individually is out of the question, you need to look at a deployment using SMS.

Deploying Windows 2000 Professional with SMS 2.0   To deploy Windows 2000 Professional with SMS 2.0, follow these steps:

1. Set up the distribution point as outlined earlier in the chapter, including all answer files and drivers.

2. From the Administrator Console in SMS, from the Action menu, select Packages, then New, and Package From Definition. A Welcome screen opens.

3. Choose Next; in the Package Definition Pane, choose Windows 2000 Professional.

4. Select Create a Compressed Version of the Source in the Source Files pane and choose Next.

5. Enter the distribution directory path that you created earlier in the Source Directory. Select Next and then Finish.

Now that you have the packages completed, you must distribute them. Follow these steps to "quickstart" the SMS distribution process:

1. From the Administrator console, select Packages, and choose your Windows 2000 Professional package and then Distribution Points.

2. Select the Action menu, New, and then Distribution Points. This process starts the wizard for New Distribution Points that will walk you through the necessary procedures.

3. Click Finish to initiate the distribution.

CAUTION

Once again, be very aware that this is not a complete description of the SMS package; I strongly recommend that you familiarize yourself with the software program or rely on someone who knows how to use it.

Upgrading from Windows 95/98 with SMS   You need to take special steps when upgrading a system from Windows 95/98. Neither of these operating systems actually becomes a part of a domain when they are logged on; only Windows NT computers are considered a part of the domain. For this reason, you need to specify that the computer should join a domain in the answer file. This is done in the [Identification] section of the Unattend.txt file by entering the following value:

```
JoinDomain = "DOMAINNAME"
```

You also need to ensure that the *Win9xUpgrade* entry is set to *Yes* in the *[Unattended]* section, as well as having *InstallDefaulComponents* = *Yes* in the *[Networking]* section. You will also need to set an Administrator password because there will be a local Administrator account created on the computer as well.

If you are upgrading Windows 9x clients, running Winnt32.exe will cause the installation to fail. This failure is due to the differences in the way that Windows 9x and Windows NT access the distribution files. After Winnt32.exe has been executed, it returns quickly and causes SMS to disconnect from the share point. This action effectively kills the file transfer and the setup process.

To avoid this failure, create a Windows 9x upgrade program under SMS in the Windows 2000 deployment package by following these steps:

1. In the Administrator console, select the Windows 2000 Professional Package that you created earlier and then select Programs.
2. Select the Action menu, New, and then Program.
3. In the Program Properties window, give the program a name.
4. Use the command line WIN95NTUPG SETUP.BAT.
5. Enter a descriptive comment so that the users will be provided with some information as to who they can call for further instructions if necessary.
6. For the *Start In* directory, list the distribution directory that you created (such as i386).
7. In the *After Running* list, select the Program Restarts Computer option.
8. Select the Requirements tab and enter 650MB as the Estimated Disk Space and One(1) Hour for the Estimated Run Time.
9. Select the This Program Can Run Only on Specified Platform option, and then choose All Win9x Clients.
10. Create the SETUP.BAT file using the command *win95ntupg Winnt32 /"Unattend":%0\..\Unattend.txt.* Place the file in the share directory for the Windows 2000 package.
11. Into the same directory, copy the WIN95NTUPG.EXE file and _OSW32RC.DLL file. (These files can be found in the \SMS\Scripts\00000409\NT4\i386 directory which is located in the SMS server.)
12. Modify the Unattend.txt file as discussed earlier in this section for Windows 9x clients.

When you have completed these steps, you can move on to the SMS distribution process outlined in the preceding section of this chapter.

Part

I

Ch

6

Adding and Modifying Hardware

Managing Hardware

In this chapter

An Overview of Windows 2000 Hardware Technology Updates

Windows 2000 offers users a few benefits not available to Windows NT users. Although still reliant on the Hardware Compatibility List, Windows 2000 loosens the apron strings a bit and provides support for more multimedia and gaming hardware and includes a newer implementation of DirectX. Windows 2000 also supports newer hardware technology such as:

- *MMX.* Intel's Multimedia Extensions added to its line of microprocessors for dealing specifically with multimedia applications and the video and audio requirements of multimedia

- *OpenGL.* An industry standard *application programming interface (API)* that is used by software developers for the purpose of 2D and 3D graphics

- *IEEE1394.* A standard developed as a high-speed serial bus interface by the Institute of Electrical and Electronics Engineers

Windows 2000 also comes equipped to handle DVD, multiple monitors, scanners, and digital cameras.

 TIP Windows 2000 Professional comes with several screen savers that were written using the OpenGL API. You can see the 3D screen savers by choosing one from the list of available screen savers in the Display Settings under Control Panel. The OpenGL screen savers all start with 3D in the name and contain OpenGL in parentheses. Note, however, that OpenGL Support is not new to Windows 2000.

Along with these new hardware capabilities, Windows 2000 includes tools that ease the installation and configuration of hardware devices. Microsoft includes the Add/Remove Hardware Wizard (a tool familiar to Windows 9x users) that helps troubleshoot devices, in addition to simplifying hardware installation and removal.

Windows 2000 supports Plug and Play (PnP), Universal Serial Bus (USB), and Advanced Configuration and Power Interface (ACPI). To help you manage all this new technology, Microsoft adds the Device Manager to Windows 2000. (Device Manager is covered in detail later in the chapter.)

 TIP If you would like more information on the PnP capabilities of Windows 2000 Professional, Microsoft has a downloadable document available online at the following URL:
`http://www.microsoft.com/Windows/professional/technical/whitepapers/PlugnPlay.asp`

The Add/Remove Hardware Wizard

Managing hardware in Windows 2000 is much simpler than it used to be under Windows NT. Rather than needing to go to the Control Panel, jump through hoops, and stand on your head, you can now use the Add/Remove Hardware Wizard and Device Manager.

The Add/Remove Hardware Wizard walks you through the process of installing, removing, unplugging, and troubleshooting hardware devices. Although it cannot help with every possible hardware situation, it certainly makes most hardware operations much easier.

Checking for Compatibility and Conflicts

Before you run the Add/Remove Hardware Wizard to install a new piece of hardware, check to see if the hardware is included on the Hardware Compatibility List (HCL) or that it contains a Windows 2000 device driver.

Next, plug the device into the socket or the slot inside the computer. When you turn the computer back on, Windows 2000 should see the new hardware and begin a search for the new driver. If the new device is not seen, you might need to verify that there are no IRQ, I/O, or DMA conflicts.

To verify that the device driver has no conflicts, follow these steps:

1. Select Start, Control Panel.
2. Double-click the Administrative Tools icon and then the Computer Management icon. Or you can simply right-click My Computer and choose Manage.
3. From the Computer Management console, expand the System Tools branch and then the System Information branch to display a listing of system resources such as DMA, I/O, and so on.
4. Check the Conflicts/Sharing entry. Any hardware devices that are conflicting or sharing resources are listed here.

Using the Wizard to Install New Hardware

If you are installing an older non-PnP device, you will need to use the Add/Remove Hardware Wizard to manually install the device. To use the wizard to add a new hardware device, follow these steps:

NOTE To add or remove hardware devices using the Add/Remove Hardware Wizard, you must be a member of the Administrator's group or a member of a group that has administrative rights. The only exception to this rule is when the Administrator has already installed the drivers on the computer for you. You can then install the device yourself.

1. Choose Start, Settings, Control Panel, and double-click the Add/Remove Hardware icon. The Welcome screen opens.

Part
II

Ch
7

2. Click **N**ext; in the dialog box that opens, choose Add/Troubleshoot a Device, and then click **N**ext again. The wizard immediately begins searching for any newly installed hardware devices that it does not have listed as installed on this computer. If your device is a PnP-compliant device, Windows 2000 should find it and begin a search for the appropriate drivers.

3. When Windows has found the new hardware, it displays the Found New Hardware Wizard welcome screen. Click **N**ext to display the **S**elect a Device Driver screen (see Figure 7.1).

FIGURE 7.1

The Select a Device Driver Screen enables you to indicate the manufacturer and the precise model of the hardware device you're installing.

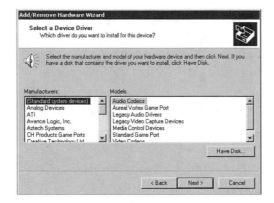

4. Choose a selection option. You can choose to have Windows 2000 search for the drivers or have the wizard display a list of known drivers for this device so that you can select the correct driver yourself. Choose the latter option if you're installing a non-PnP device for which Windows either doesn't have or cannot detect the proper driver.

5. Click **N**ext; the wizard displays a screen that asks you to choose the locations where it should search for the drivers from these options:

    ● Choose the CD-ROM Drives option if, as in most cases, the hardware is on the HCL and Windows supplies the drivers on the installation CD-ROM.

    ● Choose the Floppy Disk option if the drivers are located on an installation floppy disk.

    ● Choose Specify a Location if you want Windows to search network shares or hard drive directories.

    ● Choose Microsoft Windows Update to invoke Internet Explorer, connect to the Internet and navigate to the Windows Update Web page where it will search for updated drivers for the device.

6. Click **N**ext; the wizard searches for the drivers in the specified location. If it finds a driver, Windows installs it and configures the device to work under the OS.

If it does not find any drivers, it prompts you either to disable the device for now and to configure it later or to choose to skip the driver installation at this time and to have Windows reprompt you on the next reboot. Select the appropriate option and click the Finish button.

Using the Wizard to Troubleshoot a Device

You also run the Add/Remove Hardware Wizard to troubleshoot problems with hardware devices. To troubleshoot a device, follow these steps:

1. Choose Start, Settings, Control Panel, and double-click the Add/Remove Hardware icon. The Welcome screen opens.

2. Click Next; in the dialog box that opens, choose Add/Troubleshoot a Device.

3. Click Next again. Windows searches for new hardware, and when it doesn't find any, it displays the Choose a Hardware Device screen, which lists all the hardware that it has detected on your computer and prompts you to choose a device that you want to troubleshoot (see Figure 7.2). If there are any devices that are not functioning correctly, they are listed here with a yellow question mark next to the device name.

FIGURE 7.2
When Windows 2000 realizes that you don't want to add a new hardware device, it asks you to choose which device it should troubleshoot.

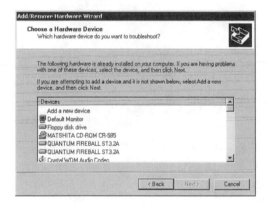

4. Select the device from the list that you want to troubleshoot and click the Next button. The wizard displays a device status screen that tells you what the particular or suspected problem is with that particular device. Most common errors or problems are a hardware resource conflict or drivers not installed.

5. At this point, you can click the Finish button and the troubleshooting wizard starts. The actions of this wizard depend on the device problem that Windows encountered. For example, if you don't have the drivers installed for a device, the Update Device Driver Wizard starts and walks you through the process of locating the necessary drivers.

Part
II

Ch
7

Uninstalling/Unplugging a Device

Sometimes, you might want to remove a hardware device from the computer. You might need to do this to add a newer model such as a better video adapter or faster CD-ROM drive.

Although it might seem like a simple solution, never remove a device by simply powering down the computer, removing the device, and restarting the computer. Instead, uninstall the device, so you free up the hardware resources that it was using. To uninstall a hardware device, follow these steps:

1. Choose Start, **S**ettings, **C**ontrol Panel, and then double-click the Add/Remove Hardware icon.

2. Click the **N**ext button to advance past the Welcome screen to the Choose A Hardware Task screen (see Figure 7.3).

FIGURE 7.3

The Choose a Hardware Task Screen is the first stop for uninstalling a device in Windows 2000.

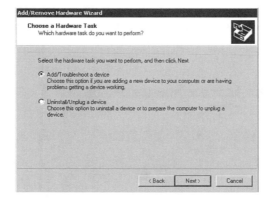

3. Select Uninstall/Unplug a Device and click the **N**ext button; the Choose a Removal Task screen is displayed.

4. If you want to permanently remove a device and its associated drivers from the computer, select Uninstall a Device, and then go on to step 5.

   Alternatively, if you are using a docking station or a portable computer and want only to unplug or eject a device, select the Unplug/Eject a Device option and skip to step 7.

5. Click the **N**ext button. The Installed Devices On Your Computer screen appears (see Figure 7.4)

6. Select the hardware device that you are removing and click **N**ext. The wizard will prompt you to verify that you want to remove the device. If you are sure you want to remove it, select the Yes option and click **N**ext. Skip to step 9.

7. If you selected the Unplug/Eject a Device option, Windows 2000 prompts you to select a device from the list to unplug (if no devices are listed here, none of your installed devices support the unplug feature). Select the device you want to unplug and then click **N**ext. The wizard tells you when it is safe to unplug the device.

FIGURE 7.4
The Installed Devices On Your Computer Screen depicts the hardware devices that Windows 2000 has detected.

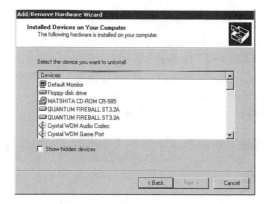

8. Click **N**ext to confirm the unplug operation.
9. Click **F**inish to close the wizard.

CAUTION

If you have an "unpluggable" device that you use for data storage, be certain to run this wizard before unplugging the device to ensure that you don't lose any data.

N O T E To undock a notebook computer, click the Start button and choose the Eject PC option. A message appears when it is safe to undock your notebook, or if you have a motorized docking station, the notebook is ejected automatically.

Some notebook computers do not support the undocking feature with Windows 2000. If this is the case with yours, perform a normal Windows 2000 shutdown.

The Device Manager

The Device Manager is a powerful troubleshooting tool that enables you to monitor and configure your hardware devices. Device manager helps you to determine the status of hardware devices on your system while also enabling you to perform driver updates. You can use Device Manager to disable or uninstall hardware devices, to view the properties of the devices, and to scan for any changes to the hardware.

N O T E You must have administrative privileges to be able to use the Device Manager.

Part

II

Ch

7

You can start the Device Manager program in two ways:

■ From Control Panel, select the Administrative Tools icon and then choose the Computer Management applet. Device Manager is found in the console tree on the left.

■ Alternatively, you can open Control Panel, double-click the System icon, and click the Hardware tab and then Device Manager. Figure 7.5 shows Device Manager as it appears when you open it with this method.

FIGURE 7.5
Use the Device Manager to install, manage, and troubleshoot system hardware devices.

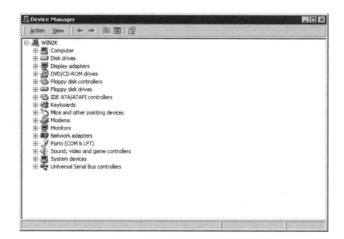

Device Manager also tracks four system resources that control how the systems on your computer function. Those resources are interrupt request lines (IRQ), input/output ports (I/O), direct memory access channels (DMA), and memory addresses.

Viewing and Managing Devices

You can view the properties of devices on your computer by expanding their listing in Device Manager. For example, if you want to take a look at the properties for your video display adapter, click the + preceding the Display Adapters listing in Device Manager to expand the Display Adapters category and view your video card.

You can view devices in one of four views:

■ *Devices by Type*, the default display type, lists devices by category.

■ *Devices by Connection* displays the devices based on the type of connection they have—for example, a modem is listed under Communications Ports.

■ *Resources by Type* displays the devices based on the type of resources they use: DMA, I/O, IRQ, and Memory. So, for example, you can expand the IRQ list for a quick look at what device is using which IRQ.

■ *Resources by Connection* displays the resources by connection type.

To use any of these views, choose a view option from the View menu in the Device Manager window.

To view the Properties sheet for a specific device, right-click the device in the details pane and choose Properties. Each property sheet might differ based on the type of device that you have selected. Figure 7.6, for example, displays the 3COM Etherlink Properties for the NIC installed on my computer.

FIGURE 7.6

The 3COM Etherlink Properties sheet provides the details about this device and enables you to troubleshoot it if necessary.

Though the Properties sheet varies from device to device, the tabs on each sheet offer the same basic types of information. The Etherlink properties sheet includes four tabs: General, Advanced, Driver, and Resources.

The General tab lists basic information about the device, such as its type, the manufacturer, and its drive location, and it offers a troubleshooter for the device. You can also enable or disable the device in the current hardware profile by selecting the Device Usage option at the bottom of the General tab. There are two options available, Use This Device (Enable) and Do Not Use This Device (Disable).

If you are using a laptop computer and want to set up a hardware profile that will be used when the laptop is docked and connected to a network and another that will be used when you are on the road and not docked, this option provides that opportunity.

If you get the "No Domain Controller Found" message when you are away from the network, you can set up a separate hardware profile as a workaround for that problem.

The Advanced tab contains advanced configuration information that pertains to the current device only. Some of the available options are as follows:

■ *Network Address.* This is the address that the network card, if present, is using on the network. This address listing is important if you have more than one network card in the computer.

Part

II

Ch

7

■ *Media Type.* This is used to determine whether the network card will be using full-duplex or half-duplex operation and speeds.

N O T E It is important to note here that this tab will contain different information, dependent on the hardware device and its manufacturer.

The Driver tab is available for all hardware devices and displays information such as the selected driver's version number, provider, digital signer, and the date of the driver's last update. The digital signer is new for Windows 2000 and requires driver developers to electronically sign their device drivers. You can use this information to determine whether you're using an approved and appropriate driver for that device.

You can view details about the driver by clicking the Driver Details button. A Driver Details Window is shown in Figure 7.7.

FIGURE 7.7
The Driver Details window lists the manufacturer name, driver filename and location, provider name, file version, and copyright notice. Click OK to close the window.

Many Driver tabs also include an Uninstall button to enable you to uninstall the driver from this tab. The Driver tab might also offer an Update Driver button that enables you to run the Upgrade Device Driver Wizard. Again, you should remember that the contents of the Driver tab vary from device to device.

Viewing and Managing Device Resources

The Resources tab of the Device Manager Properties sheet shows you what IRQ, I/O, and DMA resources are being used by this device. If you have legacy devices on your system and one of those devices is causing a resource conflict with another device, you can use this listing to change the resource and resolve the conflict. When you have selected the appropriate resource, you need to clear the Use Automatic Settings box to change the resource that you chose.

The Properties sheet for some devices, such as the Creative AWE 64 example shown in Figure 7.8, offers a Settings Based On drop-down list of configurations. These configurations are a set of IRQ, DMA, and I/O settings that are considered common for that hardware device.

N O T E You might need to change the configuration settings if your hardware device is not PnP-compliant. In this case, Windows 2000 might have trouble assigning resources to that device, or the device might cause conflicts with other hardware in the computer.

You can use the information found in the Viewing and Managing Devices section earlier in the chapter to determine the resources that specific devices are using to choose settings that will not conflict.

 TIP When installing legacy and PnP devices into the same computer, install and configure the legacy or non-PnP devices first because most legacy devices are limited in the resources that they will accept.

FIGURE 7.8
The configuration you choose from the Settings Based On list controls the settings in the Resource Settings list at the top of the tab.

You don't have to follow these listed settings, and you can change your resources one at a time by selecting the resource from the list and then clicking the Change Setting button. This action displays an Edit Interrupt Request dialog box similar to the one shown in Figure 7.9. Use this dialog box to change resource settings.

Part
II

Ch
7

FIGURE 7.9
In the Value list of the
Edit Interrupt Request
box, you can use the
arrows to scroll through
the available IRQ
resource settings for
the selected device.

The Conflict Information section displays the conflict status of the chosen resource. Do not select a resource that conflicts with other hardware devices, or your system will become very unstable or possibly inoperable.

When you have found an appropriate resource setting, click the OK button to close the dialog box and return to the Properties sheet. Click the OK button to close the Properties sheet and apply the changes. Depending on the device, you might be prompted to restart the computer.

Most Plug and Play devices will not enable you to change the settings displayed in the Properties sheet, so these options might not be available for those devices.

Printing Device Reports

If you want to generate a hard copy of the devices and settings as they exist in Device Manager, you can do so by following these steps:

1. Select the device that you want to print information about from the Device Manager listing.
2. Click the **V**iew menu and choose **P**rint; the Print dialog box is displayed.
3. Select one of these report types from the Report Type section of the dialog box by clicking the appropriate radio button:
    - *System Summary*. This report summarizes information such as product version number, bus type, registered owner, and resources used for all the devices on your computer.
    - *Selected Class or Device*. This printed report contains information—such as device name, driver location, driver version, and the resources that the device is using— for the device you selected in step 1.
    - *All Devices and System Summary*. This option prints an individual report for each device on your computer in addition to a system summary report. If your computer contains a lot of devices, this report type can generate a rather large report.
4. Click the Print button, and the report type you have selected is sent to the printer.

Setting Device Manager Options

By clicking the <u>V</u>iew menu and choosing Customize, you can change the way Device Manager looks. The Customize View dialog is displayed in Figure 7.10.

FIGURE 7.10
Use the Customize View dialog box to change the appearance of the Device Manager.

By checking or clearing options in the Customize View dialog box, you make these changes to the Device Manager display:

- *Console Tree.* Shows or hides the console tree in the left column.
- *Standard Menus.* Shows or hides the Action and View menus.
- *Standard Toolbar.* Shows or hides the Help, Show/Hide Console, Up One Level, Forward, and Back toolbar buttons.
- *Status Bar.* Displays or hides the status bar on the bottom of the MMC console.
- *Description Bar.* Checking this option displays a descriptive text bar above the details pane that describes the selected item in the console.
- *Taskpad navigation tabs.* Checking this option makes navigation tabs available in the Taskpad.
- *Menus.* If you have other snap-ins (in addition to the Device Manager) in the MMC, checking this option displays the menus from those snap-ins.
- *Toolbars.* Shows or hides snap-in toolbars for those snap-ins that have them.

Part

II

Ch

7

Managing Hardware Profiles

In this chapter

Using Hardware Profiles

Windows 2000 enables you to maintain multiple hardware profiles and choose from those profiles when the system boots. Each profile references its own set of devices (many of which are naturally duplicated in each profile), and you can enable or disable a device for a specific profile. When Windows 2000 starts, it loads only the device drivers and services for the devices in the selected profile.

 TIP If it can't determine the correct hardware profile, Windows 2000 displays a profile menu from which you can choose a profile.

Windows 2000 automatically recognizes most docking stations and supports *hot docking*, which enables you to dock and undock your portable without shutting down Windows 2000 or powering down the computer. Hardware profiles enable you to selectively enable/disable devices for each situation. For example, your docking station might contain a network adapter used when the computer is docked, but you use a PC card NIC when the computer is undocked. In the docked configuration, the PC card would be disabled. In the undocked configuration, the docking station's NIC would be disabled. The devices could then share resources without conflicting because they wouldn't be active at the same time.

You also can use hardware profiles to help your system when you occasionally use a device that puts an abnormal load on the system or conflicts with other devices; in those situations, you boot with that device's profile only when you need to use the device. In the case of a device conflict, you can remove one of the conflicting devices from each of the profiles, eliminating the conflict. The ideal solution is to resolve the conflict within the profile by changing the resource requirements of the device, but that isn't always possible.

 TIP Although Windows 2000 doesn't store different resource settings for a device in different profiles, you can add multiple instances of a device, specifying different resource settings for each one. You then can enable an instance for one profile and a different instance for another profile. See "Using Different Resource Settings" later in this chapter for more information.

Creating Hardware Profiles

You create and manage hardware profiles separately from individual devices in a profile. You use system properties to manage hardware profiles and Device Manager to manage individual devices and their profile assignments.

N O T E You must log on as a local administrator to manage hardware profiles. ■

To create or manage profiles, right-click My Computer and choose Properties. On the Hardware tab, click Hardware Profiles to access the Hardware Profiles dialog (see Figure 8.1).

FIGURE 8.1
The Hardware Profiles dialog box controls profiles globally but doesn't enable you to change individual device properties.

Click an existing profile and then click Copy to create a new profile. Enter a unique profile name when prompted. You can select a profile and click Rename or Delete, respectively, to rename or delete the profile. Use the Device Manager as explained in the following section to assign devices to a specific profile.

Assigning Devices to a Profile

By default, devices are assigned to all hardware profiles. You can selectively enable and disable devices to limit their use to specific profiles. Follow these steps to assign a device only to a specific profile:

1. Open the Device Manager and double-click the device in question to access its Properties sheet, as shown in Figure 8.2.

FIGURE 8.2
In the General tab of the device's Properties sheet, you can set resource usage and troubleshoot problems with the device, in addition to assigning it to a specific profile.

2. From the **D**evice usage list, select one of the following options:

- *Use This Device (Enable)*. Select to enable the device for the current hardware profile.
- *Do Not Use This Device in the Current Hardware Profile (Disable)*. Select to turn off (disable) the device for the current hardware profile.
- *Do Not Use This Device in Any Hardware Profiles (Disable)*. Select to disable the device in all hardware profiles.

3. Specify resource settings and other properties for the device using the Resource, Driver, and Advanced property tabs and then click OK.

4. Repeat the steps above for any additional devices you want to assign.

5. Click OK to close Device Manager; reboot to select the desired profile.

Using Different Resource Settings

You can't maintain different sets of resource settings from one profile to another for the same instance of a device. You can, however, add multiple instances of a device and then apply different resource settings to each instance. When you add and remove instances of the driver from various profiles, you're maintaining different resource settings for the same physical device.

To install multiple instances of a device, follow these steps:

1. Run the Add/Remove Hardware wizard in the Control Panel, and choose to install a new device. Windows 2000 will not detect any new PnP hardware (assuming you haven't installed any) and will give you the option to manually specify a device to add. Select No when prompted to search for the new hardware, and then manually select the device.

2. Complete the process to install another copy of the device and then use the Device Manager (as explained in the preceding section of this chapter) to set its resource properties as necessary.

3. Finally, add and remove devices from hardware profiles as necessary.

Moving Devices Between Profiles

Because every device exists in every profile and is simply enabled or disabled for a specific profile, you can't actually move a device from one profile to another. By disabling the device in one and enabling it in the other, however, you achieve the same thing. See the section, "Assigning Devices to a Profile," earlier in this chapter to learn how.

Switching Between Profiles

In most cases, Windows 2000 is able to detect and select the appropriate hardware profile. In some cases, however, Windows 2000 can't determine which profile to use, and you need to choose one at startup.

When you have more than one hardware profile, you can designate one as the default profile for Windows 2000 to select automatically when the system boots. Alternatively, you can have Windows 2000 prompt you to select a profile at boot. You can't switch between profiles on-the-fly, but instead must restart the computer to choose a different profile, with one exception. If you insert or remove a portable computer from a docking station, Windows 2000 detects the change and switches hardware profiles accordingly.

To configure how Windows 2000 handles hardware profiles on startup, right-click My Computer and choose Properties. Click Hardware Profiles to access the Hardware Profiles dialog. Use the up and down arrows beside the Available Hardware Profiles list to move the desired default profile to the top of the list and otherwise arrange the list to suit your needs.

Two options are available at the bottom of the dialog control profile selection at startup:

- *Wait Until I Select a Hardware Profile.* Windows 2000 waits indefinitely for you to select a hardware profile at startup if it is unable to determine automatically which profile to use.

- *Select the First Profile Listed if I Don't Select a Profile in* nn *Seconds.* Use the profile at the top of the list if you don't select a profile at startup within the specified amount of time.

Ejecting a Portable PC from a Docking Station

Prior to physically ejecting a portable PC from a docking station, you should inform Windows 2000 that you're ejecting the PC to enable it to shut down network connections and properly switch profiles. Click Start, Eject to inform Windows 2000 that you want to physically eject the PC. When it is ready, Windows 2000 will display a message indicating that it's safe to eject the PC.

You don't have to do anything special to insert a computer in a docking station. You can insert the computer when it is either on or off. Windows 2000 will adjust to the new docked status automatically.

 Full support for hot docking requires that the system be configured for ACPI power management. If your portable computer doesn't support ACPI, you can't use hot docking. In addition, some power management features, such as the capability to place the unit in standby mode through the Start menu, are not available without ACPI support.

Printing

Adding and Removing Printers

Windows 2000 provides extensive printer support, incorporating drivers for over fifty manufacturers and several hundred printers. The process for installing printers in Windows 2000 is simple and straightforward. As in Windows 9x/NT, Windows 2000 provides a wizard to help you install a printer, making the job painless. With Plug and Play, Windows 2000 can automatically detect and install support for any printer that supports PnP.

You need the following information to install and configure a local printer:

- Port to which the printer is connected (LPT, COM, IR, or TCP/IP).
- Printer manufacturer and model, or model with which your printer is compatible or emulates.
- Name for the printer to be used to identify it in Windows 2000.

You also are asked to make certain decisions when installing your printer:

- Whether you want to assign the printer as the default printer for Windows applications.
- Whether to share the printer with other users, and the name by which the printer is shared.
- Optional location description and comment for the printer; helpful to identify the printer to other users browsing for printer resources across the LAN.
- Whether to print a test page after installation to verify that the printer works.

In addition to the information listed previously for a local printer, you need the pathname when setting up a network printer (one connected to a remote computer across the LAN, rather than your own computer). The pathname is in the form \\server\sharename, where server is the name of the computer to which the printer is connected and sharename is the name by which the printer is shared. You can browse for the printer if you don't know its pathname.

When you have the information you need to perform the installation, use Control Panel, Printers, Add Printer to install a print driver. In the wizard, select the type of printer you want to create, and then follow the remaining prompts to complete the installation.

After installation, you can configure several printer-specific options such as installed memory, paper trays, forms, and so on, by using the printer's Properties sheet. These options vary by printer type and model, but Figure 9.1 shows an example of one printer's Properties sheet. Right-click a printer in the Printers folder and choose Properties to set its properties.

 TIP   A quick way to install a network printer is to browse in My Network Places to the remote computer and then double-click on the printer. Windows 2000 automatically installs the printer driver.

FIGURE 9.1
Printer property sheets vary from one printer to another, but they all provide access to option settings.

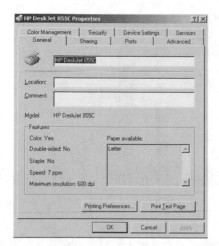

Using Windows 2000 Pro as a Print Server

You can share one or more printers from a computer running Windows 2000 Professional, although you're limited to a maximum of ten concurrent connections. In most cases, this limitation poses no problem, particularly in a small LAN or workgroup environment.

Sharing a Printer

Sharing a printer is easy. If you didn't share the printer when you installed its driver, simply open the Printers folder, right-click the printer, and choose S̲haring. On the Sharing tab of the printer's properties, click S̲hared As and specify the name by which you want the printer shared. This is the name that users will see when they browse your computer for shared resources.

You might also want to install files for additional operating systems if your LAN contains computers running other versions of Windows 2000, Windows NT, or Windows 9x. Having these additional driver files on your computer enables remote users to install the drivers from your computer across the LAN, eliminating the need for them to have the driver files, installation diskette, or OS CD-ROM on hand. They can simply browse to your printer and double-click it to install the driver on their systems.

To install these additional drivers, click A̲dditional Drivers on the Sharing tab to access the Additional Drivers dialog (see Figure 9.2). You need to have the printer driver files available (such as the CD-ROM for the applicable OS) at this point, and Windows 2000 will also prompt for the Windows 2000 Server CD. If you don't have the CD, but have access to the files locally or across the network, specify that path instead.

 TIP You can share a remote printer from your workstation; the printer doesn't have to be connected locally. This can simplify shared printer setup. In the case of a JetDirect printer, for example, you only have to install the JetDirect software on the computer that will be sharing the printer. All other computers can connect to that server to access the printer, rather than requiring the JetDirect software on each one to access the printer directly.

FIGURE 9.2
Select all other operating systems in use on the LAN to provide complete support.

Setting Printer Security

After sharing a printer, you'll want to review and possibly modify security settings to control the actions users can perform on the printer. Open the Printers folder and access the properties for the printer. On the Security tab (see Figure 9.3), select a user or group and select Allow or Deny as desired for each print permission (Print, Manage Printers, Manage Documents). These permissions determine the tasks a given user can perform with the selected printer. By default, everyone can print, but only selected groups can manage printers.

▶ For a full discussion of permissions, **see** "Understanding Permissions," **p. 242**

If a check box is shaded, the permission has been inherited, and you must change the permissions for the parent object. If neither Allow nor Deny is selected for a given permission, the group or user can obtain the permission through group membership. If this implied permission does not exist, the permission is implicitly denied.

You can add and remove users and groups from the list. Click Advanced to open the Access Control Settings properties for the printer (see Figure 9.4). Select names from the list, and then click the Add and Remove buttons to make the appropriate changes to the list.

N O T E Auditing enables you to track the actions performed on a given object, such as a printer, user account, shared folder, and so on. In addition, each object has an *owner*, which typically is the user who created the object. Ownership grants certain privileges to the owner over the object. ■

FIGURE 9.3
Set security for a shared printer to control the tasks other users can perform.

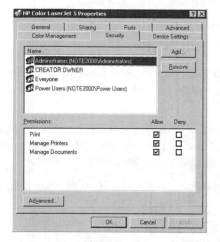

FIGURE 9.4
Configure advanced permissions, auditing, and ownership for the printer.

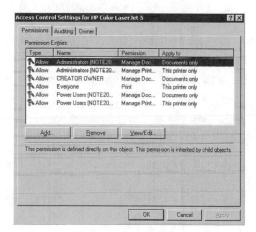

▶ To learn more about advanced security settings and options, **see** "A Checklist for Optimizing Security in a Windows 2000 Environment," **p. 209,** "The Security Configuration Tool Set," **p. 336,** and "Managing Group Policies," **p. 225**

▶ For an in-depth discussion of auditing resources, **see** "Auditing Resource Access and Use," **p. 250**

▶ To learn more about ownership, **see** "About Ownership," **p. 246**

Using Separator Pages

When you share a printer with several users, you might want to use separator pages to separate print jobs and make it easier for users to locate and retrieve their finished jobs. A separator page is a special print job Windows 2000 inserts between each user job. The separator page typically includes the name of the user who printed the document, date and time, and other pertinent information.

Windows 2000 includes four separator pages; you can customize the pages or use them as they are. Each page is designed to work best with a specific type of printer (PCL, PostScript, and so on). To assign a separator page to a printer, follow these steps:

1. Open the Printers folder, then right-click on the appropriate printer's icon, and choose Properties from the pop-up menu.

2. Click to open the Advanced tab, and then choose Separator Page.

3. Click Browse to locate and select the file you want to use. By default, the separator pages are located in the \systemroot\System32 folder. Click Open to use the selected file.

4. Click OK to close the Separator Page dialog box, and then click OK to close the printer's Properties sheet.

5. Print a test document to the printer to preview the separator page.

To customize a separator page, simply open the page in Notepad or WordPad and make the desired changes. Customizing separator pages requires a working knowledge of printer codes and print control languages and falls outside the scope of this book.

 TIP Leave the Separator Page field blank in the printer properties to disable separator pages for the selected printer.

Using Printer Pools

A *printer pool* enables you to connect multiple identical printers to a single computer and treat the printers collectively as a single object. This enables you to manage all the printers through a single instance of the printer driver because the printers function as clones of one another. Printer pools enable Windows 2000 to balance the load among the printers. When you send a print job to the driver, Windows 2000 automatically delegates the print job to whichever printer is available or has the fewest jobs. The result is easier administration and quicker, more efficient printing.

N O T E Although printer pools are most applicable to shared printers, there is no direct connection between sharing and printer pools. You can pool local printers without sharing them, but pooling only benefits local print jobs in such a case. You'd have to do a lot of local printing to make pooling worthwhile in this situation.

Setting up pooling is easy:

1. Connect the printers to the desired ports on the computer and install a print driver on one of the ports.
2. Open the Printers folder, right-click the print driver, and choose P**r**operties.
3. On the Ports property tab, select E**n**able printer pooling, as shown in Figure 9.5.
4. Select each port to which a printer is attached, and then click OK.

FIGURE 9.5
Use the Ports page to enable printer pooling.

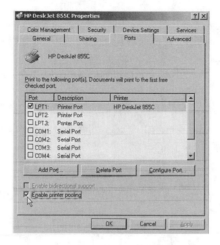

When you set other properties for the print driver, those properties affect all printers in the pool. Enable sharing, and you effectively share all printers in the pool. Change device settings, and those settings are applied to each printer.

To determine which printer a given job is assigned to, open the Printers folder and double-click the printer to view pending jobs. Port assignment appears for each job at the far right side of the window. Note that only currently printing jobs show a port assignment because pending jobs have not yet been allocated to a port.

Multiple Configurations with One Printer

If you change printer settings often, wouldn't it be nice to be able to just click a few times and have all the changes in place? Because of the way Windows 2000 handles print driver settings, you can do just that.

For example, assume you switch between four different forms throughout the day, using different paper trays and other device assignments. If your printer only has one tray slot, you couldn't leave the forms in two different trays and simply select the appropriate tray when you print. You'd have to not only physically change trays, but also change the settings in the print driver for each one each time you switched.

You can easily handle this situation and any other that involves multiple sets of printer settings by simply installing multiple instances of the same print driver. When you do, you can create a separate and unique configuration of settings for each instance. If you create four configurations for your printer, the Printers folder will contain four different instances of the same printer, and each instance will have different settings. When you need a specific configuration, print to the desired instance of your printer. You don't have to open the printer's properties to change settings; instead, you select the printer instance that already has those settings.

N O T E   Installing a new instance of a print driver doesn't add another copy of the print driver files. All instances share a single set of driver files. Make sure you use a unique name for each instance of the driver to help identify it and its function.

Use the following steps to install multiple instances of a print driver:

1. Open the Printers folder, and run the Add Printer wizard to install the first driver. Specify a unique name for the printer that identifies its function (see Figure 9.6). Complete the installation of the printer.

FIGURE 9.6
Specify a descriptive name for each instance of the printer.

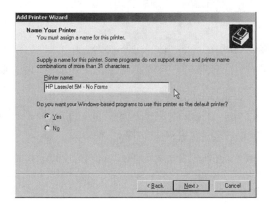

2. Right-click the printer's icon and choose Properties to set the properties of your choice for the printer.
3. Run the Add Printer wizard again to install the same printer. When prompted whether you want to keep the existing driver or install a new driver, choose the existing driver. Make sure you use a unique name to help you identify the function/settings for this instance (see Figure 9.7).
4. Set properties as desired for this new instance of the driver.
5. Repeat steps 3 and 4 as many times as necessary to create all the printer instances necessary to accommodate the unique printer configurations you use often.

FIGURE 9.7
The name for the new instance should be different from the original and should describe its function.

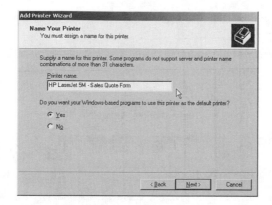

6. In the Printers folder, right-click the instance you use most often, click Properties, Set as Default Printer.

7. When you need to use a specific printer instance (other than the default), click File, Print in your application (or equivalent print command). In the Print dialog, select the desired printer instance from the Name drop-down list, and print the document.

To use a specific group of printer settings, just select the desired printer in your application and print. The settings already assigned to that instance are used automatically.

Printing to UNIX Hosts

Windows 2000 expands printing capabilities by allowing you to print to LPR devices attached to UNIX systems. You can print to printers connected to UNIX hosts by installing Print Services for UNIX. You then can add and print to an LPR printer as if it were a local printer. Follow these steps to configure your computer to print to a UNIX host:

1. Open the Network and Dial-Up Connections folder, and click Advanced, Optional Networking Components.

2. Select the Other Network File and Print Services check box, and then click Next.

3. Insert the Windows 2000 CD-ROM or specify the path to the Windows 2000 source files when prompted, and then click OK.

4. Open the Printers folder and double-click Add Printer to start the Add Printer wizard.

5. Select Local Printer and deselect Automatically Detect and Install My Plug and Play Printer. Click Next.

6. Click Create a New Port, and select LPR Port from the drop-down list. Click Next.

7. Specify settings in the Add LPR Compatible Printer dialog box, as shown in Figure 9.8, and click OK.

8. Select the printer manufacturer and model, and complete the setup process as you would for a local printer.

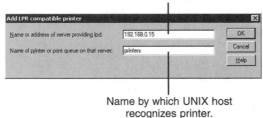

DNS name or IP address of UNIX host
where printer located.

FIGURE 9.8

Specify settings for the printer and UNIX host in the Add LPR Compatible Printer dialog box to configure your printer to a UNIX host.

Name by which UNIX host
recognizes printer.

Printing Across the Internet or an Intranet

You can share printers connected to computers running Internet Information Services (IIS) through a Web interface, making them available across the Internet or an intranet. The printers are subject to the security restrictions you apply to the printer. Remote users can connect to the printer through a Web browser or specify the printer's URL rather than UNC name when adding the printer.

N O T E   Printing across the Web employs the Internet Printing Protocol (IPP) developed jointly by Microsoft and Hewlett Packard. IPP provides secure printing across the Internet or an intranet and opens interesting new possibilities for printing and data transmission. For example, IPP could potentially replace facsimile (fax) use in many situations. Rather than fax a document to a remote fax server, you'd simply open your document and print to the remote site's printer through a standard Internet connection. As another example, hotels could provide printing services for guests, enabling a guest to process and receive a print job via room service.

Configuring Printer Sharing Via the Web

To provide printers via HTTP, the server computer must be running IIS and you must configure the Printers virtual directory under the desired Web site in IIS if it doesn't already exist. After you create the Printers virtual directory, users can connect to http://*servername*/Printers, where *servername* is the host name or IP address of the server, to view the list of shared printers.

The folder you assign as the Printers virtual directory is \systemroot\Web\Printers, such as \Winnt\Web\Printers. This folder contains several Active Server Page (ASP) files that provide the server-side print enumeration and control that users see when they connect to the site. The default page is Page1.asp. You can use the ASP pages as-is or modify them to support custom directory structure or printer capability (see the section "Customizing Printer Web Pages" later in this chapter for more information).

Follow these steps to configure a Windows 2000 computer to share its printers via the Web:

1. Install IIS on the computer if it is not already installed.

   ▶ To learn how to install IIS, **see** "Installing IIS," **p. 444**

2. Open the IIS management MMC console by choosing Start, **P**rograms, Administrative Tools, Internet Services Manager.

3. Expand the server in the left pane to view the Web sites it hosts, and then expand the site under which you want to make printers available, or expand the Default Web Site, as shown in Figure 9.9.

FIGURE 9.9
Open the default Web site or other site under which you want the Printers virtual directory added.

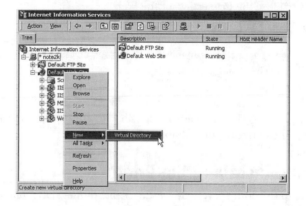

4. Right-click the site name (or Default Web Site) and choose **N**ew, Virtual Directory.

5. Click **N**ext when the Virtual Directory Creation Wizard starts, then type **Printers** in the **A**lias text box, and click **N**ext.

6. For **D**irectory, type or browse to the \systemroot\Web\Printers folder (for example, C:\Winnt\Web\Printers), and click **N**ext.

7. Set access permissions to include **R**ead and Run **S**cripts, as shown in Figure 9.10, and then click **N**ext.

Part II · Ch 9

FIGURE 9.10
Set access permissions on the new virtual directory.

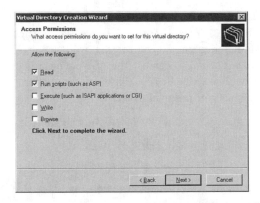

8. Right-click the virtual directory you just created and choose P**r**operties.

9. Click the Documents tab and select Enable Default Do**c**ument.

10. Click A**d**d, type **page1.asp**, and click **OK**.

11. Click **OK** to close the Properties for the Web site.

12. Close the IIS management console.

 TIP If you're unable to connect to `http://servername/Printers` to view shared printers, stop and restart the Web site in the IIS management console.

You don't have to do anything special to make newly added printers appear to clients when they browse for printers. The ASP page responsible for displaying the printer list automatically enumerates the currently shared printers.

Connecting to and Installing the Printer

You can connect to the print server and view available printers or connect directly to a specific printer. Open a browser and connect to `http://servername/Printers` to view all shared printers, where *servername* is the host name or IP address of the server (example: `http://192.168.0.15/Printers`). Connect to `http://servername/Printers/sharename` to view a specific printer's queue, where *sharename* is the name by which the printer is shared (example: `http://www.somedomain.com/Printers/LaserJet`).

 TIP If you prefer to hide your printers from the outside world, name the virtual folder something other than Printers and give the name to those individuals to whom you want to grant printer access. Choose a name not easily guessed. For example, you might create the virtual folder as "aardvaark", and users would connect using `http://yourdomain.com/aardvaark` when they needed to print.

When you connect to a computer that is sharing its printers through IPP, you see a page in your browser similar to the one shown in Figure 9.11. Click a printer to view its queue and controls (see Figure 9.12).

FIGURE 9.11
The remote server enumerates its shared printers automatically through IIS.

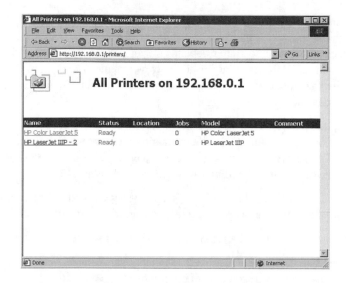

FIGURE 9.12
You can control a printer's queue through the browser connection much as you can through the Printers folder.

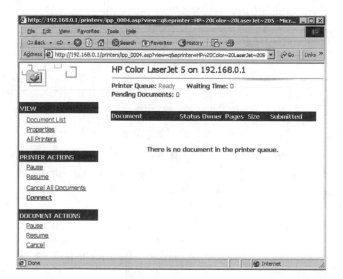

NOTE   Full support for IPP, including the capability to connect to and install printers through IPP, requires an IPP client installed on the client computer. The Windows 2000 Server CD-ROM includes an IPP client for Windows 9x in \Clients\Win9xipp.cli. (No client is included on the Windows 2000 Professional CD-ROM, although both Windows 2000 Professional and Windows 2000 Server fully support IPP.) There is no IPP client for Windows NT on either CD-ROM. Microsoft has stated that no IPP client is planned or supported for NT, although that position could change. Check the Microsoft Web site at http://www.microsoft.com/windows for future developments. ∎

You can install the drivers for the printer through the browser if your system doesn't already contain it, assuming that the remote system contains the necessary driver files. How the files are transferred to your computer depends on your connection to the print server. Windows 2000 bypasses HTTP in favor of RPC if the two computers can communicate via RPC (as is usually the case in an intranet connection). In this situation, Windows 2000 installs the print driver in the usual manner.

For situations where RPC isn't possible, Windows 2000 uses HTTP to install the driver. The server packages a cabinet (CAB) file containing the printer's INF file and all required installation files. The server sends the CAB file to the client, where it is expanded and starts the Add Printer Wizard to install the printer using the provided files.

You also can run the Add Printer Wizard and specify the URL of the printer explicitly without even connecting to the server's Printers folder or printer page.

Follow these steps to install a printer through a Web browser:

1. Open your browser and connect to http://*servername*/Printers, where *servername* is the host name or IP address of the print server.
2. Click the printer you want to install; its page opens.
3. Click Connect in Printer Actions list of options.
4. Follow the prompts provided to install the print driver on your system.

In cases where you know the remote printer's URL and model ahead of time, you can run the Add Printer Wizard and specify the URL explicitly without first connecting to the remote printer. Follow these steps to install the remote printer in this situation:

1. Open the Printers folder and run the Add Printer Wizard.
2. Click N̲etwork Printer and click N̲ext.
3. Click C̲onnect to a Printer on the Internet or on Your Intranet. Type the URL for the printer in the URL text box, using the form http://*servername*/printername, where *printername* is the printer's share name.
4. Complete the printer installation process as you normally would.

TIP With a printer added using the preceding method, the client will always connect to the print server using HTTP. You must use this method when installing a printer that contains its own network card and that is not connected to a server (but that is instead connected directly to the network, as in the case of JetDirect printers). The network printer must support IPP, however.

After the printer is installed, it appears in the Printers folder. You can print to it as you would any other installed printer.

TIP Add the printer's management URL to your Favorites list to make it easier to access its queue.

Customizing Printer Web Pages

As explained in the previous section, Windows 2000 supports IPP, enabling clients to print across the Internet or intranet and manage a printer's queue through a Web browser.

The Web documents that the client sees when it connects to the printer's URL are generated by ASP files. The standard ASP files provided with Windows 2000 generate the following pages:

■ Print server page referenced by `http://servername/Printers` that contains links to a page for every printer installed on the server (`page1.asp`).

■ Print queue page for each print queue. These pages are provided as links on the main Printers page or you can access them directly by pointing the browser to `server/printername` for the printer.

■ Pages for queued documents, printer properties, and printer-specific details. These pages are displayed within a frame when you view a printer's queue.

You can customize the way a server presents printer information by customizing existing ASP files or writing your own. The sections that follow provide a good overview of the available processes for customizing printer-specific details pages.

NOTE This section assumes you are experienced with ASP programming and doesn't cover specific customization methods; rather, it focuses on the overall process and capabilities for customizing printer-specific Web pages within Windows 2000. For additional information on the print server process, consult the Microsoft Device Developer Kit (DDK) documentation. ■

Customizing the Printer Details Page

Customizing a printer's details Web page enables you to provide links to additional customized pages, to provide information for users, and to fully control what users see when they browse and manage printers via the Web.

You can replace the default files for a printer type, manufacturer, or port monitor. If the printer uses Microsoft's standard TCP/IP port monitor (`tcpmon.dll`), you can replace printer details pages on a per-printer type or per-manufacturer basis. You can only replace the default printer details pages for printers that use other port monitors; replacements on a per-printer type or per-manufacturer type basis are not supported.

Which printer detail's Web page is displayed depends on which port monitor is used with the printer. The print server uses the following criteria to determine which page to display when the standard TCP/IP port monitor is used:

1. Printer type-specific ASP files, if installed, are used.

2. When no printer type-specific files are available, the server uses manufacturer-specific files, if installed.

3. When manufacturer-specific files are not available and the printer supports the Printer MIB (RFC 1759) for SNMP, the default ASP files are used.

4. No details page is displayed if the printer does not support SNMP.

When a printer doesn't use the standard port monitor, the server checks for monitor-specific ASP files and displays them if they exist. If they do not, no details page is displayed.

When you modify or create a custom ASP file to replace a default printer details page, you can use predefined ASP variables, ActiveX objects, and COM objects to tailor the page's function.

Using ASP Session Variables   Table 9.1 lists the predefined ASP session variables you can use to query and manage printer data. The MS Port Monitor Only column indicates whether the variable is valid only when the printer uses the standard Microsoft TCP/IP port monitor.

Table 9.1   ASP Printer Sessions Variables

Variable	Value	MS Port Monitor Only
MS_ASP1	Path to initial Web page describing printer-specific details	No
MS_Community	Print server's SNMP community name	Yes
MS_Computer	Print server's computer name	No
MS_DefaultPage	Default ASP file for printer-specific details	No
MS_Device	Printer's SNMP device index	Yes
MS_IPAddress	Printer's IP address	Yes
MS_LocalServer	Print server's identifier such as IP address or computer name	No
MS_Model	Name of printer driver	No
MS_Portname	Printer's port name	No
MS_Printer	Printer's share name	No
MS_SNMP	TRUE when SNMP used with printer; FALSE if not	Yes
MS_DHTMLEnabled	TRUE if client supports DHTML; FALSE if not	No
MS_URLPrinter	Printer's name in URL format	No

The ASP session variables described in Table 9.1 enable you to view properties of the printer for which the ASP page was invoked (*current printer*).

Using ActiveX Objects to Retrieve Printer Information   Two ActiveX objects provided with Windows 2000 enable you to retrieve information associated with a specific printer. This enables you to retrieve information not provided by the ASP session variables for the current printer or for printers other than the current printer. The two objects, IAspHelp and ISNMP are supplied in the file Oleprn.dll and support any scripting language such as VBScript.

IAspHelp enables you to retrieve information associated with a specific printer, including data not supplied for the current printer by the ASP session variables or for printers other than the current one.

ISNMP enables you to set and retrieve values for a printer if the printer supports SNMP and uses the standard Microsoft TCP/IP port monitor.

IoleCvt enables you to convert strings from ANSI to Unicode and Unicode to ANSI , convert strings to UTF8 format, and convert Unicode strings using a different code page.

Installing Pages for a Printer Type

You can install a custom printer details page for printers that use the standard Microsoft port monitor. You need to create a custom printer INF file, including in it information about the ASP file(s) and related files (image or other ASP files, for example) required to display the page. Following is a portion of a sample printer INF file:

```
[Manufacturer]
"ACE"

[ACE]
"ACE Color Laser Deluxe" = ACE01.PPD

[ACE01.PPD]
CopyFiles=@ACE01.PPD,PSCRIPT,ACE1WEB
DataSection=PSCRIPT_DATA

[ACE1WEB]
PAGE1.ASP, ACECLR1.ASP; renamed to PAGE1.ASP during installation
ACECLR2.ASP
ACECLR3.ASP
ACE001.GIF
ACE002.GIF
ACE003.GIF

[DestintationDirs]
DefaultDestiDir=66000
ACE1WEB=66004
```

As noted in the sample, you must precede the main ASP page for the printer with Page1.asp (see the first line of the ACE1WEB section). The installation procedure renames this file to

Page1.asp in the target directory. Installation also creates the directory *systemroot\ manufacturer\printer*, where *manufacturer* and *printer* are derived from the first two sections of the previous sample INF file, respectively.

N O T E Microsoft reserves the filenames structured as Page*N*.asp, so you should avoid using filenames with that format. ▮

The DestinationDirs section defines the directory where the files are installed. The DefaultDestiDir setting specifies the location of any files not otherwise directed by other settings in the section. For example, the ACE1WEB setting defines where the files specified in the ACE1WEB section are placed. Table 9.2 lists the printer-related values you can use in the DestinationDirs section.

Table 9.2 Printer DIRIDs

DIRID	Location	Contents
66000	Path returned by GetPrinterDriverDirectory function	Driver files and dependent files
66001	Path returned by GetPrintProcessorDirectory function	Print processor files
66002	Path to additional files to be copied to \systemroot\System32 folder on local system	Print monitor files, other dependent files
66003	Path returned by GetColorDirectory function	ICM color profile files
66004	Path to which printer type-specific ASP files are copied	ASP files and associated files

Installing Pages for a Manufacturer

Windows 2000 determines a printer's manufacturer through its INF file when it installs the printer. When a client tries to connect to a specific printer page, the system checks for the file Page1.asp in the folder \systemroot\Web\Printers\Manufacturer\PrinterType, where *Manufacturer* is replaced by the printer manufacturer name and *PrinterType* is replaced by the printer type. If no Page1.asp file is found, the system checks in \systemroot\Web\Printers\Manufacturer for a file.

To install a printer details page specific to a certain manufacturer and for all printer types by that manufacturer that use the standard Microsoft TCP/IP port monitor, copy the APS file

and any related files (GIF, other ASP, and so on) to the
systemroot\Web\Printers*Manufacturer* folder either manually or using a custom installation program.

Installing Pages for a Port Monitor

Custom printer details files for printers that use a nonstandard port monitor should be placed in the monitor's subdirectory at *systemroot*\Web\Printers*monitor*, where *monitor* matches the port monitor name returned by a PORT_INFO_2 structure.

Part

II

Ch

9

PART III

Administering Windows 2000 Professional

Exploring the Control Panel

The Control Panel is the control center for Windows 2000. With it you can control almost every hardware and software setting, stop and start services, install and uninstall programs, set up new hardware, and more. The following sections explain the functions of each Control Panel applet.

> **TIP**
> You can configure Windows 2000 to expand the Control Panel item on the Start menu, making it possible to pick individual Control Panel items from the Start Menu, rather than opening the Control Panel. To configure this behavior, right-click the Taskbar and choose Properties. On the Advanced tab, select Expand Control Panel then click OK. To open the Control Panel from the Start menu rather than expand it, right-click Control Panel on the menu and choose Open.

Many settings in the Control Panel applets are self-explanatory for the majority of users. Rather than document every setting in every dialog, this chapter focuses on explaining why you would use certain features and how they impact configuration. Only those options that are not self-explanatory for the average user or for users switching from other operating platforms are documented for each applet.

Setting Accessibility Options

Accessibility Options in Windows 2000 offer enhanced video, sound, and input (keyboard/mouse) options to help people with disabilities or who simply have difficulty using Windows 2000's standard features. For example, you can use Accessibility Options to enlarge fonts on the screen for easier viewing.

The standard Accessibility Options sheet, opened by double-clicking the Accessibility Options icon in the Control Panel, includes five tabs: Keyboard, Sound, Mouse, Display, and General properties. The following sections explain each page of settings.

The Keyboard Tab

The Keyboard tab (see Figure 10.1) enables you to customize the way the keyboard works, making it easier for users with difficulty using standard keyboard functions to work with the keyboard.

The Keyboard tab offers the following customizable features:

- Use StickyKeys. The StickyKeys feature makes the Ctrl, Alt, and Shift keys work as if they stay down when pressed.
- Use FilterKeys. Use the FilterKeys feature to help prevent accidental repeated keystrokes and to slow down the key repeat rate.
- Use ToggleKeys. The ToggleKeys feature causes Windows 2000 to play a sound when the Caps Lock, Num Lock, or Scroll Lock keys are pressed or released.
- Show Extra Keyboard Help in Programs. Select this option if you want programs to prompt you with additional information about keyboard features.

FIGURE 10.1
The Keyboard tab of the Accessibility Options sheet lets you make changes to keyboard accessibility properties.

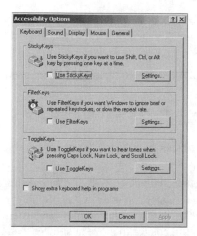

The Sound Tab

The Sound tab of the Accessibility Options sheet lets you apply visual clues to audio events in Windows 2000. This is helpful for assisting users with hearing difficulties to recognize audio events generated by Windows 2000, such as the beep that accompanies an error dialog box. The Sound options include SoundSentry and ShowSounds.

The following list explains the options on the Sound page:

- Use SoundSentry. Enable this option to have Windows 2000 display a visual warning when it plays a sound. Click the Settings button to specify which action Windows 2000 should perform for window and full-screen programs when an audio event occurs.

- Use ShowSounds. Enable this option to have your programs display captions for sounds and speech.

N O T E Programs must be written specifically to take advantage of ShowSounds. Programs, by default, do not support ShowSounds. ■

The Display tab

Use the Display tab to access the High Contrast feature. This option changes the color scheme to increase the contrast in the display, making text and icons more prominent and easier to see.

The Mouse Tab

Use the options on the Mouse tab to enable the MouseKeys Accessibility feature. MouseKeys enables you to control the mouse pointer using the arrow keys on the keyboard's numeric keypad.

Place a check in the Use MouseKeys check box to turn on MouseKeys. Click the Settings button to display the Settings for MouseKeys dialog box. The Settings for MouseKeys dialog box contains the following options:

- *Use Shortcut*. Choose this option to enable the shortcut key sequence for turning on or off MouseKeys.

- *Top Speed*. Use this slider to set the pointer's top speed when controlled by the cursor keys.

- *Acceleration*. Use this slider to specify how fast the pointer accelerates when you hold down a cursor key.

- *Hold Down Ctrl to Speed Up and Shift to Slow Down*. Choose this option to turn on the Ctrl and Shift modifiers. When this option is turned on, holding down the Ctrl key while pressing a cursor key causes the pointer to move in larger-than-normal increments. Pressing Shift causes the pointer to move in smaller-than-normal increments.

- *Use MouseKeys when NumLock Is*. This setting determines whether MouseKeys is active if the Num Lock key is active. Set this option to Off if you use the numeric keypad to enter numbers.

- *Show MouseKey status on screen*. Select this option to display a MouseKey status indicator on the taskbar to indicate when MouseKeys is active.

The General Tab

The General tab of the Accessibility Properties sheet lets you specify general accessibility options. The General page contains the following options:

- *Turn Off Accessibility Features After Idle for n Minutes*. Choose this option if you want the accessibility features to turn off when the computer has been inactive for the amount of time specified by the associated drop-down list.

- *Give Warning Message when Turning a Feature On*. Choose this option if you want the accessibility features to notify you with an onscreen message when they are activated.

- *Make a Sound when Turning a Feature On or Off*. Turn on this option to have Windows 2000 play a sound every time you turn on or off an accessibility feature using its keyboard shortcut.

- *Support SerialKey Devices*. Enable this option to have Windows 2000 support *SerialKey* devices—optional input devices that connect to the PC's serial port. Click the Settings button to specify the serial port to which the SerialKey device is connected, as well as the data communications rate.

N O T E SerialKey devices provide easier input methods than typical pointing devices, making it easier for people with motor-skill difficulties to use the computer. ▪

■ *Apply All Settings to Logon Desktop.* Select this option to apply all accessibility options to the desktop present at logon.

■ *Apply All Settings to Defaults for New Users.* Select this option to apply the accessibility option settings as the default settings for any new users.

Add/Remove Hardware Object

The Add/Remove Hardware object lets you install and uninstall hardware from your Windows 2000 computer via a wizard that guides you through each step of setting up or removing a piece of hardware.

In addition to providing a means of installing and removing hardware, the Add/Remove Hardware object lets you unplug a device and troubleshoot hardware.

▶ For a detailed look at the Add/Remove Hardware object, **see** "The Add/Remove Hardware Wizard," **pg. 113**

Part

III

Ch

10

Using the Add/Remove Programs Object

The Add/Remove Programs object lets you install and uninstall programs and install additional Windows 2000 *components* (optional features). The following sections explain how to install and remove programs and add Windows 2000 components through the Add/Remove Programs object (see Figure 10.2).

FIGURE 10.2
Use Add/Remove Programs to add applications and Windows 2000 components to the computer.

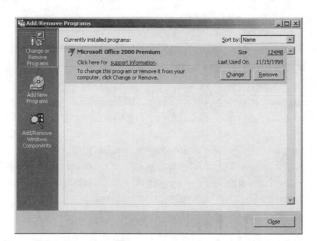

CAUTION

When you remove a program, pay close attention to any prompts that Windows 2000 might display. Occasionally, Windows 2000 might not be able to remove all the components for a program and will inform you of that fact. Also, some programs share components, and Windows 2000 warns you if you are about to remove a shared component.

Pre-Installation Planning

Before you install a program, you should consider the following:

- *Available disk space.* Even programs distributed on CD-ROM typically require at least some space on the hard disk. Check the program's requirements for hard disk space (see the package or installation instructions), and then check your hard disk(s) for enough available disk space to accommodate the program. If you don't have enough disk space, you'll need to remove unused programs or document files to make space available. Consider clearing out the Internet cache. To do so, right-click the Internet Explorer icon on the desktop and choose Properties. On the General page, click the Delete Files button.

- *Where to locate the program.* If you have more than one hard disk, decide which disk will contain the program. Most Windows 95/98/NT programs, by default, install themselves in the \Program Files folder on drive C. Most programs give you the option of specifying a disk and folder other than the one recommended by the program.

- *Will you want shortcuts in the Start menu or on the desktop to the program?* The setup process for most programs will ask this question. If the Start menu is already cluttered, you might choose not to have Setup create the shortcuts, but instead create your own shortcuts in a location you choose.

- *Do you have the necessary permissions to install the program?* Typically, this means having the necessary permissions to create folders and write to those folders. If you log in as Administrator on your workstation, you should have no trouble installing programs.

N O T E Most programs designed specifically for Windows 9x/NT/2000 that are distributed on CD-ROM include an Autorun program that causes the setup program to run as soon as you insert the CD-ROM. Installation of these programs is almost automatic—you have to specify only a few options on where and how you want the program installed. ▓

Installing Programs with the Add/Remove Programs Wizard

Regardless of whether or not the program comes on CD-ROM, most Windows programs use a file called Setup.exe to install the program. Windows 2000 includes a wizard that automatically searches for the setup program. Here's how to use this wizard to install a program:

1. Place the program's installation floppy disk (typically disk 1 of a multidisk set) into drive A, or place the program's CD-ROM into the CD-ROM drive.
2. Open the Control Panel; then open the Add/Remove Programs item.
3. On the Install/Uninstall page, click the Add New Programs button, and then click the CD or Floppy button to start the wizard.
4. Click Next and the wizard searches for a setup program.
5. If Windows finds the setup program, it displays the location of the setup program. Click Finish to start the setup program.
6. Follow the setup program's prompts to complete the installation process. Refer to the program's installation instructions for additional help.

Installing Programs Without the Wizard

Occasionally you might need to install a program without using the wizard. For example, the program might use a program other than Setup.exe for installation. In these cases, follow the program's installation instructions to locate and start the installation program.

If the program does use Setup.exe, you can locate it on the program's disk or CD-ROM by using Windows Explorer, and then open the file. Setup starts the installation process.

Uninstalling Programs

You can uninstall programs almost as easily as you install them. Although you could simply delete the folder in which the program is installed, you should always try to use Windows to uninstall the program instead. Using the Uninstall feature helps ensure that all components of the program are removed from your system.

To uninstall a program, follow these steps:

1. Choose Start, Settings, Control Panel.
2. Open the Add/Remove Programs item.
3. Scroll through the list of installed programs and select the program you want to remove.
4. Click Change/Remove and follow the prompts to remove the program. If the program you want to remove doesn't appear in the list of installed programs, it probably doesn't support the Uninstall feature. You should be able to delete the program's folder.

Add/Remove Windows Components

The Add/Remove Windows Components button in the Add/Remove Programs window starts the Windows Components Wizard (see Figure 10.3), which lets you view the Windows 2000 components that are installed, add components, and remove components. Nearly all Windows 2000 components and features can be added through this wizard.

Part
III

Ch
10

FIGURE 10.3

The Windows Components Wizard lets you add or remove major features from Windows 2000.

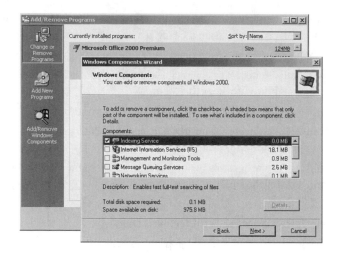

To add optional features to Windows 2000, follow these steps:

1. Open the Control Panel, and then open the Add/Remove Programs object.

2. Click the Add/Remove Windows Components button, which starts the Windows Components Wizard. Click Next.

3. Scroll through the list of available Windows 2000 components. Installed components have a check next to them. Select the component(s) you want to install by placing a check next to them.

4. To view which items will install or to select only a subset of available components, click the Details button. In the resulting list, place a check next to the items you want to install.

5. When you've selected all the items you want to add, click Next. Windows 2000 prompts you for the Windows 2000 CD-ROM if needed.

N O T E If you have a disk containing additional Windows 2000 components, click the Have Disk button and insert the disk when prompted by Windows 2000. Note that some of the folders on the Windows 2000 CD-ROM contain optional components not listed in the Windows 2000 Setup list in the Add/Remove Programs box. ■

Use a similar process to remove Windows 2000 components you no longer want or need. Open the Windows 2000 Setup page and clear the check box next to each item you want to remove. Then click Next. Windows 2000 removes the items and, if necessary, restarts the computer.

Configuring Administrative Tools

The Administrative Tools object in the Control Panel (see Figure 10.4) lets you make changes to the system as an administrator. From here, you can manage hardware, turn on and off system services, and so on.

FIGURE 10.4
The Administrative Tools object contains various controls for making changes to Windows 2000's hardware and system services.

Part

III

Ch

10

The objects contained in Administrative Tools are, with one exception, links to MMC consoles. The exception is the Data Sources (ODBC) object, which functions as a standalone tool. The Administrative Tools folder points to \Documents and Settings*user*\Start Menu\Programs\Administrative Tools. The number of objects in this folder varies depending on which services you have installed.

▶ For a detailed discussion of the objects in the Administrative Tools folder, **see** Part IV, "The Administrative Tools," beginning on **pg. 257**.

Setting Date/Time Options

The Date/Time object in the Control Panel enables you to set your system's date, time, and time zone. You also can configure Windows 2000 to automatically adjust your PC's time for daylight savings time. The time and date are stored in your computer's CMOS chip, which provides long-term storage for general information about your PC. Storing the date and time in CMOS means that your PC has the current time and date even after you turn off the PC.

Setting the Date and Time

To set the computer's time, open the Date/Time object in the Control Panel. You'll see the Date/Time Properties box shown in Figure 10.5.

FIGURE 10.5
The Date/Time
Properties box lets you
designate a time zone
and choose display
types.

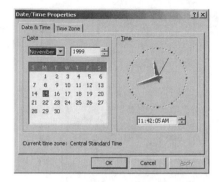

Choose the month and date by using the calendar and clicking the date. Click the hour, minutes, or seconds, and then use the spin control (small up and down arrows) to change the time. Click A.M. or P.M.; then click the spin buttons to change the time of day. Click OK when the time and date are correct.

N O T E   You can open the Date/Time Properties sheet by double-clicking the time on the tray. ■

Setting the Time Zone

To set the time zone in which your computer is located, and to enable or disable automatic adjustment for daylight savings time, first open the Date/Time object in the Control Panel. Then click the Time Zone tab to display the Time Zone page.

Choose your local time zone from the Time Zone drop-down list. Place a check in the check box labeled *Automatically Adjust Clock for Daylight Saving Changes* if you want Windows 2000 to automatically change your PC's time when daylight savings time comes and goes. Choose OK to save your settings.

Controlling the Display

The Display object in the Control Panel enables you to set a variety of settings for your display adapter and monitor. Figure 10.6 shows the Display Properties sheet.

The following sections explain the features and controls on each of the Display Properties tabs.

N O T E   You can open the Display Properties sheet by right-clicking the desktop and choosing Properties from the context menu.

FIGURE 10.6
The Display Properties sheet lets you view and change the properties for your display.

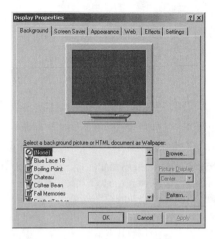

Part

III

Ch

10

The Background Tab

Use the Background tab to specify the desktop wallpaper and pattern. The background pattern, if any, appears behind the wallpaper image. You can use BMP, JPG, RLE, and Web page (HTML) files as wallpaper. The controls on this page are self-explanatory.

N O T E   If you use anything other than a bitmap (BMP) file as wallpaper, Windows 2000 must turn on Active Desktop.

To create a custom pattern, select a pattern and click the Edit Pattern button to open the Pattern Editor dialog box. Type a new name and click Add to add a new pattern or to edit the existing pattern, and then click Change. Click the Remove button to remove the selected pattern from the list. Choose OK when you're satisfied with the pattern.

The Screen Saver Tab

Use the Screen Saver tab to configure and preview screen savers. A persistent image on a monitor can cause a permanent degradation of the coating on the inside surface of the monitor's glass that leaves a ghost image on the display (called *burn-in*). Although today's monitors are not as susceptible to burn-in as older monitors, long term display of the same image can still cause burn-in. Using a screen saver prevents burn-in by blanking or changing the display. A screen saver also can help secure your system if you use the password option.

The following are selected controls on the Screen Saver tab:

- *Password Protected*. Place a check in this box if you want Windows 2000 to prompt you for your logon password to stop the screen saver and return to the desktop. Use this feature to prevent someone from using your PC if you leave it unattended.

■ *Power.* Click this to change how your monitor deals with energy-saving features, such as going into standby or idle mode. Different monitors present different prompts based on the power features available in the monitor.

The Appearance Tab

Use the Appearance sheet to specify a desktop scheme or to set various options for the appearance of specific desktop elements such as icons, fonts, window borders, and other elements.

The controls on the Appearance sheet are self-explanatory. When you have a group of settings you like, you can click the Save As button to save the settings as a named theme. The next time you want to select this particular group of settings, select its name from the Scheme drop-down list. To delete a scheme, select the scheme from the Scheme drop-down list, and then click Delete.

The Web Tab

Use the controls on the Web tab to view the Active Desktop as a Web page. You also can add and configure active content to your Windows 2000 desktop through the Web Properties sheet.

▶ For a detailed discussion on how to configure the Active Desktop, **see** "Using the Active Desktop," **pg. 62**

The Effects Tab

The Effects tab lets you control a handful of desktop special effects. The following list explains the settings on the Effects page:

■ *Desktop Icons.* Use this control to view and change icons for specific desktop items such as My Computer. Select the icon you want to change, and then click the Change Icon button to browse for a different icon. Click the Default Icon to restore the default icon for the object.

■ *Use Transition Effects for Menus and ToolTips.* Place a check in this box if you want the appearance and disappearance of menus and ToolTips to be accompanied by a special visual effect. Choose the effect from the drop-down list to the right of the check box: Fade effect (which causes the items to fade in and out) or Scroll effect (which causes the items to scroll in and out of view).

■ *Smooth Edges of Screen Fonts.* Enable this check box to have Windows 2000 automatically smooth screen fonts to improve their appearance. Turn off this option to improve performance on slower systems.

■ *Use Large Icons.* Place a check in this box if you want Windows 2000 to use larger-than-normal desktop icons. Using large icons is helpful with high-screen resolutions or if you have difficulty seeing the standard-size icons.

- *Show Icons Using All Possible Colors.* Enable this check box to have Windows 2000 display icons using as many colors as possible. Turning off this option can speed performance on slower systems.

- *Show Window Contents While Dragging.* Place a check in this box to have Windows 2000 show the entire window when dragging, rather than showing just an outline of the window.

- *Hide Keyboard Navigation Indicators Until I Use the Alt Key.* Place a check in this box if you want to hide keyboard shortcuts (the underscore that signifies which Alt+keystroke combination is used to execute a command on a menu) until you press the Alt key.

The Settings Tab

Use the Settings tab to set display resolution and color depth, as well as other settings that are specific to your display adapter and monitor. Increase color depth to improve image quality but at the cost of somewhat slower performance. Higher screen resolution gives you more desktop area with which to work.

The following list describes the controls on the Settings page:

- *Colors.* This drop-down list contains selections for each of the color depths supported by your video adapter. Select the desired option from the list.

NOTE Using a higher number of colors improves video appearance but can reduce the computer's performance, especially on older graphics cards.

- *Screen Area.* Use this slider control to specify the resolution of the desktop in pixels. Slide the control to the right to fit more information on the desktop or slide it to the left to decrease the size of the desktop.

- *Troubleshoot.* Click this if you are having problems with your display and want to have Windows 2000 provide you with some possible fixes for common problems.

- *Advanced.* Click the Advanced button to open the Advanced Display Properties sheet, which controls many more options relating to the display.

 TIP See the section, "Using Multiple Displays" in Chapter 4, "Configuring Interface and Systems Options," to learn how to configure multiple display adapters for a single system.

The General Tab of the Advanced Display Properties Sheet   Use the General page to configure global font size for the display, which increases the size of all screen text elements proportionally to the sizes specified in the Appearance tab. You also can configure how Windows 2000 handles display configuration changes. Select the Apply option if your applications work properly after resetting the display; select the Restart option if they don't work properly. Choose the Ask option if you want to choose which option to use each time you change display settings.

The Adapter Tab   The Adapter tab of the Advanced Display Properties sheet contains controls that directly relate to the type of video adapter you have.

The following is a list of the options in the Adapter tab:

■ *Properties*. Click this to open the Properties page for the video adapter currently installed in your system. Use the resulting property sheet to troubleshoot the adapter, update its driver, and assign resources to it (IRQ, I/O base address, and so on).

■ *List All Modes*. Click this button to display a dialog box containing a list of all valid display modes. Choose a mode and click OK.

The Monitor Tab   The Monitor tab of the Advanced Display Properties page contains controls that let you make detailed adjustments to your monitor.

The following is a list of options in the Monitor tab:

■ *Properties*. Click this button to bring up the Properties sheet for the current monitor, which lets you troubleshoot and change drivers for the monitor.

■ *Refresh Frequency*. Select a refresh frequency for your monitor from this drop-down list. Higher frequencies produce a display that you can view more comfortably for extended periods of time.

■ *Hide Modes that this Monitor Cannot Display*. Check this box if you don't want the Refresh Frequency list to show refresh frequencies not supported by your monitor.

CAUTION

If you try to set your monitor to a refresh frequency it doesn't support, you can run the risk of damaging the monitor. Check with the manufacturer's specifications before you try to use a refresh rate you're not completely sure of.

The Troubleshooting Tab   The Troubleshooting tab of the Advanced Display Properties sheet lets you turn off more advanced video driver features if they seem to be causing problems with the system's behavior. Drag the Hardware acceleration slider from right to left to turn off acceleration features that could be causing video problems.

The Color Management Tab   The Color Management tab of the Advanced Display Properties sheet lets you add or remove color management profiles for your monitor. Color management profiles are supplied by the monitor manufacturer, either on a floppy or as a downloadable file, and they tell Windows 2000 how to adjust the color display to produce the most accurate possible color.

To add a color profile, click **A**dd, browse to the color profile file, and then click OK. To remove a profile, select the name of the profile from the list and click Remove. If you select a profile and click Set As Default, this profile will be used as the default color profile for this user.

Fax

Double-click the Fax icon in the Windows 2000 Control Panel to access and edit the settings used by the Windows 2000 Fax service. These include the name and address to put on outgoing faxes, fax cover sheets, notification of faxes sent or received, and other options.

N O T E You won't be able to take advantage of fax functionality unless you have a fax-capable modem installed. If you have no such modem present in your Windows 2000 system, the fax icon will not be shown. ▨

The User Information Tab

The User Information tab of the Fax Properties sheet (see Figure 10.7) contains fields used by the fax service to place on outgoing fax cover pages. These fields should be self-explanatory.

Part

III

Ch

10

FIGURE 10.7
The User Information tab contains information about the current user that will be sent with an outgoing fax.

Cover Pages

The Cover Pages tab of the Fax Properties sheet lists the available cover pages used by the fax service when sending faxes. To create a new fax cover page, click New. This launches the Fax Cover Page Editor, which lets you design and edit fax cover pages.

To use an existing cover page, select a cover page and click Open. To delete an existing cover page, select a cover page and click Delete. If you want to add a cover page from another directory or disk, click Add and then browse to the cover page you want to add.

The Status Monitor Tab

The Status Monitor tab of the Fax Properties sheet lets you change options that control how fax activities are monitored in Windows 2000. The following is a list of the options in the Monitor tab:

- *Display the Status Monitor*. Select this check box to have Windows 2000 notify you with a dialog box when a fax is sent or received.
- *Status Monitor Always On Top*. Select this check box if you want the dialog box that signifies an incoming or outgoing fax to always appear on top of other windows.
- *Display Icon On Taskbar*. Select this check box if you want Windows 2000 to place an icon in the taskbar when a fax is sent or received.
- *Play a Sound*. Select this check box if you want Windows 2000 to play a sound when a fax is sent or received. For more on assigning sounds to system events, see the section titled "Sounds and Multimedia," later in this chapter.
- *Enable Manual Answer for the First Device*. Select this check box to have the highest-priority fax device answered manually. This lets you distinguish between voice and fax calls, so clear this check box if the line is being used for faxes only.

The Advanced Options Tab

The Advanced Options tab in the Fax Properties sheet contains a button marked Launch Fax Service Management. Clicking it launches the Fax Service Management console. The Fax Service Management console uses the Microsoft Management Console interface to let you make changes to fax device settings or to change how fax events are logged. The Help button launches the Fax Service Management Help content. The Add a Fax Printer button starts a wizard to help you install a fax printer.

Setting Folder Options

The Folder Options object in the Control Panel lets you control the way folders appear in Windows 2000 and other options that relate the file display and general Windows 2000 interface options. For a detailed discussion of folder options, see the section, "Customizing Folders," in Chapter 4, "Configuring Interface and Systems Options."

Configuring Fonts

Windows 2000 includes many fonts for use in Windows applications. These fonts enable you to create professional-looking, visually appealing documents. The Fonts object in the Control Panel enables you to view, install, and remove fonts. Before you learn about the Fonts folder, however, you need some background on fonts.

What Are Fonts?

Generally, the term *font* is used interchangeably with *typeface,* even though the two are different. A typeface is the basic design of a character set, defined by the shape of the characters. Each typeface is identified by a name, such as Arial, Times New Roman, and so on.

A font is a complete set of characters of a given typeface at a particular point size and style. All the characters in the Arial typeface at 12 points and in bold, for example, constitute a font. All the characters in the Arial typeface at 14 points constitute a different font from the same character set in 12 points.

N O T E   A font family is the entire range of sizes and styles of a single typeface. ▪

Many types of fonts exist, and Windows 2000 uses many of them. The following list explains the most common types of fonts:

- *Bitmap or raster fonts.* These fonts are created using patterns of pixels (dots) to define the shape and size of the characters. Each character requires a unique bitmap to define the character in each point size and style. Each bitmap or raster font file contains one set of characters in the given size and style. Defining two different font sizes, therefore, requires two separate font files. Defining a bold font requires yet another font file. These types of fonts are often called *screen fonts.* You cannot download screen fonts to a printer, which typically results in a comparable printer font that looks somewhat different from a screen font and printed output that looks different from its representation on the display.

- *TrueType fonts.* These fonts are often referred to as *outline fonts.* TrueType fonts are generated from an outline, which is a set of instructions that define the contours of the characters. Because the font is defined by its contour, only one font file is required to define the font in a given style. A single font file can define a set of TrueType characters in a size range from 2 points to nearly 700 points. TrueType fonts are compatible with nearly all types of devices, including displays and printers.

- *OpenType fonts.* OpenType is the successor to TrueType, a font format jointly developed by Microsoft and Adobe. OpenType fonts work the same as TrueType fonts and have added features to make fonts more useful on different platforms and in different languages as well.

- *Vector fonts.* These are scalable fonts that consist of line segments and dots. Vector fonts are often used for output to plotters and some types of printers. Vector fonts don't offer the same quality of output as TrueType fonts.

- *Device-specific fonts.* These fonts are specific to a certain device, such as a printer. You install the fonts in the printer's firmware or download them to the printer on a per-job basis. PostScript fonts are considered to be device-specific fonts.

Each of the types of fonts used in Windows 2000 has different applications and advantages. Because of their versatility and scalability (change of size) without loss of resolution or quality, TrueType fonts are the most commonly used fonts in Windows

N O T E Windows 2000 includes TrueType fonts to support five different font families: Arial, Times New Roman, Courier New, Symbol, and Wingding. , In addition to these standard TrueType fonts, many applications include their own fonts. Many other TrueType fonts are available commercially, as shareware or as freeware, making literally thousands of fonts available for use in Windows 2000. ■

In addition to being categorized in Windows 2000 as TrueType, raster, or vector, fonts also are categorized by intended output device, or as *screen* or *printer* fonts. As their names imply, Windows uses screen fonts to represent characters onscreen and printer fonts to create characters on a printer. TrueType fonts serve as both screen fonts and printer fonts.

Printer fonts are divided into three types, as described in the following list:

- ■ *Printable screen fonts.* These are screen fonts that also can be rendered on the printer.
- ■ *Device fonts.* These fonts are stored in the printer in its hardware or in a font cartridge.
- ■ *Downloadable soft fonts.* These fonts are downloaded from your hard disk to the printer's memory, per need.

TrueType fonts are identified in font selection dialog boxes by a special TT icon; printer fonts are sometimes identified by a Printer icon. In other applications, only TrueType fonts are identified by icon in the Font dialog boxes; other types of fonts, such as printer fonts, have no icon associated with them. OpenType fonts are identified by an OT icon.

To use a particular font in a document, select it from the Font dialog box and specify any settings, such as bold, italic, and so on. When you're ready to print the document, you might need to download the font or specify other options to control the way the printer handles the fonts.

Working with the Fonts Folder

Windows 2000 provides access and control over fonts through the Fonts folder, which you access from the Control Panel. The Fonts folder itself is the \systemroot\Fonts directory.

Opening the Fonts folder displays a folder window similar to the one shown in Figure 10.8. By default, the Fonts folder shows an icon for each of the fonts in the Fonts folder. TrueType and OpenType fonts are represented by TrueType and OpenType icons. Screen and printer fonts are represented by an A icon.

To view a sample of a font, double-click the font's icon or select the icon and press Enter. Windows displays a window that contains sample text in various sizes and other information about the font. To print a page of sample text in the selected font, click the Print button. After you view the sample, choose Done to close the window.

Each of the icons in the Fonts folder represents a font file in the \systemroot\Fonts directory. You can select a font and press Alt+Enter, or choose Properties from a font's context menu to display a standard file properties page for the font file.

FIGURE 10.8
The Fonts folder contains all your available fonts.

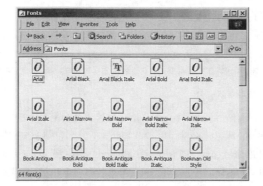

Font Folder Views   As with other types of folders, you can control the appearance of the Fonts folder and change the way in which the fonts appear in the folder. The view options for the Fonts folder are somewhat different, however, from a typical folder window:

■ *Large Icons*. Choose this command to display the font files in the folder as a large icon.

■ *List*. Choose this command to display the fonts in the folder as a list.

■ *Details*. Choose this command to display the fonts in the folder as a detailed list.

■ *List Fonts by Similarity*. Choose this command to organize the fonts according to their similarity to one another. You can sort the fonts according to their similarity to the Arial font, for example. The fonts appear in the folder as a simple list with a description of the degree of similarity to the selected font. Fonts are listed in descending order of similarity—fonts that are most similar in appearance are listed at the top of the list. To view a particular font, double-click its name in the list.

The List Fonts by Similarity command enables you to locate fonts that share the same general appearance. If a particular font isn't quite what you want but is very similar, sort the Fonts window by similarity to locate all other fonts that have a similar appearance. After you display the fonts by similarity, you can choose a different font from the drop-down list in the Font folder's toolbar. The list then re-sorts to show the degree of similarity to the newly selected font. To switch back to an icon, list, or detail view, choose View, followed by the appropriate view option.

Other Views of the Font Folder   If you have many fonts installed in the Fonts folder, you might want to simplify the view to include only one reference to each font family. Rather than display separate icons for Arial, Arial Bold, and Arial Italic, for example, the Fonts folder can display a single icon to represent the entire Arial family. To hide font variations and display a single icon for each font family, choose View, Hide Variations.

N O T E   Dragging a font's icon from the Fonts folder moves or copies the font file, depending on how you drag the font. This behavior is identical to any folder that represents files in a directory. ■

Part
III

Ch
10

Font Installation and Removal

Although you easily can copy new font files to the Fonts folder, simply copying the files doesn't make those fonts available in your applications. Instead, you must install the fonts, which adds the new fonts to the Registry and thus makes the fonts available to your applications.

To install a font, follow these steps:

1. Open the Fonts folder and choose File, Install New Font. Windows opens an Add Fonts dialog box that you use to locate the font files for the fonts you want to install.

2. When you select a directory, Windows 2000 scans the directory and lists in the List of Fonts list any font files that it finds. You can select one or more font files to install. To select all font files, choose the Select All button.

3. Use the Copy fonts to Fonts folder check box to control whether the font files are copied to the \systemroot\Fonts folder. If you enable this check box, the font files are copied from their source location to the \systemroot\Fonts folder, and references to the new fonts are added in the Registry. If the check box is cleared, the font files remain in their source location, but the font references still are added to the Registry.

4. After you select the fonts you want to install and specify whether the associated font files should be copied to your local Fonts folder, choose OK. Windows installs the fonts, and you can begin using them in your applications.

NOTE If you install fonts from a network server, you might want to leave the font files on the server to conserve disk space on your computer. Windows can then read the font files from the server whenever necessary.

If you never use certain fonts on your system or if you run very low on disk space, you might want to remove some of the fonts. You remove a font in the same way you remove a file from a folder. Select the font(s) you want to remove; then choose File, Delete, or press the Del key. Windows 2000 deletes the font files and removes the font from the Registry.

Setting Game Controllers Options

The Game Controllers object in the Control Panel, as shown in Figure 10.9, lets you add and configure joysticks, flight yokes, and game pads to use with video games under Windows 2000.

Some video game devices, such as Microsoft's SideWinder game pad, are automatically detected if they're plugged in. Many are not and have to be specified manually. If you want to add a new controller, click the Add button, which brings up the Add Game Controller window. Select the game controller to add from the list and click OK.

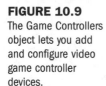

FIGURE 10.9
The Game Controllers object lets you add and configure video game controller devices.

If you've got a game controller that doesn't appear on the list, but that plugs into a standard joystick port, you can add it by clicking Custom, which brings up the Custom Game Controller window. From here you can describe the controller you have by selecting the appropriate options.

The Advanced tab of the Game Controllers window lets you modify which controller ID to assign to a given controller. To change a controller's ID, click the controller and then click Change.

Setting Internet Options

The Internet Options object in the Control Panel lets you configure the way Windows 2000 connects to and handles objects on the Internet. This includes security, types of content, connections to be used for Internet access, and many other options.

The General Tab

Figure 10.10 shows the General tab of the Internet Options sheet.

The Home Page group lets you define the page that opens by default when you first start Internet Explorer. The History group lets you specify how many days to keep the history of visited sites, and clear the History folder. The Temporary Internet Files group lets you delete files from the Internet Explorer cache. Use the Settings button in this group to specify how often Internet Explorer checks for page updates, set the size of the cache, and view the cache contents.

FIGURE 10.10
The General tab of Internet Properties holds the most basic options for Internet Explorer.

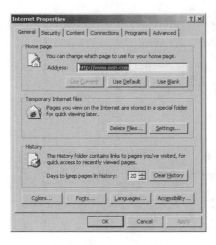

The Colors, Fonts, Languages, and Accessibility buttons let you configure Internet Explorer interface options.

The Security Tab

Internet Explorer lists security settings by "zones"—different areas of your network for which you may want to have different access rules. For instance, you may want to heavily restrict content to some sites and allow complete access to others. You control these settings in the Security tab of the Internet Options sheet, shown in Figure 10.11.

FIGURE 10.11
Security zones let you handle different Internet sites with different types of security restrictions.

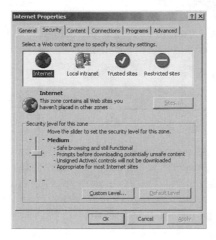

Internet Explorer gives you four basic zone types to start with:

- *Internet.* Everything not listed in any of the other categories is automatically placed in this category.
- *Local Intranet.* This zone contains options that are usually appropriate for intranets and local networks.
- *Trusted Sites.* These are sites where you have no need to worry about security, and almost all restrictions are relaxed.
- *Restricted Sites.* These are sites where you want to disable many advanced options, such as cookies or ActiveX controls. These can also be sites with content you may not want viewed by minors.

The following is a list of options available in the Security tab:

- *Select a Web Content Zone to Specify Its Security Settings.* Click one of the zones listed here to change its security settings.
- *Sites.* Click this button to place a given Web site in the selected zone.
- *Security Level for This Zone.* Drag the slider to change the security level for the selected zone. A higher level of security restricts more types of content.
- *Custom Level.* Click here to change the exact restrictions for each level of security.
- *Default Level.* Click here to restore the current level of security to its default settings.

The Content Tab

The Content tab of Internet Properties, shown in Figure 10.12, lets you control the types of content. Web pages, ActiveX objects, and so forth—that are allowed on your Windows 2000 computer via the Internet.

FIGURE 10.12
Use the Content tab to control how different kinds of Internet content are screened on your machine.

The following list describes the options available on the Content tab:

- *Enable*. Select this option to enable Content Advisor ratings in Internet Explorer, which use tags embedded in Web pages to inform the user about what kinds of content (sexual, violent, and so on) may be present.

- *Settings*. Select this option to change what kinds of content the Content Advisor will allow or deny.

- *Certificates*. Select this option to see what security certificates have been sent to you by certification authorities. Certificates enable you to authenticate your identity to remote users. See Chapter 15, "Certificate Manager," for detailed information on using certificates.

- *Publishers*. Select this option to see the list of publishers for the various certificates you have received.

- *Autocomplete*. Select this option to have Internet Explorer suggest possible matches for what you type based on what you've typed before.

- *Wallet*. Select this option to examine and securely store private information, such as credit cards, in Internet Explorer for shopping. Requires that Microsoft Wallet—an Internet Explorer add-on—be installed.

- *My Profile*. Select this option to provide Internet Explorer with personal information—address, phone numbers, and so on. Internet Explorer can give this information to sites that request it without you having to enter it each time.

The Connections Tab

The Connections tab of Internet Properties, shown in Figure 10.13, lets you configure the ways Windows 2000 connects to the Internet. If you are not connected at the time you attempt to access an Internet resource, such as a Web site, the computer will attempt to make an Internet connection according to what's specified in the Connections tab.

FIGURE 10.13
The Connections tab contains configuration options for making Internet connections.

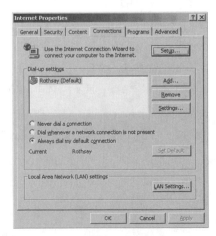

N O T E These settings are not used exclusively by Internet Explorer, but are shared by all programs that attempt to use the Internet.

The following is a list of the options available through the Connections tab:

- *Setup*. Click Setup to start the Internet Connection Wizard.
- *Add*. Select this option to add a connection type to the Dial-Up Settings list. The connection is set up through the Internet Connection Wizard.
- *Remove*. Select this option to delete the selected dial-up setting from the list.
- *Settings*. Select this option to edit the settings for the selected dial-up setting.
- *Never Dial a Connection*. Select this option to ensure that Windows 2000 never attempts to establish an Internet connection on its own. This option enables you to control when the computer dials a connection.
- *Dial Whenever a Network Connection Is Not Present*. Select this option to let Windows 2000 attempt to establish a network connection whenever no network connection is currently established.
- *Always Dial My Default Connection*. Select this option to force Windows 2000 to always use the default connection when a connection to the Internet is needed.
- *Set Default*. Select this option to make the currently selected Internet connection your default connection.
- *LAN Settings*. Select this option to configure how Internet Explorer works with proxies on local area networks.

The Programs Tab

The Programs tab of Internet Properties, shown in Figure 10.14, lets you configure which programs Windows 2000 uses automatically with different Internet services.

FIGURE 10.14
The Programs tab lets you configure which programs to use for different Internet activities.

The following is a list of the options available through the Programs tab:

- **_H_TML Editor**. Select a program from the drop-down list that will be used whenever you want to edit an HTML document.
- **_E_-mail**. Select a program from the drop-down list that will be used whenever you want to send email.
- **_N_ewsgroups**. Select a program from the drop-down list that will be used whenever you want to read Usenet newsgroups.
- **In_t_ernet Call**. Select a program from the drop-down list that will be used whenever you want to place a call to another user across the Internet.
- **_C_alendar**. Select a program from the drop-down menu that will be used when you want to schedule events and meetings.
- **Contact _L_ist**. Select a program from the drop-down menu that will be used when you want to look up a name or an address.
- **_R_eset Web Settings**. Select this option to restore all Internet Explorer defaults for home and search pages.
- **Internet Explorer Should Check to See Whether It Is the Default**. Check this box to have Internet Explorer ensure that it is the default Web browser each time it is loaded.

The Advanced Tab

The Advanced tab of Internet Properties lets you make very detailed changes to Internet Explorer behavior and aspects of Internet connectivity. Many of these options are self-explanatory. If you need help with a specific option, click the question mark button at the top-right corner of the window then click the option.

Configuring Keyboard Functions

The Keyboard object on the Control Panel contains options for changing the way the keyboard behaves in Windows 2000. When opened, it shows the Keyboard Properties sheet. The options on the Speed page are self-explanatory.

The Input Locales tab of the Keyboard Properties sheet lets you specify the language and the keyboard layout associated with your keyboard, which associates specific characters with specific keys. You can use multiple input languages at one time and switch between them with a button on the taskbar. Or, you can use the Hot keys group to define and use a key sequence to switch between input locales. Use **_A_**dd, **_R_**emove, and **_P_**roperties to configure input locales.

The Hardware tab of the Keyboard Properties sheet lists the name and device properties for your current keyboard. You can use the Hardware tab to troubleshoot the keyboard and set its properties (driver, resources, and so on).

Configuring Mouse Functions

The Mouse object in the Control Panel opens the Mouse Properties sheet. The Hardware tab in this sheet lists the name and device properties for the mouse currently installed on your computer. The remaining tabs in this sheet contain settings and options that control the mouse movements and button functions.

The Buttons Tab

The settings in the Buttons tab control the mouse button functions. The following list explains the functions of each option:

- **Right-handed.** Select this option if you are right-handed or prefer to use the mouse with your right hand.

- **Left-handed.** Select this option if you are left-handed or prefer to use the mouse with your left hand. The right mouse button will be the primary button, taking on all the functions normally associated with the left button (select, open, and so on). The left button will take on the functions of the right button (context menu).

- **Single-click to Open an Item.** Select Select this option to open items with a single click instead of a double click. To select the item, simply point to it.

- **Double-click to Open an Item.** Select this option to open items by clicking twice and to select items by clicking once.

- **Double-click Speed.** Use the Double-click Speed slider to specify the speed at which you must double-click the primary button to have Windows recognize the action as a double-click. Place the pointer in the test area on the page and double-click to test the speed. If Windows Win2000 recognizes the action as a double-click, the jack-in-the-box will pop up.

Part

III

Ch

10

The Pointers Tab

The Pointers tab lets you specify which mouse pointers are assigned to specific events. You can select a predefined pointer scheme from the Scheme drop-down list.

The following list explains the options available on the Pointers tab:

- **Scheme.** Select a scheme, which is a list of available pointers, from the drop-down list to use in Windows 2000.

- **Save As.** Click this button to save the current collection of pointers as a new pointer scheme.

- **Delete.** Click this button to delete the currently selected pointer scheme.

- **Customize.** Double-click a pointer type to browse to a new pointer on disk (an ANI or CUR file).

- **Enable Pointer Shadow.** Click this check box to turn on a small shadow underneath the pointer, which makes it slightly more noticeable in certain color schemes.

- *Use Default.* Click this to reset the currently selected pointer to its original factory setting.
- *Browse.* Click this to browse for a new pointer (an ANI or CUR file) to replace the currently selected one.

The Motion Tab

Use the Motion page to control the mouse pointer's motion. The following list explains the available options:

- *Speed.* This slider lets you specify how fast the pointer moves when you move the pointing device (mouse, trackball, and so on).
- *None.* Select this option if you want the mouse pointer to have no acceleration when it is moved faster.
- *Low.* Select this option if you want the mouse pointer to accelerate slightly when it is moved faster.
- *Medium.* Select this option if you want the mouse pointer to accelerate a fair amount when it is moved faster.
- *High.* Select this option if you want the mouse pointer to accelerate a lot when it is moved faster.
- *Move Pointer to the default button in dialog boxes.* Select this option if you want the mouse pointer to snap to the default selection whenever a dialog box pops up.

Setting Network and Dial-Up Connections Options

The Network and Dial-Up Connections object in the Control Panel lets you add and manage LAN and dial-up network connections. If you installed a networking connection (either a LAN or a dial-up) when you installed Windows 2000, it will be shown in the Network and Dial-Up Connections window.

N O T E You can open the Network and Dial-Up Connections folder page by right-clicking the Network Neighborhood icon and choosing Properties.

▶ Because network configuration can be such a critical and important part of configuring a Windows 2000 system, **see** "Networking Installation and Configuration," **pg. 49** for complete coverage of this topic.

▶ For a complete discussion of TCP/IP or dial-up connection configuration, **see** "Understanding TCP/IP," **pg. 398**

Setting Phone and Modem Options

The Phone and Modem Options object in the Control Panel lets you control how Windows 2000 works with modems and telephone connections.

The settings in the Dialing Rules tab let you change the way Windows 2000 dials the phone depending on what *location* you have selected when you make a Dial-Up Networking connection. Different Dial-Up Networking connections can use different locations.

NOTE Locations are useful if you need to use special dialing instructions in different places. For instance, calling out when you're on the road might be done differently than when dialing from home. ■

The Locations sheet lists all the currently available dialing locations. To delete an existing location, select it from the list and click Delete.

If you want to create a new location or edit an existing one, click New or Edit as needed, and the Edit Location sheet (see Figure 10.15) appears.

FIGURE 10.15
The Edit Location box lists all the properties of the current location.

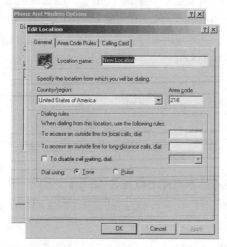

The Edit Location Sheet

The Edit Location sheet contains three tabs: General, Area Code Rules and Calling Card. The following is a list of available options on the General tab:

- *Location **N**ame*. Type a short, descriptive name for this location here.
- *Country/**R**egion*. Select from this drop-down list the country or region you are calling from when using this location.
- *Area **C**ode*. Type the area code you are calling from.
- *To Access an Outside Line for **L**ocal Calls, Dial*. Type any numbers that must be dialed before a local call is made from this location. If nothing must be dialed to make an outgoing call, leave this blank.
- *To Access an Outside Line for Long-**D**istance Calls, Dial*. Type any numbers that must be dialed before a long-distance call is made from this location.

- *To Disable Call __Waiting__, Dial.* Check this box and select a number from the drop-down list to disable call waiting from this location before you dial.
- *__T__one.* Select this option if you want to use tone dialing from this location.
- *__P__ulse.* Select this option if you want to use pulse dialing from this location.

Setting Area Code Rules and Designating Calling Cards

The Area Code Rules tab lists rules that determine how Windows 2000 makes calls from your current area code to other area codes or to other numbers within your own area code.

To add a new area code rule to the list, click New, which brings up the New Area Code Rule window. Fill in the area code and supply any other information on how you want calls from that area code to be handled, and then click OK to add the new rule to the list.

To edit an existing area code rule, select the rule from the list and click Edit. To delete an area code rule, select the rule from the list and click Delete.

The Calling Card tab lets you choose or add a calling card to be used when dialing from this location. A list of commonly used calling-card types is available, and you can add your own as well.

To add a new calling card to the list, click New and enter in the information about the calling card. To edit an existing calling card, select the card and click Edit. To delete a card from the list, select it and click Delete. You can also supply an account number and PIN number for calls using the selected card.

The Modems and Advanced Properties Tabs

The Modems tab of the Phone and Modem Options object lists all the modems currently installed in your system.

To remove an existing modem, select it from the list and click Remove. To change the properties of an existing modem, select the modem and click Properties.

To add a new modem, click Add, which starts the Install New Modem Wizard. Normally, when you click the Next button on the wizard, Windows attempts to automatically detect and install modems. If you would rather specify a modem from the Windows hardware list (or if you have a modem driver on disk), select the Don't Detect My Modem; I Will Select It from a List box.

The Advanced Properties tab of the Phone and Modem Options object, shown in Figure 10.16, lists all the available drivers for telecommunications. Most of the time, no changes will be needed to this list, but you can add, remove, or configure components in this list by selecting them and clicking Add, Remove, or Configure, respectively.

FIGURE 10.16
The Advanced Properties tab lists all the available telephony drivers in Windows 2000.

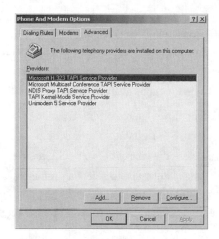

Setting Power Options

The Power Options object in the Control Panel, as shown in Figure 10.17, lets you control the power management options available in your PC or laptop.

NOTE If you are using an older PC that does not support APM (Advanced Power Management), the standard that PCs use for power management, the Power Options object may not be visible or may have some of its functions disabled. Some property pages might not appear on your system.

FIGURE 10.17
The Power Options object lets you control how your PC's power management works.

The Power Schemes tab in the Power Options object lets you organize various ways your PC can use power-management options and arrange them into power schemes. Several preprogrammed schemes are available, and users can edit the listed options and save the results into their own schemes.

The following list describes the basic functions available in the Power Schemes tab:

- *Power Schemes*. Click this drop-down list to select an existing power scheme.
- *Save As*. Click this button to save the existing power scheme under a new name.
- *Delete*. Click this button to delete the current power scheme from the list.
- *Turn Off Monitor*. Click this drop-down list to select a time interval after which to shut off the monitor when the system has not been in use.
- *Turn Off Hard Disks*. Click this drop-down list to select a time interval after which to turn off hard disks when they have not been in use.
- *System Standby*. Specify the time interval at which the system goes into standby mode.

Alarms and Power Meter

The Alarms and Power Meter tabs control, respectively, how Windows 2000 notifies you when battery power runs low and shows status of the batteries in the system.

Advanced and Hibernate Tabs

The Advanced tab of the Power Options object features several additional options that may vary depending on the kind of power management available in your computer. The following list describes the available options in the Advanced tab:

- *Always Show Icon on the Taskbar*. Check this box to show a power management icon on the taskbar, which also indicates the current state of the system's power. Double-clicking the icon brings up the Power Options Properties box.
- *Prompt for Password when Computer Goes off Standby*. Check this box to have the machine ask the user for a password when it wakes up from standby mode.
- *When I Press the Power Button on My Computer*. Select an action from this drop-down list that describes what the computer will do when the power button is pressed.

The Hibernate tab of the Power Options object describes how the hibernation feature of your PC is configured. *Hibernation* lets you write the entire contents of the PC's memory to a special section of the hard drive, and then power the computer off completely. The next time the machine is restarted, the hibernation file is read into memory, and the computer continues where it left off. This feature is most commonly found on laptops, but it can be implemented on desktop PCs as well.

To enable hibernation support, check the Enable Hibernation Support box. To make hibernation work, you need to have at least as much disk space as is stated in the Disk Space Required to Hibernate prompt.

Controlling Printer Functions

Clicking the Printers icon in the Control Panel opens the Printers folder (see Figure 10.18), which contains an icon for each of the printers installed on your computer—both those attached directly to your PC, and those printers available across the network.

You can use options in the Printers folder to add, configure, and remove printers. You also can view the jobs waiting to be printed and manage pending print jobs.

FIGURE 10.18
The Printers object lists all the available printers in your system.

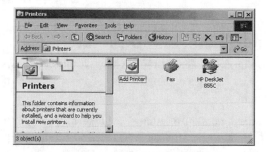

▶ For more information on using printers and printing—including Internet Printing Protocol (IPP) to print across the Internet—**see** "Printing," **pg. 131**

Configuring Regional Settings

The Regional Options object in the Control Panel lets you localize your settings for number, currency, time, date, and input locale. This enables you to configure Windows to use the standards for these items that prevail in your country or region. You can use the options in the General tab (see Figure 10.19) to choose an overall group of settings based on your language and country or locale.

FIGURE 10.19
The Regional Options tab lets you make global interface changes based on where you are in the world.

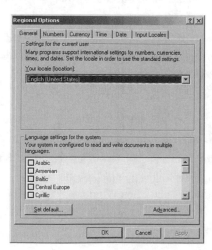

Part
III

Ch
10

To add extensions that let you read and write documents in different languages, check the boxes corresponding to the languages you want support for in the <u>L</u>anguage Settings for the System list.

To set the default language and locale for the whole system, click the <u>S</u>et Default button and choose a locale from the drop-down list.

The Ad<u>v</u>anced button lets you set code page conversion tables for different language standards. These settings are configured automatically, so there is usually no reason to change them.

The Numbers, Currency, Time, and Date Tabs

Use the settings in the Numbers tab to configure how Windows displays numbers, number groupings, and other characteristics of numeric data. The settings on the Numbers tab are generally self-explanatory.

In the Currency tab, you can configure settings that determine how Windows displays characters related to currency, including the currency symbol, number of digits displayed after the decimal sign, and digit grouping arrangements.

Use the Time tab to specify how Windows displays time. The settings on this tab are generally self-explanatory. To switch to 24-hour time, from the Time format drop-down list, choose either the H:mm:ss or HH:mm:ss options. Use the remaining options in this drop-down list to switch to a 12-hour time display.

The Date tab lets you specify the format your computer uses to display dates. The calendar type is based on your regional selection. Use the other controls to define how dates appear and are interpreted by Windows. The controls on the Date tab are self-explanatory.

The Input Locales Tab

The Input Locales tab of the Regional Options sheet lets you specify the language and keyboard layout associated with your keyboard.

Input Locales also enables you to type in languages that your keyboard may not directly support, such as Far Eastern languages. This is done through the Input Method Editor, or IME. Each language comes with its own IME.

The following list explains the language controls on the Input Locales tab:

- *A<u>d</u>d*. Click this button to add a new language to the list of installed languages.
- *<u>R</u>emove*. Click this button to remove the selected language from the list.
- *<u>P</u>roperties*. Click this button to change the layout associated with the selected language.
- *<u>S</u>et as Default*. Click this button to specify the selected language as the default, which will cause it to be used automatically when Windows 2000 starts.

- *Press Caps Lock Key*. Select this option to use the Caps Lock key to turn off Caps Lock.

- *Press Shift Key*. Select this option to use the Shift key to turn off Caps Lock.

- *Key Sequence*. Use these option buttons to specify which keyboard shortcut, if any, will cause Windows 2000 to switch between languages in the list.

- *Enable Indicator on Taskbar*. Place a check in this box to have Windows 2000 place a special language icon on the tray. This tray icon enables you to quickly switch keyboard languages and layouts.

- *Change Key Sequence*. Click this button to change the key sequence used to toggle between languages.

 TIP The Input Locales tab also appears on the Keyboard dialog box. You can use either tab to configure Input Locale settings.

Part

III

Ch

10

Setting Scanners and Cameras

The Scanners and Cameras object in the Control Panel lets you add, configure, troubleshoot, and remove scanners and cameras from your Windows 2000 computer.

To add or remove scanners or cameras from the list, click the Add or Remove buttons, respectively. To troubleshoot an existing piece of hardware, select it from the list and click Troubleshoot. To bring up the dialog box for the selected scanner or camera, which will let you configure its options, click Properties.

Scheduling Tasks

The Scheduled Tasks object in the Control Panel lets you create lists of tasks to be executed by Windows 2000 at predetermined intervals—daily, weekly, hourly, the first day of a month, and so on.

▶ To use Scheduled Tasks, you need to have the Task Scheduler service running. For more on working with system services, **see** "Services," **pg. 323**

To add a new task to Scheduled Tasks:

1. Double-click the Add Scheduled Task icon. This brings up the Scheduled Task Wizard. Click Next.

2. Select the program you want to run from the list. If you want to run a program not on the list, click Browse and browse to the program you want to use.

3. Provide a name for the task in the Type a Name for This Task box and then select an interval for the program: Daily, Weekly, Monthly, One Time Only, When My Computer Starts, and When I Log On.

4. Depending on the choice you made, you may be prompted for a more specific time and day of the week to run the task.

5. Type the username and password of the user account you want to run the program under. Most of the time this is your own username and password.

6. If you want to further edit the program's runtime parameters, check the Open Advanced Properties for This Task When I Click Finish.

7. Click Finish to add the new task to the list.

Configuring Sounds and Multimedia

The Sounds and Multimedia object in the Control Panel, shown in Figure 10.20, lets you choose which sounds are associated with which system events. You can also edit system settings for audio hardware, software used for audio coding and decoding (known as *codecs*), and change speech synthesis settings.

FIGURE 10.20
The Sounds and Multimedia object lets you change sound settings and hardware.

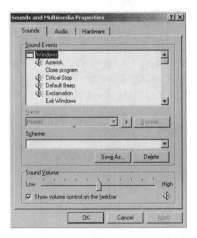

The Sounds tab of the Sounds and Multimedia object lets you control which sounds are played at particular system events. Collections of sounds and events can be saved as sound schemes. These controls are generally self-explanatory.

The Audio tab of the Sounds and Multimedia object lets you choose which hardware devices are associated with sound recording and playback.

The following list describes the controls in the Audio tab:

■ *Sound Playback, Preferred Device.* Select a default device for sound playback from this drop-down list.

■ *Sound Recording, Preferred Device.* Select a default device for sound recording from this drop-down list.

- *MIDI Music Playback, Preferred Device.* Select a default device for MIDI music playback from this drop-down list.
- *Use Only Preferred Devices.* Check this box to use only the listed devices for recording and playback.

The Speech tab of the Sounds and Multimedia object lets you make changes to software engines that analyze speech input and produce speech output. The Microsoft Speech Synthesis Engine is usually the only engine configured here when Windows 2000 is installed. Most of the settings should be self-explanatory.

The Hardware tab of the Sounds and Multimedia object lets you examine and troubleshoot the multimedia hardware in your Windows 2000 system. Many of the prompts here are also self-evident, and the Properties button simply brings up the dialog box for the selected hardware.

Controlling System Functions

The System object in the Control Panel lets you make system-wide changes to your Windows 2000 computer. This includes how your computer is represented on the network, how hardware devices are configured, and many other key settings.

 TIP You can display the System Properties sheet by right-clicking My Computer and choosing Properties.

The General tab lists several basic pieces of information about this Windows 2000 computer: registration information, serial numbers, and the type of computer it's running on.

The Network Identification, Hardware, and User Profiles tabs of the System property sheet and their controls are covered in other chapters in this book.

▶ For a detailed discussion of the Network identification settings, **see** "Modifying Identification Settings," **pg. 55**

▶ To find a complete description of managing hardware settings in Windows 2000 Professional, **see** "The Device Manager," **pg. 117**

▶ User and account profile management is detailed in "Managing User Profiles," **pg. 232**

The Advanced tab of the System Properties object contains a number of system-configuration options that some users (particularly power users) find useful. These options control performance, environment variables, and startup / recovery options.

The following list explains the options available:

- *Performance Options.* Click this button to change options relating to system performance, including application response and paging-file (virtual memory) size and location.

■ *Environment Variables.* Click this button to change Windows 2000 environment variables, such as the default path for executables.

■ *Startup and Recovery.* Click this button to change the options presented to the user when the machine is booted and to change options when the machine stops unexpectedly.

Setting Users and Passwords Options

The Users and Passwords object in the Control Panel lets you add, change, and make changes to the list of users on your Windows 2000 computer. Every user who has access to your Windows 2000 computer must have a unique user account, and each user can be assigned different levels of permissions (allowing or denying access to certain system objects) as well.

▶ For more detailed information on managing user passwords and user accounts, **see** "Managing User Accounts and Groups," **pg. 217**

Setting Wireless Link Options

The Wireless Link object appears in the Control Panel if the system contains infrared ports (see Figure 10.21). Use the Wireless Link object to specify how Windows 2000 handles file transfers through the IR port, configure image transfer via IR from a digital camera, and configure and troubleshoot the IR hardware.

FIGURE 10.21
Use the Wireless Link property sheet to configure properties for the system's infrared port(s).

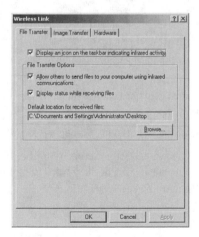

The File Transfer page defines options for transferring files through the wireless link, including enabling file transfer, specifying the default location for received files, and displaying status indicators for wireless transfers.

The Image Transfer page lets you configure your system to receive images from a digital camera via the wireless link. You can enable image transfer, specify the storage folder for incoming images, and direct Windows 2000 to open the folder after images are transferred.

Use the Hardware tab to troubleshoot and set properties (IRQ, I/O, etc.) for the wireless device(s) in your system.

## CHAPTER 11

Understanding System Administration and Security

In this chapter

The Role of System Administration

System administration involves a broad range of tasks and responsibilities, but most of them fall within two major categories: server management and user management. Managing a server typically means applying security to folders and files to control both local and remote access, sharing printers, and monitoring connections to the server. Managing users includes creating user accounts and groups, assigning group membership, granting rights and permissions to individuals and groups, and auditing user access to the system.

Woven throughout these tasks is the critical function of security management. The following sections look at each of these major categories of system administration responsibilities (and the tasks they encompass) in more detail.

NOTE Because this book focuses specifically on Windows 2000 Professional, some common administrative tasks and topics are discussed only in passing. Managing objects in the Active Directory, for example, is specific to Windows 2000 Server and is therefore not covered in this book.

Security administration is an extremely complex topic, an in-depth explanation of which would require an entire book. In most cases, this chapter provides an overview of system administration tasks to make you familiar with the tasks and tools involved. Other chapters in the book cover the actual implementation of these administrative tools and explain administration tasks in detail. These other chapters are noted in this chapter where appropriate. ▆

Managing Servers

Managing a server (including Windows 2000 Professional running as a peer server) involves a number of tasks, depending primarily on what services the server provides. On most servers, system administration comprises the following general tasks:

- Enabling file resources sharing
- Enabling printer resources sharing
- Managing the file system
- Managing user accounts
- Managing software licenses
- Monitoring and tuning server performance

The following sections explore these general management issues to give you an idea of how these tasks are handled under Windows 2000.

Sharing File Resources

Sharing file resources typically includes setting up shared directories and assigning user access privileges to those directories. The level of control you have over the shared resources depends on the type of file system on which the shared resource resides.

On a FAT file system, you can control access on a directory-by-directory basis through *share permissions*, assigning access levels to each shared directory. You can assign access permissions to a directory by group and by user. The only privileges you can assign, however, are read, change, and full control—a fairly limited set of access privileges that offer little security flexibility.

You have many additional security options on an NTFS partition through *NTFS permissions*. In addition to controlling access on a per-directory basis, you can control access on a per-file basis. This capability gives you much greater flexibility than the FAT file system. For example, you can give access to a directory to a specific user, but restrict access by that user to specific files in that directory. Using NTFS also enables you to audit file access for added security.

▶ **See** "Sharing Disk Resources," **p. 246**

Regardless of file system type, you manage shared disk resources through Explorer or through the Computer Management MMC console snap-in. Both enable you to share and unshare directories and files, assign permissions, and perform other tasks, such as security auditing.

Part
III

Ch
11

Sharing Printer Resources

Another common system administration task is sharing and managing printers. Windows 2000 provides integrated access to local and remote printers through the Printers folder located in the Control Panel or under Settings on the Start menu. Through the Printers folder, you can share local printers, install printers on remote workstations, and manage local and remote printers and their queues.

▶ **See** "Adding and Removing Printers," **p. 132**

Windows 2000's capability to install printer drivers across the network and to share remote printers enables you to manage all your network's printers from a central location, including through a dialup connection to the network. Basically, you can control a remote printer in the same manner that you control a local printer. Simply right-click the printer's icon in the Control Panel, choose Properties to display the printer's property sheet, and then set the properties according to your needs.

TIP You also can manage printers through a Web browser by connecting to `http://servername/Printers`, where `servername` is the name or IP address of the remote print host. See Chapter 9, "Printing," to learn how to configure a Windows 2000 Professional computer for IP-based printing and print management.

Managing the File System

Managing the file system is a major administrative function that includes managing disks (formatting, backup, compression, and so on), setting and managing access privileges for directories and files, and setting up and managing fault-tolerance options.

Most disk-related operations such as formatting, partitioning, and compression can be handled through Disk Management in the Computer Management MMC console (see Figure 11.1). You can also perform many of those same functions using Windows Explorer.

▶ **See** "Overview," **p. 336**

FIGURE 11.1
Use the Computer Management MMC console snap-in to manage most aspects of your system, including disks.

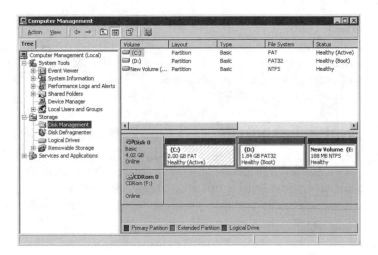

You can accomplish security-related tasks such as setting access privileges on directories and files in a variety of ways, but the most direct is to use Explorer. For example, to set access privileges on a directory, right-click the directory in Explorer. Choose Properties to access the directory's properties. Then click the Security tab, which enables you to set permissions, control auditing, and view or take ownership of the directory (see Figure 11.2).

FIGURE 11.2
Use Explorer to manage folder properties for sharing and security, as well as Web sharing if IIS is installed.

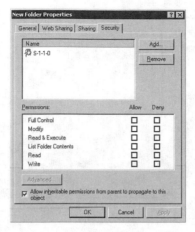

Managing Domains and Workgroups

Another aspect of server administration involves managing domains and workgroups. A *workgroup* is a logical grouping of computers on the network that simplifies browsing for shared resources. Basically, workgroups give you a means of organizing computers and resources under a common workgroup name.

Domains add distributed security to the workgroup model. If a user has an account in the domain, he can log on to the network from any workstation in the domain. The user's access to shared resources on the network is determined by the privileges of his domain account. Only Windows 2000 Server computers can function as domain controllers. The information in this chapter focuses on managing local user accounts and groups.

Tools for Monitoring and Tuning Server Performance

Ensuring fast and trouble-free operation is a critical part of any administrator's job. Windows 2000 includes a number of tools that enable you to track and manage server performance. The Performance management console snap-in enables you to view the behavior and performance for objects such as processors, memory, cache, threads, and processes (see Figure 11.3). Performance provides charting, alerting, and reporting features that display current activity and logging, as well as logging of past performance data.

N O T E A snap-in is a management tool that works within the framework of the Microsoft Management Console (MMC). You'll find more information about MMC and snap-ins in Part IV, "The Administrative Tools." ■

Part
III

Ch
11

FIGURE 11.3
Access the
Performance MMC
snap-in through Start,
Programs,
Administrative Tools.

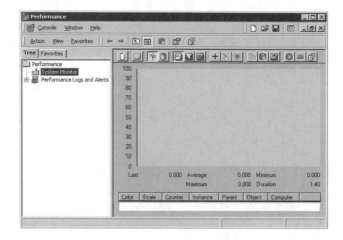

Unfortunately, performance problems are sometimes caused by hardware problems. To help you track down and troubleshoot problems, you can use the System Information MMC snap-in, which provides information about system hardware, drivers, services, memory, and other information about the workstation to help you overcome problems and tune performance. The Device Manager is the tool of choice for managing device properties and conflicts. Right-click My Computer and choose Manage to access System Information and Device Manager.

▶ To learn more about Device Manager, **see** "Viewing and Managing Devices," **p. 118**

▶ For a more in-depth discussion of the System Information snap-in and its use, **see** "System Information," **p. 320**

▶ To learn more about how Windows 2000 reports and records performance issues, **see** "Performance Logs and Alerts," **p. 318**

TIP The Windows 2000 Resource Kit contains additional tools for monitoring system and network performance.

Tools for Managing User Accounts and Groups

Every administrator knows that managing user accounts and groups can take a considerable amount of time, particularly in dynamic organizations where the number or location of users changes frequently. Windows 2000 provides a good set of utilities that enable you to quickly create, delete, and modify user accounts and groups and to assign access permissions.

TIP Because they centralize account management, domains offer a much better security structure as a LAN grows beyond 15 to 20 workstations. The Active Directory adds another layer of structure that is helpful for managing multiple domains.

TIP | Remember that to access resources on a workstation, a remote client must have an account on the workstation. If users in your organization need access to several computers on a peer-to-peer basis, consider implementing a Windows 2000 Server computer and domain model.

For example, you can use Local Users and Groups in the Computer Management console to manage most aspects of user accounts and local groups. You can use the Computer Management console to create and delete accounts and groups, assign group membership, and apply security profile settings.

As described earlier in this chapter, you assign access privileges primarily using Explorer and the Printers folder (or File Manager and Print Manager).

▶ Read more about creating and managing accounts in "Creating Local Accounts," **p. 218**

▶ To learn how to secure and share resources, **see** Chapter 13, "Managing and Sharing Workstation Resources," **p. 241**

Windows 2000 moves most administrative functions in the Microsoft Management Console (MMC). Whether you're adding a single user or configuring a complex service such as IIS (Internet Information Services, which provides HTTP and FTP services), you do it through a management console snap-in. In most cases, you can manage remote computers using the snap-ins in addition to the local workstation. Most of the management snap-ins that relate to Windows 2000 Professional administration are covered throughout this book.

You also can manage certain Windows 2000 services and functions through a Web browser. For example, you can manage the IIS service by pointing a browser to http://*servername* /IISAdmin, where servername is the IP address or host name of the IIS server.

▶ Learn more about server management in "Configuring the Web Server," **p. 446**

Although not released as of this writing, two other administrative tools might show up for Windows 2000. The Web Administrator 2.0 tools for Windows NT 4.0, which enable you to manage a Windows NT 4.0 server running IIS via a Web browser, will likely be updated for Windows 2000. The Windows NT Server Management Tools for Windows 95, which enable you to manage Windows NT systems across a LAN from a Windows 9x client, might also be updated for Windows 2000. Check the Microsoft Web site at http://www.microsoft.com /downloads for availability of both administrative tools.

Understanding Windows 2000 Security Models

Before you begin to manage accounts and groups on Windows 2000 systems, you need to have an understanding of the different security models you'll be working under, as well as other security-related issues. The following sections of the chapter examine these issues.

Part
III

Ch
11

It can be a complex task to configure security for a single user and much more so for multiple users. Windows 2000 simplifies security management through *policies*, which enable you to apply security settings on, for example, a group-by-group basis. This enables you to apply a specific set of security settings and restrictions to users based on their group membership.

Group policies in Windows 2000 are different from Windows NT 4 policies. Windows 2000 group policies integrate with the Active Directory and provide a means for more effectively managing policies across a domain, organizational unit, or enterprise.

Group policies control a wide variety of settings and restrictions for both computers and users. With group policies, you can do the following:

- Use administrative templates to apply registry settings on a per-computer or per-user basis.
- Assign scripts to automate tasks at startup, shutdown, logon, and logoff.
- Redirect folders in the Documents and Settings folder on the local computer to network folders.
- Use the Software Installation extension to assign, publish, update, or repair applications.
- Apply security settings and restrictions on a per-computer and per-user basis.

Group policies are a complex topic. Chapter 12, "Managing User Accounts and Groups," provides detailed information on using group policies. For now, simply understand that rather than try to manage security for users and computers individually, you should employ group policies to make the process easier.

▶ To learn more about group policies, **see** "Managing Group Policies," **p. 225**

N O T E You use the Group Policy MMC snap-in to manage group policy settings. You use other snap-ins such as Security Configuration and Analysis and Security Templates to further manage policies. ▇

The Workgroup Model

In Windows 2000—as well as in Windows for Workgroups, Windows NT, and Windows 9x—a *workgroup* is a collection of computers on a network that are grouped together by a logical workgroup name. When you browse for resources on the network, you first see those computers on the LAN that are part of your workgroup. In Windows 2000, for example, My Network Places displays an icon for each of the computers in your workgroup (see Figure 11.4).

FIGURE 11.4
Workgroups provide a logical structure for grouping computers on the network.

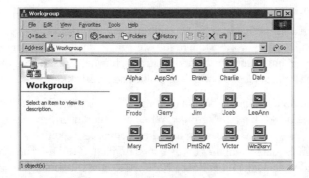

A computer can belong to any workgroup on the network, and it's simple to reassign a computer from one workgroup to another. You might need to do so if you move computers from one department to another or simply decide to restructure your network. Follow these steps to reassign a computer to a different workgroup:

1. Right-click My Computer and choose Properties.
2. Click the Network Identification tab and then click Properties.
3. Click Workgroup and specify the name of the workgroup to which you want to assign the computer.

Creating new workgroups is also easy. On any computer, simply specify a new workgroup name in the Network Identification tab of the computer's properties. Specifying the same workgroup on other computers adds those computers to the workgroup. Follow these steps to create a new workgroup:

1. Log on to a computer as administrator.
2. Right-click My Computer, choose Properties, and then click the Network Identification tab.
3. Click Properties.
4. Select the Workgroup option, type the new workgroup name in the text box, and then click OK.
5. Close the System Properties sheet.

The Domain Model

Workgroups simplify network browsing, but they do little—if anything—to simplify system administration. However, domains do simplify system administration. A *domain* is a group of computers that share a user account database. In effect, a domain is a single security boundary within the network.

Part
III

Ch
11

Domains enable centralization of account access and account management. Unlike a workgroup, in which a user must have an account on the computer she is logging on to, a domain user can log on from any workstation in the domain. Domains can span more than one physical location. More important for the administrator, however, is that you can administer accounts in one central location, which simplifies administration.

In addition to simplifying network administration, domains provide the same organization of resources to the network as workgroups. When a domain user browses the network for resources, she sees the resources organized by domain. My Network Places, for example, displays an icon for each computer in the user's domain. If the user needs to access a resource outside her domain, the Entire Network icon in the folder provides quick access to those resources.

Windows for Workgroups and Windows 95 clients on the network can enjoy the benefit of domains along with Windows NT/2000 clients. Setting the workgroup name of a Windows for Workgroups client to the name of a domain on the network adds that client to the domain. When the user browses for network resources, she sees the computers and other resources in the domain. If the user logs on to Windows for Workgroups with the correct account and password, the user is automatically logged on to the domain.

TIP You also can configure Windows 9x clients to log on to and become part of a domain. As with Windows for Workgroups clients, Windows 9x clients see the other computers in their domain when they browse for resources. To control Windows 9x domain logon, double-click the Network icon in the Control Panel. Click the Identification tab in the Network property sheet, and then enter the desired domain name in the Workgroup text box.

Domain Controllers   Within a domain, one or more servers acts as a *domain controller*. These domain controllers manage the domain account database and handle authentication requests within the domain. In the Windows NT model, one server in a domain acted as the Primary Domain Controller, or PDC. Other computers functioned as Backup Domain Controllers (BDCs), maintaining a copy of the account database to handle authentication requests when the PDC was unavailable.

Windows 2000 domain controllers function as peers, each maintaining a synchronized copy of the account database. The main difference from Windows NT is that account changes can be made on any domain controller and can be synchronized automatically with the other domain controllers in the domain. In Windows NT, changes had to be made on the PDC (although you could make those changes across the network from a workstation or BDC).

Trust Relationships Between Domains   A *trust relationship* is a special logical relationship between domains. In a trust relationship, one domain trusts another domain's users. The *trusting domain* enables users who have accounts in the *trusted domain* to access resources in its domain. For example, assume that domain A is the trusting domain and domain B is the trusted domain. A user from domain B can access resources in domain A.

If you are familiar with Windows NT, you'll probably know that a trust relationship can be unidirectional or bidirectional. Just because domain A trusts domain B, that doesn't mean that domain B trusts domain A. You must explicitly set up the trust relationship between the two domains to be bidirectional if you want it to be so. Figure 11.5 illustrates the concept of trust relationships in Windows NT.

FIGURE 11.5
Trust relationships in NT can be unidirectional or bidirectional.

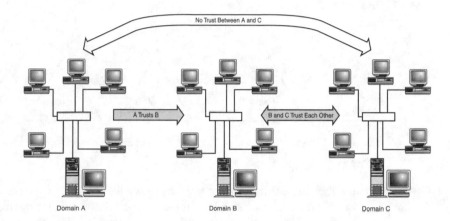

Domain trust relationships in NT are not *transitive*. This means that trusts do not pass from one domain to another. For example, if domain A trusts domain B and domain B trusts domain C, that doesn't mean that domain A trusts domain C. If you want domain A to trust domain C, you must explicitly set up the relationship between domain A and domain C.

In Windows 2000, however, domains have a somewhat different structure because of the Active Directory. A domain tree in Windows 2000 is a group of domains connected by a trust relationship that share a common schema, configuration, and global catalog. Multiple domain trees can be grouped together to form a domain forest.

N O T E   A *schema* defines the types of objects a given container within the Active Directory can contain and the attributes of those objects.

Windows 2000 trust relationships are transitive because they implement the relationship using the Kerberos security protocol (explained later in this chapter). As Figure 11.6 shows, domains A and B have an established trust. Domain C has an implicit trust with domain A.

Part

III

Ch

11

FIGURE 11.6
Trust relationships in
Windows 2000 are
transitive. This figure
shows Domains in a
Forest; Domain C trusts
Domain 3 through tran-
sitive trust.

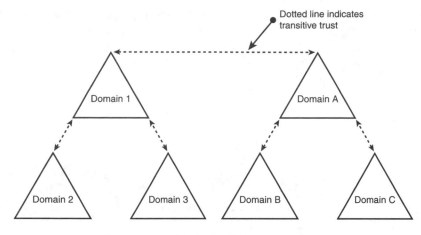

Domains in a Forest
Domain C trusts Domain 3 through transitive trust

Although the Active Directory certainly imposes a higher level of complexity on the Windows 2000 security model, it also simplifies management where multiple domains are involved. Rather than establish and manage multiple explicit trust relationships, you can simply structure the domains in the Active Directory and rely on the transitive trust relationships to accomplish the same ends.

N O T E   The section "The Active Directory" later in this chapter offers additional information on the Active Directory and its benefits. ▦

Managing Security for User Accounts and Groups

You must have a valid, preexisting user account to log on to a computer running Windows 2000. If the workstation is participating in a workgroup and not a domain, you must have an account on that workstation itself. If you are logging on from a computer in a domain, you must have an account in the domain (or in a trusted domain).

A user account identifies each user with a name and other optional information, and it defines how and when a user can log on, what resources the user can access, and what level of access the user has to those resources. Basically, the user account defines all aspects of the user's access to the computer and network through its assigned rights and associated permissions. Each user account includes a password for security.

In addition to existing as an individual account, users can belong to specific *groups*. A group is a collection of users who have similar job or resource access needs. Groups simplify resource administration by enabling you to assign and control rights and permissions on a broad basis.

Instead of assigning permissions for a specific resource to every user, you can associate a specific set of permissions with a group; you can then give those permissions to users simply by making them members of the group. In this way, groups provide a means of logically organizing users and their rights and permissions.

Windows 2000 supports two types of groups:

- *Local groups* can contain individual local user accounts and other local groups. Local groups are used primarily to control access to local resources in a workgroup environment, both for users who log on locally and those who access local resources from across the network.

- *Domain groups* serve to enable domainwide, and in some cases enterprisewide, security and resource sharing. Windows 2000 supports three types of scope for domain groups: domain *local*, *global*, and *universal*. Each group resides within a single domain, but its scope determines how the group is used and the privileges its members have.

Depending on their scope, groups in the Active Directory can be used for domainwide access or local control of resources. Windows 2000 does maintain backward-compatibility for local groups for mixed environments containing Windows NT and Windows 2000.

The most important point to understand is that groups enable you to simplify administration and resource access. Instead of having to grant specific rights to each user, you simply create groups with specific rights and then assign users to those groups as needed. It's also important to understand that a user can be a member of many groups and that one group can contain another group. In addition, you can add specific rights to a user if that user is the only one who needs those rights; you don't have to create a group with those specific rights. You might consider doing so anyway, however, because you might have another user in the future who also needs the same rights.

N O T E Don't confuse *permissions* and *rights*, which are different. Permissions provide specific types of access to resources (such as folders, files, and printers). Rights define the actions a user or group can perform. See the section "Understanding Permissions and Rights" later in this chapter for an explanation of both. ▪

Working with Built-In Groups

Windows 2000 includes a selection of built-in user accounts and groups. The Administrator account, which you create when you install Windows 2000, is essentially a built-in account. You can't delete or disable the Administrator account, but you can rename it. The Guest account is another built-in account. You can't delete the Guest account, but you can rename and disable it.

Table 11.1 lists the built-in groups supported by Windows 2000 in a workgroup environment. Table 11.2 lists built-in groups supported by Windows 2000 in a domain/Active Directory.

Table 11.1 Built-In Groups—No Domain

Group	Automatic Contents	Purpose
Administrators	Domain Admins	Full control to administer system
Backup Operators	None	Back up files and folders
Guests	Domain Guests, Guest	Use but not configure system
Power Users	Authenticated Users	Use and configure system but not access other users' files
Replicator	None	Supports file replication in a domain
Users	Authenticated Users	Use but not configure system

Table 11.2 Built-In Groups—Domain

Group	Automatic Contents	Purpose
Cert Publishers	None	Enterprise certification and renewal agents
DHCP Administrators	None	Administer DHCP server
DHCP Users	None	View-only access to DHCP server
Domain Admins	Administrator	Administer the domain
Domain Computers	Computers added to domain	Allow domain access by member computers
Domain Controllers	Domain controllers in domain	Handle authentication and Active Directory replication
Domain Guests	Guest account	Use but not configure computer in domain
Domain Users	All dom. accounts	Use but not configure computer in domain
Enterprise Admins	Administrator	Administer enterprise
Grp. Pol. Creator	Administrator	Modify group policy for domain
RAS and IAS Servers	None	Servers can access RAS properties of users
Schema Admins	Administrator	Users can administer schema

Working with the Everyone and Authenticated Users Groups

In both Windows NT and Windows 2000, the built-in *Everyone* group is controlled not by the Administrator but by the operating system itself. In Windows NT, every user authenticated within the domain becomes a member of the Everyone group, including anonymous and guest users. You can use the Everyone group to assign permissions.

In Windows 2000, the Everyone group still exists, but Windows 2000 adds a new built-in group, *Authenticated Users*. This group is the same as the Everyone group with the exception that it does not include anonymous and guest users.

How Windows 2000 Manages the Logon Process for Security

When a user logs on from a Windows 2000 workstation, the logon dialog box prompts for a User Name, Password, and domain (Log on To). In a workgroup, the Log on To drop-down list is omitted. The User Name and Password text boxes need a user account name and its associated password. From Log on To, the user can select a domain in which he has an account or select the local computer.

When the user specifies a domain in the Log on To box, the workstation passes the logon request to a domain controller for the specified domain, which checks the security database for a matching account and password. If one is found, the domain controller directs the workstation to authorize the logon.

If the user instead specifies the local workstation name in the Log on To box, the workstation checks its internal security database for a matching account. If one is found, the logon succeeds.

Logon in Trusted Domains

In a trust relationship, one domain trusts another. The trusting domain recognizes all the users and global group accounts from the trusted domain, enabling users to log on at the workstation in the trusting domain. Basically, the trusting domain is saying to the trusted domain, "If a user can log on to workstations in your domain, I'll let him log on in my domain."

When a user logs on from a trusting domain, she enters the name of the domain where her domain account resides in the logon dialog box. Windows 2000 then passes the logon request to a domain controller for that domain for authentication.

Remote Logon

With Windows 2000 Remote Access Services (RAS) , a user can log on through a dialup connection. Depending on how the RAS server is configured, the remote user can gain access to either the shared resources on the server or those resources and the resources on the network to which the RAS server is connected.

Remote logon is authenticated in much the same way as local logon. If the RAS server is not part of a domain, the remote user must have an account on the RAS server. If the RAS server belongs to a domain, the remote user can use a domain account to log on.

Part
III
Ch
11

The Active Directory

Although not explicitly a part of Windows 2000 Professional, the Active Directory is an important topic to understand because Windows 2000 Professional computers can reside in a network where Active Directory is used.

N O T E This section provides only a brief overview of Active Directory because this book focuses specifically on Windows 2000 Professional. For a detailed discussion of the Active Directory, refer to *Microsoft's Active Directory: Administration, Management, and Security*, from Que.

The Active Directory is a *directory service* new in the Windows 2000 Server family of products. A *directory* in this context is an information store containing information about essentially every object in the enterprise, including files, accounts, computers, printers, domains, and so on. A *directory service* is the combination of the directory and the services that make the directory available to users.

The Active Directory serves as a management tool as well as a user tool. It simplifies administration by providing a container in which objects can be cataloged and categorized, and it makes possible such tasks as browsing for specific types of objects (such as all printers in a specific building).

How is the Active Directory important in the context of Windows 2000 Professional? As far as administering a Windows 2000 Professional computer is concerned, it's only relevant in considering the workstation's participation in the domain and thereby in the Active Directory. Certain features—for example, IntelliMirror, which enables Windows 2000 to automatically install applications for roaming users—rely on the Active Directory. In this sense, the Active Directory is simply a server-side feature that Windows 2000 Professional workstations take advantage of, but which you don't manage directly on the workstation.

Working with Kerberos Security

Windows 2000 includes support for the Kerberos authentication protocol, which defines interaction between a client and a server-side authentication service referred to as a Key Distribution Center (KDC). The KDC processes authentication requests, issuing a Kerberos *ticket* that grants the client access to the requested resource. The ticket is cached on the client computer and can be reused for future connections to the same server. If the ticket expires during an active session, the client requests a new ticket.

N O T E Kerberos is the primary domain authentication mechanism in Windows 2000, replacing NTLM authentication.

Because of the way Kerberos functions on the server side compared to NTLM authentication, connection requests can be processed more quickly and can reduce server overhead. This ultimately improves performance for the client. Because of the way Kerberos is designed and implemented, it also simplifies client logon and resource access.

As with the Active Directory, Kerberos is really a Windows 2000 Server feature that affects Windows 2000 Professional workstations operating within a domain. This information is provided to give you an understanding of what Kerberos is and what it does; there are no configuration or management issues relating to Kerberos authentication specific to Windows 2000 Professional.

A Checklist of Tasks for Optimizing Security in a Windows 2000 Environment

Ensuring optimum security has become increasingly important in today's business environment, whether your systems are connected to the Internet or only connected to an internal LAN. Tightening security in a Windows 2000 environment requires several steps to ensure as secure a network as possible. The following sections define a checklist of tasks to perform to secure a Windows 2000 system and network.

N O T E The following security optimization checklist Is patterned after recommendations developed and promoted by the SANS (System Administration, Networking, and Security) Institute . SANS offers regular security news, related subscription content, and many other useful services. For additional information on security and other topics of interest to system administrators, check out the SANS Institute Web site at http://www.sans.org. ▪

Part

III

Ch

11

Secure Computer Physically

Lock up servers and critical workstations to keep users away from them, preventing unauthorized physical access to computers, particularly when FAT volumes are present. Although this is particularly important for servers, it's also important for workstations. If you neglect to secure the system from unauthorized boots or don't enforce a requirement for password-protected screen savers, it's quite possible for a user to gain access to the system and its files with the computer already booted and logged on or by booting from a bootable diskette. Although this last possibility is most dangerous when FAT volumes are used instead of NTFS, it's still possible for a person to boot a system from a diskette and access files stored in NTFS volumes.

Secure the Boot Process

In the system's BIOS configuration utility, configure the system to prevent boot from diskette and password-protect the BIOS to prevent a user from changing boot options. Without these changes, it's possible for a user to boot the system from diskette and potentially retrieve data from the system, even when the data is stored in NTFS volumes.

TIP On most systems, pressing Delete, F1, or F10 when the initial boot screen is displayed opens the BIOS configuration utility for the computer. The key varies from system to system depending on BIOS type and manufacturer.

Require Screen Savers with Password Protection

Require all users to apply a screen saver with password protection to prevent unauthorized access by others at an unattended, unlocked workstation. Use group policies to enforce screen saver settings.

▶ For a discussion of group policies and how to apply them, **see** "Managing Group Policies," **p. 225**

Use NTFS

FAT offers nothing in terms of local security and very limited control of security for shared access across the network. Place critical data in NTFS partitions to ensure local security for the data and make additional options available for sharing the data on the LAN. If you don't need to maintain FAT volumes on your systems, convert them to NTFS when you install Windows 2000 or use the Convert command-line utility.

Maintain Current ERD and Backup Set

Put in place a regular backup strategy and make sure you always have a current backup set that includes the system state data as well as a current Emergency Repair Disk (ERD). Having both will ensure that you can perform an authoritative restore if a drive or system failure occurs. Use the Windows 2000 Backup program to create and update the ERD.

Protect Backups

Make sure that you perform regular backups, but also make sure that you secure those backup sets. Move the backup sets off-site to guard against a disaster (flood, fire, terrorist attack, and so on), and protect the backup sets adequately, such as in a fire safe. A backup set is worthless if it gets destroyed along with your data and/or hardware.

Prevent Logon Caching

It's much easier for someone to break into a system if he knows a valid username for the computer or domain than if he doesn't, even if he still has to guess or attempt to crack a password. For this reason, you should prevent Windows 2000 from displaying the last logon account in the logon dialog box. Although this means that you'll have to retype your user name even if you were the last one who logged on, it increases security. Enable the setting Do Not Display Last User Name In Logon Screen in `\Local Computer Policy\Computer Configuration\Windows Settings\Security Settings\Local Policies\Security Options` of the group policy. Run the Groupu Policy snap-in (`gpedit.msc`) to modify this value.

Require Logon

You can configure Windows 2000 to automatically log you on at startup, bypassing the Ctrl+Alt+Delete action and logon dialog box. To prevent someone from gaining access to your system by simply turning it on, you should disable automatic logon. Open Users and Passwords in the Control Panel, click the Advanced Tab, and select Require Users to Press Ctrl+Alt+Delete Before Logging On.

Display a "No Trespassing" Sign at Logon

Unless you display the equivalent of a "No Trespassing" sign in the logon dialog (or logon message of an FTP or Telnet server), any legal action you attempt to take against an intruder could fail. Here's an example (check with your legal counsel to ensure the message has the necessary weight of law in your region):

WARNING: Access to this system by authorized personnel only. All users will be monitored for security purposes and potential law enforcement. Unauthorized use will be subject to criminal and civil prosecution and penalties.

You can set the logon banner through the settings Message Text for Users Attempting to Log On and Message Title for Users Attempting to Log On located in `\Local Computer Policy\Computer Configuration\Windows Settings\Security Settings\Local Policies\Security Options` of the group policy. Set the banner message for an FTP server using the Message tab of the server's properties in the Internet Information Services MMC snap-in.

Set options for the Telnet service through the registry at `HKLM\Software\Microsoft \TelnetServer\1.0`. Set the banner message for a Telnet server by editing the file `\systemroot\System32\Login.cmd`. Use Echo statements to define the message that appears when a user logs in. Following are specific steps to accomplish the Registry changes:

1. Click Start, Run.
2. In the Run text box, type **Regedt32**, and click OK.
3. Open the window for `HKEY_LOCAL_MACHINE`.
4. Open the branch `Software\Microsoft\TelnetServer\1.0`.
5. Set the value of LoginScript to point to the script you want executed for each user at logon (by default, `\systemroot\System32\login.cmd`.
6. Close the Registry Editor.
7. Use Notepad or WordPad to edit the script specified in step 5 to include echo commands that display the logon warning message.

▶ To learn more about working with a Telnet server, **see** "Configuring a Telnet Server," **p. 426**

Part

III

Ch

11

TIP You can run the `Tlntadmn.exe` application to administer the Telnet service, although modifying `Login.cmd` is not available through it.

Maintain Log Files

Although you can configure the event logs to automatically overwrite when they fill up, you should consider actively managing the logs and archiving them when they near capacity. Prosecuting an intrusion will rely heavily on proving that the intrusion occurred, and by whom. Your event logs are primary evidence. Use the Event Viewer MMC console to manage and save the event logs to disk.

Require Strong Passwords

Develop a strategy and policy for requiring strong passwords. Rather than short passwords containing only letters, require that passwords have a minimum length of 10 characters or more, with numeric and special characters required. Set password options through `\Computer Configuration\Windows Settings\Security Settings\Password Policy` in the group policy:

1. Click Start, Run, type **gpedit.msc**, and click OK.
2. In the Group Policy console, open the branch `Computer Configuration\Windows Settings\Security Settings\Account Policies\Password Policy` (see Figure 11.7).

FIGURE 11.7
Use Group Policy to enforce password restrictions.

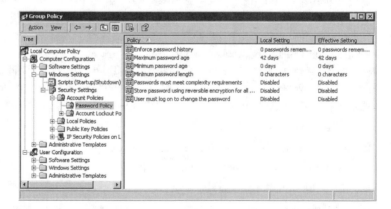

3. Set password policy settings according to your needs, and then close the Group Policy console.

Secure Event Log

The event logs often contain information that could be used by a hacker to gain access to the system or LAN, so you should protect the event logs from being viewed by unauthorized personnel. To do so, apply permissions to the log files in `\systemroot\System32\Config` so that only the system and administrators have access to the log files. You also should audit access to the log files.

Secure Printers

Printers that contain sensitive documents such as checks and purchase orders should be protected to prevent unauthorized users from printing to them. Apply permissions to the printers so that only authorized users can print to them. To apply printer permissions, open the Printers folder, right-click the printer in question, and choose Sharing. Click the Security tab and allow/deny access as needed.

Restrict Anonymous Logon

IIS provides for anonymous access as a primary means of serving Web documents to users. This can create a security hole if you inadvertently give the IIS anonymous account permissions in folders where it should have none. Check the settings for anonymous access on the Directory Security tab for any Web sites shared on the computer through the IIS console snap-in. Also make sure that the IIS anonymous user has not been assigned permissions in any directories where anonymous users should not have access.

NOTE The IIS anonymous user typically has the user name IUSR_*computername*, where *computername* is the name of the computer on which IIS is installed. ∎

Part III

Ch 11

Control Remote Registry Access

Windows 2000 provides for remote registry viewing and modification, which opens a security hole for potential compromise across the network. Unless you specifically need it for cross-network administration, restrict network access to the registry by following these steps:

1. Click Start, Run, type **regedt32.exe**, and click OK.
2. Select the branch
   `HKEY_LOCAL_MACHINE\System\CurrentControlSet\Control\SecurePipeServers \winreg`.
3. Choose Security, Permissions, and in the Permissions dialog, allow and deny access to groups and users as needed.
4. Close the Registry Editor.

Restrict Anonymous Network Access

You can restrict anonymous (null session) logons when they connect to specific named pipes and restrict the ability for null session connections to list account names and share names. Restricting these null session connections closes potential security holes that could allow remote users to gain access to accounts and shares.

To edit the list of restricted named pipes, edit the value of `HKLM\SYSTEM\CurrentControlSet \Services\LanmanServer\Parameters`, adding or removing restricted named pipes as needed. Modify the value of `HKLM\SYSTEM\CurrentControlSet\Control\Lsa\RestrictAnonymous` to restrict null session connections from enumerating accounts and shares. Use `Regedt32.exe` to modify these registry settings.

Enforce Account Lockout

You should create and enforce account lockout policies to prevent unauthorized users from attempting to gain access by guessing account passwords. Configure all non-Administrator accounts to lock out after a small number of logon attempts (such as three). Set password options through `\Computer Configuration\Windows Settings\Security Settings\Account Policies\Password Policy` in the group policy.

Secure the Administrator Account

Consider renaming the Administrator account to decrease the chance of a hacker gaining access to the system by guessing or cracking the Administrator password. Also require administrators to use their personal accounts when not performing administrative tasks, and ensure that those personal accounts do not have administrative permissions or rights.

Secure Everyone Group and Guest Account

For optimum security, eliminate use of the Everyone group and replace it with Authenticated Users. This protects against unauthorized access by anonymous logon and helps ensure that anyone who gains access to a resource has first been authenticated with a valid account. You also should consider renaming the guest account or disable it altogether.

Apply Permissions by Group Rather Than User

Although you can apply permissions and rights on a per-user basis, it's much more difficult to track permission assignments. Assign permissions and rights by group, and then grant them to individual users by placing them in the group.

Limit Shared Accounts

Require all users to have and use their own account, except in situations where it is impractical and where you can provide adequate restrictions to the shared accounts.

Employ and Monitor Auditing

You should enable auditing of at least the following minimum set of events to help monitor access to your systems: success and failure of logon and logoff, failure of file and object access, failure of use of user rights, success and failure of security policy changes, and success and failure of system startup and shutdown. Monitor the logs on a regular, frequent basis.

> **CAUTION**
>
> Be careful of how many events you audit because some events can cause the event logs to grow very rapidly.

Secure IIS

You should make sure you tighten security on any computer running IIS to prevent unauthorized access or denial-of-service attacks across the intranet or Internet. See Chapter 24, "Installing and Configuring Internet Information Services," for more information on configuring IIS security.

Use a Firewall

Locking your file cabinets and desk drawers is great, but you're still vulnerable if you leave your office door unlocked. Consider implementing a firewall to enable you to filter and control traffic in and out of your network, particularly when the network is connected to the Internet.

Part

III

Ch

11

Maintain System Updates

Make sure you apply service packs as they become available to ensure that any security flaws detected in previous releases are sealed.

CHAPTER 12

Managing User Accounts and Groups

In this chapter

Account Management in Windows 2000

One of the primary tasks of administering a Windows 2000 workstation or server is managing user accounts, groups, and policies. Account management has a direct bearing on other administrative tasks such as resource sharing, as you typically apply permissions and rights based on group membership and in some cases, individual accounts. Windows 2000 provides a handful of different means for managing accounts and groups. This chapter focuses primarily on the Local Users and Groups console snap-in, which you access through the Users and Passwords object in the Control Panel. It also covers the Users and Passwords Control Panel object, as well as the Security Policy snap-in, which you use to assign rights and configure other security properties.

Security management is closely linked to account management in Windows 2000. In addition to account management, this chapter also explains other tasks that help you define security policies, enable users to roam (maintain the same profile regardless of logon location), assign rights, and so on.

Creating Local Accounts

You can use the Users and Passwords object in the Control Panel to create user accounts, although your options are somewhat limited using this method. You can create accounts, for example, but assign the account to only one group. To assign an account to more than one group or perform other advanced tasks such as assigning a user profile or logon script, you need to use the Local Users and Groups snap-in. This lack of flexibility in the Users and Passwords object is why this chapter focuses on the snap-in instead.

 TIP The Users and Passwords object is useful when you want to create an account that is a member of a single group or you want to change the password of an existing account.

To access Local Users and Groups, open the Control Panel and then the Users and Passwords object. Click the Advanced tab and then the Advanced button to access the Local Users and Groups snap-in (see Figure 12.1). You also can access Local Users and Groups through the Computer Management console snap-in (right-click My Computer and choose Manage). Alternatively, open the MMC in author mode (run MMC /A) and add Local Users and Groups to any custom console by choosing Console, Add/Remove Snap-In, Add.

> **N O T E** Because this book focuses on Windows 2000 Professional, this chapter focuses on creating local accounts and groups rather than domain accounts or global groups. ▪

Creating the Account

Right-click the Users folder and choose New User to access the New User dialog (see Figure 12.2). Specify properties as described in the following list and click Create.

FIGURE 12.1
You can add the Local Users and Groups snap-in to any custom console.

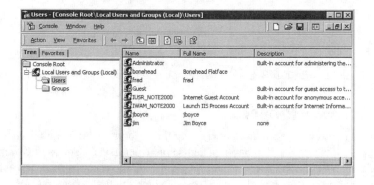

FIGURE 12.2
Use the New User dialog box to set and configure passwords.

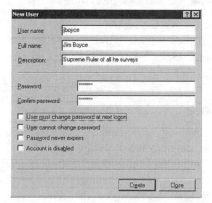

Part

III

Ch

12

- **User Name.** Name under which user will log on. Define and implement a naming scheme that provides consistency throughout an organization. Some use first initial of first name plus last name, whereas others use different naming schemes such as first name and first two or three letters of the surname. The user name must be unique on the local computer.

- **Full Name.** Typically, the user's first name and surname.

- **Description.** Optional description to further identify user or user's group, department, and so on.

- **Password and Confirm Password.** Specify user's password. Both entries must match to protect against mistyping.

- **User Must Change Password at Next Logon.** Select to force the user to change his password at the next logon. This helps ensure that if you use a standard password (such as PASSWORD) to create the account, the user can't continue to use that password, opening a potential security hole.

- **User Cannot Change Password.** Select to prevent the user from changing his password. This is most useful for shared accounts to prevent one user from locking the others out. It's also a good idea to prevent password changes for service accounts.

■ *Password Never Expires*. Select to allow the password to be used indefinitely. Deselect to enforce the account policy for password age (if defined).

▶ **See** "Defining Password Policy," **p. 231**

■ *Account Is Disabled*. Select to disable the account, preventing it from being used.

Setting Account Properties

You can modify an account after creating the account to change its properties, such as password options, group membership, and so on. Open Local Users and Groups, click Users, and then double-click the user account (or right-click the account and choose Properties). The resulting properties include three tabs, of which the first—General—offers the same properties presented when you created the account (see preceding section).

One additional option, Account Is Locked Out, applies only when you're setting the properties for an account that has been locked out through the security policy. If the account is locked out, the option is automatically selected; deselect the option and click OK to unlock the account.

Changing Group Membership

The Member Of tab enables you to specify group membership for the account. When you create an account, it is automatically made a member of the Users group. You can change group membership to another group or add other groups. Display the properties for the account and click the Member Of tab. To remove a group membership, select the group in the Member Of list and click Remove. Click Add to access the Select Groups dialog to add other groups. Double-click each desired group or type the group names separated by semicolons. Click OK when you're satisfied with the group memberships.

N O T E   When you add the group it takes the form *hostname\group*, where *hostname* is the name of the local computer and *group* is the name of the group for which you're adding membership, indicating that the group resides on the local computer rather than in a domain. ■

Setting Profile Properties

The third tab of the user properties, Profile, enables you to define the user's profile, logon script, and home folder.

Specifying a Profile Path   The file you specify in Profile path, if any, determines operating environment settings for the user at logon, subject to overriding settings (such as defined by group policy settings). Specify the path to the user's policy file. See the section, "Managing User Profiles," later in this chapter if you need detailed information on using profiles.

N O T E Although you can employ a Windows NT–style profile using the method described previously, you might prefer to use group policies to implement environment and security settings within a domain, particularly when you have a homogenous Windows 2000 network. Using group policies provides for additional options and features with simplified administration. ■

Specifying the Logon Script The Logon Script setting specifies the script to run at logon, which can be a batch or command file (BAT or CMD), executable (EXE), or Windows Scripting Host script (VBScript and JScript). The logon script is typically used to automate drive mapping, set environment variables, or start background processes. Specify a script filename located in the NETLOGON share of the domain controller or local computer, or in the \systemroot\System32\ Repl\Import\Scripts folder on the local computer. Specify a relative path to the script if the script is located in a subfolder of the NETLOGON share. For example, admin\logme.bat would reference the file Logme.bat in the Admin folder of the NETLOGON share.

See the section, "Managing Scripts," later in this chapter for a detailed discussion of logon scripts for local and domain accounts, as well as scripts (logon and logoff) defined by the group policy.

Defining the Home Folder The Home folder group of controls on the Profile tab enables you to define the folder Windows 2000 makes active at logon. Typically, this is the folder in which the user stores his documents, but it can be any folder, either local or on a network server. Choose Local Path if you want to specify a local folder, and then include the path to the folder. Choose the Connect button and select a drive letter to specify a network share as the user's home folder, and then type the path to the folder in the To field. You can use a UNC pathname in the form \\server\share\folder, where server is the name of the server, share is the network share containing the shared folder, and folder is the folder itself.

TIP In Windows NT, the path specified in To must be the name of a share, rather than a folder within a share. The ability to assign a folder within a share in Windows 2000 simplifies home folder configuration because you no longer have to share each user's folder individually.

Part
III

Ch

12

Creating Local Groups

You can use Local Users and Groups to create new local groups and assign users to groups, as well as remove existing groups. To create a group, open Local Users and Groups, right-click Groups, and choose New Group. Windows 2000 opens the New Group dialog. Type a unique name for the group in Group name, and then click Add to select accounts to add to the group. The following section explains how to assign rights to groups.

▶ For detailed information on assigning permissions on resources by group membership, **see** "Sharing Disk Resources," **p. 246**

Assigning Rights to Groups

A *user right* grants a user (or group) the authority to perform a specific action. When a user logs on to an account to which a right has been granted, either directly or through group membership, that user can perform the task associated with the right.

Understanding User Rights

Windows 2000 recognizes two types of user rights: *privileges* and *logon rights*. Table 12.1 describes the specific privileges that are assignable to users. Table 12.2 describes logon rights.

Table 12.1   Privileges

Right	Purpose
Act as part of the operating system	Lets the user act as trusted part of the operating system; granted automatically to certain subsystems.
Add workstations to domain	User can add workstations to domain, enabling domain logon from those workstations.
Back up files and directories	User can back up files and directories on the computer, supersedes file and directory permissions. Does not enable user to view file or directory contents without explicit permission.
Bypass traverse checking	Lets user traverse directory trees even if she lacks permission to traverse a specific directory; doesn't supersede ownership or permissions (can only traverse, and not view or manipulate, contents without specific permissions).
Change the system time	User can set computer's system clock.
Create a pagefile	Allows user to create a page file.
Create a token object	User can create security access tokens.
Create permanent shared objects	Enables user to create permanent shared objects such as device instances.
Debug programs	Allows user to debug programs.
Enable Trusted for Delegation on User and Computer Accounts	Lets user enable Trusted for Delegation on user and computer accounts.
Force shutdown from a remote system	Lets user force a system to shut down from a remote node (such as a dial-up connection).
Generate security audits	Allows user to generate security log entries.
Increase quotas	Enables user to increase object quotas.
Increase scheduling priority	Enables user to boost scheduling priority of a process.
Load and unload device drivers	Allows user to dynamically load and unload device drivers for PnP devices. Applies to domain controllers within a domain. Outside of a domain, applies only to computer on which right is assigned.

Right	Purpose
Lock pages in memory	User can lock pages in memory, preventing her from being paged to disk.
Manage auditing and security log	Enables user to manage auditing of files, directories, and other objects.
Modify firmware and environment values	Allows user to modify system environment variables.
Profile single process	Enables user to profile a non-system process.
Profile system performance	Enables user to profile system processes and performance.
Replace a process level token	Enables a user to modify a process's access token.
Restore files and directories	User can restore files previously backed up. Having backup permission does not give a user restore permission, and vice-versa.
Shut down the system	Enables user to shut down the computer.
Take ownership of files or other objects	User can take ownership of files, directories, and printers. Applies to domain controllers within a domain. Outside of domain, applies only to computer on which right is assigned.
Unlock a Laptop	User can unlock a laptop.

Table 12.2   Logon Rights

Right	Purpose
Access this computer from network	Lets user connect to the computer from across the network.
Log on locally	User can log on to system locally. In most cases, you don't want users to have the right to log on locally to a server for security and performance reasons.
Log on as a batch job	Enables user to log on to system as a batch queue facility.
Log on as a service	Allows processes to register with the system as a service.
Deny Access to this Computer from the Network	Holder can deny the Access This Computer from the Network right.
Deny Logon as a Batch Job	Holder can deny the Log On as a Batch Job right.
Deny Logon as a Service	Holder can deny the Log On as a Service right.
Deny Local Logon	Holder can deny the Log On Locally right.

Part

III

Ch

12

N O T E Don't confuse *rights* with *permissions*, which are different. A right applies to systemwide objects and tasks, and permissions apply to specific objects such as files and printers. Also, many of the advanced user rights listed in this chapter are only applicable within the framework of a custom application or Windows 2000 subsystem. ■

Some privileges can take precedence over object permissions. For example, a member of a Backup Operators domain group can perform backup operations on files whose owners have set the files' permissions to deny access to all other users. In this case the right to back up files and directories takes precedence over the files' object permissions.

▶ To learn more about permissions, **see** "Understanding Permissions," **p. 242**

Generally, you control user rights by placing the user in a group whose rights you've already assigned. You also can assign rights on an account-by-account basis, but it's a better practice to assign rights by group for simplified management. If you need to add a right for a specific user, create a specific group for that right and make the user a member. Remove a user from a group when you need to remove a given right.

Assigning Rights

You can assign rights with either the Security Policy snap-in (`Secpol.msc`) or Group Policy snap-in (`Gpedit.msc`). This section explains the Security Policy snap-in, but you can use the same process for the Group Policy snap-in on a local computer.

Click Start, **P**rograms, Administrative Tools, Local Security Policy to open the Security Policy snap-in. Open Local Policies\User Rights Assignment to view current rights assignments.

TIP If the Administrative Tools folder is missing from your Start menu, right-click the taskbar and choose P**r**operties. Click Advanced, and in the Start Menu Se**t**tings group, select Display Administrative Tools.

Double-click a right to view or modify its assignment. The properties sheet for the right shows group/account assignments (see Figure 12.3). Select and deselect rights in the Local Policy Setting column to grant or deny the right, respectively, to the selected group or user. Click **A**dd to assign new groups or users the specified right. Click OK when you're done.

FIGURE 12.3
Select or deselect a group or user to allow or deny the right, respectively.

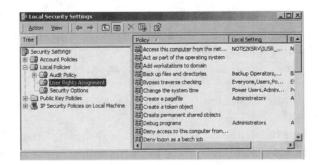

The Effective Policy Setting column for the selected right indicates how the right is currently enforced on the system by listing users and groups to whom the right is assigned. Any defined domain-level policies will override the local policy setting, resulting in the effective setting.

Managing Group Policies

In Windows 2000, *group policies* make it possible for you to assign security settings and other properties to users based on account or group membership. Group policies are the primary means of distributing and controlling a user's configuration in Windows 2000.

Windows 2000 supports two types of group policies: local and nonlocal. Only one set of local policies exists on each computer. Nonlocal group policies apply only within the framework of the Active Directory (AD) and are stored on domain controllers. Nonlocal group policies apply at the site, domain, or organizational unit with which the particular group policy is associated. When policies defined by the local and nonlocal group policies conflict, the nonlocal policies take precedence by default over local policies. If no conflict exists, both apply.

N O T E Although this chapter explores nonlocal group policies and their implications (particularly to local policies), local policies remain the focus of the chapter. ■

Policy Inheritance and Exclusion

As with permissions, policies can be inherited with policies passed down from the parent container to the child container in the AD. The following list summarizes inheritance and exclusion:

- Policies applied at the highest level container pass down through each successive level, subject to restrictions described as follows:
  - Policy settings explicitly set at a child container override policies defined by the parent container(s).
  - Settings not defined by the parent are not inherited by the child.
  - Settings disabled in the parent are inherited as disabled by the child.
  - When settings are configured at the parent but not at the child container, the settings are inherited by the child.
  - Policy settings are inherited as long as they are compatible. When parent and child settings are compatible, the child inherits the parent settings and applies additional, related settings. When settings are not compatible, the child does not inherit but instead applies its own settings.

 You can block inheritance at the site, domain, or organizational unit level. Select Block Policy Inheritance on the Group Policy tab for the selected object in the appropriate Active Directory snap-in. You also can select Allow Inheritable Permissions from Parent to Propagate to this Object on the Security tab of the object's properties to control inheritance for individual child objects. Group policy objects set to No Override can't be blocked and are always applied (applies within the AD only; this is not applicable to the local group policy.)

Part
III

Ch
12

Applying Policies

Windows 2000 uses a specific procedure to apply policy settings and the user profile:

1. During boot, the network starts along with network-required services.

2. Windows 2000 obtains an ordered list of group policy objects, which depends on several factors, including membership in a domain, location of the computer object in the AD, location of the User object in the AD, and so on.

3. Computer policy is applied synchronously using the following order: Windows NT 4.0 system policy and then group policies for local, site, domain, organizational unit, child organizational unit, and so on. The user interface is hidden by default while the group policies are applied.

4. Startup scripts defined by the group policies execute.

5. Windows 2000 requests the user to log on (the user presses Ctrl+Alt+Del) or Windows 2000 automatically logs on the user, depending on how you have logon configured.

6. The user profile is loaded after valid authentication.

7. User policy is applied synchronously using the following order: Windows NT 4.0 system policy, followed by group policies for local, site, domain, organizational unit, child organizational unit, and so on. The user interface is hidden by default while the user policies are applied.

8. Group-policy–based logon scripts execute first, followed by the user object script.

9. The user interface appears as defined by settings in the group policy and user profile.

N O T E Group policies take the place of the Windows NT 4.0 system policy (created with the System Policy Editor under Windows NT), but you can continue to use the system policy until you translate its settings to the group policies. Windows NT 4.0 system policies are disabled by default, but you can enable them through the group policy setting Disable System Policy (Use Group Policy Only) in Computer Configuration\Administrative Templates\System\Group Policy. ■

Assigning Group Policies

You assign group policies through the Group Policy MMC snap-in. To assign policies, you first open the appropriate container, such as the local computer or group policy for a specific domain, organizational unit, or so on.

To open the Group Policy object for the local computer, open Gpedit.msc in \systemroot\System32 or open the management console and add the Group Policy snap-in. Figure 12.4 shows the Group Policy console.

FIGURE 12.4
You can modify group policies on the local computer or other container.

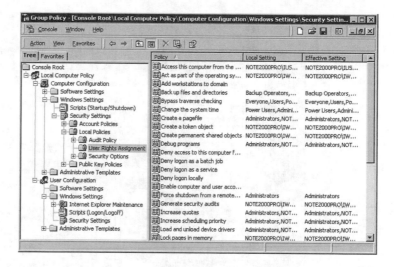

The group policy comprises a hierarchical structure of settings. The Computer Configuration branch controls computer-specific settings such as startup and shutdown scripts and other settings that relate to the computer, rather than to the user. The User Configuration branch contains settings that apply to the user, such as the logon script.

In each branch you'll find an Administrative Templates branch. Use the settings in this branch to specify various global settings that control how group policies are applied as well as general policy settings (printing, network configuration, and so on).

The Group Policy window contains numerous settings, and explaining each one in detail would take a book by itself, so they are not detailed individually here. In many cases, the settings are self-explanatory, and (in any case) Windows 2000 offers fairly detailed information about each one.

The value of a setting appears in the Setting column. A value of Not Configured indicates that the setting has not been explicitly set. Double-click a setting to configure it or view an explanation of the setting. Windows 2000 displays a tabbed Properties sheet that offers options or explanations for the current setting; an example of such a Properties sheet is shown in Figure 12.5. The contents of the Properties sheet vary, depending on the setting.

You can configure the setting by selecting the desired option, such as Not **C**onfigured, **E**nabled, or **D**isabled. Enabling a policy sometimes offers additional options you can set, depending on the policy. Windows 2000 typically provides a description of the setting. If you don't immediately see a description, look for an Explanation tab that contains a detailed explanation of the setting.

You should take some time to review all the policy settings, working one-by-one through the group policy. For now, simply understand that you can configure most settings through the group policy and that settings can also be applied through higher-level objects such as group policies in the domain.

Part **III**
Ch **12**

FIGURE 12.5
View and change policy settings through the policy's Properties sheet.

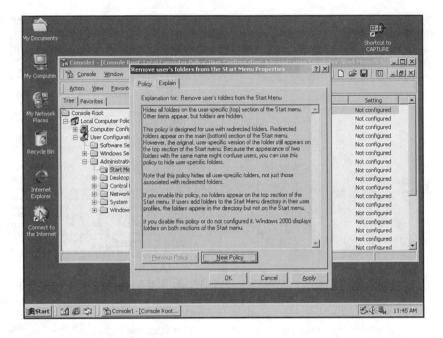

Managing Scripts

You can assign scripts to execute automatically at logon or logoff through the user's account properties as well as through the group policy. The logon script you assign through the user's account properties (called the user's *object script*) applies specifically to the selected user. Scripts that you assign through the group policy apply to the entire scope of users and groups for which the group policy applies.

Specifying the Path to the Script Location

The default path to the user's object script is *systemroot*\System32\Repl\Import\Scripts or the NETLOGON share on the local computer when logging on locally (in a workgroup) or the NETL-OGON share of the authentication server when logging on in a domain. When you specify the script path in the user's account properties, you must specify the path relative to this location. If the script file AdminScr.bat is located in *systemroot*\System32\Repl\Import\Scripts\Admins, for example, you would specify Admins\AdminScr.bat in the account properties.

The default path to logon and logoff scripts defined by the local group policy is *systemroot*\System32\GroupPolicy\Users\Scripts*type*, where *type* is either Logon or Logoff, respectively. The default path to startup and shutdown scripts defined by the local group policy is *systemroot*\System32\GroupPolicy\Machine\Scripts*type*, where *type* is either Startup or Shutdown, respectively. For both logon/logoff and startup/shutdown scripts, you can specify any folder when you modify the policy because the full script path is added to the policy itself.

TIP In Windows NT, the NETLOGON share points by default to *systemroot*\System32\Repl\ Import\Scripts. In Windows 2000, the NETLOGON share points to *sysvol**domain*\Scripts on the domain controller. To store and execute scripts from a local computer (managing multiple accounts on a single computer), place the scripts in *systemroot*\System32\Repl\Import\ Scripts (you'll probably have to create the folder) or create a NETLOGON share on the local computer and place the scripts in that shared folder.

Assigning Scripts

The section "Specifying the Logon Script" earlier in this chapter explained how to assign a user's object script in the account properties. You use the Group Policy object to assign logon/logoff and startup/shutdown scripts.

Follow these steps to assign a script:

1. Open the Group Policy snap-in and expand Computer Configuration\Windows Settings\Scripts for startup or shutdown scripts, or User Configuration\Windows Settings\Scripts for logon or logoff scripts.

2. In the right side of the window, double-click the type of script you want to assign to access the Scripts dialog.

3. Click Add to specify Script Name (name of script file) and Script Parameters, which are parameters passed to the script at execution. Click Browse if you want to browse for the script file.

4. Click OK to add the script, and then add or remove other scripts as desired.

5. Click OK, and then repeat the process for other script types.

6. Close the Group Policy snap-in when you're satisfied with the script assignments.

TIP You can use the Up and Down buttons on the Scripts tab to change the order of scripts in the list. This has no bearing on the script execution unless you configure scripts to execute synchronously (see the following section). When configured for synchronous execution, scripts execute according to list order.

Configuring Script Execution

Scripts defined by the group policy execute before the user's object script. The policy-defined startup and shutdown scripts execute hidden and synchronously; the user doesn't see them execute, and each script must complete before the next will execute (subject to policy-defined timeout value, which defaults to 600 seconds). All startup scripts must complete before the logon dialog appears.

Logon and logoff scripts defined by group policy execute hidden and *asynchronously*, meaning that they execute concurrently by default. Explorer can start while the logon scripts are still executing. You can configure the scripts for synchronous execution, which means each must

Part

III

Ch

12

complete before the next starts (useful if one script relies on another). Setting logon script execution to synchronous also prevents Explorer from starting before all scripts complete (including the user object script).

You can configure the policy-defined logon/logoff scripts to execute synchronously if you prefer (useful if an action in one script relies on an action in another). Configuring synchronous execution of the logon scripts also means that all scripts must finish before Explorer starts. You configure these script options through policy settings.

Use the Group Policy snap-in to define how scripts execute. You'll find the settings for logon/logoff scripts in User Configuration\Administrative Templates\System\ Logon/Logoff. Applicable settings include Run Logon Scripts Synchronously, Run Legacy Logon Scripts Hidden, Run Logon Scripts Visible, and Run Logoff Scripts Visible. The settings for startup/shutdown scripts reside in Computer Configuration\Administrative Templates\System\Logon. Applicable settings include Run Logon Scripts Synchronously, Run Startup Scripts Asynchronously, Run Startup Scripts visible, Run Shutdown Scripts Visible, and Maximum Wait Time for Group Policy Scripts.

Using Environment Variables in Scripts

In some cases, it can be helpful to read the value of environment variables within the script. For example, in a wide area network, you might want to set an environment variable to the name of the user's home directory server and then use the same script for multiple users to let them each map a home directory to a different server. You'd define the server variable within a policy-defined script and then use that variable in the user's object script to map the desired network share from the specified server.

Table 12.3 lists reserved variables you can use in a logon script to determine information about the user and environment at logon. You also can parse any environment variable on the system using %variable%, replacing variable with the environment variable name.

Table 12.3 Logon Script Variables

Variable	Function
%HOMEDRIVE%	User's local drive letter assigned to home folder.
%HOMEPATH%	Full path to user's home folder.
%OS%	Current operating system of logon workstation.
%PROCESSOR_ARCHITECTURE%	Processor type of logon workstation (such as x86 for Intel).
%PROCESSOR_LEVEL%	Processor level of logon workstation (example: 5).
%USERDOMAIN%	Domain containing user's account.
%USERNAME%	User's account (logon) name.

TIP You can use environment variables in user profile paths and home directory paths, as well as scripts. For example, you might define %server% as the name of the desired server and then use \\%server%\ Users\%username% to map a local drive letter to the user's home folder on the server specified by %server%. If %server% resolved to Server1, for example, and the user logged on as fred, the path would resolve to \\Server1\Users\fred.

Setting Account and Password Policies

You can specify account lockout and password settings in the local policy, controlling restrictions on passwords, how the passwords are applied, account lockout, and other options. Modify these settings using the Group Policy snap-in. (These settings are set in Windows NT through User Manager.)

▶ For tips on enforcing tighter security, **see** "A Checklist of Tasks for Optimizing Security in a Windows 2000 Environment," **p. 209**

Defining Password Policy

Settings in the Password Policy determine how passwords are treated. Define these password policy settings through the local policy at Computer Configuration\Windows Settings\ Security Settings\Account Policies\Password Policy:

- *Enforce password history.* Specify number of previous passwords to retain; range 0 to 24. System won't allow user to reuse a password in the history list. Setting of 0 turns off password history.

- *Maximum password age.* Days to use password before requiring user to specify new password.

- *Minimum password age.* Minimum days password must be used before it can be changed. Setting of 0 enables immediate change.

- *Minimum password length.* Minimum number of characters required in password. Setting of 0 allows for no password (not recommended). Use setting of 10 or higher for increased security.

- *Passwords must meet complexity requirements of the installed password filter.* Password must meet criteria, which includes not containing the username in the password and containing three of the following: English uppercase letters, English lowercase letters, Westernized Arabic numerals, and non-alphanumeric characters (!, @, #, and so on).

 TIP The default password filter is defined in the file Scecli.dll in \systemroot\System32. You can customize the filter by providing a custom Scecli.dll file, either by creating one yourself (requires programming ability) or acquiring one from a third-party vendor.

- *Store password using reversible encryption for all users in the domain.* Encrypt password.

Part
III

Ch
12

Account Lockout Policy

The Account Lockout Policy settings enable you to control how Windows 2000 treats any attempt to log on with a bad password. Defining these settings can help protect against password "guess attacks." Define these password policy settings through the local policy at `Computer Configuration\Windows Settings\Security Settings\Account Policies\ Account Lockout Policy`:

- *Account lockout threshold*. Specify number of invalid logon attempts that can occur before account is locked out. Default is 0 (lockout is disabled).
- *Account lockout duration*. Specify number of minutes account will remain locked out. Default is 30 minutes.
- *Reset account lockout counter after*. Specify number of minutes after which lockout counter is reset to 0. Default is 5 minutes.

Managing User Profiles

User profiles enable a user's desktop settings and other interface and operating parameters to be retained from session to session. If a user's profile is stored on a server on the domain, the user can have the same interface and settings regardless of which computer she uses to log on to the domain (called a *roaming profile*). In addition, profiles enable you to control the types of changes a user can make to her working environment. The following section provides an overview of profiles.

Understanding Profiles

A *profile* comprises settings stored in a special type of Registry file and a set of folders and shortcuts that create the user's working environment. When a user logs on, Windows 2000 reads the user's profile and structures the desktop according to the settings in the profile. These settings include such things as desktop colors, sounds, and other Control Panel settings; specific accessory application settings (Notepad, WordPad, and so on); network printer connections; and other user environment settings.

The first type of profile you can assign to a user is called a *personal profile*. The personal profile can be changed by the user from one logon session to another, subject to certain restrictions in the profile itself. This type of profile enables a user to make changes to his profile and retain those changes for future logon sessions.

The second type of profile is called a *mandatory profile*. A mandatory profile is almost identical to a personal profile, except that changes do not carry from one session to another. A user has the ability to change certain settings even with a mandatory profile, but those changes are not stored permanently in the user's profile. The profile reverts to its original state for the next logon session.

TIP The only real difference between a personal profile and a mandatory profile is the name of the Registry file. A personal profile has the file extension DAT, and a mandatory profile uses the file extension MAN. Profile files are explained in more detail in the next section.

If a user has no profile, Windows NT uses a *default profile* from the user's logon workstation. That profile is then saved as the user's profile (called the *local profile*) for future logon sessions.

Profiles serve three primary purposes:

■ They provide a unique user interface configuration for each user and allow that configuration to move with the user from workstation to workstation.

■ They enable users to share a single workstation but retain unique desktops.

■ They enable the administrator to control the types of changes a user can make to her working environment.

Table 12.4 lists settings stored in a user profile.

Table 12.4   User Profile Contents

Source	Settings
Windows Explorer	User-defined settings for Explorer
My Documents	User's My Documents folder
My Pictures	User's My Pictures folder
Favorites	User's Favorites folder
Mapped network drives	Network shares mapped to local drive IDs
My Network Places	User's My Network Places folder
Desktop contents	Items and shortcuts on user's desktop
Screen colors and fonts	User-specified desktop UI settings
Application data and Registry hive	Application data and user-specified Registry settings
Printer settings	Network printers and settings
Control Panel	User-specified changes made through Control Panel
Accessories	User-specified settings for Accessory programs
Windows 2000 applications	Per-user program settings
Help bookmarks	User-defined bookmarks in Help

Part
III
Ch
12

How Profiles Are Created and Stored

Profiles consist of a Registry file named NTuser.dat, which is a cached copy of the KKEY_CURRENT_USER portion of the Registry, and a user-specific directory structure. NTuser.dat contains settings that define the computer's hardware, installed software, and environment settings. The directory structure and associated shortcuts define the user's desktop environment and application environment.

Local user profiles are stored in a folder matching the user's name within the Documents and Settings folder. The Documents and Settings folder typically resides under the root of the drive containing the `systemroot` folder. The profile for a user named `joeb`, for example, would be stored in the folder `\Documents and Settings\joeb`.

When a user logs on, Windows 2000 checks the user's account to determine whether it contains a user profile path. If the path is available and the user's profile exists on the path, Windows 2000 opens and uses the profile. If no profile exists on the path or no path is specified, Windows 2000 creates a profile folder on the local computer for the user. Windows 2000 then copies the contents of the Default User profile folder to the user's profile folder. In addition, the contents of the All Users folder are used to further define the user's desktop. When the user logs off, any changes he has made to his working environment are stored in his profile folder and profile Registry file.

You specify the profile path in the Profile tab of the user's account properties. See the section "Setting Profile Properties" earlier in this chapter for more information.

Supporting Roaming Users

A *roaming user* is one who logs on to the network from more than one computer. For consistency, these users should use the same profile regardless of the logon location, giving them a consistent desktop and group of user settings from one logon session to the next. A *roaming user profile* ensures that consistency.

There is little difference between a local profile and a roaming user profile. The only difference is in where the profile is stored and how it is accessed. You can implement a roaming profile in one of three ways.

New Roaming Profile   In each of the three methods for creating a roaming profile, you rely on the user profile path to specify the location of the user's profile. This path must reside on a server to which the user will have access regardless of the logon location. You specify the profile path in the user's account when you create or modify the account as explained earlier in this chapter.

The first method for creating a roaming user profile is to only specify the profile path in the user's account and allow the user's profile to be created automatically from the default profile the first time the user logs on to the domain. Profile changes in subsequent logon sessions will be stored to the user's profile in the specified profile path.

Preconfigured Roaming Profile   You should create a profile for the user and copy it to the user's profile path if you don't want the default profile to be used to create the user's profile. When the user logs on, that preconfigured profile will be used. Note that you still must specify the path to the user's profile in his account. Profile changes in subsequent logon sessions will be stored to the user's profile.

N O T E   You can't copy a profile using Explorer or another file management utility. Instead, you
must use the System object in Control Panel to copy the profile. See the section "Copying
Profiles" later in this chapter for an explanation of how to copy profiles. ■

Mandatory Profile

If you want to restrict changes to a profile, create a *mandatory* profile. Specify the path to the
user's profile directory in his account. Then, copy a preconfigured profile to that folder.
Finally, rename the profile Registry file NTuser.dat to NTuser.man, turning the profile into a
mandatory profile. When the user logs on, Windows 2000 uses the mandatory profile to create the user's work environment. Although the user can make changes to his desktop (subject to restrictions in the profile), those changes are not stored in his profile when he logs off.

Creating a Profile

It's important to understand that there is no tool specifically for creating a user profile.
Instead, Windows 2000 creates the profile automatically when the user logs on (if none
exists). The user makes changes to his environment, which change the Registry settings that
define those elements. Therefore, the profile updates automatically (because it comprises the
applicable section of the Registry and the user's folders).

You "create" a user profile by logging on as the target user and modifying the desktop as
desired. When you log off, Windows 2000 stores the profile changes. You can create the profile on any computer, but remember that the hardware on the computer where you create the
profile might not match the hardware where the user logs on. Settings for display resolution
and color depth, in particular, could cause problems if the target computer doesn't adequately
support the settings in the profile.

After you create the profile, you can log on as Administrator and copy the user profile to the
desired server to define a roaming or mandatory profile for the user, as explained next.

Copying Profiles

You probably will want, on occasion, to copy profiles from one location to another. For example, you might need to copy a profile to a user's profile path on a network server so that profile will be applied the next time the user logs on. You can't copy a profile simply by using
Explorer or another file management utility. Instead, you must use the System object in
Control Panel.

To copy a profile, open the Control Panel and double-click System (or right-click My
Computer and choose Properties). Then click the User Profiles tab as shown in Figure 12.6.

From the list of stored user profiles, select the profile you want to copy. Then click Copy To.
In the Copy To dialog, type the path to the folder in which you want to copy the profile, or
click Browse to browse for the folder. Click Change if you want to specify users and groups
that are allowed to use the profile. By default, the user account under which the profile was
created can use the profile. Click OK when you're satisfied with the folder location.

Part

III

Ch

12

FIGURE 12.6
All profiles created on
the computer appear in
the User Profiles page.

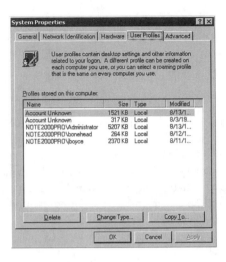

You also can define how Windows 2000 treats your roaming profile (applies only when you're logged on with a roaming profile). Selecting **R**oaming Profile causes Windows 2000 to download the profile from the server. Selecting **L**ocal Profile causes Windows 2000 to use the cached copy of the roaming profile on the local computer.

To define roaming profile behavior, click a profile and click **C**hange. On the Change Profile Type dialog, select either **R**oaming Profile or **L**ocal Profile.

Security Configuration Tool Set

Windows 2000 incorporates several MMC snap-ins to help you monitor and manage security. Of particular use for managing Windows 2000 Professional systems are the Security Templates and Security Configuration and Analysis snap-ins.

 The snap-ins discussed in this section are a subset of the Security Configuration Tool Set, a full set of snap-ins and applications that help you manage security on Windows 2000 systems. The snap-ins described here apply specifically to user and group security management on a Windows 2000 Professional computer (whether locally or in a domain). Other tools in the Tool Set help you analyze and configure other security settings. You'll find additional discussion of the Security Configuration Tool Set in Microsoft TechNet or on the Microsoft Web site at http://www.microsoft.com.

Security Templates Snap-In

Windows 2000 includes several security templates that make it easier to manage security settings. These templates, which are text files, are stored in *systemroot*\Security\Templates. Templates can define all security settings except IP Security (IPSec) and public key policies. The primary purpose for security templates is to provide a security framework for various situations and enable you to apply security settings quickly and easily in that situation. You also can use templates as a baseline to analyze security in a given situation.

For example, Windows 2000 includes templates for both basic and high security on a domain security, basic and high security for a workstation, basic and high security for a member server, and so on. If you wanted to easily configure a workstation for high security, for example, you would simply apply the predefined Hisecws template to the computer's group or local policy, which contains security settings predefined for that type of installation. You might first modify the template to tailor it to your needs.

You can use existing templates as-is, modify them, or use them to create new templates (or create templates from scratch). The template itself doesn't actually control security settings. Instead, you use the template either as a baseline against which you compare settings for a given computer or group policy object. Alternatively, you import the template into a group policy object to apply the settings in the template to the group policy.

Editing Security Templates The Security Templates MMC snap-in (see Figure 12.7) enables you to view and edit the contents of security templates. Add the Security Templates snap-in to any MMC console to work with template files. The Security Templates snap-in by default shows the contents of \systemroot\Security\Templates (as a hierarchical tree), but you can add paths to other folders as well. To do so, right-click Security Templates and choose New Template Search Path. The console prompts you to select the desired path and then adds a branch in the console for the new path.

FIGURE 12.7
The Security Templates snap-in is essentially a graphical interface for editing the security template INF text files.

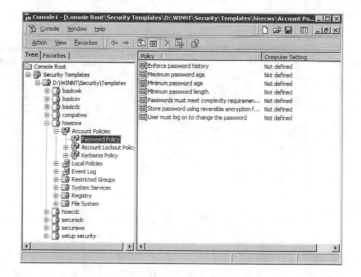

Part III

Ch 12

Security Templates imposes the same structure on all template files. Simply expand the desired template and modify settings as you would a group policy. Double-click a setting to view its properties, and configure it as needed. When you've configured the template the way you want it, right-click the template in the left tree and choose Save to save to the existing file or Save As to create a new security template.

TIP Remember that modifying a template file with the Security Templates snap-in doesn't actually modify security settings. It simply modifies the template file (the snap-in is really just a special-purpose text editor). You must apply the template to the local or group policy to apply its settings.

Creating a New Template You can create a new template if you prefer to configure all settings from scratch. Right-click the desired path in the tree (such as C:\WINNT\Security\ Templates) and choose New Template. You're prompted for the template name (the INF extension is appended automatically) and a description.

 TIP Right-click a template and choose Set Description to view or change its description.

Applying Settings with a Template You apply a template and its settings to a group policy using the Security Configuration and Analysis snap-in, discussed in the following section.

Security Configuration and Analysis Snap-In

The Security Configuration and Analysis snap-in enables you to analyze and review security settings for the local or a group policy or to apply settings from one or more templates to the selected object. You also can export settings to a template file. Figure 12.8 shows the Security Configuration and Analysis snap-in in use.

FIGURE 12.8
This snap-in compares current settings against a database of settings that you define.

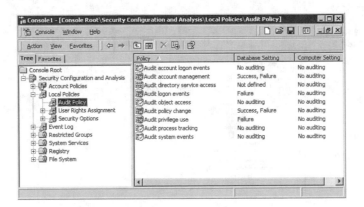

Within the snap-in you work with a security *database*. You can create and manage any number of databases, opening the one you need at any given point. The database serves as the baseline configuration against which you analyze the current settings and can also serve as the configuration you apply to the computer. You can import one or more template files into the database, either replacing existing settings with a single template or merging settings from multiple templates, as desired.

As indicated previously, you can use this snap-in to analyze the current system settings against the settings defined in the current database. You then can review the settings to identify potential problem areas where current settings don't match the database settings. The snap-in shows the current setting and database settings side-by-side. You can then change individual settings or apply the settings in the database to the system.

For example, assume that you have a computer that you believe was configured using the Basicws template (basic workstation security), but you're not sure. You want to check it against the Hisecws template (high security workstation) to identify potential security problems. So, you import the Hisecws template into the current database and then analyze the system. As Figure 12.8 illustrates, the database settings appear in one column with the current computer settings in an adjacent column. You then can review each setting, apply any desired changes to the database, and then apply the database settings to the system when you've finished reviewing. Alternatively, you can simply open the appropriate group policy in the Group Policy snap-in (such as the local policy) and make individual changes.

Defining the Database   You can open an existing database or create a new one. When you create a new database, you also typically import one or more templates into the database to define your baseline settings. Follow these steps to create a new database:

1. Open the Security Configuration and Analysis snap-in.
2. Right-click Security Configuration and Analysis, and then choose Open Database.
3. Specify a new database filename in the Open Database dialog and click Open. The snap-in displays the Import Template dialog.
4. Choose a template to import into the database and click Open.
5. Optional, to merge another template: Right-click Security Configuration and Analysis again and choose Import Template. Choose another template to merge into the database, deselect the Clear option (to cause a merge rather than replace), and then click Open.

Analyzing the System   After you define the baseline database, you're ready to analyze the system settings against the database. Follow these steps to analyze the system:

1. Open or create the desired database.
2. Right-click Security Configuration and Analysis and choose Analyze Computer Now.
3. Specify the name of the file where you want errors logged and click OK. The snap-in analyzes the system settings against the database.
4. Expand the branches you're interested in and compare settings. A green check in the icon beside each setting indicates consistency (a match). A red X indicates an inconsistency (mismatch). No icon indicates that the attribute was not part of the database and therefore was not analyzed.

Part
III

Ch
12

Configuring the System You can use the Security Configuration and Analysis snap-in to apply security settings to the local system on a global basis, applying all settings in the database to the system. Alternatively, you could open the local policy in the Group Policy snap-in and make individual changes.

Follow these steps to apply all settings in the loaded database to the local system policy:

1. Open or create the desired database.
2. Analyze the system.
3. Make any desired changes to settings. Double-click a setting, select Define This Policy in the Database, and then specify the desired setting. This defines the setting in the database only, not the local setting.
4. When you've configured the database as desired, right-click Security Configuration and Analysis, choose Configure Computer Now, and click OK.
5. Specify the log file for error logging and click OK.

Exporting the Database You might want to export a database to a security template file, particularly if you have spent a considerable amount of time analyzing and configuring the database settings. With the database exported to a template, you can later load that same template to apply to the same computer or to others. Follow these steps to export the database to a security template:

1. Configure the database settings as desired in the Security Configuration and Analysis snap-in.
2. Right-click Security Configuration and Analysis and choose Export Template.
3. Specify a filename and folder for the template INF file, and then click Save.

## CHAPTER 13

Managing and Sharing Workstation Resources

In this chapter

Understanding Permissions

Windows 2000 incorporates peer-to-peer networking, enabling computers to share resources such as folders, files, and printers with other users on the network. Although the presence of one or more Windows 2000 Server computers in a network can enhance security and resource sharing, even Windows 2000 Professional computers have extensive support for securely sharing their resources.

In Windows 2000, *permissions* and *rights* enable Windows 2000 to control which users have access to resources and what actions those users can perform.

> **N O T E** Don't confuse *rights* with *permissions*, which are different. A right applies to systemwide objects and tasks, and permissions apply to specific objects such as files and printers. ■

▶ **See** "Assigning Rights to Groups," **p. 222**

About Permissions

In Windows 2000, *permissions* play an important role in conjunction with user and group accounts to ensure a high level of security over resources such as folders, files, and printers. You can apply permissions in two different ways: through *share permissions* and *object permissions* (also called *NTFS permissions* for folders and files on NTFS volumes).

Object permissions control local access to the resource. For example, you might set the permissions on an NTFS folder so that the Users group has read-only access to the folder. Anyone in that group who logs on to the workstation locally is restricted to read-only access to that folder. (Object permissions also control access to resources across the LAN or Internet as explained later in this section.)

Share permissions determine the level of access remote users across the network have to the shared resource. Assume that you share a folder with Full Control, giving the Everyone group full control over the folder. Anyone connecting to the folder would then have full control over its contents, including the capability to read, write, and delete files and subfolders (subject to object permissions on the folder and its contents).

Object permissions and share permissions combine to provide improved security for shared resources. One type of permission does not take precedence over the other, but the most restrictive permission always becomes the effective permission when the permissions provide differing levels of access. For example, you might give Everyone Full Control through share permissions but grant individual users or groups the Read permission. For these individuals and groups, the Read permission would be effective because it is the more restrictive of the two.

Share permissions provide looser security than object permissions for the following reasons:

- Share permissions give the user the same level of access to all subdirectories and files within the shared folder.
- Share permissions have no effect for local access. (The user logs on at the computer.)

■ Share permissions can't be used to secure individual files, but instead can only be applied to folders.

Object permissions also play one other role: controlling access to local resources when the workstation is part of a domain. When you assign permissions to a resource, you can grant other members of the domain access to that resource by giving their domain accounts or global groups the necessary permissions.

N O T E The type of permissions you can apply to a folder or file depends on the file system being used: NTFS or FAT/FAT32. NTFS provides extended security features not supported on FAT volumes. FAT volumes do not support object permissions and only support limited share permissions. ■

By default, Full Control for Everyone gets applied to an NTFS folder when you share it. You can then use object permissions to fine-tune security for the folder and its contents. Think of it this way: Share permissions are the lock on the office door, and object permissions are the locks on the file cabinets. You could give each user or group specific share permissions (their own door key), but it's easier to manage the permissions at the real point of use (the file cabinet).

Table 13.1 lists standard NTFS object permissions, which represent combinations of specific types of access.

N O T E Standard permissions are slightly different in Windows 2000 from Windows NT. Although the same permissions are available, some no longer show up as basic permissions. These include Delete (D), Change Permissions (P), and Take Ownership (O). These permissions do appear on the advanced permissions tab, however. ■

Table 13.1   Standard NTFS Object Permissions

Permission	For a Folder, User Can	For a File, User Can
Full Control	Perform all actions	Perform all actions
Read (R)	Display folder names, attributes, owner, and permissions	Display file data, attributes, owner, and permissions
Write (W)	Add files and folders, change folder's attributes, and display owner and permission	Display owner and permissions, change file attributes, create data in and append data to a file
Read and Execute (X)	Display folder names, attributes, owner, and permissions; run files if executable	Display file data, attributes, owner; run file if executable
List Folder Contents	View folder contents	Not applicable

Part
III

Ch
13

TIP See the section "About Ownership" later in this chapter for an explanation of how ownership works and its impact on security.

Usually, you will use the standard NTFS permissions to secure resources. These standard NTFS permissions are combinations of the individual NTFS permissions and appear within the Security tab for the folder or file.

Table 13.2 lists individual NTFS permissions.

Table 13.2   Individual Object Permissions

Permission	For a Folder, User Can	For a File, User Can
*Traverse Folder/ Execute File	Move through folder to other folders or files	Run program
List Folder/Read Data	View file or subfolder	View data in name file
Read Attributes	View folder attributes	View file attributes
Read Extended Attributes	View extended folder attributes	View extendedfile attributes
Create Files/Write Data	Create files in folder	Write changes to/overwrite file
Create Folders/Append Data	Create subfolders	Append to end of file but not change, overwrite, or delete
Write Attributes	Change folder attributes	Change file attributes
Write Extended Attributes	Change folder extended attributes	Change file extended attributes
**Delete Subfolders and Files	Delete subfolders	Delete file
Delete	Delete folder	Delete file
Read Permissions	View folder permissions	View file permissions
Change Permissions	Change folder permissions	Change file permissions
Take Ownership	Take ownership of folder	Take ownership of file

Notes:
* Applies only when group or user not granted Bypass Traverse Checking right. When applied to a folder, it does not automatically enable execute for all files in folder.
** Allows deletion on subfolders and files even if Delete permission not granted on those objects.

Table 13.3 lists the object permissions that apply for specific standard permissions.

Table 13.3   Object Permissions in Standard Permissions

Permission	Full Control	Modify	Read and Execute	Read	Write
Traverse Folder/Execute File	✓	✓	✓		
List Folder/Read Data	✓	✓	✓	✓	
Read Attributes	✓	✓	✓	✓	

Permission	Full Control	Modify	Read and Execute	Read	Write
Read Extended Attributes	✓	✓	✓	✓	
Create Files/Write Data	✓	✓			✓
Create Folders/Append Data	✓	✓			✓
Write Attributes	✓	✓			✓
Write Extended Attributes	✓	✓			✓
Delete Subfolders and Files	✓				
Delete	✓	✓			
Read Permissions	✓	✓	✓	✓	✓
Change Permissions	✓				
Take Ownership	✓				

On a FAT file system, you can assign the No Access, Read, Change, and Full Control share permissions to a shared folder, but you cannot apply permissions to specific files on a FAT file system. Instead, files are subject to the share permissions applied to the directory that contains them.

Perhaps more important is the fact that you can't set object permissions on directories or files on a FAT file system. This limitation essentially makes it impossible to provide any degree of local protection for FAT volumes, although you still can protect FAT volumes from unauthorized access by remote users. If a user can log on to a computer, he can gain full access to any folder or file in a FAT volume on that computer.

A set of additional permissions enable you to control access to printers. These printer-related permissions are as follows:

- *No Access*. Prevents any access to printer and its queue.
- *Print*. Prints to printer, but can't change queue or any other printer properties.
- *Manage Documents*. Enables user to control settings for individual documents in the queue and to pause, resume, restart, and delete documents in a queue. Does not provide print permission, which must be granted separately.
- *Full Control*. Gives user complete control over a printer, including printing and managing documents. User also can delete a printer and change its properties.

N O T E Additional permissions apply in specific situations such as within the Active Directory. This chapter focuses primarily on NTFS and printer object permissions because those are the ones you'll deal with most often under Windows 2000 Professional. ■

▶ **See** "Printing," **p. 131**

Part
III

Ch

13

About Inheritance

Permissions can be *inherited* by a child object from a parent object. In the case of resource sharing, this means that object permissions set for a folder can be inherited by subfolders and files. Subfolders and files by default inherit the object permissions you apply to the parent folder. You can disable inheritance at the folder and file level, which enables you to assign permissions on those child objects that are different from the parent folder.

About Ownership

In Windows 2000, each folder and file has an *owner*. The owner is the user who creates a folder or file. If the user is a member of the Administrators group, then the Administrators group becomes the owner. The owner always has the ability to assign and change permissions on a folder or file that she owns.

It's also important to understand that even though the Administrators group might have complete access to the system and its contents, its members might not have access to specific folders and files if the owner of those resources has configured their permissions to exclude the Administrators group. An administrator can, however, take ownership of the resource to gain access to it, if necessary.

Sharing Disk Resources

As discussed earlier, Windows 2000 offers two mechanisms for setting security on folders and files on your workstation, thereby making it possible for you to control who can access those resources. The first of these mechanisms, NTFS object permissions, enables you to control who has access to resources locally on your computer and also to refine control of access by network users.

> **CAUTION**
>
> Before sharing a folder, be certain to set its object permissions and permissions for subfolders and files to provide the necessary security. This prevents unauthorized access to the share's contents while you are configuring its security settings (or in case you forget to set the object permissions after sharing the folder).

Setting Object Permissions on NTFS Folders and Files

The easiest way to set object permissions on an NTFS folder or file is through Windows Explorer. Right-click the object, choose Properties, and then click Security to access the Security tab (see Figure 13.1).

The Security tab shows the object permissions for the selected folder or file. Whether subfolders receive displayed permissions (in the case of a folder) depends on the settings for each subfolder for inheritable permissions. Unlike in Windows NT, you do not have the option on the Security property tab to directly apply the selected permissions to all files and subfolders under the selected folder.

FIGURE 13.1
Specify who can access the folder through the Security tab in the folder's Properties sheet.

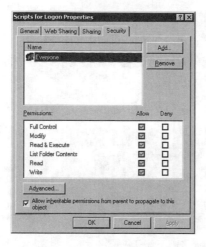

Allow and deny permissions by checking the appropriate boxes in the Allow or Deny columns. As you make selections, you might notice that some changes happen automatically. Deny Write permission, for example, and the Allow column boxes for the Full Control and Modify permissions automatically deselect.

The setting Allow Inheritable Permissions from Parent to Propagate to This Object determines whether the object permissions for the parent folder are inherited. Select this setting if you want permissions to be inherited from the parent folder. Deselect this object if you want to set permissions differently from the parent folder.

When you deselect this option, Windows 2000 gives you two options:

- **Copy.** Copy existing inherited permissions from the parent to the current folder or file. You can then modify permissions on the object.

- **Remove.** Remove all inherited permissions and retain only explicit permissions set at the object level. You then can modify permissions on the object.

 TIP A gray check in the Allow or Deny column indicates that the selected permission is inherited. A black check indicates that an explicit permission is set at the object level. You can't change an individual inherited permission but instead must copy the existing inheritable permissions to the object and then modify them explicitly.

Part
III

Ch
13

Click OK or Apply to apply the new permissions when you're satisfied with your selections.

Setting Advanced Permissions

In many cases, the standard permissions provided in the Security tab suffice to adequately secure a folder or file. In special cases, however, you might want to apply advanced permissions to fine-tune security on the resource.

Open the Security tab for the object and click Advanced to access the Access Control Settings dialog for the object, as shown in Figure 13.2.

FIGURE 13.2
Configure advanced object permissions, auditing, and ownership through the Access Control Settings sheet.

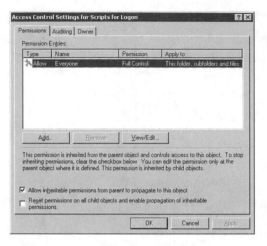

The groups and users who have permissions assigned to the resource, along with those permissions, appear in Permission Entries. Select an object and click View/Edit to edit the permission through the Permission Entry sheet. Figure 13.3 explains the available options.

FIGURE 13.3
Configure permissions for an object through the Permission Entry dialog.

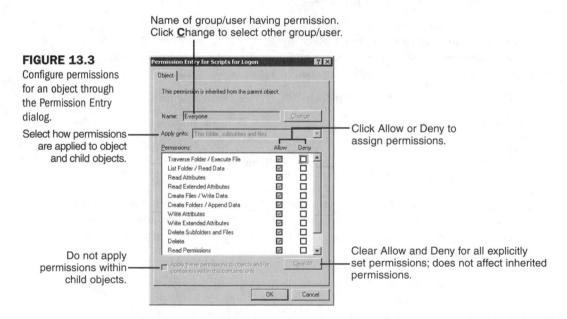

Name of group/user having permission. Click Change to select other group/user.

Select how permissions are applied to object and child objects.

Click Allow or Deny to assign permissions.

Do not apply permissions within child objects.

Clear Allow and Deny for all explicitly set permissions; does not affect inherited permissions.

Sharing Folders and Files

Setting NTFS permissions on folders or files doesn't make them available to other users across the network. You must share a folder to make its contents available to other users on the LAN. The process of sharing a folder includes specifying the share permissions. You might also want to assign NTFS permissions to further refine security for the shared folder or its contents.

To share a folder, follow these steps:

1. Locate the folder in Explorer and set object permissions (NTFS folders volumes only) as needed to control access.

2. Right-click the folder in Explorer and choose Sharing to access the Sharing tab (see Figure 13.4).

FIGURE 13.4

Configure sharing options for a folder through the Sharing tab in its Properties sheet.

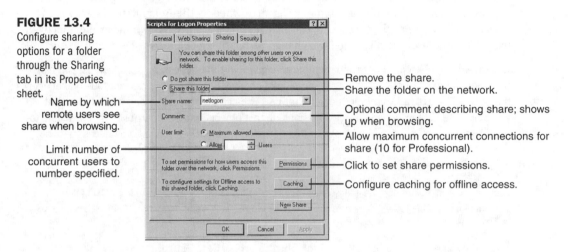

Name by which remote users see share when browsing.

Limit number of concurrent users to number specified.

Remove the share.
Share the folder on the network.
Optional comment describing share; shows up when browsing.
Allow maximum concurrent connections for share (10 for Professional).
Click to set share permissions.
Configure caching for offline access.

3. Choose options from the Sharing tab.

4. Choose OK to close the folder's properties and begin sharing the folder.

TIP

The easiest way to combine share and NTFS permissions to control shared resource access is to assign the share permission Full Control to Everyone (or Authenticated Users for somewhat tighter security) and then use NTFS object permissions to assign varying levels of security to specific users and groups. Set the object permissions first to ensure security.

Normally, the share name you specify is the name users see when they browse the workstation for shared resources. End the name with a dollar sign, such as **share$**, to hide the resource from the browse list. Users with appropriate permissions can connect to and use the resource, but they must specify it explicitly by name (because it doesn't show up in the browse list).

The User limit settings enable you to determine the number of current connections to the share. Windows 2000 Professional computers are limited to 10 concurrent network connections, so choosing Maximum Allowed means that 10 users can access the share at the same time. Use the Allow option to reduce the number of concurrent connections.

The Permissions button enables you to define the share permissions. Remember that share permissions control the level of access users have to the share across the network. Object permissions for the folder and its contents will further affect users' access.

Part
III

Ch

13

N O T E See the section, "Configuring and Managing Offline Files," later in this chapter for an explanation of caching and offline access. ■

Changing Ownership

The user who creates an object such as a folder or file is the *owner* of that object. Objects created by a member of the Administrators group are owned by the Administrators group. The owner of an object has the ability to perform all acts on the object, which means he effectively has full control over the object and can change permissions, delete the object, and so on.

If your individual account or group membership gives you the necessary permissions, you can take ownership of an object. Taking ownership of an object essentially gives you full control over the object. For example, assume that another user created an object on your workstation, but you need to delete or change the permissions on that object, and the other user isn't available to do it. In this case, you would take ownership of the object and then modify it as necessary.

> **CAUTION**
>
> Taking ownership of an object can have consequences for the previous owner, including making the resource unavailable to her. Make sure you really need to take ownership of an object before doing so.

To take ownership of an object, open the object's properties. Click the Security tab and then click Advanced. Click the Owner tab. The dialog shows your current logon account and, if you're logged on as Administrator, also lists the Administrators group. Click your logon account and, if you want to take ownership of all child objects, select Replace Owner on Subcontainers and Objects. Then click OK or Apply.

N O T E If you don't have the required permission on an object to take ownership, Windows 2000 displays an error message indicating that your attempt to take ownership failed. ■

Auditing Resource Access and Use

An important aspect of securing resources is monitoring their use. Monitoring resource use helps you determine whether unauthorized users are attempting to access the resource and can also identify other potential security problems. It also can point out access problems with a resource.

The mechanism that Windows 2000 provides for monitoring resource access is called *auditing*. Auditing causes the success or failure of events that you specify to be logged to the security log on your workstation. You can view the security log through the Event Viewer.

▶ **See** "Viewing Event Logs," **p. 376**

N O T E You can monitor folder and file events only on NTFS partitions. ■

Auditing enables you to track several types of activities on your workstation. These include the following:

- *Logging On and Off.* Audit to determine who is using your workstation and when. Also monitor to track unauthorized logon attempts.
- *Use of Folder and File Resources.* Audit these to track unauthorized attempts to access shared resources, as well as to track resource use.
- *Use of User Rights.* Audit to track system changes performed by a user.
- *User and Group Management.* Audit to track changes to users and groups on your workstation.
- *Security Policy Changes.* Audit to track changes made to user rights or the audit policy (audit settings).
- *Restarting or Shutting Down the System.* Audit to track startup and shutdown of the system, which could indicate attempts to tamper with your workstation.
- *Process Tracking.* Audit to determine which programs are being used on your computer.

You enable auditing by defining an *audit policy* in the local security policy at Security Settings\Local Policies\Audit Policy. This process consists of turning on auditing and specifying which types of events will be audited (see Figure 13.5). Group policies above the local policy, if any, can override the local audit policy.

FIGURE 13.5
You can enable auditing of success, failure, or both for each type of object.

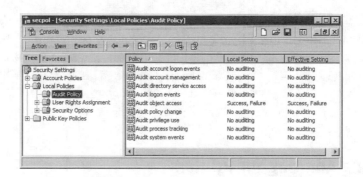

Part
III

Ch
13

After turning on auditing of object access through the local policy, you can configure auditing of specific objects. It's important to understand that turning on auditing in the local policy for object access doesn't actually cause any auditing to take place; it simply makes it possible. You have to also turn on auditing at the individual objects you want to monitor. So, it's a two-step process: Enable auditing globally for specific types of objects, and then turn on auditing at individual objects. Enabling the other auditing categories (account logon events, account management, and so on) in the group policy does cause auditing to take place without further configuration.

Configuring Auditing for Files and Folders

After you have defined the audit policy, follow these steps to configure auditing on an object (folders and files are used as the example):

1. Open in Explorer the properties for the folder or file you want to audit. Click the Security tab, click Advanced, and then click the Auditing tab to access the Auditing properties (see Figure 13.6).

FIGURE 13.6
Add groups and users whose use of the object you want to audit.

List groups and users to audit.

Allow or prevent auditing properties of parent to be inherited.

Reset existing auditing properties on child objects and propagate settings to children.

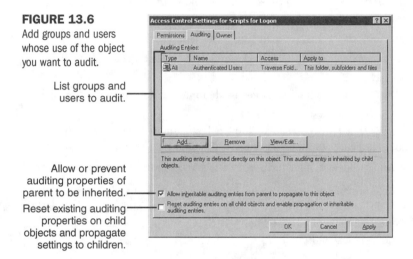

2. Click Add, select groups and/or users you want to audit for the selected object, and then click OK to display the Auditing Entry dialog (see Figure 13.7).

3. Select and deselect in the Successful and Failed columns for each access type to define which types of events are audited for the selected group or user, and then click OK. Figure 13.7 describes options in the Auditing Entry dialog.

4. Click OK on the Access Control Settings dialog, and then close the object's properties sheet.

Configuring Auditing for Printers

You configure auditing of printers in much the same way that you do for folders and files. After you enable auditing of File and Object Access in the audit policy, open the printer's Properties sheet. Choose the Security tab and then choose Advanced. Choose the Auditing tab and configure auditing as described previously for folders and files.

N O T E Every object has different auditable events; naturally, the events you can audit for a printer are different from those for a folder or file. ▪

Group or user being audited.

FIGURE 13.7
Specify the events and success/failure for each that you want to audit.

Specify how auditing applied object and children.

Type of event audited.

Apply selections to Apply **o**nto list and all applicable children.

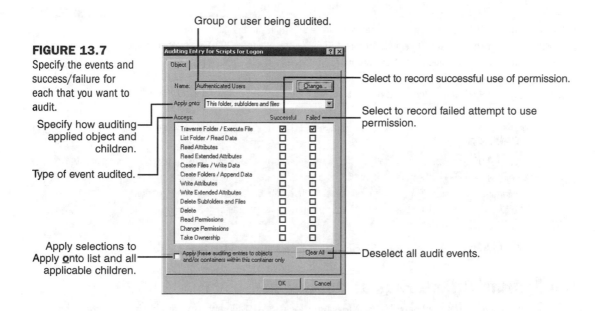

Select to record successful use of permission.

Select to record failed attempt to use permission.

Deselect all audit events.

Configuring and Managing Offline Files

Windows 2000 incorporates a new feature called *offline files* that enables you to work with shared network folders and their contents even when you're not connected to the network. For example, you can continue to work with files from the company file server from your notebook PC even when you're a thousand miles away in a plane at 35,000 feet. How? By *caching* those files on your computer when you are connected to the network.

In a nutshell, here's how offline files work: When you're connected to the network, you browse for a shared folder that you want to use offline. You right-click the folder and choose Make A**v**ailable Offline. Windows 2000 copies the folder to your workstation, retaining on your computer the permissions set at the server for the folder and any subfolders and files in it.

TIP The client user must have the necessary permissions to access a folder or file before it can be cached to his computer for offline use.

In effect, Windows 2000 copies the files to a hidden folder on your computer and makes them appear as if they were still located in the original location (such as in My Network Places). When you're disconnected from the network, you can continue to work with the shared folder, but you're actually working with the local, cached copy. When you reconnect to the network, Windows 2000 synchronizes the changes (automatic or manual, depending on how you configure Offline Files).

Part
III

Ch
13

TIP   Windows 2000 by default places the offline folders and files in the hidden folder
systemroot\CSC (CSC stands for *Client Side Cache*). Windows 2000 renames and tracks file
names for offline folders and files, so you might not recognize the contents of the CSC folder. You can
use the Cachemov.exe program included with the Windows 2000 Resource Kit to move the cache
to a different location, if desired (not enough space on the system drive, for example).

CAUTION

Before you go wild and start making shared resources available offline on your computer, consider that
doing so actually copies the contents of the selected shared resource to your computer. You probably
won't like the results if you make a folder available offline that contains several hundred Mb of data
because that data will all be copied to your computer's client-side cache folder.

Windows 2000 by default enables offline access to any folders you share.

Configuring Offline Files at the Server

Any system that supports Server Message Block (SMB) file and printer sharing can share its
resources offline. These include Windows 2000, Windows 9x, and Windows NT 4.0, but excludes
Novell NetWare networks. Only Windows 2000, however, offers you the capability to configure
any Offline Files settings at the server (where the resource is shared). This means you can't disable offline access to a shared folder on a Windows 9x or Windows NT 4.0 computer; if it's
shared, other users can cache it on their local computers. On a Windows 2000 computer, however, you can selectively disable offline access to a shared folder. Users who right-click such a
share do not see the Make Available Offline command in the share's context menu.

N O T E   Don't confuse the generic term *server* with Windows 2000 Server. A Windows 2000
Professional computer can act as a peer server, as can Windows 9x and Windows NT
Workstation computers.

Server-Side Cache Settings   On a Windows 2000 computer, you can configure caching settings on a
share-by-share basis. You can configure each shared folder for one of three cache settings:

- *Automatic Caching for Documents.* Files the user opens are automatically downloaded to
  the client's cache, and older copies are automatically deleted. The server version of the
  file is always opened if available. Recommended for folders containing user documents.

- *Automatic Caching for Programs.* Files opened by the user are automatically downloaded to the client's cache, and older copies are automatically deleted. The cached
  copy is always opened even if the server copy is available to reduce network traffic.
  Recommended for folders containing read-only documents or programs.

- *Manual Caching for Documents.* Remote users must manually specify files they want
  made available offline. The server version of the file is always opened if available.

Open the shared folder's properties and click the Sharing tab. Click Caching and specify the desired cache option.

Disabling Offline Caching for a Shared Folder

On Windows 2000 computers, you can remove offline caching ability from a shared folder, preventing clients from making the folder available offline (caching it on their computers). You should disable caching on any folders that contain sensitive data that you allow users to access over the network but don't want replicated anywhere else. You might disable caching on folders you feel don't need to be cached or where caching could lead to confusion or unsynchronized data.

To disable offline caching, preventing a shared folder from being made available offline, open the Sharing tab of the folder's Properties sheet, and then click Caching. Deselect Allow Caching of Files in This Shared Folder, then click OK, and close the folder's property dialog.

Configuring Offline Files at the Client

Caching shared files on your computer, making them available when your computer is offline, is a two-step process. First, you need to enable offline files on your computer. To do so, open My Computer (or any local folder) and choose Tools, Folder Options. Choose the Offline Files tab. Configure settings using Figure 13.8 as a guide, and then click OK.

FIGURE 13.8
Configure offline file options for your computer Offline Files tab of the Folder Options sheet.

Synchronize offline files at logoff; otherwise, requires manual synchronization.

Set frequency for reminder balloons.

Click to delete offline files.

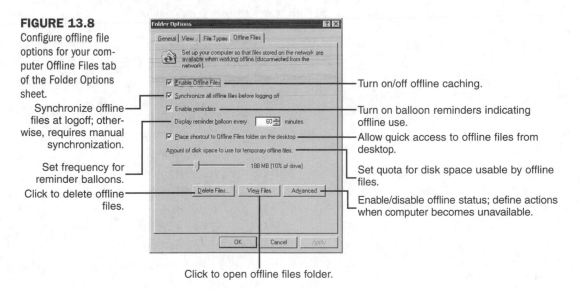

Turn on/off offline caching.

Turn on balloon reminders indicating offline use.

Allow quick access to offline files from desktop.

Set quota for disk space usable by offline files.

Enable/disable offline status; define actions when computer becomes unavailable.

Click to open offline files folder.

Part
III

Ch
13

After you have enabled and configured the use of offline files on your computer, browse to the shared folder you want to use offline. Right-click the share and choose Make Available Offline. Windows 2000 prompts you to specify how to handle subfolders if the shared folder contains them. Choose Yes to cache the shared folder and all its subfolders. Choose No to cache only the root of the share. Then click OK.

You can click Advanced on the Offline Files tab to configure advanced settings that determine how your system reacts when a network connection is lost. You configure the setting globally but can specify exceptions when specific computers become unavailable. For example, you might want to work with offline files most of the time but not when a connection to a specific server is lost.

The following list explains the controls on the Offline Files—Advanced Settings dialog:

- *Notify Me and Begin Working Offline.* When remote connection becomes unavailable, display notification and begin working with cached files offline.

- *Never Allow my Computer to Go Offline.* When remote connection becomes unavailable, display notification but do not begin working offline. Network files might become inaccessible.

- *Add.* Click to add an exception for when a specific connection is lost. You can specify either of the previously listed options.

- *Edit.* Select an exception and click Edit to change its behavior.

- *Remove.* Select an exception and click this to remove the exception.

PART IV

The Administrative Tools

System Backup and Disaster Recovery

Overview

Although today's computers are very reliable, hardware failures still occur. User error also is a possibility. Either situation can lead to accidentally lost or corrupted files. So, having backup copies of your documents is particularly important. Because the process for installing Windows 2000 and your applications can be a lengthy one, having a backup of your entire system also is important.

> **CAUTION**
>
> Backup media sets should be stored offsite whenever possible to safeguard the media. In the event of a catastrophe onsite (fire, etc.), having the media offsite ensures that your backups will not be destroyed along with your file system.

Windows 2000 includes a utility program called Backup that enables you to back up your system to a tape storage device or file. You can place the backup file on a local drive, network volume, or removable media (diskette, Zip disk, etc.).

Backup also provides a mechanism for backing up your *system state data*—a collection of various files and databases that define the system's configuration. It's important to have your system state data backed up in order to ensure a complete backup and the capability to fully restore your system.

N O T E For more detailed information regarding system state data, refer to the section, "System Repair and Recovery," later in this chapter. ▪

Should You Make Backups?

In a word, "yes!" Even casual home users can benefit from a backup and recovery plan. (Do you want to lose your banking data or great American novel?) For business and corporate users, a backup strategy can literally mean life or death to your business. Some of your data is irreplaceable or could be so difficult and time-consuming to replace that it puts you out of business. What if you suddenly lost your entire customer list? Could you re-create it easily? Would you have the staff or time to do it?

Even the loss of a job in progress can have a major impact on your business. Although you might be able to re-create the data, you're losing valuable time that could be spent on completing the job or handling new business. A day spent re-creating a job is a day's lost profit.

Choosing a Backup and Recovery Plan

Choosing a good backup strategy is an important step in planning for disaster recovery. Unless you are prepared to completely reinstall your workstation, including operating system and all software, you should have a full system backup. Use additional backups to keep your backup set current and back up important documents and files.

Here are some tips to help you define a backup strategy:

- Separate documents and program files so you can easily back up documents without backing up programs (which seldom change).
- Back up important documents regularly. Save an extra copy of important documents to disk or other removable media whenever you make changes to the documents.
- In a business environment daily backups are the norm. Do a full backup weekly and an incremental or differential backup daily.
- Back up system state data along with a full backup. This enables you to restore your system in the event of a catastrophic failure.
- Make a backup prior to all major system changes. Back up system state data before installing any new software or device. Perform a full backup prior to major changes like installing new hard drives.
- Perform at least one test restore to make sure you can restore data that you've backed up, ensuring that your storage device works properly.

Running Backup

To open Backup, choose Start, Programs, Accessories, System Tools, Backup. Figure 14.1 shows the Backup program's interface.

FIGURE 14.1
The Backup program welcome.

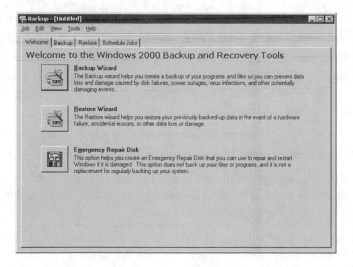

Part
IV

Ch
14

The Backup program interface comprises a tabbed window. The Welcome tab provides quick access to automated Backup tasks including wizards that help automate the backup and restore processes.

The Backup and Restore tabs each contain two areas—one that displays the drive or tape directory structure and another for selecting individual items such as files. Figure 14.2 shows the Backup page.

FIGURE 14.2

The Backup page.

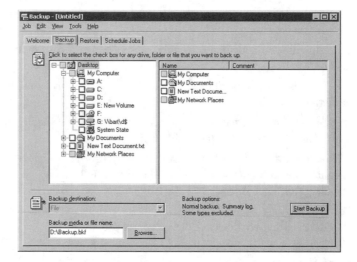

Following are some important features of the Windows 2000 Backup program:

- Back up and restore files from and to local and remote drives. Backup supports NTFS and FAT volumes. Files backed up from a Windows 2000 NTFS partition should be restored only to a Windows 2000 NTFS partition to avoid potential loss of data (because of structural changes in NTFS from Windows NT 4.0.)
- Verify files during the backup process to ensure an accurate backup copy.
- Support for standard backup methods including *normal*, *copy*, *incremental*, *differential*, and *daily copy* (explained later in this chapter).
- Span multiple tapes with file sets and files.
- Use batch files to automate backup, including scheduling unattended backups.
- Status logging, enabling you to monitor Backup's operations.

These features indicate that Backup supports several types of backup methods. These backup methods enable you to define how the program backs up files. These backup methods are described in the following sections.

TIP Prior to purchasing an offline storage device, check the Windows 2000 Hardware Compatibility List (HCL) to determine if the tape drive is supported by Backup. All tape drives supported by Windows 2000 are supported by Backup.

Microsoft's Web Site

`http://www.microsoft.com/hcl`

Normal

This option is most useful for creating a complete backup of a drive. The first type of backup operation on any volume should generally be a normal backup to ensure that the entire volume is backed up. A normal backup backs up all selected files regardless of the files' archive bit. The archive bit is then cleared to indicate that the files have been backed up.

Copy

Copy is useful when you want to back up files without affecting the archive bit. For example, you might want to perform an unscheduled backup of a small selection of files outside of your normal, routine backup schedule. This method backs up all selected files regardless of the state of the archive bit. Unlike a normal backup, however, copy does not reset the archive bit, so the backup will not affect subsequent, incremental, or differential backup operations.

Incremental

Incremental backups are typically used in combination with normal backups. Incremental backs up all selected files that have been modified since the last time the file was backed up and clears the archive bit of those files to indicate that they have been backed up. Figure 14.3 shows a typical backup scheme that uses incremental backups daily in concert with a normal backup once a week to provide a complete backup set.

FIGURE 14.3
Example of incremental backups.

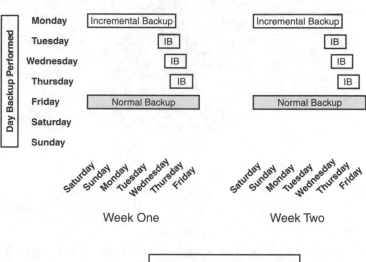

Part
IV

Ch
14

In order to restore a system from an incremental backup set, you first restore the normal backup from the previous backup set (last week), and then restore each of the incremental backups. In this example, if the system failed on Saturday, you would restore Friday's backup, because it backed up the entire system. If the system failed on Wednesday, you'd restore the full backup from Friday, plus any incremental backups that were made up through Wednesday.

Incremental backups take a relatively small amount of time to create, because only those files that have changed since the last backup are put on tape. Their disadvantage is that you have to use several tapes to restore the system (in this example, possibly five tapes).

Differential

Differential backs up files that have been modified since the last backup but does not change the archive bit. So, assuming that a normal backup is done on Friday and a file is modified Monday morning, differential backs up these modifications Monday evening. The file also will be backed up every day until the next normal backup. Figure 14.4 shows a typical differential backup scheme.

FIGURE 14.4

A typical differential
backup scheme.

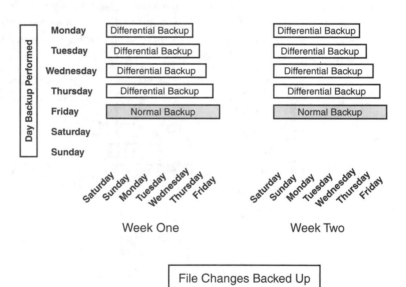

The advantage of using a differential backup scheme is that you need to restore from only two media: the last normal backup followed by the latest differential backup. The disadvantage is that you use more media space and therefore potentially more media. Also, the backup process takes longer because you are backing up more files more often than with an incremental backup.

Daily

Daily is most useful for backing up files in between the usual scheduled backups. Daily backs up only those files that have been modified on the date the backup is performed. It does not reset the archive bit. You might use daily, for example, to perform a "safety" backup prior to installing new software.

Media Rotation

You generally will want to have at least two complete backup sets—one set from the last successful backup period and the current backup set. Why not use the same set each week? If you experience a problem with some of the media or a daily backup, you have destroyed your chances of completely rebuilding the file system because your backup set is incomplete.

N O T E Having more than two sets is advantageous if you can afford the media and have a safe place to store it. For example, your system might get infected by a virus, but you might not realize that fact for a month. Having a backup set from prior to the point the system is infected enables you to restore to an uninfected system. ■

One of the simplest tape rotation schemes is the two-set rotation because you use two media sets to protect your file system; you use one set one week and the other set the next week. With this scheme you always have at least one week's worth of secure backups. Figure 14.5 shows a typical two-set rotation scheme.

FIGURE 14.5
A typical two-set rotation scheme.

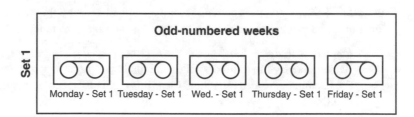

Odd-numbered weeks

Set 1

Monday - Set 1   Tuesday - Set 1   Wed. - Set 1   Thursday - Set 1   Friday - Set 1

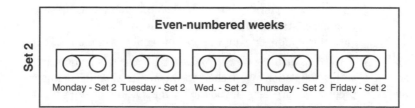

Even-numbered weeks

Set 2

Monday - Set 2   Tuesday - Set 2   Wed. - Set 2   Thursday - Set 2   Friday - Set 2

Part
IV

Ch
14

You can use other schemes as well, depending on the number of media sets you are willing to manage and how critical your data backup needs are. For most workstation environments, however, some variation of the two-set rotation is fine.

In any media rotation, some media will be used more than others. The media you use for the normal backup each week, for example, will see much more use than any media used for incremental back-ups. The more you use a media, the more wear it experiences. Within your backup scheme, you might want to rotate media within a set. As you begin using a previous tape set as the current set, for example, rotate the tapes up or back a day. Make the old Friday tape the new Monday tape. Old Tuesday becomes new Wednesday, and so on. This will ensure relatively even wear on all the tapes. Make sure to relabel the tapes accordingly.

Configuring Backup

Setup installs Backup automatically when you install Windows 2000; so, typically the only thing you need to do to begin backing up your file system is to configure your tape drive(s) and Backup program. See Chapter 10, "Exploring the Control Panel," for tape configuration tips.

▶ **See** "Setting Add/Remove Hardware Object," **p. 157**

Setting Backup Options

Backup offers several options you can configure to specify how Backup looks and performs. To configure these options, choose <u>T</u>ools, <u>O</u>ptions. The following sections explain the various properties and settings for Backup.

General   The General tab contains several options that define the way Backup appears and functions. You can use these options to control a wide range of functions:

- *Compute selection information before backup and restore operations.* Enable this to have Backup display the number of files and total byte count of selected files prior to starting the backup or restore operation. Clear this option to speed up backup or restore operation time.

- *Use the catalogs on the media to speed up building restore catalogs on disk.* Choose this to have Backup use the catalogs already on the backup media (tape or file) to build the on-disk catalog for the restore operation. If you are using several tapes from a set and the tape containing the catalog is missing or the catalog for a backup set is damaged, clear this option. Backup will scan the contents of the media to build a new catalog.

- *Verify data after the backup completes.* Choose this if you want Backup to verify the data at the completion of a backup operation. Clearing this option speeds up the backup process but presents the possibility that backup errors will not be identified, leading to an incomplete or faulty backup set.

- *Back up the contents of mounted drives.* Mounted drives are volumes that are attached to an empty NTFS folder and are assigned a label or name instead of a drive letter. Choose this to have the Backup program back up the contents of mounted drives. Clear this option to back up only the path information for the mounted drive.

- *Show alert message when I start Backup and Removable Storage Management is not running.* Choose this to have Backup notify you if the Removable Storage Management service is not running when you start Backup.

- *Show alert message when I start Backup and there is compatible import media available.* Enable this to have Backup notify you if importable media is available at startup in the Removable Storage Import pool. If you typically back up to a floppy disk, hard disk, or other removable media, you can clear this option.

- *Show alert message when new media is inserted into Removable Storage.* Choose this to have Backup notify you when new media is inserted into a unit managed by Removable Storage Management.

- *Always move new import media to the backup media pool.* Choose this to have Backup move new imported media automatically into backup pools.

Restore   The Restore tab offers a handful of options that control the way Backup handles restore operations:

- *Do not replace the file on my computer.* Backup will not restore a file if the file being copied from the backup set already exists on your computer.

- *Replace the file on disk only if the file on disk is older.* If a file being copied from the backup set already exists on your computer, Backup will restore the copy from the backup set only if the copy on your computer is older than the one being restored from the backup set.

- *Always replace the file on my computer.* Backup will always replace the file on the computer with the copy being restored from tape, regardless of the age or currency of both files.

Backup Type   Use the Backup Type tab to specify the type of backup operation Backup will use as the default. Select the desired type from the Default Backup Type drop-down list. You can override the default type when you create and schedule a backup job.

Backup Log   The Backup Log tab contains options that enable you to specify how Backup handles logging of operations. The options on the Backup Log tab are self-explanatory.

Exclude Files   The Exclude Files tab (see Figure 14.6) lets you specify certain files for Backup to exclude from the current backup operation. You can specify exclusions that apply to two types of files: those owned by all users and those owned only by you. The top list on the Exclude Files tab lists files that are excluded for all users. The bottom one lists files that are excluded for the user who is currently logged on (you).

Part

IV

Ch

14

FIGURE 14.6

The Exclude Files tab.

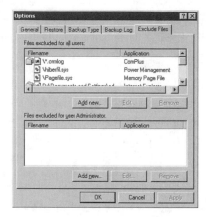

Click Add New to add files to be excluded for all users. To add files to be excluded that belong to you, click Add New. Either action displays the Add Excluded Files dialog (see Figure 14.7).

FIGURE 14.7

The Add Excluded Files dialog.

Registered File Type lists all file types currently registered with Windows 2000. Select files from the list to exclude that type of file, or type a file filter in the Custom File Mask box (such as *.exe to exclude all executables).

 TIP Although you can add files to the list of files to be excluded for all users regardless of your group membership, the files in this list will be excluded only if a member of the Administrators group performs the backup.

Use the Applies to Path text box to specify the path to which the file mask applies. Using C:\, for example, would restrict the file exclusion mask to the root folder of drive C. If the Applies to all subfolders box is selected, the file exclusion mask applies to all subfolders under the folder specified by the Applies to path box.

TIP Click **B**rowse to browse for the path level at which you want to begin excluding files from the backup operation.

Viewing and Selecting Files

One common task you will perform in Backup is to select which folders and files to include in a backup set. The left side of the Backup window contains a hierarchical tree of the volumes on your computer, your documents folder, and network resources (refer to Figure 14.2).

Selecting Files for Backup

Use these methods to select files for backup:

■ Click the check box beside an item to select it and everything underneath its branch. For example, click beside a drive's icon to select all folders and files on that drive.

■ Click the plus sign (+) or minus sign (-) beside a folder to expand or collapse the folder's branch so that you can view subfolders and files, and select individual folders and files if desired.

Selecting Files for Restore

When you are restoring files, you'll first select which files to restore. Open Restore (see Figure 14.8) to view the backup sets stored on the current tape. Locate the tape device containing the file(s) to be restored, and then double-click the tape icon to read a catalog from the tape.

FIGURE 14.8
The Restore tab.

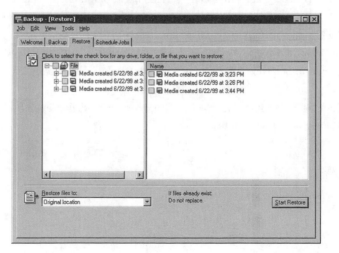

Part
IV

Ch

14

To restore everything on the tape or in the file, place a check beside the media name in the left pane. To restore selected folders and files, expand the directory structure in the left pane and select files and folders as desired in either the left or right pane.

Saving File Selections

If you back up the same group of folders and files regularly, you'll probably want to save the selection by name so you can restore the selection quickly, without having to reselect the items.

After you create the selection set you want to save, specify a filename for the current selection set by choosing Job, Save Selections.

Later when you want to use that same selection set, choose Job, Load Selections, and select the desired set. You can replace the currently opened selection set with the current file selection using Job, Save Selections.

Backing Up Files

Although the process of backing up files is simple, the Backup program includes a wizard to help automate the process. This section explains how to back up files using the manual method. The wizard automates the process of selecting files, options, etc. These options are explained in this section.

To begin the manual backup from the Backup tab in Backup follow these steps:

1. Use a saved selection list or choose folders and files for the backup from the Backup tab.
2. Click Tools, Options to specify various backup options from the Default Backup Type drop-down list; then click OK.
3. Specify the backup media to which you want to back up the data from the Backup Destination drop-down list. To back up to a disk, choose File from the drop-down list.
4. Select the appropriate media or file path for the backup from Backup media or filename. Browse if necessary.
5. Click Start Backup. The Backup Job Information dialog appears. See Figure 14.9 for a description of its options.

Identify current backup set for easy
identification later (50 characters max).

FIGURE 14.9
The Backup Job
Information dialog.

Replace existing
backup sets with
new backup set,
overwriting old
backup sets.

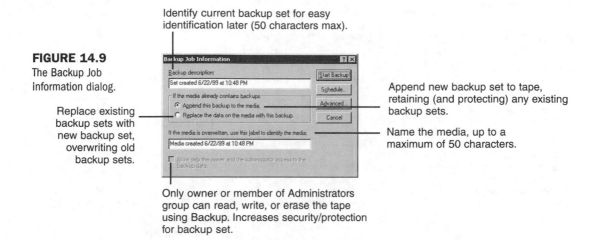

Append new backup set to tape,
retaining (and protecting) any existing
backup sets.

Name the media, up to a
maximum of 50 characters.

Only owner or member of Administrators
group can read, write, or erase the tape
using Backup. Increases security/protection
for backup set.

6. Click A**d**vanced on the Backup Job Information dialog to access the Advanced Backup
   Options dialog. Figure 14.10 explains the options.

Applies to Windows 2000 Server's
Remote Storage feature; not applicable
to Professional.

FIGURE 14.10
The Advanced Backup
Options dialog.

Specify backup type
for the set.

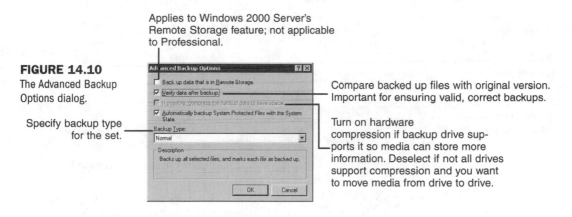

Compare backed up files with original version.
Important for ensuring valid, correct backups.

Turn on hardware
compression if backup drive supports it so media can store more
information. Deselect if not all drives
support compression and you want
to move media from drive to drive.

7. Click S**c**hedule to schedule the backup job. Windows 2000 prompts you to specify a
   name if you haven't saved it yet.

8. Specify the account and password under which you want the backup job to run using
   the Set Account Information dialog, and then click OK.

9. On the Schedule Data tab of Scheduled Job Options, specify a name by which the
   backup job will be labeled and the date and time the backup operation will occur.

10. Click **P**roperties to access the Schedule Job dialog. Figure 14.11 explains its options.

Part
IV

Ch
14

Specify start time for job.

FIGURE 14.11
Check Show m**u**ltiple schedules to create multiple jobs.

Choose frequency at which the current job will be run.

Choose dates, days, and frequencies of the backup job; changes according to selection in **S**chedule Task.

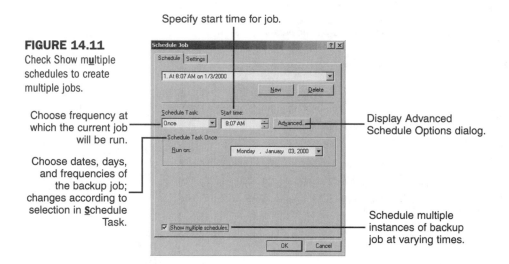

Display Advanced Schedule Options dialog.

Schedule multiple instances of backup job at varying times.

11. To specify advanced schedule properties, click Ad**v**anced. Figure 14.12 explains the Advanced Schedule Options dialog.

Have Backup repeat task according to associated settings.

Choose beginning date of range of dates during which task will run.

FIGURE 14.12
The Advanced Schedule Options dialog offers finer control over scheduling.

Time at which to end task.

Duration for the task.

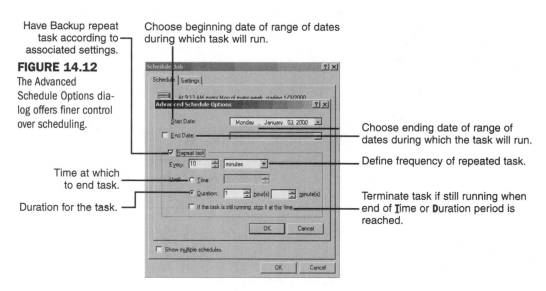

Choose ending date of range of dates during which the task will run.

Define frequency of repeated task.

Terminate task if still running when end of **T**ime or **D**uration period is reached.

12. On Schedule Job, click the Settings tab. Figure 14.13 explains its options.

13. When you are satisfied with the schedule settings, choose OK to return to the Backup Job Information dialog, and then click **S**tart Backup to schedule/initiate the backup job.

Number of hours/minutes task can run before Backup stops it.

Delete task at completion if not scheduled to run again (such as once-only or repetition time expired).

FIGURE 14.13
The Settings tab.

Task started only after computer idle for specified time.

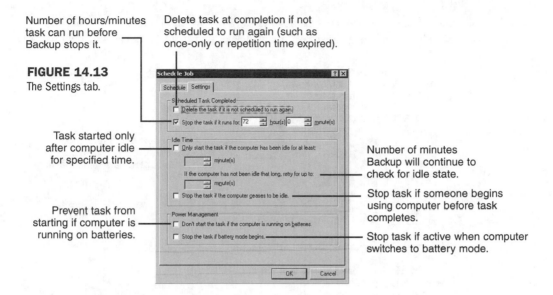

Number of minutes Backup will continue to check for idle state.

Stop task if someone begins using computer before task completes.

Prevent task from starting if computer is running on batteries.

Stop task if active when computer switches to battery mode.

Restoring Files

As with the Backup process, you can use the Restore Wizard to automate and assist you in the process of restoring files. This section explains how to perform a manual file restore procedure. The options available in the wizard are explained in this section.

Follow these steps to perform a restore operation:

1. Start Backup and click the Restore tab.

2. Select the tape device from which to restore, or click the File check box if restoring from a file archive.

3. Select the folders and files you want to restore.

4. Choose an option from the **R**estore files drop-down list using the following list as a guideline:

   ■ *Original location.* Choose this to have files restored to the locations from which they were backed up.

   ■ *Alternate location.* Choose this to redirect the files to an alternative location. Use the **A**lternate location text box or browse for the restore location.

   ■ *Single folder.* Choose this to have all files restored to a single folder, regardless of whether they were backed up from a single folder or not. Use the **A**lternate location text box or browse for the location.

Part
IV

Ch
14

5. Click Start Restore to access the Confirm Restore dialog, and then click **A**dvanced to set options in the Advanced Restore Options dialog. Figure 14.14 explains its options.

Restore permissions, ownership, and audit entries with files. Windows 2000 NTFS volumes only.

FIGURE 14.14

The Advanced Restore Options dialog.

Restore removable storage database to *systemroot*\system32\nt msdata. Erases existing removable storage database.

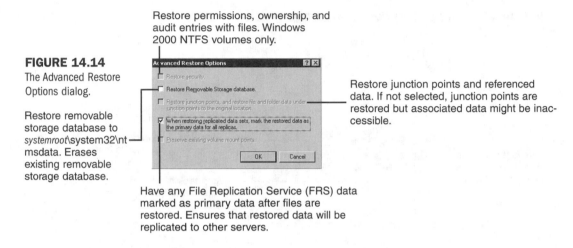

Restore junction points and referenced data. If not selected, junction points are restored but associated data might be inaccessible.

Have any File Replication Service (FRS) data marked as primary data after files are restored. Ensures that restored data will be replicated to other servers.

6. In Confirm Restore dialog, click OK to start the restore process.

Media Operations

You can perform a handful of tape operations using Backup. These operations include formatting a tape, retensioning a tape, and so on. Access these operations by choosing **T**ools, **M**edia Tools:

- *Catalog.* Choose this to view a catalog of the tape.
- *Erase.* Use this to erase all information on a tape. In the Erase Tape dialog, specify either **Q**uick Erase or **S**ecure Erase. Quick Erase rewrites only the tape header, effectively making the tape blank because no record of the data on the tape remains. Secure Erase physically erases all data on the tape and can take several hours, depending on tape drive speed and tape capacity.
- *Re-tension.* Use this to retension the tape, removing slack to make sure the tape functions properly and moves evenly past the drive heads. Retensioning is not required for 4mm and 8mm tapes.
- *Format.* Use this to format the tape. Formatting is required prior to using a new tape unless the tape is formatted by the tape manufacturer or the drive type does not require preformatting. This command is dimmed if formatting is not applicable to the drive/tape.

Using Backup from the Console Prompt

Although you might use the graphical interface for Backup most often, you also can work with the Ntbackup command from the console prompt. This enables you to create batch files that automate backup operations.

Ntbackup is the program file for Backup. You can open a command console and use the command dynamically to start a backup job, or you can include the command in batch files to automate backup jobs. Like many commands, Ntbackup supports several *command-line switches* that are optional parameters you include with the command to control the way it functions.

The syntax of the Ntbackup command appears as follows (the command you use will vary depending on the switches you use):

```
ntbackup backup [system state] "bks backup.bks"/j "daily_backup"
```

Most likely, you'll need to add more switches to the command. The basic style for writing a command is as follows: **ntbackup backup [systemstate]** *"bks filename"* **/J** {*"job name"*} **[/P** {*"pool name"*}] **[/G** {*"guid name"*}] **[/T** { *"tape name"*}] **[/N** {*"media name"*}] **[/F** {*"file name"*}] **[/D** {*"set description"*}] **[/DS** {*"server name"*}] **[/IS** {*"server name"*}] **[/A] [/V:{yes|no}] [/R:{yes|no}] [/L:{f|s|n}] [/M** {*backup type*}] **[/RS:{yes|no}] [/HC:{on|off}]**/UM

The following list describes the parameters for the Ntbackup command:

- *systemstate*. Specifies that you want to back up the system state data. All system state data is backed up when you use this option, so the /s switch does not apply. The backup type will be forced to normal or copy.

- *bks filename*. Specifies the name of the selection file (.bks extension) to be used for the backup operation (lists files to be backed up). Create the file using the graphical user interface (GUI) version of Windows Backup, and then save it by name for use in the command line.

- /J *(job name)*. Specifies the job name to be used in the log file. The job name typically should describe the files and folders being backed up in the current backup job, along with the date and time of the backup.

- /P *(pool name)*. Specifies the media pool from which you want to use media for the current backup. Usually, this is the Backup media pool. Do not use the following switches with this option: /A, /G, /F, /T.

- /G *(guid name)*. Specifies the Global User ID (GUID) for the tape when performing an overwrite or append operation.

- /T *(tape name)*. Specifies a label for the tape when performing an overwrite or append operation.

- /N *(media name)*. Specifies the new media name. Do not use /A with this switch.

Part

IV

Ch

14

■ /F *(filename)*. Specifies the logical disk path and filename for the backup archive file. You must not use the following switches with this switch: /P, /G, /T.

■ /D *(set description)*. Specifies a label for each backup set.

■ /DS *(server name)*. Backs up the Directory Service file for the specified Microsoft Exchange Server (Exchange Server requires Windows 2000 Server).

■ /IS *(server name)*. Backs up the Information Store file for the specified Microsoft Exchange Server (does not apply to Windows 2000 Professional).

■ /A. Performs an append operation. Either /G or /T must be used in conjunction with this switch. Do not use this switch with the /P switch.

■ /V: *(yes|no)*. Specifies whether a file verification takes place after the backup.

■ /R: *(yes|no)*. Restricts access to this tape to the owner or members of the Administrators group.

■ /L: *(f|s|n)*. Specifies the type of log file: f=full, s=summary, n=none.

■ /M *(backup type)*. Specifies the backup type. It must be one of the following: normal, copy, differential, incremental, or daily.

■ /RS: *(yes|no)*. Backs up the Removable Storage database.

■ /HC: *(on|off)*. Turns on or off hardware compression, if available, on the tape drive for the current backup set.

■ /UM. Finds first available media, formats it, and uses it for current backup.

 TIP Most often, you will create batch files containing the Ntbackup command to automate tasks, and then schedule these batch files for execution using the Windows 2000 AT command. For more information on the AT command, refer to Appendix B, "Windows 2000 Professional Troubleshooting Guide."

System Repair and Recovery

A complete system file backup does not necessarily ensure that you will be able to easily restore a system if a hardware or software failure causes a major system fault. In order to ensure a relatively easy way to restore your system if it fails, you should perform these tasks:

■ *Create an emergency repair disk (ERD) and update it before you make changes to the system (install software or hardware).*

■ *Perform a full system backup including the system state data.* Back up system state data *before* making software or hardware changes, and back up system state data *after* making extensive user account or group changes.

■ *Back up repair data.* You should back up the Registry and other key repair data to enable you to repair your Windows 2000 installation through the Setup program.

■ *Define and implement a backup strategy that includes a weekly full backup with incremental or differential backups all other days.*

■ *Perform a test backup and restore to make sure you can restore files from your backup media.*

■ *Use Safe mode.* You should become familiar with Safe mode, which enables you to boot and repair a system that has failed because of hardware or software configuration problems.

■ *Install the Recovery Console.* You should install the Recovery Console, which enables you to boot the system to a command prompt and use a limited set of commands to repair the master boot record, copy system files, and perform other recovery procedures.

The following sections explain these tasks.

Creating an Emergency Repair Disk

Creating a repair disk is an important part of ensuring your system against a catastrophic failure of the operating system, file system, or hardware.

To create an ERD, open Backup and click the Welcome tab to display the Welcome page. Then, click Emergency Repair Disk to create a repair disk. Insert a blank, formatted diskette when prompted and click OK to begin creating the disk.

> **CAUTION**
>
> A repair disk does not back up the file system and should not be used as an alternative to a full backup. Instead, you should use a repair disk as a complement to a system backup to ensure that you can fully recover your system if necessary. You should create an up-to-date repair disk any time you modify your system, such as installing new hardware or software.

TIP To make a backup copy of the Registry, select Also **B**ackup the Registry on the ERD dialog. This saves the Registry to *systemroot*\repair\regback.

Unlike a Windows NT Emergency Repair Disk, the one created by Windows 2000 does not contain a copy of the Registry, but instead contains only the AUTOEXEC.NET, CONFIG.NT, and SETUP.LOG files. To use the ERD to repair the system, run Setup from the Windows 2000 CD. Choose the Repair option when presented with the option of installing a new copy of Windows 2000 or repairing an installation. Windows 2000 prompts you to insert the repair disk.

N O T E The ERD presents the least useful of all the backup tools because of how little it backs up, but it should be included in disaster recovery planning and prevention. ■

Part
IV

Ch
14

Backing Up System State Data

System state data on a Windows 2000 system includes the Registry, the COM+ class registration database, the system boot files, and protected files in the dllcache folder. It is imperative that you have a current backup of the system state data in order to perform a complete backup should your system fail.

Under Windows 2000 the system state data can represent 200MB or more of data, so choose a backup location or media that will accommodate the data.

Follow these steps to back up the system state data:

1. Open the Backup tab in Backup and click beside System State in the tree.
2. Select any other data you want to back up, including performing a full backup.
3. Start the backup.

You restore the system state data as you would any other backup media set when the need arises. Restart the system after restoring the data.

 TIP When you perform your regular full backup, include the system state data in the backup to simplify system recovery.

Backing Up Repair Data

The *systemroot*\Repair folder contains backup copies of Registry and other configuration files. You can use these backup copies in concert with the Setup program and the ERD to repair the system.

Although the ERD procedure can create a backup of the Registry, you can use a manual method to back up the Registry in the event you have problems running Backup or using the ERD Wizard.

First boot to the repair console or use Safe mode with command prompt. Make a backup copy of the current contents of the Repair folder, and then manually copy the following files to the Repair folder:

- *systemroot*\System32\Autoexec.nt
- *systemroot*\System32\Config.nt
- *systemroot*\System32\Config\Default
- Documents and Settings\Default User\Ntuser.dat
- *systemroot*\System32\Config\Security
- *systemroot*\System32\Config\Software
- *systemroot*\System32\Config\System

TIP To save a lot of typing, create a batch file to back up the files, and run the batch file from the repair console.

Working with Safe Mode

A feature in Windows 2000 borrowed from Windows 98 is Safe mode, which lets you boot the system using a minimal set of drivers. Safe mode can help you boot the system when a configuration problem otherwise prevents a boot. You boot to Safe mode, correct the problem, and then reboot normally.

 TIP Safe mode is good for troubleshooting problems with specific drivers because unlike a normal boot, the system displays driver names as it loads them. Boot hanging at a specific driver can indicate a problem with that driver.

To boot in Safe mode, press F8 at the boot menu. Windows 2000 then offers the following menu options:

- *Safe Mode.* Boot the GUI with minimal drivers and no network support.
- *Safe Mode with Networking.* Boot the GUI with minimal drivers and with network support.
- *Safe Mode with Command Prompt.* Boot GUI with a command prompt (console) as the shell.
- *Enable Boot Logging.* Turn on logging of boot status messages.
- *Enable VGA Mode.* Boot the system using the standard VGA display driver (bypass improperly configured or corrupt display driver).
- *Last Known Good Configuration.* Boot the system with the same configuration used during the last successful boot.
- *Directory Services Restore Mode.* Not applicable to Windows 2000 Professional.
- *Debugging Mode.* Boot the system in debugging mode.

Using the Recovery Console

The Recovery Console provides a command-line environment in which you can boot the system to perform troubleshooting and recovery procedures. For example, you might boot to Recovery Console, restore the system state data to repair a configuration problem, and then restart the system normally. The Recovery Console is covered in detail in Appendix B.

Part
IV

Ch
14

Certificate Manager

Overview of Certificates

Certificates are a security mechanism that identify you and your data uniquely and securely. For example, you can use a certificate to log on to a secure Web site without having a user-name and password, because the certificate can securely identify you to the server. The web site must naturally support the use of certificates for authentication and must already have a record of you and your certificate.

Certificates also enable you to secure your data. You can use a certificate to digitally sign your email, for example, ensuring to the recipient that the message was sent by you and not forged. You can also use certificates to encrypt data for transmission across non-secured networks such as the Internet. You might use a certificate to encrypt an important file for transmission to someone else through email, for example.

Certificates comprise a public key and a private key. You provide the public key to people who will be receiving digitally signed or encrypted data from you. The private key encrypts the data, which can be unencrypted only with the public key.

You cannot create your own certificate, but you can request digital certificates from Certification Authorities, or CAs. Several commercial CAs exist that will provide you with a certificate for a nominal annual fee. In addition, a Windows 2000 Server can act as a CA, distributing and managing individual and group certificates in a LAN or enterprise.

 VeriSign, Inc. (http://www.verisign.com) is one of the most popular commercial CAs. In addition to providing certificates for individuals, VeriSign also provides certificates and other security mechanisms for e-commerce.

After you have a certificate, you can begin using that certificate to authenticate yourself and your data and protect that data.

Requesting Certificates

Before using a certificate, you must obtain one. You can request a digital certificate from a public CA such as VeriSign, Thawte, GTE, etc. You also can request a certificate from a CA on your LAN or within your enterprise.

Obtaining a Certificate from a Public CA

You need to obtain a certificate from a public CA if you want to use it for authentication and security for email and other services outside your LAN or enterprise. Typically, you can obtain a certificate through the CA's website. In most cases, you have to provide personal information such as name, address, phone number, and so on through a form on the CA's website. The expense for the certificate is charged to your credit card (unless the certificate is free). Typically, the CA then emails you the information needed to connect to its certificate server and obtain the certificate, which is then installed automatically through your browser. After the certificate is installed, you can begin using it to secure your data for transmission.

 TIP Some CAs offer personal certificates for free, so you should shop around to find the type of certificate and provider that meet your needs.

Finding Public Certificates on the Web

The following list identifies the current URLs for various entities that provide public certificates:

VeriSign, Inc. provides digital certificates for individuals and organizations, ISVs, and secure servers. http://www.verisign.com

Thawte, Inc. Offers personal and server certification services for Netscape, MSIE, PGP, and other generic X.509 software users. http://www.thawte.com

BelSign provides digital certification in Europe for individuals and servers. http://www.belsign.be

Certco offers digital certificates to financial institutions but not individuals.
http://www.certco.com

Trade Authority provides digital key and certificate management primarily for customers requiring multiple digital certificates. http://www.tradewave.com

Obtaining a Certificate from an Enterprise CA

Your organization can use certificates for authentication and security, gaining for local resources the advantages that certificates typically provide for Internet resources. Your network must include a Windows 2000 Server acting as a CA in order for you to request and use a certificate for these purposes.

Use the following steps to request a certificate from an enterprise CA:

1. Open the Certificate Manager in the MMC (see following section for assistance).

2. Right-click the location where you want the certificate installed, and choose All Tasks, Request New Certificate. Specify information per Table 15.1.

3. At the completion of the Certificate Request Wizard, click Install Certificate.

Table 15.1   New Certificate Properties

Option	Use
Type	Type of certificate (*certificate template*) you want to request. Certificate templates are predefined configurations that provide common settings for the certificate request.
Cryptographic Service Provider	Specify cryptographic service provider to be used for certificate. A CSP is a software program that generates security key pairs.
Certification Authority	Name of certification authority from which to request the certificate if your enterprise includes more than one CA server.
Friendly Name	Name for the new certificate.

N O T E   To request a certificate from a standalone server, connect to
`http://servername/certsrv`, where *servername* is the name of the Windows 2000 Server computer hosting the CA service. The resulting page provides the mechanism for you to request certificates, which should be similar to the information described earlier. Note that the page might differ from one server to the next, because the pages can be modified. ▪

Adding Certificate Manager to the MMC

Prior to using the Certificate Manager snap-in, you should add Certificate Manager to the MMC. To do so, follow these steps:

1. Click Start, Run, enter **MMC /A**, and then click OK to start MMC in Author mode in order to create a new console.

2. Optional: To add the Certificate Manager snap-in to an existing console layout, click **C**onsole, **O**pen to open the existing console.

3. Click **C**onsole, Add/Remove Snap-In.

4. Click A**d**d, select Certificates from the snap-in list (see Figure 15.1); then click **A**dd.

5. Only administrators and domain administrators can manage certificates for their computers or local services, in addition to their user accounts. Otherwise, you can administer certificates only for your user account. Choose the appropriate option from the Certificates Snap-in dialog (see Figure 15.2), and then click Finish, Close, OK.

6. Click **C**onsole, **S**ave to save the current MMC configuration.

FIGURE 15.1
The Add Standalone
Snap-in dialog.

FIGURE 15.2
The Certificates snap-
in dialog appears only
if you have the appro-
priate permissions.

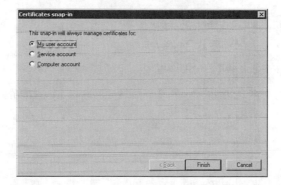

N O T E While this chapter focuses on using Certificate Manager to manage certificates for a user
account, the process is the same for service and computer accounts. ■

After you add Certificate Manager to the MMC, you'll see a console similar to the one shown
in Figure 15.3.

FIGURE 15.3
The Certificate
Manager snap-in
added to the MMC.

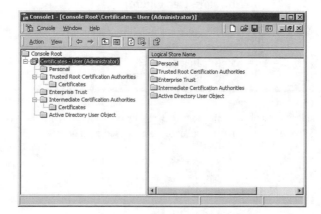

Managing Personal Certificates

The Certificate Manager snap-in for the MMC helps you manage certificates. You can use the Certificate Manager to view, find, move, delete, and modify certificates. You also can import and export certificates to move them from one computer to another. This section explains how to use Certificate Manager to manage certificates.

Overview of Certificate Stores

A *certificate store* is a collective group of certificates stored on a computer. Through the Certificate Manager you can view the contents of the certificate store(s) on a local or remote computer. Certificate Manager offers three options for viewing the certificate store: *logical mode*, *physical mode*, and *certificate purpose*. Table 15.2 describes these modes.

Table 15.2   Certificate View Modes

Mode	What It Displays	When to Use
Logical certificate stores	Logical structure of name or by category. certificate store, hiding physical structure (see Figure 15.3). For example, Registry and Group Policy branches are hidden in logical mode.	Focus on certificates by name or by category name or by category.
Physical certificate stores	Physical structure of certificate store (see Figure 15.4).	When you want to export an entire store.
Certificate Purpose	Sorts certificates by purpose of the certificates within the store (see Figure 15.5). Makes it much easier to locate and manage individual certificates for specific tasks.	Focus on certificates by function rather than name or category.

N O T E   An individual certificate will often show up under multiple categories in certificate purpose mode, because most certificates can be used for more than one purpose. ▪

FIGURE 15.4
Viewing a certificate store in physical mode.

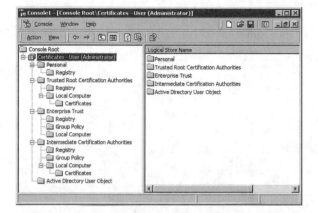

FIGURE 15.5
Certificate purpose lets you focus on certificates by their function.

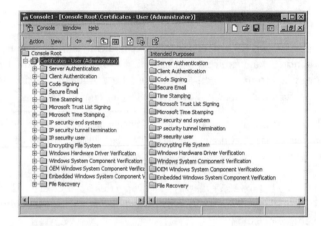

 TIP

In addition to specifying the view mode, you also can toggle the view of archived certificates. When you renew a certificate, the old copy is archived and hidden by default since you typically won't need it again. Turning them off unclutters the certificate view.

Viewing and Modifying a Certificate

You can use the Certificate Manager MMC snap-in to view individual certificates in your certificate store. Follow these steps to view a certificate:

1. Open Certificate Manager.
2. Click the certificate store; then choose View, Options, and select the mode in which you want to view the store.
3. Locate and select the branch containing the certificate you want to view.
4. Double-click the certificate you want to view. Certificate Manager displays a Certificate property sheet for the certificate similar to the one shown in Figure 15.6.

FIGURE 15.6
The General tab provides basic information about the certificate.

The General tab lists general properties for the certificate such as its purpose, to whom it is issued, the issuing CA, and expiration information about the certificate. Click Issuer Statement to view a statement or disclaimer from the CA for the certificate. Issuer Statement is dimmed if the certificate does not contain an issuer statement.

 TIP Clicking More Info on the Disclaimer page will typically open a browser at the issuer's website. The issuer statement seldom offers any useful information, but the website is usually worth the trip. In some cases the issuer statement is located on the website.

The Details tab (see Figure 15.7) displays all properties for the selected certificate. View various types of information with the Show drop-down list. Click individual fields to view the properties for the selected field.

FIGURE 15.7
The Details tab.

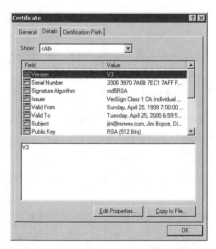

You can edit a handful of properties for the certificate by clicking **E**dit Properties on the Details tab. Doing so displays the Certificate Properties dialog shown in Figure 15.8. The figure explains the dialog options.

FIGURE 15.8
The Certificate Properties dialog.

Use to organize/identify certificates in Certificate Manager

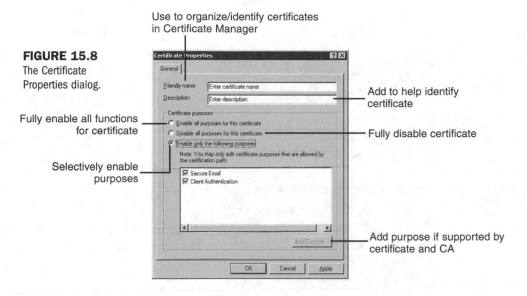

Add to help identify certificate

Fully enable all functions for certificate

Fully disable certificate

Selectively enable purposes

Add purpose if supported by certificate and CA

 TIP

Click a column header to sort the certificate list in Certificate Manager according to the selected column. For example, click Friendly Name to sort the list according to each certificate's friendly name.

You can display Certificate Properties by right-clicking on a certificate and choosing Properties from the context menu.

The Certification Path tab (see Figure 15.9) displays the *certification path* for the selected certificate. A certification path is a chain of related certificates. Use this tab to view properties of certificates within the chain.

Finding a Certificate

Locating a particular certificate can be time-consuming if you have several certificates or if you are unfamiliar with the store's structure. Certificate Manager enables you to locate certificates based on text in specific fields. Follow these steps to locate a certificate:

1. Open Certificate Manager, click Certificates in the tree, and click **A**ction, Find Certificates to access the Find Certificates dialog (see Figure 15.10).

FIGURE 15.9
The Certification Path tab.

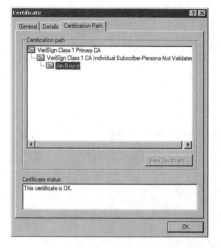

FIGURE 15.10
The Find Certificates dialog.

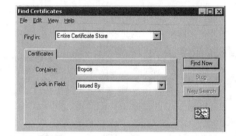

2. Enter the text you want to locate in the Contains field.

3. Select the area of the store to search from Look in Field, then click Find Now.

4. Click View and the desired option to change the view of the search results.

> **TIP** You can use the Find Certificates dialog to perform several actions on certificates, including renewing, exporting, deleting, and setting certificate properties. The File menu in the Find Certificates dialog gives you access to these functions, which are covered individually in the remainder of this chapter.

Moving a Certificate

Occasionally you might find it necessary to move a certificate from one certificate store to another. For example, you might have imported a certificate into the wrong store by accident and need to move it into the correct one.

Moving a certificate is a simple process: Locate and select the certificate; cut (or copy) the certificate to the Clipboard, and then select the correct location and paste the certificate.

Deleting a Certificate

You can use Certificate Manager to delete certificates you no longer want or need. Keep in mind, however, that deleting a certificate prevents you from decrypting data that was encrypted using the certificate. Delete a certificate only when you are sure you no longer need it or the data with which is was encrypted.

Follow these steps to permanently delete a certificate and its data:

1. Open the Certificate Manager and locate the certificate you want to delete.
2. Select the certificate and use one of the following actions: right-click the certificate and choose **D**elete; click the Delete toolbar button; or choose **A**ction, **D**elete.
3. Certificate Manager prompts you to verify that you really want to delete the certificate(s). Choose **Y**es to delete the certificate or **N**o to abort the operation.

Renewing a Certificate

Most certificates are issued with an expiration date. When the expiration date arrives, the expired certificate will be invalid and no longer function. You can, however, renew the certificate. Fee-based certificates require that you also pay a renewal fee.

Use Certificate Manager to renew certificates you've received from a Windows 2000 Enterprise CA. Renewing a certificate issued by a standalone server requires that you connect to the CA server's website.

TIP

Connect to `http://servername/certsrv`, where *servername* is the name of the standalone Windows NT CA server, to renew a certificate issued by that standalone server.

See the list in the section, "Obtaining a Certificate from a Public CA," earlier in this chapter for the web address of several public CAs.

You can renew a certificate issued by a Windows 2000 CA with the same key set or with a new key set. In most cases you'll want to retain the same key set, enabling you to continue to use the new certificate for data encrypted with the old certificate. Using a new key set guards against the possibility that someone might have compromised the old key set.

To renew a certificate issued by a Windows 2000 Enterprise CA, right-click the certificate you want to renew and choose All Tas**k**s, Renew Certificate with New Key or Renew Certificate with Same Key, depending on which option you want. Certificate Manager starts a wizard to help you complete the task.

Importing and Exporting Certificates

Occasionally, you might want to import and export certificates. The following are typical reasons for importing certificates:

- Install a certificate sent to you by another user, computer, or CA.
- Restore a damaged or lost certificate that you have previously backed up.
- Install a certificate and its associated private key from a different computer, such as from your desktop to your notebook computer.

The following are common reasons for exporting certificates:

- Back up a certificate for safekeeping.
- Back up a certificate and its associated private key.
- Copy a certificate from one computer to another so you can use it on both computers.
- Remove a certificate and its private key from one computer and install it on another.

Exporting a certificate creates a certificate file that uses one of the following standard certificate formats:

- *Personal Information Exchange (PFX)*. This format corresponds to the PKCS #12 file format, an industry standard certificate format for transporting, backing up, and restoring certificates and their keys between differing platforms such as Internet Explorer and Netscape. It is the only format supported by Microsoft for exporting a certificate and its associated key.
- *Cryptographic Message Syntax Standard (PKCS #7)*. This format enables a certificate and all the certificates in its certification path to be transferred between two computers or to removable media.
- *DER Encoded Binary X.509*. This binary format is for use only on Windows systems and does not work on other platforms. It is useful for transferring certificates to other applications (such as Netscape) on Windows-based platforms.
- *Base64 Encoded X.509*. This format is not restricted to the Windows or Intel platforms and is useful for transferring certificates to non-Windows/non-Intel platforms such as Digital Alpha systems.

Importing Certificates

You can use Certificate Manager to import certificates into your certificate store. To import a certificate, open Certificate Manager and select the store in which you want to place the certificate. Click **A**ction, All Tas**k**s, Import to start the Certificate Manager Import Wizard. The wizard prompts you for the following information:

- The filename of the certificate file. Type or browse to the file.
- For PKS files, the password by which the certificate file was encrypted.

- **E**nable strong private key protection. Choose this to be prompted for the password each time an application uses the certificate's private key. This ensures that an application can't use the private key without your okay.
- **M**ark the private key as exportable. Choose this to mark the private key as exportable. Clear this to prevent the private key from being exported from the resulting certificate file, increasing security.

Exporting Certificates

Exporting a certificate enables you to transfer a certificate to another format or use the certificate on other systems, as well as send the certificates to others to use.

Follow these steps to export a certificate:

1. In Certificate Manager, open the branch of the store containing the certificate you want to export.
2. Select the certificate to be exported, and then choose **A**ction, All Tas**k**s, Export to start the Certificate Manager Export Wizard. Click Next.
3. Specify whether you want to export the private key (along with the certificate); then click Next.

Choosing to export the private key enables you to export the certificate to a PFX (PKCS #12) file. You do not have the option of using DER, Base64, or PKCS #7 formats.

Choosing not to export the private key gives you the option of export to DER, Base64, and PKCS #7 formats, but not to a PFX file.

4. Skip to step 7 if you are not exporting the private key.
5. Choosing **Y**es to export the private key results in dialog with which you specify the following options:
    - *Include all certificates in the certification path if possible.* Choose this to have all certificates in the certification path for the selected certificate included in the exported file, if possible.
    - *Enable strong protection.* Choose this to enable strong protection, also know as *iteration count.* Note that strong protection requires Internet Explorer 5.0 or later, or another browser capable of using this feature.
    - *Delete the private key if the export is successful.* Choose this to have the private key deleted if the export operation is successful.
6. Enter and confirm a password for the certificate file. Anyone attempting to import the certificate will need to know this password. Click **N**ext to continue.
7. Type a filename for the certificate or click the B**r**owse button to browse for a location for the new certificate file, and then click **N**ext.
8. Review your settings, and then click **F**inish to complete the process.

Component Services Explorer

Using Component Services

Component Services comprises a set of administration tools that allow you to configure and administer COM components and applications. Component Services can help to automate the process of installing, removing, or updating COM+ applications on the computers in your organization. The Component Services run as a snap-in to the Microsoft Management Console (MMC).

COM (formerly known as OLE Automation) stands for *Component Object Model*. Programmers use COM to make portions of their applications available to other applications or programmers for the purpose of customization. For example, Microsoft Office 2000 can be customized through the use of VBA (Visual Basic for Applications). Each application exposes certain objects that can be customized. These objects are COM objects.

Windows 2000 uses the concept of *COM+_Services*, which are an extension of Microsoft Transaction Server and COM. COM+ provides for better security and transaction management.

N O T E You'll learn more about using COM+ applications later in this chapter. ■

To access the Component Services application, open Control Panel, double-click Administrative Tools, and then double-click the Component Services icon. The Component Services window is shown in Figure 16.1.

FIGURE 16.1

The Component Services window is where you administer the COM+ Applications and component services on the computer. Your own Component Services window might differ from this one, depending on what application you have installed.

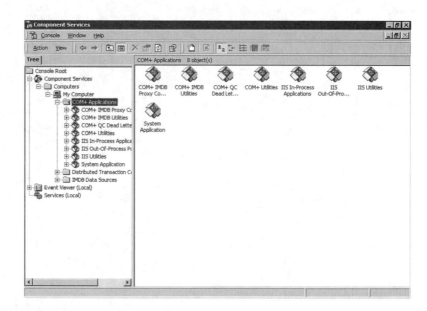

N O T E Component Services is normally installed during the initial setup of Windows 2000 Professional. If it is not present on your computer, you will need to install it using the Add/Remove Programs Control Panel Applet. ■

Installation doesn't make Component Services available for use. Before you can use the tool on the network, you must perform these tasks:

- Designate an administrator to enable secure access to the Component Services tool.
- Make computers visible to Component Services so that computers with COM+ applications can be controlled from the administrator and so you can deploy COM+ applications to those computers.
- Configure and enable Distributed COM (DCOM) . If you are running in a networked environment, DCOM must be configured in order for computers to communicate across the network. The configuration of DCOM enables its functionality. If you disable DCOM, the services will still run on the local computer, but you cannot connect to or communicate with other COM+ computers on the network.

Part

IV

Ch

16

N O T E   Distributed COM (DCOM) is the term used to describe the use of COM components over a networked environment. This could be a LAN, a WAN, or the Internet. ■

▶ To learn more about networking in Windows 2000 professional, **see** "Networking Installation and Configuration," **p. 49**

Assigning an Administrator for Component Services

As mentioned before, you need to assign an administrator who will be responsible for administering and configuring the service. The reason behind this requirement is that Component Services actually runs as a system application that allows access to areas of the operating system that should be kept open only to administrators. Assigning an administrator configures the security settings for Component Services.

CAUTION

Do not overlook the important step of assigning a user to the administrative role in Component Services. If you fail to do so, the services will not be able to be administrated, and you will have to reinstall Component Services.

TIP   You might want to consider assigning more than one user as administrator if you want to have another person responsible for working with component services on this computer. This arrangement would come in handy if you or the regular administrator should be away on vacation or absent due to illness. You don't need to assign two users, of course, but the option is available.

To assign an administrator for Component Services, follow these steps:

1. In the console tree pane of the Component Services window, click the plus (+) sign to expand the COM+ Applications list of contents. Using the same technique, expand the System Application list, the Roles list, and then the Administrator list.

2. Right-click the Users icon; from the pop-up menu, choose **N**ew, User. The Select Users or Groups window is displayed, as shown in Figure 16.2.

FIGURE 16.2
Use the Select Users or Groups dialog box to select a computer that contains the user account of the person who will administer the service.

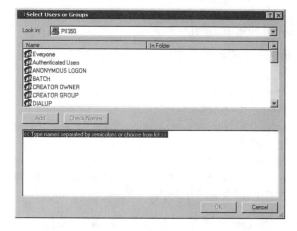

3. From the Look In drop-down list, select the computer that contains the user accounts (in most cases, the local computer is listed by default).

4. From the Name list of available user or group accounts, select the desired account, and then click the **A**dd button to add it to the list. The name now appears in the bottom pane of the dialog box. You can add additional users by holding the Ctrl key and selecting each user as in a multi-select scenario, or you can add the users one at a time by repeating this step for each user you want to add.

5. When you finish adding users, click OK to close the dialog box.

When you complete this process, you should see the added users in the details pane of the Component Services window. You must restart the computer for the changes to take effect.

▶ For an in-depth discussion of security issues involved in user accounts and groups, **see** "Understanding System Administration and Security," **p. 193**

▶ To learn more about assigning and managing rights and policies, **see** "Assigning Rights to Groups," **p. 222** and "Managing Group Policies," **p. 225**

Making Computers Visible to Component Services

With an administrator assigned and the means for secure access to Component Services in place, you are ready to make the computers visible to the Component Services tool. Follow these steps to perform this task:

1. Right-click the Computers folder in the Component Services console tree.

2. From the pop-up menu, select **N**ew, Computer. The Add Computer dialog box is displayed.

3. Enter the name of the computer to add if you know it, or you can click the **B**rowse button to locate a computer on the network.

4. Click OK. If this is the only computer that will use Component Services, there is no need to add any other computers. If you want to add more computers, repeat the preceding steps for each computer that you want to add.

After you add the computers, they appear in the details pane of the Component Services Window, and you can manage the objects on those remote computers from this administrative tool. You can also delete computers by selecting them in the details pane and pressing the Delete key.

Enabling DCOM

As mentioned earlier, for computers to communicate with COM components on another computer on the network, you need to enable DCOM.

> **N O T E** If you disable DCOM on a remote computer, you will not be able to re-enable it over the network. You will have to physically go to the computer and re-enable it there. ▪

DCOM needs to be enabled on each computer on the network that supports it. You use the same basic procedure to enable and to disable DCOM. You should only disable DCOM if you are absolutely sure that you will not be using it on a specific computer. If in doubt, leave it enabled.

To enable or disable DCOM on a computer, follow these steps:

1. Select the computer in the details pane of the Component Services window, and then choose **A**ction, P**r**operties. The Computer Properties dialog box appears.

2. Select the Default Properties tab. To enable DCOM for the computer, select the Enable Distributed COM on this Computer check box. Clear the check box to disable DCOM on the computer.

3. Click the OK button to close the dialog box.

Using COM+ Applications

A COM+ application is a group of COM components that perform identical or related functions that deal with security and administration of component services. Installing a COM+ application makes that application and its components available on the network. The installation of COM+ applications requires two steps:

1. Exporting the client- and server-side installation files.

2. Installing proxy and application information to the clients and servers.

Install COM+ applications on a *staging* computer before you deploy them into your production environment. A staging computer is a testing computer that is set up separate from your mainstream computers and network. This gives you an opportunity to "test-drive" the applications and identify any potential problems before they can interfere with your operation.

The deployment technique you use might vary from application to application. If in-house developers are creating your applications, they can provide you with a complete application package that includes an installation routine that will simplify the deployment process.

If you purchased third-party products, they might come with installation routines, and you might have to install them manually. The application process for most applications has six steps, though individual applications might not require all of them. These common installation steps are the following:

1. Export COM+ server applications.
2. Install COM+ server applications.
3. Export COM+ application proxies.
4. Install COM+ application proxies.
5. Remove COM+ applications.
6. Replicate COM+ applications.

Exporting COM+ Server Applications

COM+ server applications consist of an .msi file and can be installed using the Component services Administrative tool.

 An .msi file is an information file that is created for the purposes of installing the applications. The extension actually stands for Microsoft Installation. ▨

However, if the application requires additional components, they must be installed outside of the Component Services tool. This information will be provided by the programmer of the application, and the necessary steps will be included.

The Component Services administrative tool can be used to export a server application to one or more computers on the network. You might use this feature to copy a server application from a staging computer to a production computer. To perform this function, follow these steps:

1. Open Control Panel, double-click the Administrative Tools icon, and then double-click the Component Services icon to start the administrative tool.
2. Expand the Component Services list to reveal the COM+ applications icon, and then expand the COM+ applications list.
3. Right-click the application that you want to export, and then choose Export from the pop-up menu. The COM Application Export Wizard opens.

4. Click <u>N</u>ext on the COM Application Export Wizard opening screen. The Application Export Information window opens (see Figure 16.3).

5. In the text box, enter the full path to the application file or use the <u>B</u>rowse button to locate it.

FIGURE 16.3

The COM Application Export Wizard automates the process of exporting server applications to other computers on the network.

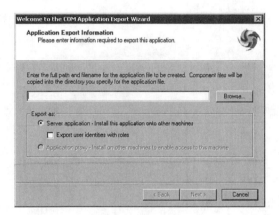

6. Make sure the Server Application - Install this Application onto Other Machines radio button in the Export As area is selected.

7. Click <u>N</u>ext; the Wizard generates an .msi file with the appropriate information needed to export the application.

8. When the Wizard has finished performing the export, click <u>F</u>inish to close the dialog box.

Installing COM+ Server Applications

To install a COM+ application on a remote computer, you must have Administrative privileges on that computer. You can install COM+ applications using the Component Services administration tool, Windows Explorer, or from the command prompt. In this chapter, I discuss using the Component Services tool.

N O T E COM+ server applications can only be installed on Windows 2000 computers. ■

Open the Component Services tool, and then follow these steps to install the applications:

1. In the Tree pane of Component Services, click the plus sign next to the computer that you will install the application on and then right-click the COM+ Application icon; choose <u>N</u>ew, <u>A</u>pplication from the pop-up menu (see Figure 16.4). The COM Application Installation Wizard opens.

FIGURE 16.4

To install COM+ applications, you use the Component Services tool to access the COM Application Installation Wizard.

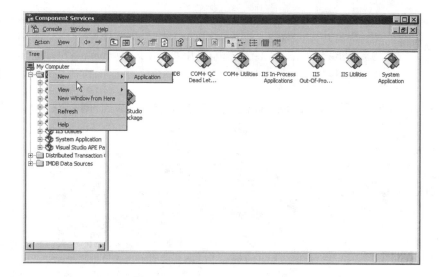

2. Click Next in the Wizard Welcome screen.

3. Click the Install Pre-built Application(s) button; the Install from Application File dialog box opens.

4. Select the .msi file for the application that you are installing, and then click Open; the Select Application Files dialog box appears.

5. Click the Browse button to search for and add any extra applications that you want to install. When you have finished adding applications, click Next.

6. Specify the application identity in the Set Application Identity dialog box. (Interactive User is the default, but you can click This User and enter another user or group.) Click Next; the Application Installation Options dialog box opens.

7. Specify the destination directory for the application by typing the directory path in the text box provided.

8. Click Finish; the application is installed and appears in the details pane.

NOTE To install COM+ applications using Windows Explorer, locate the server application .msi file on the computer and double-click it. The Windows Installer will proceed to install the application.

You can also install from the command prompt using this command-line syntax:

```
msiexec -i [<property overrides>] <application name>.msi
```

See the online help for the available overrides. ▪

Exporting COM+ Application Proxies

COM+ application proxies enable the client applications to search for COM+ server applications, using DCOM.

To export the proxies, follow these steps:

1. Right-click the application in the console tree and choose Export. The COM Application Export Wizard opens.

2. Click Next on the Welcome screen; the Application Export Information dialog box opens.

3. Enter the path for the location into which you want to install the application proxy, or click the Browse button to locate the directory.

4. In the Export As area, choose the Application Proxy - Install on Other Machines to Enable Access to this Machine option, and then click Next.

5. Click Finish when the Wizard has completed the export.

The application proxy file contains information that points to the server from which it was exported. If you want to specify a different remote server, follow this procedure:

1. Right-click the computer that you are exporting from in the console tree.

2. Select Properties from the pop-up menu, and then open the Options tab in the Properties dialog box.

3. In the Export section, enter the name of the remote server in the Application Proxy RSN text box, and then click OK.

Installing COM+ Application Proxies

Installing COM+ application proxies is a relatively simple procedure. You can perform the installation using the Windows Explorer or the command prompt.

To install an application proxy using the Windows Explorer, double-click the application proxy .msi file (this file can be on your local computer or on a network share); the Windows Installer installs the application proxy on the computer.

You can also perform the install using the command prompt. The syntax is identical to the COM+ Server command line:

```
msiexec -i [<property overrides>] <application name>.msi
```

Once again, see the online help for the Windows Installer for the overrides.

Removing COM+ Applications

You might want to remove COM+ applications as well. Follow the procedure listed here to remove an application:

1. Open the Component Services tool and expand the Computer and COM+ Applications lists to reveal the installed applications.

2. Select the application that you want to remove.

3. If the application is a server application, you must shut it down first by right-clicking it and choosing Shut Down. If the application is a library application, ensure that all processes that are accessing the library are shut down.

4. Right-click the application again and choose **D**elete.

5. Choose Yes when prompted to delete the application.

Replicating COM+ Applications

As mentioned previously in regards to installing COM+ applications, you should install them on a staging computer first for testing before a final implementation in your production environment.

When you have determined that the COM+ application works correctly and you want to deploy it, the easiest way is to replicate it to a production computer.

To replicate the application, you use the COMRepl.exe utility provided with Windows 2000. This utility copies COM+ applications and configurations from a master computer to the target computer. The syntax for the command is as follows:

```
COMREPL <source_computer> <target_computerlist>[/n[/v]]
```

<source_computer> indicates the computer that contains the application to be replicated.

<target_computerlist> indicates the name of the target computer. If you are using more than one computer as a target, list those names here, separated by a space.

/n prevents the confirmation prompt from displaying when the replication starts.

/v activates verbose mode; this mode echoes the log file output to the screen.

To ensure a smooth replication, you need to make sure your system meets the following requirements:

- Component Services must be installed on the target computers.

- Role checks for the application must be passed by the user on both the source and target computers. Role checks are used to determine that the user has the correct privileges to perform the requested tasks.

- Local machine accounts that might be used by roles are not replicated.

- Any database files or other data not related to Component Services must be replicated by the user manually.

Working with the Distributed Transaction Coordinator (DTC)

Distributed transactions are used to update data on computers over a network. The advantage of using a distributed transaction environment is that the application does not have to keep track of failures related to network or computer downtime. The distributed transaction system can handle these details for the application.

Each system using DTC contains a local *transaction manager* with which the applications communicate. This local transaction manager communicates and coordinates with the transaction manager on remote computers.

NOTE Normally, each system has its own DTC manager. The Administrator, however, can configure a computer to use a Manager on another system. ▪

When your application makes a request to send data, your local transaction manager establishes an outgoing relationship with the remote transaction manager. The remote manager establishes an incoming relationship with your transaction manager. The outgoing and incoming relationships are also known as superior and subordinate relationships, respectively.

Together, these relationships are known as a transaction commit tree. Should a network or computer fail during a transaction session, the two managers will query each other when brought back online as to the status of the transaction outcome. This status-check can help considerably in ensuring complete and accurate transactions.

In addition to the DTC Transaction Manager, a typical DTC also contains these components:

- *DTC Proxy*. The DTC proxy is actually a DLL file that implements OLE Transaction interfaces. The OLE Transaction Interface consists of various functions within the DLL that provide or define the interfaces that applications call to perform transactions.

- *GUI Administrator*. You use the Component Service MMC snap-in to manage the DTC system. The Component Services tool uses *remote procedure calls (RPC)* to communicate with the DTC transaction manager. By using the Component Services tool, you can administer local and remote DTC managers. This procedure can be a timesaver for Network Administrators because it offers the capability to manage multiple DTC transaction managers from one computer or site.

- *Log File*. This log file is stored on the local computer and contains all the information regarding transactions. It contains an ID for a transaction and any resource managers that were used by the transaction manager. This file acts like a revolving door; information remains in the log only for a short time. When the log is filled, new information overwrites the old. If you have a transaction that has not completed yet and the log file is about to be rewritten, DTC rewrites the information for that transaction so that it doesn't get lost.

Configuring the DTC Service

DTC is installed automatically when you install Windows 2000; however, you might have to perform some configuration. For example, for applications to use the DTC service, DTC must be running on the computer. By default, the DTC service is set to be started manually. To configure DTC to start automatically, follow these steps:

1. Open the Component Services tool and double-click the Services icon.

2. Double-click the Distributed Transaction Coordinator service entry; this brings up the DTC Properties sheet.

3. Open the General tab, and then click the Start button to start the service. (Click the Stop button to stop it or the Pause button to pause the service.)

4. Select Automatic from the Startup Type drop-down list to have the service start automatically when the computer boots up.

5. Click the OK button.

Change the Logon Identity   Normally, DTC runs under the System account. In the event that you need to change this logon identity, you must select an account that has Administrative privileges. Follow these steps to change the logon identity:

1. Double-click the Distributed Transaction Coordinator service entry to open the DTC Properties sheet; open the General tab, and click the Stop button to stop the service (as described in the previous steps).

2. Open the Log On tab and click the This Account radio button.

3. Enter a username and password, or use the Browse button to display the available user accounts and select one.

4. Go back to the General tab and click the Start button to restart the DTC service.

5. Click OK.

Specify a Site Coordinator   As mentioned earlier in this section, you can specify that any site computer be managed or coordinated by the transaction manager located on another computer. Working from the site computer, follow these steps to accomplish that task:

1. From the Component Services tool, right-click the computer that contains the DTC service and choose Properties. Select the MSDTC tab on the Properties sheet (see Figure 16.5).

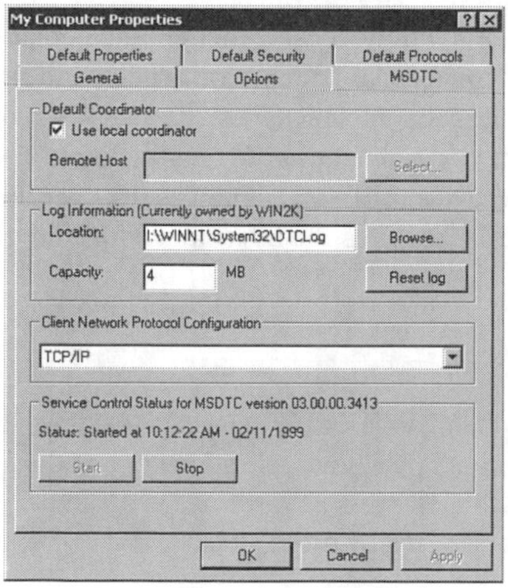

FIGURE 16.5
Use the MSDTC tab of the Computer Properties dialog box to determine which computer will manage the site. The status information at the bottom of the tab indicates when the DTC Service was last started.

2. In the Default Coordinator area, clear the Use Local Coordinator check box.

3. Enter a hostname in the Remote Host field, or choose one using the Select button.

4. If you are going to be using a remote coordinator, you must set the correct protocol to be used for communication. Use the drop-down list to select the protocol in the Client Network Protocol Configuration area of the MSDTC tab.

5. Click OK to close the Properties sheet.

Edit the Registry to Run DTC Through a Firewall If you need to run DTC through a firewall, you will need to make some changes in the system registry; specifically, you need to add some values to the registry that don't appear there by default. Because DTC uses RPC dynamic port allocation, it makes it hard to configure a port on the firewall to allow the incoming and outgoing transactions.

Part

IV

Ch

16

> **N O T E** RPC (Remote Procedure Call) is used by a networking application when it needs to access something on a remote computer over the network. The port used for this procedure call is not hard-coded, but it changes on an as-needed basis—thus, the term *dynamic port allocation*. If you are familiar with DHCP (Dynamic Host Configuration Protocol) for IP addresses, you are familiar with the processes involved in dynamic port allocation. ■

> **CAUTION**
>
> Editing the registry is always a dangerous task to perform if you are not familiar with the keys and values. You can render a computer unbootable if you delete or modify keys without understanding their purpose. Further, the procedure described in this section requires that the firewall be configured to enable incoming access to the ports. If you are unable to configure the firewall or if you have any concerns about your ability to edit the registry, *ask your administrator or other appropriate personnel to assist you with this procedure.*

The following steps outline the registry editing procedure you use to add the necessary values:

1. Choose Start, **R**un, then type **regedt32** in the Run text line, and click OK. The Registry Editor is displayed.

> **N O T E** Regedt32.exe is the 32-bit registry editor that comes with Windows 2000. Users of Win9x might be familiar with the regedit.exe application used for the same purpose on those operating systems. Although regedit.exe exists on Windows 2000 systems as well, it doesn't support the REG_MULTI_SZ data type that is required for configuring ports. ■

2. Open the HKEY_LOCAL_MACHINE on the Local Machine window by selecting the title bar, as shown in Figure 16.6.

FIGURE 16.6
When you select the HKEY_LOCAL_MACHINE entry in the Registry Editor window, you can search and edit the subkeys as necessary.

3. Expand the tree to display the following path: HKEY_LOCAL_MACHINE\Software\ Microsoft\Rpc.

4. Select the Rpc folder; choose **E**dit, Add Key. The Add Key dialog box is displayed.

5. In the Key Name field, type **Internet**; click OK. (Don't worry about the Class value in this dialog box.) The Add Key dialog box closes, and the new Key is added to the RPC folder. You will need to expand the RPC folder to see the new key as shown in Figure 16.7.

FIGURE 16.7
The newly added Internet key under the RPC folder in the left pane of the registry editor.

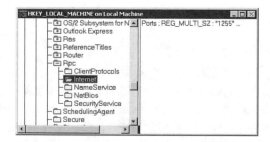

6. Select the newly created Internet Key in the left pane; choose **E**dit, select Add Value. The Add Value dialog box opens.

7. Enter the name Ports in the Value Name field, then choose the REG_MULTI_SZ data type. Click OK. The Multi-String Editor dialog box opens.

8. In the Data field, enter the port number(s) that you want RPC to use (ports must fall in the range of 0 to 65,535.

   To specify multiple ports, enter each one on a separate line or you can enter a range of ports such as "1255-1300".

9. Using steps 6 through 8, add another value under the Internet key with a name value of PortsInternetAvailable. Give it a data type of REG_SZ and enter Y for the data.

10. Add another value under the Internet key with a value of UseInternetPorts, a data type of REG_SZ, and a data value of Y.

11. Configure your firewall to allow incoming access to these ports.

Managing DTC

You can start and stop the DTC service from the Component Services tool. Simply right-click the computer that you want to start or stop the service on, and choose the Start MS DTC or Stop MS DTC option from the pop-up menu that is displayed.

When the service is stopped, you will notice that the computer icon contains a red, downward-pointing arrow to indicate that the service is not running as shown in Figure 16.8.

FIGURE 16.8
The red, downward-pointing arrow next to the My Computer icon indicates that the DTC service has been stopped on this computer.

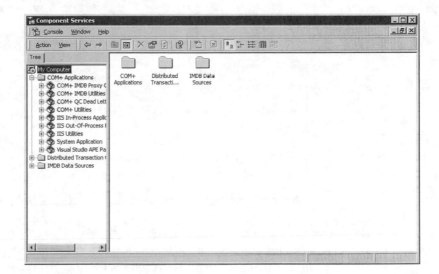

Alternatively, you can start or stop DTC by using the Computer Management tool, selecting the Distributed Transaction Service from the list of services, and using the Stop or Start buttons on the toolbar.

If you are the command-line kind of person, you can use `msdtc -start` or `msdtc -stop` at the command line.

Viewing Transaction Information

In the Component Services tool, you can expand the Distributed Transaction Coordinator icon in the console tree to view the Transaction List and the Transaction Statistics.

If you want to change the view of the transaction list, right-click a blank area in the details pane and choose View from the pop-up menu. You can select Large or Small icons, List view, or Details view.

Monitoring DTC

You can monitor the performance of DTC using one of two methods—System Performance Monitor or the Component Services Administrative tool.

Start the Performance Monitor tool from the Administrative Tools window by double-clicking the Performance icon (see Figure 16.9).

FIGURE 16.9
The Performance Monitor can be started from the Administrative Tools window by double-clicking the icon.

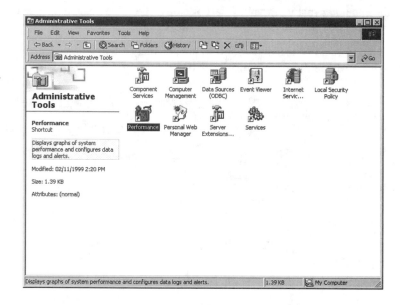

To add a counter to the graph, select the + button in the details pane. In the Add Counters dialog box, choose the computer that you want to monitor, and under the Performance object drop-down list box, select Distributed Transaction Coordinator. You can now select counters that you would like to monitor.

To monitor DTC from the Component Services tool, expand the DTC icon and choose the Transaction Statistics icon. The details pane now displays the statistics screen.

Using IMDB Data Sources

The In-Memory Database is a database cache that resides in the computer's memory and gives the COM+ applications on that computer rapid access to the data held in that cache.

IMDB can also cache temporary information, using the Transacted Shared Property Manager (TSPM), and you can use that cached information to create temporary tables.

IMDB also can cache data from back-end databases, but it does so through the use of OLE DB technology. IMDB supports the following OLE DB providers:

- ODBC (Kagera) to SQL 6.5 and SQL 7.0
- ODBC (Kagera) to Oracle 7 and 8
- Native OLE DB provider (Luxor) for SQL
- Native OLE DB Provider (Canoe) for Oracle

TIP For more specific information pertaining to these database access methods, you can perform a search on the Microsoft developer Web site at http://msdn.microsoft.com.

Oracle also provides information pertaining to accessing its database offerings at http://www.oracle.com/html/dev_it.html.

On Intel-based computers, IMDB can use up to 3GB of cache memory. If you have an Alpha-based system that supports the Very Large Memory architecture on Windows 2000, IMDB can use that memory for its cache.

Part
IV
Ch
16

Creating and Assigning an Account to IMDB

The IMDB service operates under the local system account on the computer on which it is installed. This arrangement is fine if you are accessing data on the local computer only. If you need to access data on a back-end database that resides on another computer on the network, however, you will need to configure security for IMDB. To accomplish this, you must set up a user account that has access to the necessary data sources on the network and then assign that account to IMDB.

You should create a group or set of groups that will include user accounts for the purpose of accessing the IMDB service. Creating a group first and then assigning users to the group is a better way of assigning access. In this way, if any changes are necessary, you can make those changes to the group instead of to each individual user.

N O T E For these accounts to access IMDB, they must be added to the IMDB Trusted User Roles. This is accomplished using the Component Services administration tool, as described later in this chapter. ■

▶ For an in-depth discussion of group security issues, **see** "Tools for Managing User Accounts and Groups," **p. 198**

▶ To learn more about managing group accounts, **see** "Managing User Accounts and Groups," **p. 217**

Configuring IMDB

To access data on a back-end database, you must configure the connection and permissions between IMDB and the database.

To configure IMDB, follow these steps:

1. Open the Component Services.
2. When you have the Component Services window displayed, expand the Component Services icon to gain access to the computer icon. Right-click the computer icon and choose Properties; the My Computer Properties sheet opens.
3. Select the Options tab, shown in Figure 16.10.

FIGURE 16.10
Use the Options tab of the My Computer Properties sheet to configure IMDB.

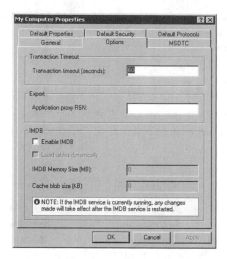

4. The first option that you must select is the Enable IMDB check box, which is located in the IMDB area at the bottom of the tab.

5. If you want tables to load as they are requested and not when the service starts, select the Load Tables Dynamically check box.

6. In the IMDB Memory Size text box, enter the amount of memory that you want IMDB to use for the cache. (If you leave this value as 0, IMDB uses a default setting; for the default settings, see the online help file.)

7. In the Cache BLOB Size field, enter the maximum size of Binary Large Object (BLOB) data that can be stored in the cache.

8. Click the OK button to close the dialog. You will need to stop and restart the service for the changes to take effect.

Adding User Accounts to the IMDB Trusted Users Role Group

For users to access IMDB, their accounts must be added to the IMDB Trusted User Role. You can do this by creating a group and then assigning users to that group. You can then assign the group to the IMDB Trusted User Role. Assigning accounts as a group simplifies administration. When you assign an account to the IMDB Trusted User Role group, you in effect configure secure access to IMDB and to other data stores.

▶ Create a group using the procedures outlined in "Managing Security for User Accounts and Groups," **p. 204**

To assign a group to the IMDB Trusted User Role, follow these steps:

1. Open the Component Services tool, and double-click the System Application icon under the COM+ Applications listing.

2. Expand the Roles entry and double-click the IMDB Trusted User icon. This will expand to display a Users folder.

3. Right-click the Users folder, and then choose New, User from the menu. The Select User or Groups dialog box opens.

4. Double-click the account group you created earlier to add it to the list box.

5. Click the OK button to close the dialog box and add the user to the details pane.

If you need to access data on another computer, you must assign the IMDB service to a user account that has access to the other computer and the data store. To perform this procedure, follow these steps:

1. In the Component Services console tree, select Services.

2. In the details pane, right-click the IMDB Server icon and choose Properties. The IMDB Properties dialog box is displayed.

3. Open the Log On tab. By default, the service uses the Local System Account; clear this option by selecting the User Account option. This action fills in the Account, Password, and Confirm password fields with the default LocalSystem account information. You must select a user account that is able to access the necessary resources.

4. Click the Browse button. This displays the Select User dialog box.

5. From the list of available users, select the account you want to use and click OK. You are returned to the IMDB Service Properties dialog box.

6. Enter the password for the user account that you selected, and then click OK. A message box appears, indicating that the service must be shut down and restarted for the changes to take effect.

7. To verify that the changes have taken effect, in the Services details pane, locate the IMDB Server entry and verify that the user account is listed in the Log On As column.

Defining a Data Source for IMDB Tables

If you will be accessing data from back-end databases, you must configure the information necessary to gain access to that data. This information is known as a *data source name (DSN)* and is used by IMDB to locate the data source.

NOTE The procedure outlined in this section defines the data source for IMDB, but the steps don't provide details concerning the various data source requirements. You should consult the online help files and the data source provider's documentation for details regarding their specific implementations. ■

To define a back-end data source, follow these steps:

1. In the Component Services window, right-click IMDB Data Sources, and then select New, Data Source from the pop-up menu. The New IMDB Data Source dialog appears.

2. Type a name for the data source in the Name field. This name must be unique and typically consists of the computer name and database name. (This string is not case-sensitive.)

Part
IV

Ch
16

3. In the OLE DB Provider Name field, type the exact name of the provider that will be used to access this data source.

4. Type the name of the computer that is hosting the database in the Provider Data Source field.

5. In the IMDB Catalog Name field, type the name of the database that the data will come from.

N O T E If you will be accessing an Oracle database, this field must be left empty. ▨

6. Enter any provider-specific properties in the Provider Properties field.

7. Click OK.

Adding or Removing Tables in IMDB

You can set up dynamic loading of tables and have IMDB load the tables that are requested by users. Another method is to specify the tables to load at startup. These tables will exist when the service is running and be available to the users.

To add a table, follow these steps:

1. Double-click the IMDB Data Sources icon in Component Services.

2. Double-click the data source that you want to update.

3. Right-click the Tables folder, and then choose New, Table from the pop-up menu.

4. In the IMDB Data Source Table dialog box, enter the name of the table that you want to load at startup.

5. If you no longer need a table in the list, right-click that table and choose Delete to remove it. The table will not be loaded at the next startup.

Creating a Log File for Troubleshooting IMDB

One of the best tools that you can possibly have for troubleshooting IMDB is an up-to-date log file. This log file can be useful for determining the state of the service at certain times.

N O T E If the IMDB Service is stopped, the log file information is not maintained. A new log file is started with the service. ▨

To create a log file, you set start parameters in the IMDB Properties dialog. Follow these steps to create a log file:

1. Open the Properties sheet for the IMDB Service.

2. Select the General tab.

3. Select Stop to stop the service.

4. In the Start Parameters field, enter the following string:
```
-f imdbsrv.log -fo SEWI
```

The -f option is used to give the log a filename.

The -fo option is used to specify a set of messages to record. You can select any combination of the letters in SEWI. (SEWI stands for Success, Error, Warning, and Informational messages.)

5. Click the OK button.

In the online help file are tables that list the error messages returned by IMDB and those written to the log file. You should review these tables for explanations regarding specific error messages.

Part

IV

Ch

16

Computer Management: System Tools

Overview

Windows 2000 integrates many administrative functions that formerly were standalone applications into various Microsoft Management Console (MMC) snap-ins. The Computer Management snap-in lets you manage several system configuration items. Use one of the following methods to open the Computer Management snap-in:

- Open Computer Management in Control Panel/Administrative folders.
- Double-click the file COMPMGMT.MSC located in the *systemroot*\System32 folder.
- Right-click My Computer and choose Manage.

This chapter focuses on system tools in the Computer Management snap-in. Many of the functions these tools offer were handled by standalone utilities in previous versions of Windows NT. Local users and groups, for example, were previously handled by User Manager. The Event Viewer tool has taken the place of the Event Viewer application. Each section identifies not only the current tool but also the Windows NT utility it replaced.

N O T E Some items in the System Tools branch are referenced in passing in the following sections because they are covered in detail in their own chapters. These sections are noted and their respective chapters identified within each applicable section. ▧

Performance Logs and Alerts

You can monitor your system performance with Performance Logs and Alerts in System Tools. Moreover, you can define events and properties to be monitored and logged as well as generate system alerts when specified events or performance criteria occur. Performance Logs and Alerts replaces Performance Monitor in Windows NT 4.x.

The following are available in Performance Logs and Alerts:

- *Counter Logs.* Use to record data about hardware performance and system activities and services to track your system's performance and utilization. Typical objects you can track include (but are not limited to) processor, logical disk, physical disk, print queue, redirector, etc. You can track multiple properties for each of the monitored objects.
- *Trace Logs.* Use to monitor specific event occurrences related to processes, threads, disk I/O, TCP/IP, page faults, and file I/O. When the event occurs the data is sent to the log service.
- *Alerts.* Set an alert on a counter to define a message to be sent, program run, or log started when the selected counter meets a specified criteria. Alerts enable you to trigger an action when an event occurs.

While Performance Logs and Alerts gives you access to the settings for the counter logs, trace logs, and alerts, it doesn't give you access to the actual Performance Monitor graphs (see Figure 17.1).

FIGURE 17.1
The Performance Monitor offers more information than Performance Logs and Alerts.

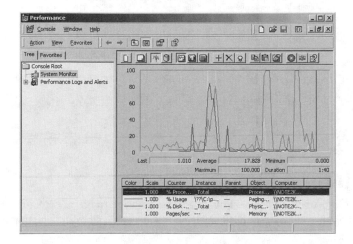

Configuring and using performance counters, logs, and alerts goes beyond the scope of this book. For detailed information on monitoring system performance, refer to *The Windows NT Workstation Advanced Technical Reference*. Although not written for Windows 2000, the material in the ATR is germane to Windows 2000 performance monitoring.

Local Users and Groups

Local Users and Groups lets you view and modify selected properties for user and group accounts, just as the User Manager does in Windows NT 4.x. Figure 17.2 shows Groups expanded to show groups on the local computer.

You can create new user accounts and groups as well as modify properties of existing accounts and groups (assuming you have the appropriate rights and permissions). Creating and managing user accounts and groups is such an important topic that it, as well as the Local Users and Groups tool, are covered in detail in their own chapters. See Chapter 12, "Managing User Accounts and Groups," for complete coverage.

FIGURE 17.2
Groups on the local computer.

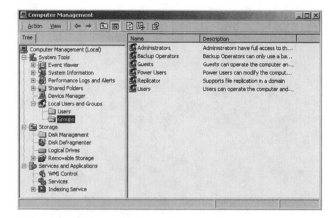

System Information

System Information gives you quick access to a wide range of configuration and status information about your system hardware and resources. System Information is divided into four branches:

- *System Summary.* Displays an overview of the system showing operating system version, system name, system type, information about memory, and other basic system information.

- *Hardware Resources.* Provides information about resource conflicts, DMA utilization, IRQ settings, and other hardware resource properties.

- *Components.* Provides information about specific hardware components, such as the display adapter, modem, I/O ports, and so forth.

- *Software Environment.* Offers information about drivers, environment variables, services, and other operating system software settings that determine the way your hardware functions and Windows 2000 operates.

- *Internet Explorer 5.* Provides information about Internet Explorer's configuration settings, files, and cache.

- *Applications.* Offers information about installed applications.

The following sections provide more detail about the settings and objects in System Information.

TIP Click System Information and choose **V**iew, and then choose either Advanced or Basic depending on the type of view you want. The Advanced view includes all the information provided by the Basic view, including additional information most useful to advanced users or system support technicians.

System Summary

System Summary displays basic information about your computer, which generally is self-explanatory. Information provided includes operating system version, memory properties, BIOS revision, etc., and can be useful for troubleshooting system problems and taking a system inventory for potential upgrades.

You can perform limited tasks within System Summary. Right-click in the System Summary and choose All Tasks to access the following tasks:

- *Find.* Choose this to locate information in the System Information node based on a search string that you specify. See the section, "Finding Specific Data in System Information," later in this chapter for more information.

- *Save As System Information File.* Choose to save all data in System Information, including resources and other information, to a file that can be loaded and viewed in the MMC. This feature is useful for sending the data file to a support technician for troubleshooting and archiving your system configuration.

- *Save As Text File.* Choose this to save only the System Summary data to a text file. You then can use Notepad, WordPad, or another text editor to view, modify, and print the file.

You also can print a report from System Summary. Unfortunately the Computer Management snap-in doesn't provide a means of customizing the report so you'll end up with several pages of detailed information about your system. If you want to print only the system summary, first save the summary to a text file, and then open the file in Notepad or WordPad to print it.

Hardware Resources

Hardware Resources provides information about the resources used by your computer. Figure 17.3, for example, shows IRQ utilization for the target system. The resources reported by Hardware Resources include the following:

- *Conflicts/Sharing.* Lists the Interrupt Request Lines (IRQs) that are shared or that indicate a conflict between two or more devices.

- *DMA.* Shows Direct Memory Access (DMA) assignments for each device that uses DMA.

- *Forced Hardware.* Lists hardware for which resource settings are forced, overriding Plug-and-Play or hardware defined settings.

- *I/O.* Lists the input/output base address ranges and the addresses assigned to each device that requires one. The I/O base address typically is used by the system as an entry point to communicate with the device. Address ranges that are not used are marked as "Free."

- *IRQs.* Lists Interrupt Request (IRQ) assignments for each device requiring one. IRQs are used to signal the CPU that a device needs the CPU's service. IRQs that are available are marked as "Free."

Part

IV

Ch

17

■ *Memory.* Lists memory ranges in the Upper Memory Area (UMA), which is the memory address range between 640KB and 1MB, and the devices to which the various memory ranges are assigned.

Hardware Resources provides a means of viewing current assignments and status, but does not provide a means of modifying resource usage. Use the Device Manager to make changes to resource assignments.

▶ **See** "The Device Manager," **p. 117**

FIGURE 17.3
IRQ utilization in the Hardware Resources node.

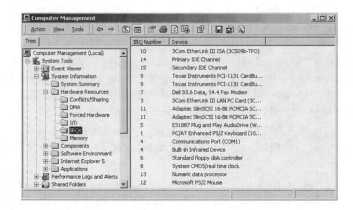

Components

Components organizes and displays information about the various system components and their drivers and settings. As with the other nodes under System Information, you can only view the information, not change settings.

Software Environment

Software Environment displays a wide range of information about your system's operating system configuration, including driver status, active network connections, services status, and much more. You can only view information in Software Environment, not change it.

Finding Specific Data in System Information

System Information provides a search feature you can use to locate specific information about hardware or settings in the System Information branch, which is particularly helpful because the amount of data in System Information is extensive.

Use the following steps to search for specific data in System Information:

1. Open Computer Management and click the level at which you want to search (System Summary, Hardware Resources, and so forth).

2. Click **A**ction, **F**ind, and enter your search text in the Find **W**hat text box.

3. Choose between the following options:

   Check **R**estrict Search to Selected Category to search only the currently selected category. Uncheck this to search all categories.

   Check Search Categories **O**nly to search only the console (left) pane and not the results (right) pane for the specified text. Uncheck this to search the results pane as well.

4. Click **F**ind Next to begin the search.

Saving System Information to a File

You can take a *snapshot* of your system, saving its current settings to a file at any time. Snapshots are useful for recording system status and generating a system configuration file that can be reviewed by a support technician for troubleshooting purposes. You also can use snapshots to monitor system configuration for users across the LAN.

You can save the data to a System Information file, which uses a proprietary binary file format that can be viewed only with the Computer Management snap-in, or to a text file that can be viewed with any text editor.

Choose **A**ction, Save As System **I**nformation File to save the file in binary format. Choose **A**ction, **S**ave As Text File to save the data to a text file. In either case, you are prompted to specify the name of the file to create. System Information Files do not receive a file extension by default. Text files receive a standard TXT file extension.

 TIP System Information files by default are stored in your My Documents folder unless you specify a different location. Your own My Documents folder is located in the folder \Documents and Settings*username*\My Documents, where *username* is the name under which you are logged on. Double-click a System Information file to open the file in the MMC for viewing or printing.

Running System Tools

You can use the **T**ools menu in Computer Management to access several additional system management tools that are described elsewhere throughout this book. The Computer Management snap-in organizes these tools under a single menu.

Services

Services in the Computer Management snap-in lets you view the status of system and application services, as well as start, stop, restart, pause, and resume these services. Services takes the place of the Services Management tool in the Windows NT 4.x Control Panel. Figure 17.4 shows the Services branch opened to display these services.

Part
IV

Ch
17

FIGURE 17.4
Service status displayed in the Services branch.

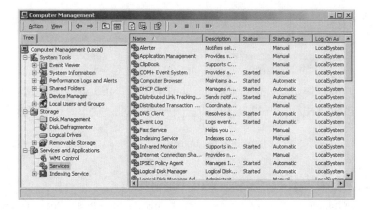

Understanding Services

In Windows 2000, as in Windows NT, *services* are applications that perform specific functions within the operating system. Device drivers, for example, function as services. Other system-wide functions are handled by services. These services include, for example, networking, logon, scheduling, print spooling, remote access, and many more. In addition to the services that are included with Windows 2000 Professional, third-party applications often include or are designed to run as services. You might install a virus scanner, for example, that starts automatically as a service when the computer boots and constantly monitors the system for viruses.

Starting and Stopping Services

A running service processes requests and otherwise performs the functions for which it was designed. Stopping a service terminates the service, ceases its function, and removes it from memory. Starting a service initializes the service and activates it so it can perform its job.

You also can *pause* and *resume* services. Pausing a service is similar to stopping a service with the exception that the service remains in memory and can be started again more quickly than if it were stopped.

Resuming a paused service reinitializes the service and "turns it back on" so it will again accept requests and perform its job.

One of the easiest methods for starting, stopping, pausing, and resuming services is to use Services in Computer Management\System Tools. Follow these steps to control a service's operation:

1. Open the Computer Management snap-in, and then click Services.
2. Right-click the desired service and click Start, Stop, Pause, Resume, or Restart, as appropriate.

N O T E   An alternative to the previous steps is to double-click the service to open its properties (refer to Figure 17.4) and click Start, Stop, Pause, or Resume as appropriate. ■

> **TIP** Choosing Restart from the service's context menu pauses then resumes the service. This is the same as manually pausing and resuming the service except it combines both tasks into a single command.

Starting and Stopping Services from the Console Prompt

You also can start and stop services from the Windows 2000 command console by using the NET START and NET STOP commands. You must know the name of the service, however, in order to use the console to start or stop it. For example, you would use the following command to start the Microsoft Fax Service:

```
net start fax
```

Double-click a service in the Services list to display its properties. You'll find the service name listed on the General tab. This is the service name you can use with NET START and NET STOP to start and stop the service.

> **TIP** You can use NET STOP and NET START to control services on a remote computer if the Telnet service is running on the remote computer. Telnet to the computer, and then issue the NET STOP or NET START commands at the console prompt.

Setting Service Properties

You can specify several properties for each service that determine how the service starts and functions. Double-click on a service in the list or right-click on the service and choose Properties to view its properties. The following sections describe service properties.

General The General tab (see Figure 17.5) displays general information about the service and enables you to start and stop the service and control its startup options.

Name by which service is listed in the Services node. Modify the name if you choose.

FIGURE 17.5
The General service tab.

Optional description to identify service or its function.

Start the selected service.

Stop selected service and remove from memory.

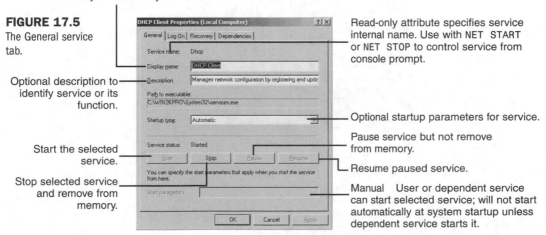

Read-only attribute specifies service internal name. Use with NET START or NET STOP to control service from console prompt.

Optional startup parameters for service.

Pause service but not remove from memory.

Resume paused service.

Manual   User or dependent service can start selected service; will not start automatically at system startup unless dependent service starts it.

Part
IV

Ch

17

Log On   The Log On tab (see Figure 17.6) lets you specify how the service will log on to the system and under which hardware profiles it will operate.

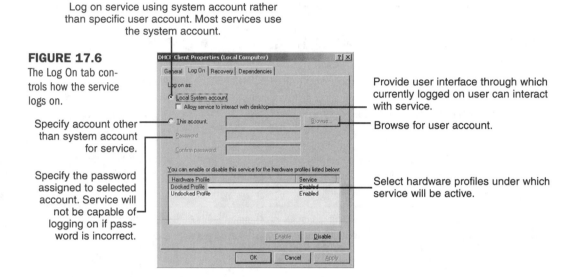

Log on service using system account rather than specific user account. Most services use the system account.

FIGURE 17.6
The Log On tab controls how the service logs on.

Specify account other than system account for service.

Specify the password assigned to selected account. Service will not be capable of logging on if password is incorrect.

Provide user interface through which currently logged on user can interact with service.

Browse for user account.

Select hardware profiles under which service will be active.

Recovery   The Recovery tab (see Figure 17.7) defines the course of action to be taken if the service fails. These options enable you to automate system recovery and troubleshoot service startup problems. Table 17.2 explains these options.

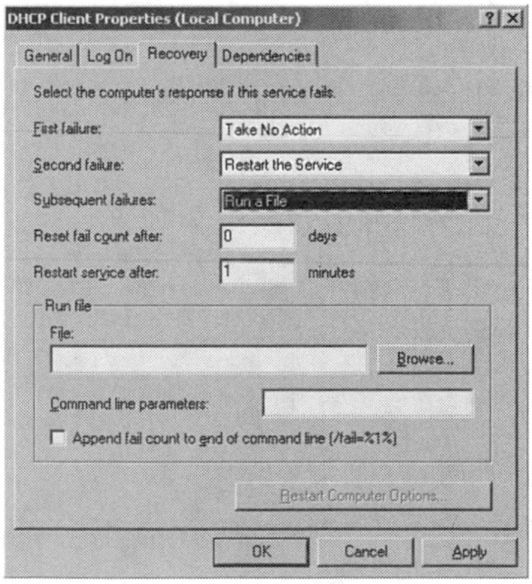

FIGURE 17.7
Control what happens when a service fails using the Recovery tab.

Table 17.2 Service Recovery Options

Option	Use
First failure, Second failure, and Subsequent failures	Define action Windows should take on first, second, and subsequent attempts to recover after service fails. Choose from one of following four options:
Take No Action.	No attempt is made to recover or restart service.
Restart the Service.	Attempts to restart service.
Run a File.	Executes file specified by Run File control group.
Reboot the Computer.	Reboots computer if service fails.
Reset 'Fail Count' to zero after *n* day(s)	Specifies number of days after which fail counter is reset to zero.
Restart service delay	Specifies delay in minutes between service failure and attempt to restart service. Providing delay enables system to stabilize after failure.
Run the following file	Runs script or other file upon failure of service.
Command line parameters	Specifies any optional command line parameters to include with application or script that will run upon service failure.
Append 'Fail Count' to end of command line	Enables option to have current fail count appended to end of command line specified in Run the following file text box. The string /fail=%1% is appended to command line, and %1% is replaced by actual fail count value.
Reboot Computer Information	Click to view Reboot Computer Information dialog and specify a delay before booting and optional reboot message.

Dependencies   The Dependencies tab (see Figure 17.8) identifies services on which the selected service depends, as well as services that depend on it.

FIGURE 17.8
The Dependencies tab.

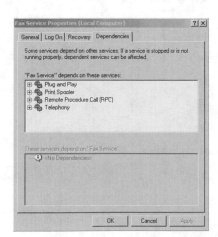

Any services on which the selected service depends must be running in order for the dependent service to start and function properly. The dependency list is hierarchical, giving you a view not only of directly dependent services, but also of dependent services farther down the chain.

Shared Folders

Shared Folders in System Tools provides functions previously handled by Server Object in the Windows NT Control Panel. You can view the number of connections to a share, view and change share properties, and see information about open files through Shared Folders. You also can close files and disconnect users.

N O T E Before modifying or creating shared resources you should review Chapter 11, "Understanding System Administration and Security," if you don't already have an understanding of how permissions affect the availability of shared resources. ■

Shares

Shares under Shared Folders lets you view your computer's shared resources (see Figure 17.9). These include administrative shares as well as normal shares. Administrative shares are defined automatically by Windows 2000 for administrative purposes and include a dollar sign ($) at the end of the share name to make the shares hidden from browsing. These administrative shares include:

- *C$, D$, etc.* Each local hard disk is shared.
- *ADMIN$.* This is the *systemroot* folder (the folder containing Windows 2000).
- *IPC$.* Named pipes are shared under this share name.
- *print$.* This share supports shared printers.

FIGURE 17.9
The Shares node shows normal and hidden shares.

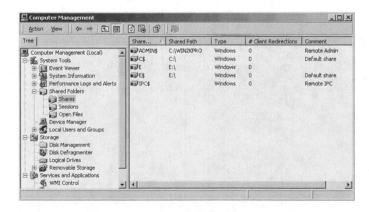

Any additional shares that your system hosts also appear in the shared folder list.

Viewing Share Properties Double-click a share or right-click a share and choose Properties to view the share's properties. The General tab, described in Figure 17.10, shows the name by which the folder is shared, the path to the folder, and other general information.

FIGURE 17.10
Control a shared folder through its properties.

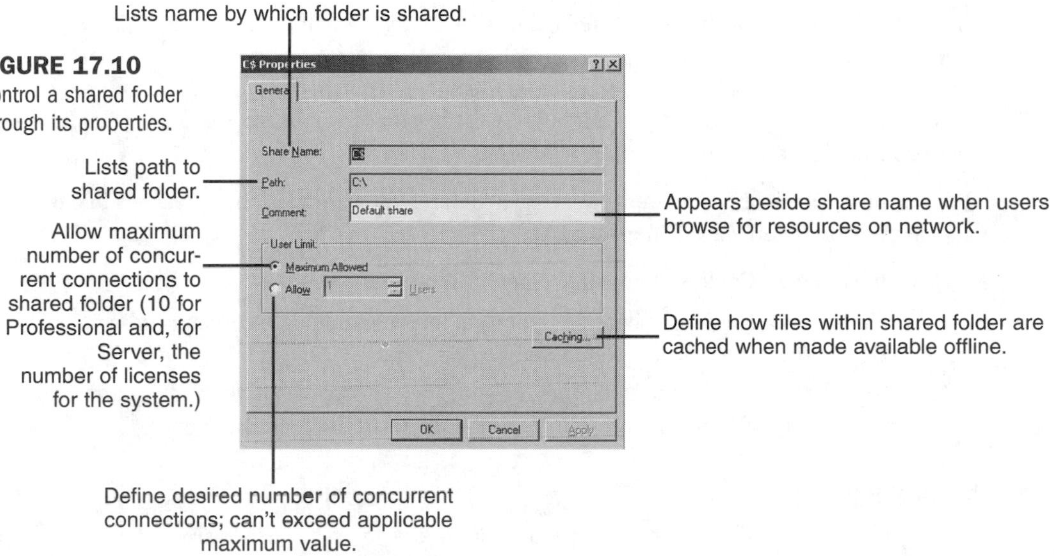
C$ Properties
General
Share Name:
Path:
C:\
Comment:
Default share
User Limit
Maximum Allowed
Allow
Users
Caching...
OK
Cancel
Apply
Lists name by which folder is shared.
Lists path to shared folder.
Allow maximum number of concurrent connections to shared folder (10 for Professional and, for Server, the number of licenses for the system.)
Appears beside share name when users browse for resources on network.
Define how files within shared folder are cached when made available offline.
Define desired number of concurrent connections; can't exceed applicable maximum value.

TIP See Chapter 13, "Managing and Sharing Workstation Resources," for more information on offline access and caching.

NOTE These options are not available for administrative shares created automatically by Windows 2000.

The Share Permissions tab lets you modify the groups and permissions that apply to the share. Refer to the section, "Creating New Shares," below for more information about share permissions.

Stopping a Share Stopping a share removes the share from access by other users. It does not affect the folder or contents of the folder in any way other than to prevent access to it by remote users.

Right-click a share and choose Stop Sharing to stop the share. You also can select a share and choose Action, Stop Sharing to stop a share.

Creating New Shares Creating a new share makes the selected folder available for access by other users across the network. The type of access these users have, if any, is determined by the permissions applied to the shared folder, files, and subfolders.

N O T E Access to shared resources is determined by two sets of permissions: *share* and *NTFS* (if the shared folder resides on an NTFS partition). One type of permission does not override the other, but the most restrictive permission takes precedence. ▨

By default, folders are shared with full control for Everyone, which means that unless you change the share permissions or use NTFS permissions to restrict access to the share and its contents, all users will have full control over the share. This includes the ability to delete files and make other changes that you might not want to grant to all users. Consider what level of access you want others to have prior to sharing a folder.

You can use either of two methods to share a folder. Follow these steps to share a folder using the Computer Management snap-in:

1. Open Shared Folders\Shares in Computer Management.
2. Click **A**ction, **N**ew, **F**ile Share or right-click in the Results (right) pane and choose New File **S**hare to start the Create Shared Folder Wizard.
3. Browse to and select the folder you want to share or type its path in the Folder to share box. Modify the share name and description if desired; then click **N**ext.

CAUTION

Sharing the root folder of a disk makes the entire disk available to remote users, subject to the share/NTFS permissions you apply to the folder and its contents.

---

4. Choose permission options using Table 17.3 as a guide.

Table 17.3   Set Permissions Dialog Options

Option	Use
All users have full control	This default allows everyone full control.
Administrators have full control; other users have **r**ead only access	Retain full control and grant others read permission.
Administrators have full control; other users have **n**o access	Retain full control and deny others any access.
Customize share and folder permissions	Select and click **C**ustom to assign custom permissions.

 TIP Use a dollar sign ($) at the end of a share name to hide the share, preventing others from seeing the share when they browse for resources. Others can connect to the share if they know its name.

5. Click Finish to begin sharing the folder, **B**ack to make changes, or Cancel to cancel the process.

You also can share a folder from the folder's context menu, bypassing the Computer Management snap-in and the Create Shared Folder Wizard. This lets you share folders from Explorer.

▶ **See** "Sharing Disk Resources," **p. 246**

Exporting the Share List You might on occasion find it useful to be able to export your list of shared folders to an external file. For example, you might want to export a large share list to a database for manipulation or for inclusion in a web document or report. Through the Computer Management snap-in you can export the share list to either a tab-delimited or comma-delimited text file.

Use the following steps to export a share list to a text file:

1. Open the Computer Management snap-in, and then open the Shared Folders branch.

2. Click Shares; then choose **A**ction, Export **L**ist to access the Save As dialog.

 TIP You also can right-click in the Results pane (not on a share) and choose Export **L**ist from the context menu.

3. Specify the location and filename for the export file. Choose the format for the file based on the type of application in which you'll later import the list. Then click **S**ave to export the list to the file.

Sessions

Sessions under Shared Folders (see Figure 17.11) lists the client connections to your computer, the number of files open by each session, and other information about each connection.

FIGURE 17.11
The Sessions node displays information about client connections.

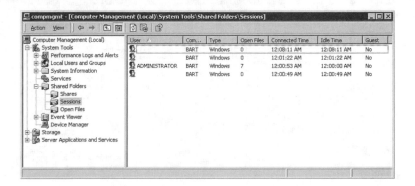

Refreshing the View   You can refresh the view of the Sessions results pane to make sure that the view shows the current status of all client sessions. Right-click in the Results pane or on Sessions and choose Re*f*resh to update the contents of the results pane based on the current connection status.

Disconnecting Sessions   You can use Sessions to disconnect client connections from your computer. Note, however, that disconnecting a session could result in lost data if the remote user has files opened through the session. You should attempt to warn users prior to disconnecting them.

Use the following steps to disconnect one or more sessions:

1. Open Shared Folders\Sessions in Computer Management.
2. To disconnect all sessions, right-click Sessions and choose Disconnect **A**ll Sessions from the context menu.
3. To disconnect a single session, right-click on the session in the results pane and choose Close **S**ession from the context menu.

Exporting the Sessions List   As with the Shares list, you can export the list of current sessions to a tab- or comma-delimited file for analysis or reporting. Click Sessions and choose **A**ction, Export **L**ist or right-click Sessions and choose Export **L**ist. See the section, "Exporting the Share List," earlier in this chapter for additional information on exporting data.

Open Files

Open Files (see Figure 17.12) lists the files that are open by other users on your computer. The information displayed includes the filename, user who has the file open, session type, number of file locks, and mode in which the file is opened.

FIGURE 17.12
Open Files shows files opened by other users on your computer.

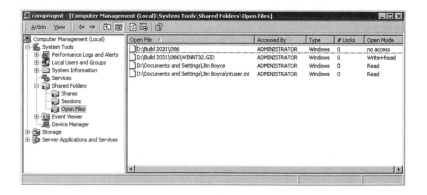

Use Open Files not only to view which files are open and by whom, but also to close files. Closing a file can potentially cause a loss of data if the user has modified the file but not saved changes, so you should attempt to notify the remote user prior to closing a file.

Right-click on a file and choose **C**lose Open File from its context menu to close the file. Right-click the Open Files node and choose Disconnect **A**ll Open Files to close all files that are opened by remote users.

Event Viewer

Event Viewer in Computer Management lets you view the System, Application, and Security logs for your computer. The Application log contains event messages generated by applications and certain Windows 2000 operating system components. The Security log contains event messages generated by security events such as logon, resource access (when auditing is enabled), and so forth. The System Log primarily contains event messages generated by the various operating system components.

Event Viewer in Computer Management takes the place of the Event Viewer application in Windows NT. Viewing events and managing the event logs is such an important management feature that it is covered in detail in Chapter 20, "Event Viewer."

Part

IV

Ch

17

Device Manager

Device Manager in System Tools lets you view the properties of and configure hardware in your computer. The Device Manager is useful not only for configuring hardware but also for troubleshooting device conflicts and problems with individual devices. The Device Manager also lets you enable and disable devices for specific hardware profiles. As shown in Figure 17.13, the Device Manager by default displays the various system component categories as individual expandable branches in the results pane.

FIGURE 17.13
Use Device Manager to configure and troubleshoot devices.

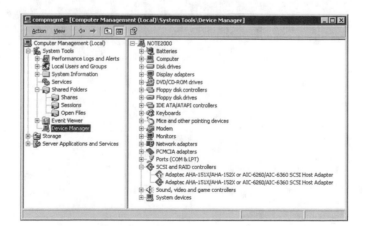

The Device Manager takes on some of the tasks from the Devices, SCSI Devices, Ports, and other hardware configuration tools in the Windows NT Control Panel. Much of the functionality in the Device Manager is new for Windows 2000 in support of Plug and Play and the new hardware management mechanisms offered by Windows 2000.

 TIP When you are managing a remote computer through the Computer Management snap-in, the Device Manager functions in read-only mode for the remote computer. You must run Device Manager locally on the computer in order to make changes to hardware settings. Connecting through the Computer Management snap-in to a Windows NT 4.x workstation results in no information being displayed in the Device Manager, as Windows NT 4.x does not support Plug and Play or the hardware management mechanism employed by Device Manager.

Device management is a major function of configuring and managing a computer, so Device Manager is covered in detail in Chapter 7, "Managing Hardware."

18

Computer Management: Storage

> **N O T E** This chapter assumes you are using the Computer Management snap-in to manage your
> local workstation. You can, however, connect to and manage other computers through the
> Computer Management snap-in. Any pertinent differences between managing the local computer ver-
> sus a remote computer are noted throughout this chapter where appropriate. ■

Overview

This chapter focuses on the Storage branch of the Computer Management snap-in, which
offers functions that were handled by standalone utilities in Windows NT. Disk Management,
for example, takes the place of the standalone Disk Management utility. Each section in the
rest of this chapter identifies not only the current tool but also the Windows NT utility it
replaced or supplemented, where applicable.

> **N O T E** For comprehensive coverage of the Removable Storage Manager, see Chapter 21,
> "Removable Storage Manager." ■

Disk Defragmenter

You can use Disk Defragmenter in Computer Management (see Figure 18.1) to analyze the
fragmentation of disks in your system and to defragment drives if desired. The capabilities
provided by Disk Defragmenter are new in Windows 2000. Previous versions of Windows NT
did not include a defragmenting utility, although third-party applications are available that perform the same function.

Disk Defragmenter can analyze and defragment FAT, FAT32, and NTFS partitions.

FIGURE 18.1
The Disk Defragmenter
tool is new in Windows
2000.

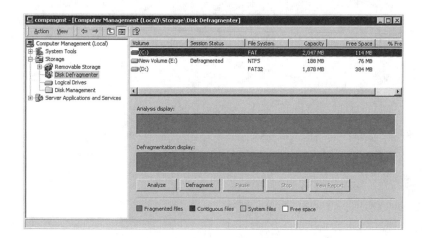

Understanding Fragmentation

The smallest unit of logical disk storage space is the *cluster*, which is a group of *sectors*. Clusters are arranged on a disk in circular *tracks*. Windows 2000, by default, attempts to store files in contiguous clusters on the disk for best performance. Having a file in contiguous clusters means that Windows can read the entire file in one pass without having to move the heads to (potentially) several different locations on the disk to reassemble the entire file or file segment being read. Reducing head movement improves disk access speed.

As files are erased, rewritten, and modified, the contiguous free space on the disk becomes used and files begin to become *fragmented*, or scattered into non-contiguous clusters. Because the system is perfectly capable of reassembling all the "pieces" of a file to re-create the whole, fragmentation doesn't pose a problem per se. Jumping around the disk to read data does, however, impose a performance penalty. As CPU and bus speeds increase, hard disk performance becomes more critical for overall system performance.

You therefore should *defragment* your system hard disk(s) periodically to ensure optimum system performance. Defragmenting a drive rearranges the data on the disk into contiguous clusters. Figure 18.2 shows a disk before and after analysis and defragmentation. A color legend provides at-a-glance information about the drive.

FIGURE 18.2
A disk after defragmentation.

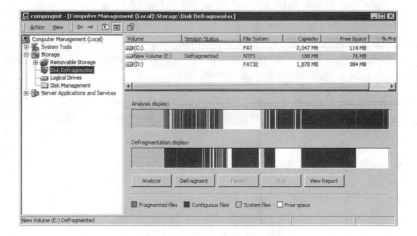

Part
IV
Ch
18

N O T E Defragmenting a disk does not increase the amount of free space on the disk. Remove files, compress folders and files, or change the default cluster size to increase free space. You can't change cluster size without reformatting a disk in Windows 2000 (and therefore deleting all of the data on the disk). Some third-party utilities are available, however, that can change cluster size without reformatting.

You can increase free space on FAT partitions by switching to FAT32. Windows 2000 provides native support for FAT32. See http://www.sysinternals.com for a FAT32 driver for Windows NT 4.x systems.

Consolidating free space and increasing free space are separate issues. Disk Defragmenter does not consolidate all of the free space on the disk into a contiguous area. The defragmentation process does consolidate free space to some degree, but having all free space in a contiguous area does not offer a significant performance improvement.

Disk Defragmenter can't gain exclusive access to certain system files on a disk and therefore can't defragment these files. The paging file (virtual memory) and the Master File Table (NTFS volumes) are examples of files that Disk Defragmenter can't defragment.

Analyzing Disks for Fragmentation

Although you don't have to analyze a disk prior to defragmenting the disk, you might want to do so to determine the state of the disk and whether it really needs defragmenting. Defragmenting a disk can be relatively time-consuming, so you'll probably only want to do it when necessary or perhaps on a weekly basis.

 TIP Time to defragment a disk varies according to several factors including disk size, number of files, percentage of fragmentation, and available system resources.

When you click on a disk in the Disk Defragmenter window, the previous status of the disk is loaded and displayed graphically (refer to Figure 18.2).

To analyze a disk for fragmentation, select the disk in the Volume pan, and then choose **A**ction, **A**nalyze. Or, right-click the drive and choose **A**nalyze from the context menu. Upon completion, Disk Defragmenter displays a dialog with a recommendation on whether or not the disk needs to be defragmented.

Click View **R**eport to display a report window similar to the one shown in Figure 18.3. The report offers general information about the drive as well as the results of the fragmentation analysis.

FIGURE 18.3
A disk analysis report.

Defragmenting Disks

Defragmenting a disk is a simple process but can take some time if the disk is large. You therefore might want to defragment a disk when you are not using the system. Follow these steps to defragment a disk:

1. Open Disk Defragmenter and select the volume you want to defragment.
2. Choose **A**ction, **D**efragment, or right-click the volume and choose **D**efragment.

Disk Defragmenter Reports

Disk Defragmenter stores an analysis/defragmentation report for each drive showing status as of the last analysis or defragmentation operation. Follow these steps to view, save, or print Disk Defragmenter reports:

1. Select the volume with the report you want to view and choose **A**ction, View **R**eport. Or, right-click the drive and click View **R**eport from the context menu.
2. Click **P**rint to print the report or click **S**ave As to save the report to a text file.

Unattended Defragmentation

Unfortunately, the Disk Defragmenter tool in Windows 2000 does not include a feature to schedule defragmentation. You must manually start the defragmentation process. The command-line components of Disk Defragmenter, Dfrgfat.exe and Dfrgntfs.exe, do not support command-line arguments, which otherwise would enable you to use the AT command to perform a defragmentation. Unless you use a third-party application to perform defragmentation, you'll have to manually start the defragmentation tool at a convenient time, such as when you leave your computer at the end of the day.

 TIP For security reasons you should enable a screen saver with password protection to prevent other users from accessing your system while you are away from it (for example, if you leave it defragmenting at the end of the day.)

Logical Drives

You can view the status and properties of logical drives in your system with Logical Drives in Computer Management\Storage (see Figure 18.4). You also can use Logical Drives to change the label of a volume and set permissions on NTFS volumes.

Part
IV

Ch
18

FIGURE 18.4
Use Logical Drives to
set basic properties on
a drive.

Viewing and Changing General Properties

You can use Logical Drives to view general properties for a drive such as total capacity, space used, free space, partition type, etc. You also can change the volume label of a logical drive.

Double-click a drive in the drive list, select a drive and choose **A**ction, P**r**operties, or right-click a drive and choose P**r**operties to view the General tab for the drive (see Figure 18.5).

The only property you can set on the General tab is the volume label. Volume labels are useful for applying an optional description to a drive and appear under a drive's icon in Explorer and in other locations such as file dialogs. Simply click in the **L**abel text box and type a label up to 11 characters; then click either OK or **A**pply.

FIGURE 18.5
The General tab for a
drive shows basic drive
information, but most
properties are informa-
tion only.

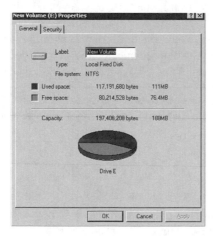

Setting Security on NTFS Volumes

NTFS volumes include an additional tab labeled Security. You can use the Security tab (see Figure 18.6) to apply NTFS permissions to the volume.

FIGURE 18.6
Use the Security tab to set NTFS permissions.

The Security tab shows the NTFS permissions for the root folder of the logical drive. Whether subfolders receive these permissions depends on the settings for each folder for inheritable permissions (discussed in more depth shortly). Unlike in Windows NT, you do not have the option on the Security tab to directly apply the selected permissions to all files and subfolders under the selected folder.

Place a check mark beside each permission as desired in the Allow or Deny columns to set permissions. As you make selections you might notice that some changes happen automatically. Deny Write permission, for example, and the Full Control and Modify boxes in the Allow column automatically deselect.

Click OK or **A**pply to apply the new permissions when you're satisfied with your selections.

> **N O T E** You can click Ad**v**anced to set advanced properties for the volume. Setting advanced NTFS permissions most often will apply to individual folders rather than an entire volume. For that reason, setting advanced NTFS permissions is discussed in Chapter 11, "Understanding System Administration and Security."

Disk Management

Every operating system needs some mechanism through which you can manipulate the file system at the lowest level to manage partitions and perform other disk management tasks. Disk Management in Computer Management\Storage serves that purpose and takes the place of the Windows NT Disk Administrator.

Disk Management lets you perform a variety of administrative tasks on disk drives, including the following:

- Create and delete partitions on a hard drive and create and delete logical drives within an extended partition.
- Format disks and apply volume labels.
- View information about a drive, although the information given is the same as you will find in the disk's properties, which you can access by right-clicking a drive icon in Explorer and choosing Properties.
- Assign drive letters to hard drives and CD-ROM drives.
- Create and delete *spanned volumes*. A spanned volume consists of areas of two or more disks that are grouped together to form a logical drive or volume. Spanned volumes let you gather together smaller blocks of free disk space into a single, larger logical drive. Spanned volumes are referred to as *volume sets* in Windows NT.
- Extend the size of a spanned volume.
- Create and delete *striped volumes*. Striped volumes are similar to spanned volumes in that they enable you to create a logical drive that spans more than one physical disk. The primary advantage to striped volumes is that they offer improved performance over standard disks because each disk in a striped volume can read and write simultaneously. Striped volumes do not offer any fault tolerance, however. If a disk in the set fails, all data on the stripe set is lost. So, you should combine some form of fault tolerance or use a good backup scheme when employing striped volumes. Striped volumes are referred to as *stripe sets* in Windows NT.

N O T E Striped volumes represent RAID (Redundant Array of Inexpensive Disks) Level 0. Windows 2000 Professional does not support RAID above RAID 0, which means you will need to employ hardware-based RAID if you need fault tolerance on your Windows 2000 Professional system. You can, however, use Disk Management on a Windows 2000 Professional computer to create and manage mirrored volumes and RAID-5 volumes on Windows 2000 Servers. This book does not cover creation or management of mirrored or RAID-5 volumes. ▥

When you install Windows 2000, Setup formats the installation drive according to your specifications. You can use Disk Management after installation to modify your workstation's file system.

N O T E Disk Management does not offer a means for changing the size of FAT or NTFS partitions. You can, however, change the size of spanned volumes. ▥

> **CAUTION**
>
> Unlike its predecessor Disk Administrator, Disk Management performs most functions right away rather than requiring that you commit the changes. When you delete a partition, it is gone. You can't recover it by exiting Disk Management without committing changes. So, be careful with the operations you perform with Disk Management.
>
> Also, whenever you modify the file system using Disk Management you should update your Windows NT repair and system state data.

▷ **See** "System Repair and Recovery," **p. 276**

Support for Dynamic Volumes

In addition to replacing the functions in Windows NT's Disk Administrator, the Disk Management tool also supports *dynamic volumes*, which are new in Windows 2000. Windows 2000 now refers to older, partition-based volumes as *basic volumes*. Disks that contain dynamic volumes are called *dynamic disks* and those that contain basic volumes are called *basic disks*. Dynamic volumes use a different on-disk structure than basic disks.

Dynamic disks are not limited to four volumes as are basic disks. Dynamic disks support all the same logical volume types as basic disks including simple, spanned, striped, mirrored, and RAID-5 volumes. Dynamic volumes can be formatted in FAT, FAT32, and NTFS. In most cases, you perform the same types of tasks in the same way regardless of whether the disk or volume is basic or dynamic. Functions that differ for dynamic volumes are covered in the section, "Special Operations with Dynamic Disks and Volumes," later in this chapter.

In addition, Windows 2000 offers only limited support for spanned and striped volumes on basic disks, supporting these volumes fully only on dynamic disks.

▷ **See** "Working with Spanned Volumes," **p. 352**

▷ **See** "Working with Striped Volumes," **p. 354**

Part
IV

Ch
18

 TIP Dynamic disks and their volumes are inaccessible to non-Windows 2000 operating systems on *multiboot systems* (those which contain other operating systems in addition to Windows 2000). In addition, you can't mix dynamic and basic volumes on a dynamic disk. Dynamic disks and their volumes are, of course, accessible by other operating systems across the network when shared from a computer running Windows 2000.

A Quick Tour of Disk Management's Interface

You can manage disks using any of three views: Volume List, Disk List, and Graphical. Figure 18.7 shows Disk List view on top and Volume List view on the bottom. Figure 18.8 shows Graphical view, and the bottom pane has been turned off.

FIGURE 18.7
The Disk List and
Volume List views.

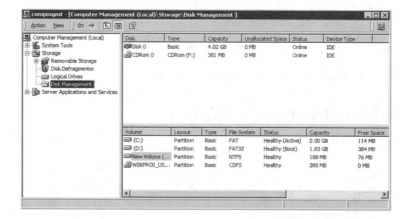

FIGURE 18.8
The Graphical view
offers a more intuitive
view of the disks.

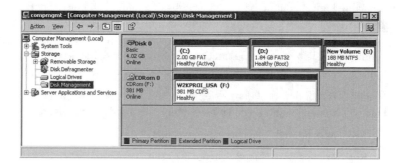

The advantage in using Graphical view is that you can see at a glance which physical drives are associated with which logical drives. Volume List view offers additional information not shown in Graphical view, such as percent free. Disk List simplifies the display if you're interested in physical rather than logical drives. The rest of this chapter assumes you are using Graphical view except as noted where other views are more useful.

 TIP Disk Management by default displays the top pane in Volume List view and the bottom pane in Graphical view. To hide the bottom pane and work with a single pane, choose **V**iew, Botto**m**, Hidd**en**.

To work with a particular drive or block of unpartitioned space, click on the drive or unpartitioned space in Disk Management.

Installing New Disks in a System

After you install a new disk in a system, use Disk Management to scan for the new disk and prepare the disk for use (create partitions, dynamic volumes, format, etc.).

Using a New Disk   After installing the new disk, start the system and log on. Open Disk Management and click **A**ction, **R**escan Disks.

> **N O T E**   New disks are added as basic disks. See the section, "Upgrading a Basic Disk to a Dynamic Disk," later in this chapter if you want to make the new disk dynamic.

Moving Disks Between Systems   When you move a disk from one system to another the new drive will typically be recognized automatically. You can manually force Disk Management to recognize and import the new disk if for some reason it does not import automatically.

Follow these steps to move a disk from one system to another:

1. Shut down both systems and move the drive to the new system.
2. Turn on the system, log on, and open Disk Management.
3. Disks that have not completed the import process are marked as Foreign in the Status column. Right-click the disk and choose Import Foreign Disk.

Working with Basic Disks and Volumes

You can use Disk Management to create partitions from unpartitioned space on a basic disk. You also can delete partitions, format drives, and assign drive letters.

> **CAUTION**
> Deleting a partition deletes all data contained in that partition. Make sure you have backed up the partition prior to deleting it (if you want to be able to restore the data from the partition).

Creating a Partition   A basic disk can contain up to four primary partitions or three primary partitions and one extended partition. Extended partitions can contain multiple logical drives. To create a partition, follow these steps:

1. Click on a block of unpartitioned space (labeled *free space*) in Disk Management.
2. Choose **A**ction, All Ta**s**ks, Create **P**artition to start the Create Partition Wizard; then click **N**ext to access the Select Partition Type page.

TIP You can also right-click an area of free space and choose Create Partition from the context menu.

3. Choose **P**rimary partition or **E**xtended partition, as desired.

4. Specify the desired partition size in the Specify Partition Size dialog (see Figure 18.9). A partition can be as small as 1MB or as large as the amount of free space available. Click **N**ext to continue.

FIGURE 18.9

The Specify Partition Size dialog.

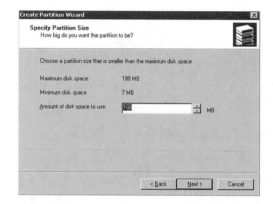

5. *Primary partitions only:* Choose a drive letter for the new partition. (This does not apply to extended partitions.)

   Or, choose the **D**o not assign a drive letter or drive path option if you do not want to assign a drive letter at this time. Click **N**ext to continue.

6. *Primary partitions only:* Use Figure 18.10 as a guide for your selections in the Format Partition dialog; then click **N**ext:

7. *Primary and extended partitions*: Click Finish to complete the partition creation process.

You can format a partition after creating it if you prefer (refer to step 6). A partition must be formatted before you can store data on it. Refer to the section, "Formatting a Drive," later in this chapter for additional information on formatting using Disk Management.

TIP See the section, "Working with Mounted Volumes," later in this chapter for an explanation of how to create a new logical drive from an empty NTFS folder.

FIGURE 18.10
The Format Partition
dialog.

Choose desired drive
format (FAT,
FAT32, or NTFS).

Cluster size for
the new drive.

Optional label for drive.

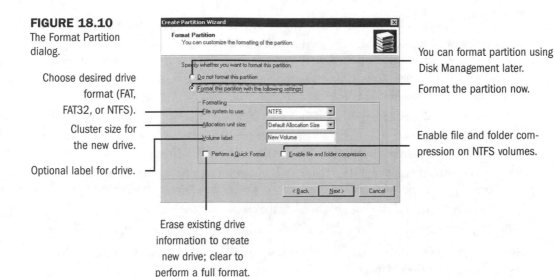

You can format partition using
Disk Management later.

Format the partition now.

Enable file and folder compression on NTFS volumes.

Erase existing drive
information to create
new drive; clear to
perform a full format.

Deleting a Partition You might, on occasion, need to delete a partition. For example you
might want to completely reinstall your system, and deleting the partition is the quickest way
to destroy the old data. Deleting a partition removes the partition information for that partition and reassigns the space in the partition as free space. You then can use that space to create another partition, spanned volume, or striped volume.

To delete a partition, follow these steps:

1. *IMPORTANT*: Make sure you have backed up all data in the partition if you want to
   retain the data.
2. Click the partition and choose **A**ction, All Tas**k**s, **D**elete Partition. Or, right-click the
   partition and choose **D**elete Partition from the context menu.
3. Disk Management prompts you to confirm the deletion. Click **Y**es to delete the partition or **N**o to cancel the operation.

Creating a Logical Drive An extended partition differs from a standard partition in that it
can contain multiple logical drives. A physical disk can contain only one extended partition.

You create an extended partition in much the same way you create a standard partition:

1. Create the extended partition per the instructions in the section, "Creating a Partition,"
   earlier in this chapter.

Part
IV

Ch
18

2. Select the extended partition, and then choose **A**ction, All Tas**k**s, Create **L**ogical Drive.

 Or, right-click the extended partition and choose Create **L**ogical Drive from the context menu. Either action starts the Create Partition Wizard. Click **N**ext to display the Select Partition Type dialog.

3. The **L**ogical drive option is automatically selected. Click **N**ext to continue.

4. Specify the desired drive size, and then click **N**ext to continue.

5. Choose a drive letter for the new logical drive or choose **D**o not assign a drive letter or path if you don't want to assign one at this time. Then click **N**ext.

6. In the Format Partition dialog, choose options for formatting the new logical drive based on the options described previously in the section, "Creating a Partition."

7. Click **N**ext; then click Finish to complete the creation of the logical drive.

8. Repeat the steps to create additional logical drives in the extended partition, if desired.

Formatting a Drive   Before you can use a newly created drive, you must format the drive. Use these steps in Disk Management to format a volume:

1. Select the partition or logical drive to format in Disk Management.

2. Choose **A**ction, All Tas**k**s, **F**ormat, to access the Format dialog (see Figure 18.11).

FIGURE 18.11
The Format dialog.

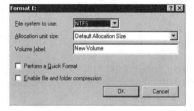

3. Specify the desired file system type (FAT, FAT32, or NTFS) from **F**ile system to use.

4. Choose the desired cluster size from **A**llocation unit size.

5. Specify a label in the **L**abel text box.

6. Choose **Q**uick Format if you want the partition to be formatted without checking the drive for errors.

7. Select **E**nable file and folder compression, if desired, for an NTFS volume.

8. When prompted to confirm that you want all data in the partition to be overwritten, choose OK.

Reformatting a Drive   You can use Disk Management to reformat any drive—with two exceptions. You can't change the Windows 2000 system or boot partitions within Windows 2000. Instead, you must run the Setup program again to reinstall Windows 2000, which will give you the option of reformatting the partition. All data on the disk will be deleted, so make sure you have a backup of the data if necessary.

TIP   See the section, "Converting a FAT Volume to NTFS," later in this chapter to learn how to convert a FAT partition to NTFS without reinstalling Windows 2000.

Specifying Drive Letters   When you create a logical disk by creating a standard partition, creating logical drives in an extended partition, or creating a dynamic volume, you have the option of assigning a drive letter to the drive. You can, however, change the letter assigned to the drive. This is particularly useful for rearranging drives, such as moving a CD-ROM drive's letter to the end of your hard drives.

To assign a drive letter, follow these steps:

1. Select the drive you want to change in Disk Management.

2. Choose Action, All Tasks, Change Drive Letter and Path to display the Change Drive Letter and Paths for (X:) dialog.

    Or, right-click on the drive and choose Change Drive Letter and Path from the context menu.

3. Click Edit to display the Edit Drive Letter or Path dialog (see Figure 18.12).

Part
IV
Ch
18

FIGURE 18.12
The Modify Drive Letter
or Path dialog.

4. Select a drive letter and click OK, and then click Yes to confirm the change or No to cancel.

TIP   You can create a volume with no drive ID associated with it. This is useful if you are creating more than 24 volumes (using all available drive letters). You cannot, however, access a drive unless you assign a letter to it or mount it to an empty NTFS volume.

Designating the Active Partition   Although a disk can contain more than one partition, only one partition at a time can be the *active partition*. When the system boots, it boots the operating system found in the active partition.

N O T E In the case of a multiboot system containing Windows 2000, Windows NT, or Windows 95/98, all operating systems can reside in the same partition. Therefore, it isn't necessary in this case to change the active partition to switch from one to the other. The Windows 2000 boot loader offers you the option of booting each operating system.

You must activate the desired operating system's partition if you want to switch from an operating system in one partition to the operating system in another partition, such as boot UNIX. Select the partition you want to make active, and then choose **A**ction, All Tas**k**s, **M**ark Partition Active.

Special Operations with Dynamic Disks and Volumes

Although you perform most tasks in the same way whether on a basic disk or dynamic disk (or volume), some tasks are different on dynamic disks or not available on basic disks. The following sections describe tasks you can perform on dynamic disks and volumes.

N O T E Although Windows 2000 offers limited support for spanned and striped volumes on basic disks, dynamic disks offer full support for these volume types. The sections later in this chapter that deal with spanned and striped volumes focus primarily on dynamic disks.

Upgrading a Basic Disk to a Dynamic Disk   Before you can begin working with dynamic volumes, you must create a dynamic disk. When you install a new disk in a system, Windows 2000 installs it as a basic disk. You then can upgrade the basic disk to a dynamic disk. After the dynamic disk is created you can begin creating dynamic volumes in the disk.

The following notes apply to upgrading a basic disk to a dynamic disk:

- You can't change dynamic volumes back to partitions. You instead must delete the dynamic volumes then convert the disk back to a basic disk. (See the section, "Convert a Dynamic Disk to a Basic Disk," later in this chapter for more information.)

- Prior to upgrading a basic disk to a dynamic disk you should close all applications and files that are open on the disk.

- A basic disk to be upgraded to a dynamic disk must contain at least 1MB of unallocated space.

- A dynamic disk can't contain partitions or logical drives, but instead can only contain dynamic volumes.

- Dynamic disks can't be read locally by operating systems other than Windows 2000 (applicable only to multiboot systems).

- Upgrading a basic disk containing existing partitions to a dynamic disk causes the existing volumes to be converted to simple volumes on the dynamic disk. Mirrored, striped, spanned, and RAID-5 volumes on a basic disk are converted to their dynamic counterparts, respectively.

Follow these steps to upgrade a basic disk to a dynamic disk:

1. Install the new disk as described previously in the section, "Installing New Disks in a System."

2. Start the system, log on, and open Disk Management.

3. Click the basic disk you want to upgrade to a dynamic disk and choose **A**ction, All Tas**k**s, **U**pgrade to Dynamic Disk.

   Or, right-click the disk and choose **U**pgrade to Dynamic Disk from the context menu.

4. Verify that you have selected the correct drive in the Confirm Upgrade to Dynamic Disk dialog, and then click **U**pgrade. Windows 2000 initializes the disk and brings it online.

Creating a Simple Volume   After you create a dynamic disk you can create simple volumes on the disk. Simple volumes are much like individual partitions or logical drives in that they represent a single, logical file system.

Follow these steps to create a simple volume on a dynamic disk:

1. Select the area of unallocated space in which you want to create the simple volume.

2. Choose **A**ction, All Tas**k**s, Create **V**olume, or right-click the unallocated space and choose Create **V**olume from the context menu to start the Create Volume Wizard.

3. Click Next to access the Select Volume Type dialog, and with **S**imple Volume automatically selected, click **N**ext again.

4. Specify the size for the new volume in the Select Disks dialog; then click **N**ext.

5. Choose a drive letter, specify the path to an empty NTFS folder, or choose the option **D**o not assign a drive letter or drive path, as desired, on the Assign Drive Letter or Path dialog. Click **N**ext.

6. Specify options for formatting the new volume in the Format Volume dialog (see the section, "Formatting a Drive," earlier in this chapter for more information). Click **N**ext.

7. Review your settings, and then click **F**inish to complete the task.

Reactivating a Dynamic Disk or Volume   A dynamic disk or volume might show up as Missing or Offline in Disk Management if the disk has become corrupted, was powered down, or was disconnected. You can bring a missing or offline disk or volume back online through Disk Management. Open Disk Management and click the disk or volume you want to bring online. Choose **A**ctions, All Tas**k**s, Rea**c**tivate Volume, or Rea**c**tivate Disk, as appropriate. Or, right-click the disk or volume and choose Rea**c**tivate Disk or Rea**c**tivate Volume, as appropriate, from the context menu.

The disk or volume's status should change to show Online after the disk is reactivated.

Deleting a Dynamic Volume   You can easily delete a dynamic volume from a dynamic disk. Doing so removes the volume and all its data. Deleted volumes can't be recovered, so you should make sure you have a backup of the data if you want to retain the data.

Open Disk Management and select the volume you want to delete. Choose **A**ction, All Tas**k**s, **D**elete Volume. Or, right-click the volume and choose **D**elete Volume from the context menu. Click **Y**es to delete the volume or **N**o to cancel the operation.

Convert a Dynamic Disk to a Basic Disk   You can convert a dynamic disk back to a basic disk to enable create partitions, extended partitions, and logical drives on the disk. Converting a dynamic disk back to a basic disk requires that you first delete all dynamic volumes from the disk, so you should make sure you have the data in those volumes backed up if you intend to keep the data.

Follow these steps to convert a dynamic disk back to a basic disk:

1. Back up all data that you want to retain from all volumes in the dynamic disk.

2. Open Disk Management and delete all volumes from the dynamic disk using the steps described in the previous section of this chapter.

3. Select the disk to be converted, and then choose **A**ction, All Tas**k**s, **R**evert to Basic Disk. Or, right-click the disk and choose **R**evert to Basic Disk from the context menu. Disk Management converts the disk without any further prompting.

Working with Spanned Volumes

As briefly explained earlier in this chapter, a spanned volume brings together free space of varying sizes from two or more drives. Spanned volumes enable you to piece together a logical drive from bits and pieces here and there on your drives. It's a little like making a quilt from scraps of fabric, but the result is a fully functioning logical drive.

Spanned volumes offer one other major advantage: They enable you to combine as many as 32 hard drives to create a single, possibly huge volume. However, the space allocated to a spanned volume does not have to consist of the entire drive, which makes it possible to use smaller amounts of free space from one or more drives to create the set. Remember that spanned volumes do not offer any fault tolerance. If one drive in the spanned volume fails, all data in the set is lost.

Although Windows 2000 recognizes and supports spanned volumes created on basic disks with Windows NT, Windows 2000 does not enable you to create or expand spanned volumes on basic disks. These functions are available only on dynamic disks.

 TIP   Although you can't create or expand spanned volumes on a basic disk, you can use Disk Management to delete spanned volumes from basic disks.

Creating a Spanned Volume   To create a spanned volume, follow these steps:

1. Open Disk Management and select the first area of free space on a dynamic disk to be added to the spanned volume. Choose <u>A</u>ction, All Tas<u>k</u>s, <u>C</u>reate Volume.

   Or, right-click the unallocated space and choose <u>C</u>reate Volume from the context menu. Either action starts the Create Volume Wizard.

2. In the wizard click <u>N</u>ext, choose Spanned Volume, and click <u>N</u>ext again.

3. In the Select Disks dialog, select at least one additional drive to add to the set (see Figure 18.13) and click <u>A</u>dd.

4. Click <u>N</u>ext, and then follow the remaining wizard prompts to specify a drive letter or mount to NTFS folder, format type, and other options as you would a standard volume.

FIGURE 18.13
Choose one or more additional drives to add to the set.

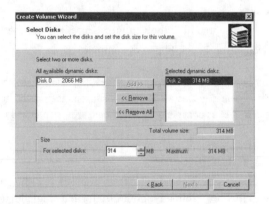

Part
IV

Ch
18

Extending a Simple or Spanned Volume   You can make a simple or spanned volume larger by adding more free space to the volume. If you extend a simple volume, it becomes a spanned volume. The following notes apply to extending simple and spanned volumes:

- You can only extend volumes that contain no file system or that are formatted as NTFS. You can't extend FAT or FAT32 volumes. You can, however, extend such a volume after converting the volume to NTFS.
  ▶ **See** "Converting a FAT Volume to NTFS," **p. 357**

- You can't extend simple volumes that were upgraded from basic volumes. You can only extend simple volumes that were created on dynamic disks.

- The system and boot volumes can't be extended.

- Striped, mirrored, and RAID-5 volumes can't be extended.

- You can extend a simple volume within its original disk or onto additional disks.

- A simple volume extended onto multiple disks becomes a spanned volume and can't be mirrored or striped.

- After you extend a spanned volume you can't delete any portion of the volume without deleting the entire spanned volume.

To extend a simple volume or spanned volume, follow these steps:

1. Open Disk Management and select the simple volume or spanned volume; then choose **A**ction, All Tas**k**s, E**x**tend Volume, or right-click the volume and choose E**x**tend Volume from the context menu.

2. Click Next to access the Select Disks dialog.

3. Add and remove dynamic disks from the **S**elected dynamic disks list using **A**dd and **R**emove. The disks listed in **S**elected dynamic disks are the ones that will be used to expand the volume.

4. Specify how much space to add to the volume using Size, and then click **N**ext.

5. Review your selections and click Finish to complete the task.

N O T E   After you extend a spanned volume, you can't reduce it by removing selections. You must back up the set, remove it, re-create it at the new size, and then restore the data. A spanned volume must be formatted as or converted to NTFS before you can extend it.

Working with Striped Volumes

Windows 2000 lets you create striped volumes, which represent RAID level 0. A *striped set* comprises multiple disks that are grouped together to form a single logical drive. When data is written to the disk, it is broken into stripes that are written sequentially to each of the drives in the stripe set. So, a single file would potentially be spread across all drives in a set.

Striped volumes offer increased performance. In an SCSI subsystem, each drive can read and write independently of the others, meaning that all drives can be reading and writing at the same time. Striping the data onto multiple disks improves the read/write performance of the logical drive. If you need to read a file, the disk subsystem can read each stripe at the same time and reassemble them into the file. With large files, this process is quicker than if the disk had to read the entire file from a single disk.

CAUTION

Striped volumes offer no fault tolerance. If a drive in a stripe set fails, all data in the set is lost. Windows 2000 Professional doesn't support any RAID levels that offer fault tolerance. If you require fault tolerance, you must switch to Windows 2000 Server or use a hardware-based RAID solution for your Windows 2000 Professional computer.

Creating a Striped Volume The process for creating a striped set is virtually identical to that for creating a spanned volume. Refer to the previous section on spanned volumes for more information, and choose Striped Volume instead of Spanned Volume in the Create Volume Wizard.

Deleting a Striped Volume If a drive in a stripe set fails, the stripe set is invalidated and must be deleted. Refer to the section, "Deleting a Dynamic Volume," earlier in this chapter for an explanation of how to delete a striped volume.

 TIP Striped volumes with parity, which are supported by Windows 2000 Server but not by Windows 2000 Professional, can be rebuilt if a single drive in the set fails. Switch to Windows 2000 Server if you need this capability on your computer.

Working with Mounted Volumes

Windows 2000 adds a new and very useful feature called *mounted volumes* not offered by Windows NT. This new feature lets you associate a volume with an NTFS folder, thereby making the volume appear as the contents of that folder. Rather than being recognized by a drive letter, the volume is recognized by the folder path. For example, you could mount a CD-ROM that has the drive ID of D into a folder called Library on drive C. To access the CD-ROM you could simply read from C:\Library or you could still access it as drive D.

Mounted volumes bring the benefits to the Windows 2000 operating environment that UNIX's distributed file system brings to that operating system. Volumes do not have to be contained on the same physical disk or partition to be seen as a homogenous file structure.

Following are some examples of how mounted drives can be useful:

- *Apply disk quotas on a selective basis.* You can mount a folder for your users to C:\Users and apply quotas to that folder without applying the quotas to the rest of drive C.

- *Increase apparent volume size without repartitioning or resizing a disk or volume.* You might prefer to maintain all applications in C:\Program Files, but the disk might be too small to contain any additional programs. Add a new drive to the system, format it as NTFS, and then mount it as C:\Program Files to expand the apparent size of drive C.

- *Create an apparently homogenous, virtual file structure from different disks.* You can mount volumes from various disks to create a file structure that you or users see as a single, homogenous file structure. For example, your drive C might appear to have 10 folders, but those folders could actually be 10 separate disks.

- *Overcome the 26-letter limitation imposed by using drive letter IDs.* Because you do not need a drive letter for a mounted volume, you can overcome the 26-letter limitation by using mounted volumes.

Part

IV

Ch

18

N O T E Mounted volumes are different from the Distributed File System (DFS) that enables a Windows 2000 server to build a homogenous file structure from local folders as well as remote shares. Mounted volumes apply only at the local computer. ■

Creating a Mounted Volume You use Disk Management to create mounted volumes. You can mount a local drive only at an empty folder on an NTFS volume. The NTFS volume can be basic or dynamic.

Follow these steps to create a mounted volume:

1. Open Disk Management tool and select the volume or partition you want to mount; then choose **A**ction, All Tas**k**s, Ch**a**nge Drive Letter and Path. Or, right-click the volume or partition and choose Ch**a**nge Drive Letter and Path from the context menu. Disk Management displays the Drive Letter and Paths dialog.

2. Remove the existing drive letter, if desired, by selecting the drive letter from the list and clicking **R**emove.

3. Click **A**dd to display the Add New Drive Letter or Path dialog (see Figure 18.14).

FIGURE 18.14
The Add New Drive Letter or Path dialog.

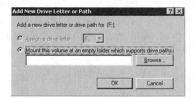

4. Select **M**ount this volume.

5. Type the path to the local, empty NTFS volume in the associated text box or browse for the folder; then click OK to mount the volume.

N O T E You can browse only when creating a mounted volume on the local computer. You must specify the path in the text box if using Disk Management to manage a remote computer. ■

Unmounting a Volume Disk Management lets you unmount a volume, making it no longer accessible under the selected path. Unmounting a volume has no effect on the data it contains, nor is the volume automatically removed from any other current mounts. Unmounting a volume simply disassociates the volume from the specified path.

Follow these steps to unmount a volume:

1. Open Disk Management and select the volume or partition you want to unmount; then choose **A**ction, All Tas**k**s, Ch**a**nge Drive Letter and Path.

2. Select the path you want to remove in the Drive Letter and Paths dialog, and then click **R**emove.

3. Click **Y**es to verify the operation or **N**o to cancel it.

Setting Disk Management Display Options

You can control Disk Management's display through the **V**iew menu. **V**iew, S**e**ttings displays its properties. The Legend tab lets you specify the color and pattern Disk Management uses to display various disk elements. The options on this property page are self-explanatory.

The Scaling tab (see Figure 18.15) lets you select between having Disk Management display disks based on their size or size them equally. This option determines the size of the box in which Disk Management shows the information about a drive in Graphical view. It has no effect on the actual size of the drive itself.

FIGURE 18.15
The Scaling tab determines the visual relationship between capacity and size on the screen.

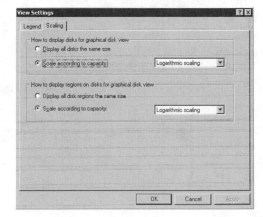

Part
IV
Ch
18

N O T E If a drive contains logical disks or partitions of considerably different size, choosing the option to display regions based on actual size option could cause the smaller partitions/logical disks to effectively disappear. To make them reappear, choose the option to display all disks/regions the same size. ▪

Converting a FAT Volume to NTFS

You might decide to convert a FAT or FAT32 partition to NTFS to take advantage of increased security, quotas, or other NTFS features. You can easily do so without risk of losing any of the data in the partition. However, keep in mind that if you boot any other operating systems on the computer that does not support NTFS (such as Windows 9x, DOS, or UNIX), you will not be able to read the FAT partition after it is converted to NTFS.

CAUTION

The version of NTFS in Windows 2000 is different from NTFS in Windows NT. Therefore, if you dual-boot your system with Windows NT after converting the drive under Windows 2000, you could experience problems in using the drive while running Windows NT.

You can't convert a FAT volume to NTFS using Disk Management, but the conversion process is germane to other topics covered in this chapter, so the conversion process is covered in this section.

To convert a FAT or FAT32 partition to NTFS, use the Convert command from a console prompt. The syntax of the Convert command is as follows:

```
Convert drive: /FS:NTFS [/V]
```

The following list describes the options for the Convert command:

- drive: Specify the drive letter of the drive to be converted.
- /FS:NTFS   This specifies that the drive should be converted to NTFS.
- /V   Use this optional switch to run the Convert utility in Verbose mode, which offers additional status information as the conversion takes place.

To convert drive D from FAT to NTFS, for example, use the following command:

```
Convert D: /FS:NTFS
```

Note that you can't convert the current drive without rebooting the system.

Data Sources (ODBC)

In this chapter

Overview

Open DataBase Connectivity (ODBC) provides a standard for database applications to share their databases with a wide variety of clients. A good example is Expertelligence's WebBase, a database connectivity server you can use to create web documents based on database queries. WebBase makes standard SQL database queries through the ODBC drivers to create web pages based on the data retrieved by the query.

ON THE WEB

http://www.expertelligence.com   Expertelligence Web Site

TIP   In effect, an ODBC driver acts as a transaction coordinator and translator between a client application and a database engine. It's a database middleman of sorts.

Client applications can access data held by data management systems after you install and configure your ODBC drivers and settings with the ODBC Data Source Administrator, located in the Administrative Tools folder of the Control Panel. This chapter explains how to configure data sources using the ODBC Data Source Administrator.

N O T E   For information regarding the available options for specific drivers, refer to the section, "Configuring Specific ODBC Drivers," later in this chapter. The following sections examine only common procedures and settings. ■

User DSN and System DSN

You can add, remove, and configure ODBC drivers with the User DSN (Data Source Name) and System DSN pages. A User DSN is visible only to the logon account that was active when the DSN was set up. System DSNs are visible local services to all users who log on to the local machine. The process for creating user and System DSNs is identical on their respective pages. Figure 19.1 shows the User DSN page. The System DSN page is nearly identical.

FIGURE 19.1
The User DSN and System DSN pages are nearly identical.

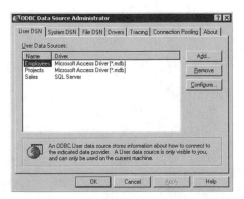

User Data Sources lists all user data sources currently installed. This section explains how to set up User and System DSNs.

To create a User or System DSN, follow these steps:

1. Select the User DSN or System DSN page as appropriate.
2. Click Add, select the driver you want to install, and then click Finish.
3. Define specific driver settings in the resulting dialog per later sections in this chapter.

To remove a data source driver, select the driver and click Remove.

To configure an existing data source, select the data source and click Configure. Modify settings as desired using the resulting dialog or wizard (which is the same one used to install the driver).

 TIP You can add more than one instance of a specific driver type. You might, for example, add an SQL data source for several different SQL servers in your enterprise.

File DSN

The File DSN page, which is very similar to User DSN and System DSN, enables you to add, remove, and configure individual file DSNs, which can be shared by all users who have the same drivers installed (subject to permissions assigned to each file DSN). You might choose to create a file DSN when you want to share a data source on a very broad basis, such as across the LAN, rather than restrict it to a single user or group of users.

Adding a File DSN

Adding a file DSN is very similar to adding a user or system DSN except that you first specify the file under which the data source settings are stored:

1. Open the File DSN page and click Add.
2. Select the driver for the data source you want to install; then click Next.
3. Specify the path to the file in which you want to store the driver configuration or click Browse to browse to the file. Click Next to continue.
4. Define specific settings in the resulting dialog or wizard.

Specifying the Default Directory

You can easily specify the default directory that will appear in the Look In drop-down list by default. Follow these steps:

1. Open the ODBC Data Source Administrator, and then open the File DSN page.
2. Choose the folder you want to define as the default using the Look In drop-down list.

3. Click **S**et Directory.

4. Click **Y**es to verify that you want to assign the folder as the default, or click **N**o to cancel.

Drivers

The Drivers page (see Figure 19.2) enables you to view information about available drivers. The information includes the driver name, version, authoring company, driver filename, and driver file date.

N O T E The Drivers page provides information; it does not enable you to change drivers. ∎

FIGURE 19.2
The Drivers page.

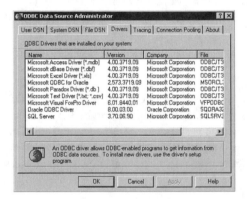

Tracing

The Tracing page (see Figure 19.3) enables you to implement tracing of ODBC tasks to troubleshoot problems with a client application or connection. You can start and stop tracing and configure tracing options through the Tracing page. When tracing is turned on, ODBC actions are logged to a file that you specify. You can monitor the contents of the file with a text editor to assist in identifying and correcting problems.

Table 19.1 explains the options in the Tracing page.

FIGURE 19.3
The Tracing page.

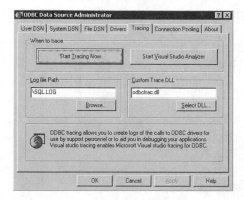

Table 19.1   Tracing Options

Option	How to Use	Why Use It
Start **T**racing Now/ Stop **T**racing Now	Toggle to start/stop tracing.	Trace ODBC tasks to troubleshoot problems with a client application or connection.
Start **V**isual Studio Analyzer/Stop **VI**sual Studio Analyzer	Toggle to start/stop Visual Studio Analyzer.	Use to assist in debugging and analyzing client-side applications.
Log File Path	Specify the path to or click **B**rowse to define the trace log file.	Specify the name and location of the log file.
Custom Trace DLL	Specify the DLL in the text box or click **S**elect DLL to browse for the file. The default DLL ODBCTRAC.DLL.	You can use a custom DLL supplied with another application or development included with Windows 2000 is environment (or one you create yourself) to provide tracing functions.

Part

IV

Ch

19

Connection Pooling

The Connection Pooling page (see Figure 19.4) lets you define whether ODBC device drivers can reuse open connection handles to the database server. Eliminating the need for applications to establish new connections to a server can improve performance, because the time and overhead involved in establishing the connection is considerably reduced. By default, Oracle and SQL connections are pooled but others are not.

FIGURE 19.4

The Connection Pooling page.

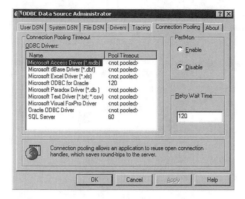

The Connection Pooling page includes the following controls:

- **_ODBC Drivers._** This lists the available drivers and their pool timeout values. The Pool Timeout column indicates drivers whose connections are not pooled. Double-click a driver to specify connection pooling options for the driver in the Set Connection Pooling Attributes dialog (see Figure 19.5).

FIGURE 19.5

The Set Connection Pooling Attributes dialog.

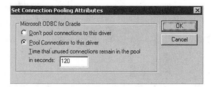

- **_Enable/Disable._** Use the PerfMon group of controls (**E**nable and **D**isable) to specify whether Performance Monitor will monitor ODBC connections.
- **_Retry Wait Time._** Use this to specify the number of seconds between connection retries.

About

You can use the About page (see Figure 19.6) to view file name and version information about the ODBC core components. The page is useful to help you determine if your core ODBC components are current but it does not enable you to configure any ODBC settings.

FIGURE 19.6
The About page.

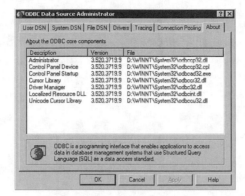

Configuring Specific ODBC Drivers

Windows 2000 includes several ODBC drivers that enable applications to communicate with various database engines. This section explains how to configure these individual ODBC drivers.

General ODBC Settings

You can configure most ODBC drivers through one or two dialogs. While dialogs are specific to each driver, many of the options are the same from driver to driver. So, rather than focus on each driver, this section explains the options. Table 19.2 lists the driver options and their applicable drivers. The following sections explain the SQL driver configuration, which you perform using a wizard.

Part
IV

Ch

19

Table 19.2 Common ODBC Options

Option	Access	dBASE	Excel	MS Oracle	Oracle	Paradox
Advanced	✓					
Approximate Row Count		✓				
Buffer Size	✓			✓		
Collating Sequence		✓				✓
Compact	✓					
Connect to Database in Read-Only Mode					✓	
Create	✓					
Data Source Name	✓	✓	✓	✓	✓	✓
Database Type						
Default						
Define Format						
Deleted						
Description	✓	✓	✓	✓	✓	✓
Enforce ODBC DayOfWeek Standard				✓		
Exclusive	✓	✓				✓
Extension/Extensions List						
Fetch Data in Background						
Include REMARKS in Catalog Functions				✓		
Include SYNONYMS in SQLColumns				✓		

Text	FoxPro	Use and Tips
		See, "Advanced Excel Options," later in this chapter.
		Determines whether or not table size statistics are approximated.
		Access: specifies size of the buffer used for disk I/O. Larger values increase memory use but can improve performance. Oracle: Specifies size, in bytes, to be allocated to buffer that holds fetched data. With Oracle driver you specify number of rows to fetch; Microsoft driver returns enough rows to fill buffer.
	✓	Selected language affects way items are sorted.
		Remove empty space in records to conserve space. Do not compact password-protected databases; you'll risk data loss or inability to access the database.
		Enable option to open database in read-only mode, preventing changes to data.
		Click to create new Access database compatible with Microsoft Access version 7.x or later.
✓	✓	Specify a name for the data source to appear in the Data Sources list.
	✓	Choose either Visual FoxPro database or Free Table directory depending on type of data in data source.
✓		Enable if you want all files to be listed in data source folder.
✓		Click to display Define Text Format dialog to specify file format for data source (define how data is interpreted).
	✓	Enable to include deleted records in the data source.
✓	✓	Specify optional description for data source.
		Select to set result set to ODBC day-of-the-week format, with Sunday=1 and Saturday=7 (Sunday as the first day of the week). Deselect to define Monday as the first day of the week (Sunday=7 and Monday=1).
	✓	Select to specify exclusive access to database file, locking file for use only by single user. Deselect to open in shared mode.
✓		Shows file extensions displayed for data source. Type new extension in the Extension field and click Add.
	✓	Enable to improve performance by having data fetched in background.
		Select to have driver return Remarks columns for SQLColumns result set. Deselect to improve performance if not required.
		Select to return column information for Tables, Views, and Synonyms with SQLColumns() API call. Deselect to speed response time.

Part

IV

Ch

19

continues

Table 19.2   Continued

Option	Access	dBASE	Excel	MS Oracle	Oracle	Paradox
Library					✓	
Net Style						✓
Null						
Option					✓	
Options	✓	✓	✓			✓
Page Timeout	✓	✓				✓
Path						
Prefetch Count					✓	
Read Only	✓		✓			
Repair	✓					
Rows to Scan			✓			
Select	✓					
Select Directory		✓	✓			✓
Select Indexes		✓				
Select Network Directory						✓
Select Workbook			✓			
Server/Service Name				✓		
Show Deleted Rows		✓				
System Database	✓					
Translation				✓		
Use Current Directory		✓	✓			✓
User Name/UserID				✓	✓	✓
Version		✓	✓			✓

Text	FoxPro	Use and Tips
		Specifies name of translation library to be used; not supported on all versions.
		Choose network style for this data source.
	✓	Enable to have driver include null fields.
		Specifies numeric value passed to translation library when library is called by Oracle ODBC driver; not supported on all versions.
✓	✓	Displays Driver section of the dialog to show additional options.
		Specifies amount of time unused page remains in buffer.
	✓	Specifies FoxPro database file or click **B**rowse.
		Specifies number of rows that application can fetch at one time from Oracle database. Increasing this number increases amount of memory required to hold the rows. Specifies a value that matches number of rows you want to see.
		Select to prevent the database from being changed.
		Click to select and repair an Access database.
		Specify integer from 1–32767 that defines number of rows driver will scan in the data when setting columns and column data types.
		Browse for and select existing Access database file.
✓		Specify path to folder containing the database file.
		Specify index file(s) to use with the data source.
		Specify network directory after you enter a username.
		Click to select Excel 5.0, 95, 97, or 2000 file used as data source.
		Specify name of Oracle database from which driver will retrieve data.
		Select to make retrievable rows marked as deleted. Deselect to hide deleted rows.
		Select a shared system database.
		Select ODBC translator to use for connection. By default, no translation is performed.
✓		Select to make application's current directory the directory from which data source is opened.
		Specifies account to be used to access data source.
		Select client version to which data source is connecting.

Part

IV

Ch

19

Advanced Excel Options

The Excel ODBC driver offers a handful of advanced settings:

- **_Login_ name.** Specifies username for data source if data source uses a system database that requires authentication. The default Access username is Admin.

- **_Password._** Specifies password associated with the username specified by **_Login_** name. The password for the default Admin username is an empty string.

- _DefaultDir._ Specifies default directory for driver to use.

- _Driver._ Enter a custom name for the Access driver, if desired.

- _FIL._ Specifies file type of data source. Default is "MS Access" for Microsoft Access.

- _ImplicitCommitSync._ Specifies how changes that occur outside transaction are written to the database. With default of Yes, Access driver will wait for commits in an internal/implicit transaction to be completed. This helps ensure that changes are correctly written to the database but can affect performance.

- _MaxBufferSize._ Sets same option for data transfer buffer as the Buffer Size control in the Setup dialog.

- _MaxScanRows._ Specifies number of rows to be scanned when setting a column's data type based on existing data. Valid values are from 1–16, with a default of 8. A value of 0 causes all rows to be scanned.

- _PageTimeout._ Specifies length of time, in tenths of a second, that an unused page remains in the buffer. The default value is 0.5 seconds and must be greater than 0.

- _ReadOnly._ Specifies a value of 1 to make the database read-only, preventing changes. A value of 0 allows changes to the database.

- _SafeTransactions._ All transactions are committed immediately if this value is set to 0. All transactions are saved to disk only upon a commit operation when set to a value of 1, but performance is slightly degraded. Use a value of 1 to decrease the likelihood of data loss.

- _Threads._ Specifies the number of background threads for the engine to use. Increase the value beyond the default of 3 to improve performance if the database has a large amount of activity.

- _UserCommitSync._ When set to Yes (the default), the driver waits for commits in user-defined transactions to be completed. When set to No it is possible for a transaction to override another, with unpredictable results. This setting should be left at its default value of Yes in a multiuser environment, but can be set to No to improve performance in a single-user environment.

SQL Server

The ODBC Data Source Administrator provides a wizard for adding and configuring an SQL Server data source. Follow these steps to install and configure an SQL Server data source.

1. Open the ODBC Data Source Administrator and open the User DSN, System DSN, or File DSN page, as desired.

2. Select an existing SQL Server data source and click Configure, or click Add to add a new SQL Server data source.

   To add a new SQL Server data source, select SQL Server from the list of drivers and click Finish. The dialog shown in Figure 19.7 appears.

FIGURE 19.7
The first step in configuring the SQL driver for a data source.

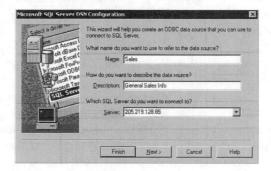

3. Enter the name for the data source in the Name field. This name appears in the Data Sources list on the DSN tab.

4. Specify an optional description for the data source in the Description field.

5. Specify the name or IP address of the SQL Server computer, and then click Next to display the next page of the wizard (see Figure. 19.8).

FIGURE 19.8
Specify connection and authentication options.

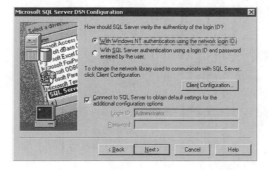

Part
IV

Ch

19

6. Configure options on this page of the wizard using the following list as a guide:

- **_With Windows NT authentication using the network login ID._** Use to have the SQL Server ODBC driver request a trusted connection to the server. Driver uses current client logon username and password to authenticate request on server. This user name and password must have an association on the SQL Server computer to a SQL Server login ID.

- **_With **S**QL Server authentication using a login ID and password entered by the user._** Use to have the SQL Server ODBC driver require the user to specify a SQL Server login ID and password for all connection requests.

- **_**C**onnect to SQL Server to obtain default settings for additional configuration options._** Use to have the SQL Server ODBC driver connect to the SQL Server (specified in the first page of the wizard) to obtain settings for options in remaining configuration wizard pages. When you click **N**ext with this option selected, the driver connects to the SQL Server and obtains the data. Disable to use default settings so the driver will not connect to the SQL Server to obtain the information.

- **_**L**ogin ID._** Specify the username you want to use to connect to the specified SQL server to retrieve the settings for subsequent wizard pages (refer to the preceding bullet for more information). This username and the associated **P**assword field are used only to retrieve information from the SQL Server for the remaining configuration pages and are not used for actual data connections after the data source is created.

- **_**P**assword._** Specify the password to use with the username specified in the **L**ogin ID field.

- **_Clien**t** Configuration._** Click to use the Network Library Configuration dialog shown in Figure 19.9 (discussed in the next step).

FIGURE 19.9

The Network Library Configuration dialog.

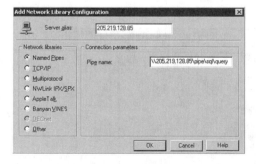

7. Usually, you do not have to configure the network client configuration for the data source. Occasionally, however, you might need to specify the network connection mechanism and other options that define how the client connects to the data source. The options in Connection parameters are specific to the network connection type you select from the Network Libraries list of options.

8. Click **N**ext to continue and open the next page of the wizard (see Figure 19.10).

FIGURE 19.10

Specify the database name and other database options.

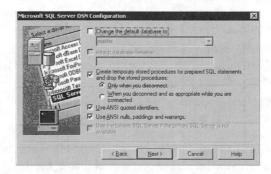

9. Specify options for database parameters based on the following list:

- *Change the **d**efault database to.* Choose a database from its drop-down list to define the database for the data source; this will override the default database for the specified login ID. Disable to use the default database defined for the login ID on the server.

- *Attac**h** database filename.* Specify name of primary file for an attachable database. The specified database is used as the default database for the data source. Specify the full path and filename for the file.

- *Create temporary stored procedures for prepared SQL statements and drop the stored procedures.* Select this and choose an associated option button to cause the driver to create temporary stored procedures to support the SQLPrepare ODBC function. Deselect if you do not want the driver to store these procedures.

- *Only when you disconnect.* Use to have the stored procedures created for the SQLPrepare function dropped only when the SQLDisconnect function is called. Doing so reduces the overhead involved in dropping the stored procedures (improving performance) while the application is running but can lead to a buildup of temporary stored procedures. This particularly applies to applications that issue many SQLPrepare calls or that run for a long time without disconnecting.

Part
IV

Ch
19

- *When you disconnect and as appropriate while you are connected.* Use to have the stored procedures dropped when SQLDisconnect is called, DQLFreeHandle is called for the statement handle, SLPrepare or SQLExecDirect is called to process a new SQL statement on the same handle or when a catalog function is called. Using this option entails more overhead while the application is running but helps prevent a building of temporary stored procedures.

- *Use ANSI quoted identifiers.* Use to enforce ANSI rules for quote marks so that they can only be used for identifiers (such as table and column names), and character strings must be enclosed in single quotes.

- *Use ANSI nulls, paddings, and warnings.* Use to specify that the ANSI_NULLS, ANSI_WARNINGS, and ANSI_PADDINGS options are set on when the driver connects to the data source.

- *Use the fallover SQL Server if the primary SQL Server is not available.* Use to have the connection attempt to use the fallover server if supported by the primary SQL Server. When a connection is lost, the driver cleans up the current transaction and attempts to reconnect to the primary SQL Server. If the driver determines that the primary server is unavailable, the driver attempts to connect to the fallover server.

10. Click Next to open the next page of the wizard. (see Figure 19.11).

FIGURE 19.11
Specify miscellaneous database options.

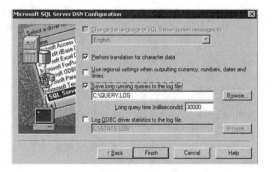

11. Specify options based on the following list:
    - Change the language of SQL Server system messages to:.
    - Perform translation for character data.
    - Use regional settings when outputting currency, numbers, dates, and times.
    - Save long running queries to the log file.
    - Long query time (milliseconds).
    - Log ODBC driver statistics to the log file.

Event Viewer

Viewing Event Logs

Windows 2000 provides a good set of features for trapping and logging *events*. Microsoft defines an event as any significant occurrence in the operating system or application that requires users to be notified. These can include system, security, and application events. For example, Windows 2000 can log such things as user logon, service startup, service termination, and much more.

Windows 2000 maintains three different logs, which include the following:

- *System.* Includes system-related events such as service startup and shutdown, system warning messages, network-related events, and so on.

- *Security.* Includes various security-related events such as log on and log off and whichever events, if any, you configure for auditing (such as resource use, object access, and so on).

- *Application.* Windows 2000 as well as other applications record application-related events in this log. Events recorded to the application log can vary widely because any application designed to do so can write to the application log.

The Event Viewer MMC snap-in (see Figure 20.1) lets you view and manage the event logs. Click Start, <u>P</u>rograms, Administrative Tools, Event Viewer to use the Event Viewer by itself, or right-click My Computer and choose Mana<u>g</u>e to view it within the context of the Computer Management snap-in.

FIGURE 20.1
The Event Viewer console snap-in.

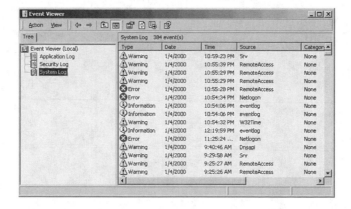

Events range in severity from informational notifications to potentially serious—such as services failing. These categories include information, warning, error, success audit, and failure audit.

Each event also has other common properties such as the event ID, date, source, time, and so on. Event Viewer displays events in columnar format so you can quickly identify the information you need. Each event includes an icon to represent its severity.

The categories for event information include the following:

- *Date.* Indicates the date the event occurred and helps you quickly locate events for a specific period.
- *Time.* Indicates the time the event occurred.
- *Source.* Notes the source that logged the event and can be an application or file system component (such as a device driver); useful for determining what generated the event.
- *Category.* The category of the event is defined by the source and identifies the type of event that occurred. For example, security events include such categories as logon, logoff, policy change, object access, and others.
- *Event.* Lists the event ID for the event. Each event includes an integer that uniquely identifies the event. Note that the event ID is generated by the source.
- *User.* Specifies the user who caused the event to be generated, if applicable.
- *Computer.* Indicates the computer that caused the event to be generated, if applicable.

Choosing and Viewing a Log

Use Event Viewer to view any of the three event logs. To choose a log for viewing, click the log that you want to view. Scroll through the event list to locate the event in which you are interested, and then double-click on the event to open an Event Detail dialog (see Figure 20.2) that offers more information about the event. You also can select an event and press Enter to view its details.

FIGURE 20.2
The Event Detail dialog gives additional information about the event.

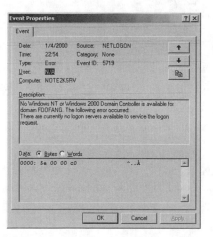

The Description text box includes a description of the event. The Data field displays additional information, if any, generated by the event. Click the Up or Down arrow to view the next or previous event in the log, respectively. Click the Document button below the Down arrow button to copy the event to the clipboard.

Part
IV

Ch
20

> **N O T E** The Bytes option displays the record data in hexadecimal. The Words option displays the data in DWORD format. This data is most useful for troubleshooting by experienced programmers or support staff.

Filtering Events

You can filter the view so that only certain events appear in the Event Viewer if a particular log is very large or you're troubleshooting a specific event or problem. For example, if you're having problems with a service failing, filter the log to only show events generated by the service or by related services.

To filter the log view, choose View, Filter. The Filter properties appear (see Figure 20.3).

FIGURE 20.3
The Filter tab lets you weed out unrelated events.

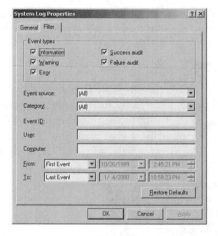

To return the view to its default of showing all events, click Restore Defaults on the Filter tab.

You also can specify how you want the event log sorted, either ascending (oldest events at the top) or descending (newest events at the top). Choose View, Newest First or Oldest First to configure this property.

TIP There is a Help file in the Windows 2000 and NT Resource Kits called NTMSGS.HLP. If you search via the index for *Event* you will find two topics: Event Source and Event Viewer. Each of these topics has a listing of event IDs and their descriptions. This file can be useful when troubleshooting errors in the event logs.

Finding Events

Event Viewer includes a feature that enables you to search through the log to locate specific events. To find an event, choose View, Find, to display the Find dialog (see Figure 20.4).

FIGURE 20.4
The Find dialog.

The controls on the Find dialog are much the same as on the Filter dialog. Specify the options you want, and then choose either Up or Down to specify the direction you want Event Viewer to search through the log.

Refreshing a Log

Events add to the event logs automatically. When you are viewing a log, however, the view of the log in Event Viewer doesn't change. To view events that have been added to the log since you opened it, choose Action, Refresh, or press F5.

> **NOTE** When you save a log file and then later open that log file, at that point the log is static. You can't refresh a log you've loaded from disk. ■

Setting Log Size and Duration

To prevent unmonitored logs from filling up the drive on which they are stored, each log has a maximum size. You also can define what action Windows 2000 should take when the log reaches its maximum size.

To configure log settings, right-click the log for which you want to set properties, and then choose Properties from the context menu. The General tab for the log appears (see Figure 20.5).

FIGURE 20.5

Set various log properties with the General tab.

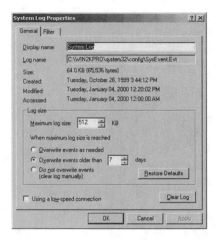

Use the General tab to specify the maximum size of the log and how Windows 2000 handles each when the log reaches maximum size. The controls on the General tab include the following:

- **Display Name.** Modify the name for the log as it appears in the Event Viewer snap-in to differentiate one log from another (such as the System logs on several different computers) in different views.

- **Log name.** Show the filename for the selected log.

- **Maximum Log Size.** Specifies the maximum size, in 64KB increments, of the selected log.

- **Overwrite Events as Needed.** Have Windows 2000 overwrite the oldest events with new ones when the event log reaches maximum size.

- **Overwrite Events Older Than.** Have Windows 2000 overwrite events that are older than the specified number of days.

- **Do Not Overwrite Events (Clear Log Manually).** Have Windows 2000 notify you when the event log is full but take no other action. New events are discarded until you clear the log, which could mean you would miss important log messages, making this the least desirable option.

- **Restore Default.** Restore the default settings for the log.

- **Clear Log.** Clear all events from the log. Event Viewer prompts you to save the events to a file if desired, and then prompts you to confirm the action of clearing the log.

- **Using a Low speed connection.** Choose this option if the connection to the selected event log is through a slow connection such as a modem. With a slow connection, Event Viewer waits until you request a specific item before retrieving it from the remote system.

Viewing a Log on Another Computer

In addition to viewing your local event logs, Event Viewer also makes it possible for you to view the event logs on other computers, assuming you have the necessary administrative permissions on those other computers.

To specify the computer whose event logs you want to view, right- click Event Viewer (Local) in the left pane, and then choose Connect to another computer. The Select Computer dialog appears. Select the computer from the list or type its name, and then click OK.

Saving and Clearing Event Logs

You might want to periodically remove all events from a log and archive them. This is particularly useful for simplifying a cluttered log or creating a log benchmark when you are troubleshooting a problem. You also might want to save a log so you have a snapshot of the system status at a given point.

To clear all events from a log, select the log. Then choose Action, Clear All Events; or right-click on the log and choose Clear all Events. Event Viewer asks you if you want to save the log contents before clearing it. To save the log, click Yes. If you want to discard all events in the log without saving them, click No.

You also can save a log without clearing the log events. Select the log and choose Action, Save Log File As, to open a standard Save As dialog in which you specify a name for the event log. You also can right-click on the log and choose Save Log File As to save the log to a file.

 TIP You can save event logs in native format (EVT), as a tab-delimited text file (TXT), or as a comma-delimited file (CSV), depending on the type of program in which you want to view or manipulate the log data.

To open an existing log, click on the Event Viewer folder, and then choose Action, Open Log File. Or, right-click Event Viewer and choose Open Log File. Type the log file name in the associated text box or browse to locate the file.

Choose the Saved option button, and then type the log file name in the associated text box or browse to locate the file.

Setting Event Viewer Columns

You can define which of the columns appear for each log in the events pane to simplify your view of the log. To define which columns appear, first select any log (the column settings apply to all logs). Then, choose View, Choose Columns to display the Modify Columns dialog shown in Figure 20.6. Add and remove columns as desired by clicking the column name and clicking Add or Remove as appropriate.

Part
IV

Ch
20

FIGURE 20.6

The Modify Columns dialog.

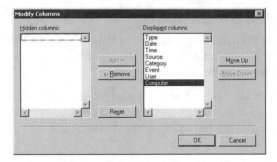

You also can define the order in which the columns are displayed. Click on a column name in the Displayed Columns lists, and then click Move Up or Move Down as desired to adjust the column order. You also can drag and drop columns into the desired order within the Event Viewer window.

Click OK when you're satisfied with the results.

## CHAPTER 21

Removable Storage Manager

Using Removable Storage Services (RSS)

RSS (Removable Storage Services) is a new feature of Windows 2000. It handles all removable media in a system and is the base component for applications such as backup programs to access removable media. RSS also manages media libraries such as CD jukeboxes and automated tape libraries by performing such functions as cleaning, inventory, operator requests, and drive or slot management.

You manage RSS through the Removable Storage window (see Figure 21.1), located in the Computer Management MMC (Microsoft Management Console). To access Removable Storage, do the following:

1. Right-click My Computer and select **M**anage from the context menu. The Computer Management window appears.

2. In the Tree pane, double-click Removable Storage to expand the list of its contents (Media Pools, Physical Locations, Work Queue, and Operator Requests).

FIGURE 21.1
Use Removable Storage in the Computer Management MMC to manage RSS and removable media.

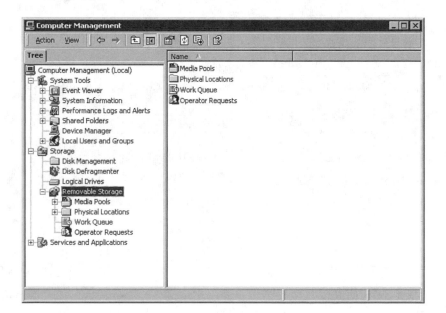

Configuring Removable Storage

Removable Storage Properties sheet provides two tabs that contain the options with which you configure general options and set security in RSS. Right-click the Removable Storage node in the Computer Management console and click P**r**operties. The General tab of the properties sheet shows information about current work items and operator requests. Use the following two options in the Options area on the General tab to configure general features:

- *Send Operator Requests to Messenger Service*. Select this option to have operator requests displayed in a Messenger Service pop-up window.

- *Tray Icon for Pending Operator Requests*. Select this option to have an icon displayed on the system tray when operator requests are waiting to be serviced.

Media Types and Classifications

To configure and begin using Removable Storage, you need an understanding of the different media types supported by RSS. This will help you not only configure Removable Storage but also install devices in preparation for using Removable Storage. Removable Storage supports three basic types of media (some examples of each are provided):

- *Read-Only Optical Disk*. CD-ROM and DVD

- *Writeable Optical Disk*. CD-R, DVD-R, MO (Magneto-Optical) disk

- *Tape*. DAT (Digital Audio Tape), DLT (Digital Linear Tape)

Each of these types can also be classified as *physical* or *logical* media. The physical media are the individual disks or tapes in their entirety. Logical media are the separate sides of double-sided media. RSS has the capability to define and allocate different sides of the same physical medium independently.

To identify each piece of media, RSS uses on-media identifiers, which are written to the media the first time they are used. The identifier has two parts: the label type, which indicates the format of the media, and the label ID, which is a unique identifying label for the media. If the media is a read-only type (CD-ROM, DVD-ROM), RSS uses the volume and serial number already burned on the media for identification.

RSS defines each piece of media as being in a particular *state* with respect to the system and the media pools (discussed next in this chapter). RSS determines media state by checking the on-media identifier and its media pool association. The states of media are the following:

- *In-use*. Currently being used by RSS or an application. Doing anything to media puts it in an in-use state.

- *Loaded*. Media in a usable drive that is ready to be accessed.

- *Mounted*. Media in a usable drive but not yet ready to be read/written..

- *Idle*. Media not currently being used. Can either be currently in an online library or cataloged in an offline library.

- *Unloaded*. Media that is idle and ready to be removed.

▶ **See** "The Device Manager," **p. 117**

Part
IV

Ch
21

Creating and Configuring Media Pools

All media in RSS, no matter its state or type, belongs to a *media pool*. Media pools are collections of a single media type, and you can assign them either to the system or to applications. Media pools have properties that you can assign depending on their use, and they are defined logically based on needs. You can create media pools in a hierarchical manner, meaning that a media pool can contain other media pools. For example, you might create individual media pools for specific applications, then create a media pool as a container to organize all of the other pools.

To view media pools in RSS, follow these steps:

1. Open Removable Storage in the Computer Management MMC and double-click to expand its contents.

2. Double-click Media Pools to expand the media pools (see Figure 21.2).

FIGURE 21.2

Media Pools in Removable Storage bring together potentially different media types into a logical group. Note that the three default system media pools (Free, Unrecognized, and Import) exist with each type of media.

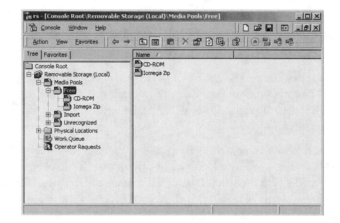

System media pools contain media that has not yet been assigned to an application and include three types of pools. Media is assigned to a system media pool based on RSS's recognition of all or part of the on-media identifier. Removable Storage automatically creates system media pools for each type of media in the system. The default system media pools are the following:

- *Unrecognized.* If RSS does not recognize the label type of the media, it becomes part of this pool. Unformatted media and new types of media are assigned to the unrecognized pool.

- *Import.* If RSS recognizes the label type of the media but does not recognize the label ID, the media is placed in the import media pool until it is either cataloged and moved to an application pool or formatted and moved to the free media pool.

■ *Free*. Each type of media has a free media pool where media available for use or reuse are kept. Application pools can be configured to draw media from or return media to the free media pool as needed, and multiple application pools can draw from the same free media pool.

Application media pools are assigned to applications for use. A single application can use media from more than one media pool, and multiple applications can share a media pool. For example: Application 1 might have some data stored on CD and might also store information to tape. Application 2 might store all its data to tape. Both applications would use a tape media pool, and Application 1 would also use a CD media pool.

Creating a Media Pool

To create a hierarchical application media pool, follow these steps:

1. Right-click Media Pools under the RSS section of the Computer Management MMC.

2. Select Create Media Pool from the context menu. The Create a New Media Pool Properties sheet will be displayed (see Figure 21.3).

3. On the General tab, type a name and description for the media pool. In the Media Information area, leave the default radio button, Contains **O**ther Media Pools, selected.

4. Click OK. The Computer Management MMC will be visible with the newly created media pool in place.

5. Right-click the media pool you just created (it will appear below Media Pools in the RSS section), and select Create **M**edia Pool from the menu. The Create a New Media Pool Properties sheet will again be displayed.

6. Type a name for your media pool, but this time select the Contains Media of **T**ype radio button in the Media Information area and select a media type from the now available drop-down list box.

7. Because this is a media pool that contains specific media, three additional options are available that enable you to draw from and return media to the free media pool and to set a maximum number of times a specific piece of media can be used (allocated). Make your selections from among these options.

8. Click OK. The Computer Management MMC will be visible with the new media pool listed below the previous one.

Part
IV

Ch
21

FIGURE 21.3
Use the Create a New
Media Pool Properties
sheet to create a hier-
archical media pool.

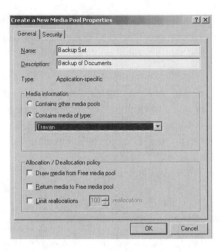

N O T E Removable Storage Services–aware applications such as Microsoft Backup will generally
create and use application media pools automatically, although properties of these might
need to be configured. ■

Managing Media Pools

Managing media within pools or moving media between pools are tasks generally handled by
RSS itself if the system is set up with automated media libraries and application pools are configured to use and return media to and from the free media pool. You might need to perform
some media tasks manually, however, particularly on systems where media storage is not
automated (standalone libraries).

Moving media between pools is simply a matter of finding the pool in which the particular
piece of media is currently located and then clicking and dragging it to the new location. You
might move media between pools to restructure existing pools or when you need to move
"spare" media to a pool that is running low on available storage space.

CAUTION

Do *not* rearrange media that are allocated to specific application pools because doing so could cause
data to be destroyed.

You can perform several operations against media, depending on their current state, by simply right-clicking the individual media and choosing from the context menu:

- *Mount/Dismount*. Allows the mounting or dismounting of idle media in a library.
  Mounting changes the state of the media to loaded.
- *Eject*. Ejects dismounted media from an online library and moves the media to the
  offline library.

■ *Deallocate*. Deallocates media that are currently allocated to an application media pool. Deallocated media can be prepared and moved to the free media pool.

■ *Prepare*. Prepares media to be placed in the free media pool (data-destructive action).

> **N O T E** If a particular operation is not possible given the current media state or location, the operation will appear grayed out in the context menu. Good examples are media that have not been allocated to an application pool cannot be deallocated and media in an offline library cannot be ejected. ■

Configuring Media Libraries and Drives in the Physical Locations Folders

The Physical Locations folder in RSS holds the various media libraries or devices for the media types. *Library* is the term Removable Storage uses to define a media inventory and storage management unit; a library contains data storage media and the device used to read the media. Removable Storage has three basic types of media libraries to which different types of media and media devices belong:

■ *Offline Library*. Contains media that have been cataloged by RSS but are currently not online. There is only one offline library, and it is the only library that can contain multiple media types. The actual location of the media doesn't matter; they can be on a shelf. The key element is that they are not currently in an online library.

■ *Standalone Library*. This is a category of online library that is defined as single disk units with media that are operator-mounted, such as a CD drive. A system can contain multiple standalone libraries (as occurs, for example, in a system with both a CD drive and a tape drive), but each library accepts only one type of media.

■ *Robotic Library*. Multislot or multidrive automated units are referred to as online libraries. Again, these libraries only take a single type of media, but the unit is managed entirely by RSS. Operator intervention is required only for cleaning, errors, and offline media requests.

Figure 21.4 shows a Physical Locations folder and the libraries it contains.

On occasion, you'll want to inventory an online library to determine its contents. You might need to retrieve data from a library, remove data to make room in the library, move some of the media, or determine whether to keep the library at all. Online libraries can be inventoried by comparing the RSS database for the library with the media actually available in the library. There are two methods of inventory: fast, where RSS checks the status of the slots, and full, where each piece of media in the library is mounted and the on-media identifier is checked.

> **N O T E** On systems where a bar code reader is available and media have been bar code–labeled, a fast inventory checks the bar codes instead of the on-media labels for media in the library. ■

Part

IV

Ch

21

FIGURE 21.4
Physical Locations
(Libraries) in RS
describe physical drives
and media.

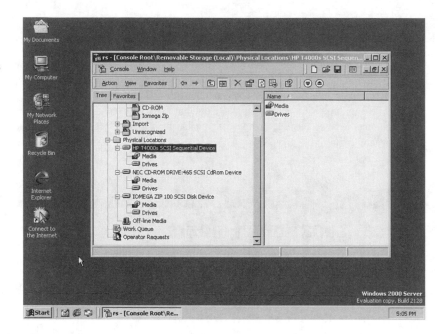

To manually inventory a library, simply right-click the library and select Inventory. To change the inventory type of a library, follow these steps:

1. Select the library to be configured and right-click.

2. Choose Properties from the drop-down menu. The Library Properties sheet will be displayed.

3. On the General tab of the properties sheet, in the Inventory area, select the type of inventory (Full, Fast, or None) that you want performed by default on that library. The General tab also enables you to require a full inventory if there is a mount failure and to enable or disable a library.

4. Click OK to return to the Computer Management MMC.

N O T E There are four additional tabs in the Library properties box: Media, Components, Device Info, and Security. With the exception of Security (discussed later), configuration of these tabs relates primarily to multislot devices and robotic media systems and will be specific to the device managed. ▨

Managing the Work Queue

The work queue section of the Removable Storage Manager is just that: a listing of all the actions that have occurred, are being processed, or have been requested for media managed by RSS. The Work Queue node is shown in Figure 21.5. Work queue requests are marked according to the current state of the request in the queue:

■ *Completed*. Requests that have completed successfully.

■ *Failed*. Requests that failed to complete.

■ *Waiting*. Requests that have not yet executed.

■ *Queued*. The next request to be executed.

■ *In Progress*. The currently executing request.

FIGURE 21.5
An operator can manually manage the Work Queue by opening its node in the MMC.

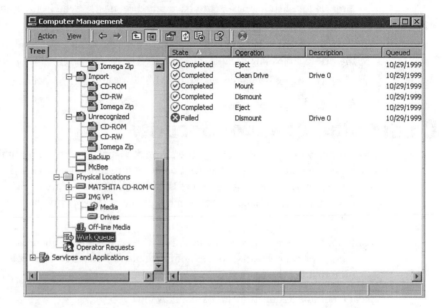

Items in the work queue can be managed manually by an operator, either to reorder mounts in the queue or to delete items from the queue. Either task can be accomplished by selecting an item in the queue, right-clicking, and selecting either reorder mounts or delete.

If the operator decides to reorder mounts in the queue, a dialog box will appear showing the current location of the mount request in the queue and the options to move the request to a different location in the queue. There are three location possibilities in the dialog box:

■ *Move to the Head of the Queue*. Next request to be executed.

■ *Move to the End of the Queue*. Last waiting request in the current queue.

■ *Make It Number X*. Where *X* is a specific location in the queue.

The Work Queue itself has properties for the automatic cleaning or removal of requests. You might want to change the default settings if you want to monitor failed requests because

Part

IV

Ch

21

you're having problems with a particular piece of equipment, if you have users attempting to perform tasks for which they don't have the necessary permissions, and so on. To set the work queue properties, follow these steps:

1. Right-click the Work Queue listing in the Computer Management tree pane.

2. Select Properties from the context menu. The Work Queue Properties sheet will appear with the General tab displayed.

3. In the Request Queue Cleaning area, the default selection is to automatically delete completed requests, including failed requests, every 72 hours. You can change the time interval for cleaning or elect to have failed requests saved in the queue for later analysis.

4. The General tab also includes buttons to delete now and clear the queue or to restore the original cleaning default selections.

5. Click OK to apply changes and close the Work Queue Properties sheet.

Configuring Operator Security

Although many of the actions of RSS are automated, particularly with multidrive or multislot robotic storage units, operator intervention is required for some tasks. Operator requests are stored in the operator request section of the RSS and are also queued in the work queue. Operator requests are cleaned in the same manner as the work queue, with the same available options.

In addition, the operator has full control over the actions in the queue and can choose either to respond to or cancel work request notifications. If the operator cancels the request, the application making the request is notified of the cancellation.

Typical Operator Requests include the following:

- Notification of errors or library failures.

- Requests for specific offline media that are needed by an application.

- Requests for additional media if none are available. This can occur because the free media pool is empty, the application pool has been configured not to use the free media pool, or the library is a standalone unit.

- Requests for new cleaning cartridges in a library.

- Requests for new media in the event that all available free media have reached maximum allocation.

Only users and groups with the appropriate permissions can manage RSS itself or objects in Removable Storage. By right-clicking the object, selecting Properties, and configuring the Security tab, you can set security at the following levels:

- The Removable Storage Application
- Individual Media Pools
- Physical Media Locations (Libraries)

The process for setting security is much the same at any level to which you set it. Follow these steps to configure security on Removable Storage:

1. Right-click the object on which you want to set security (such as the Removable Storage node in the Computer Management console) and choose Properties.
2. Click the Security tab (if the property sheet offers tabs other than the Security tab).
3. Select the user or group whose permission you want to modify, or click A**d**d and add the user or group.
4. In the **P**ermissions group, select Allow or Deny to allow or deny the specific permission for the selected user or group.
5. Click OK to close the property sheet.
6. Repeat the process for any other objects for which you want to modify security.

▶ **See** "Assigning Rights to Groups," **p. 222**

Managing Removable Storage with the *RSM.exe* Utility

Although all functions of RSM can be easily managed from the Computer Management MMC, there is a limited command-line utility, RSM.exe. Located in the %systemroot%\system32 directory, this utility provides for the management of media on the system and can be used for scripting non–RSM-aware applications. The syntax for RSM is as follows:

RSM [ALLOCATE | DEALLOCATE | DELETEMEDIA | DISMOUNT | HELP | MOUNT | VIEW]

Each command available for RSM.exe has different switches available for it to provide more granular control and identify objects. Using the /? or /help switch with the individual command will supply some additional information on the command-specific switches. Most are simply identifiers for the object to be managed. For example, to view the switches you can use with the Allocate option (and pipe it into the MORE Command for easy viewing), use the following command: RSM ALLOCATE/?|MORE

Part

IV

Ch

21

Troubleshooting Removable Storage

There are a handful of common problems you might experience with Removable Storage. This section provides some tips on troubleshooting these problems.

You might occasionally experience a problem with Removable Storage being unable to complete the automatic configuration for a robotic library. If Removable Storage stops the configuration process, it could be because Removable Storage has configured a drive inside the library before the library has been configured. Make sure that Windows 2000 recognizes the drives and that the necessary drivers are installed, and then attempt the installation again.

If Removable Storage is unable to recognize or configure a library, it could be that the library doesn't support drive-element address reporting, which prevents RSS from mapping each drive in the library to a specific drive bay. You must use libraries that support drive-element address reporting and connect all drives in a library on the same SCSI bus associated with the drive bay.

There are some general troubleshooting methods you can use when you experience problems even after RSS is properly configured and your media pools and libraries are configured properly:

- Use the Event Viewer to check the event logs to identify any RSS-related errors.
- Make sure you have media available to a pool if you're having problems with RSS not detecting the media type.
- Make sure you are logging on as a member of the Administrators Group (or another group with appropriate permissions) if you intend to make configuration changes or to configure security of Removable Storage.

Communications, Internet, and Networking

Internet and Intranet Connections

Understanding TCP/IP

The Internet's explosive growth in the last several years has stimulated a strong demand for support of TCP/IP (Transfer Control Protocol/Internet Protocol) and Internet-related utilities and programs. Windows 2000 offers a set of core components and general utilities that make it an excellent platform for TCP/IP internetworking.

> **N O T E** TCP/IP and the Internet generally are closely related; you need the TCP/IP protocol to connect to and use the Internet. Even if you don't need to access the Internet, TCP/IP still offers an excellent means of interconnecting disparate operating systems on a single network.

The TCP/IP network transport protocol is widely supported by a majority of operating systems, including all versions of UNIX, Windows 2000, Windows NT, Windows 9x, Windows 3.x, Novell NetWare, Macintosh, Open VMS, and others. TCP/IP offers a number of advantages that make it an excellent network transport protocol, particularly for connecting dissimilar computers and for enabling wide-area networking.

You can use TCP/IP as your only network protocol or in conjunction with another protocol. You might use NetBEUI within your LAN, for example, and use TCP/IP to connect to the Internet through a router or dial-up connection. Alternatively, you might decide to use TCP/IP as your LAN protocol as well.

TCP/IP is versatile but also complex. Before you can set up a TCP/IP network and correctly configure the computers and other devices on the network, you must understand many key issues. The following sections explain these issues, beginning with IP addressing.

Understanding IP Addressing

On a TCP/IP network, a *host* is any device on the network that uses TCP/IP to communicate, including computers, routers, and other devices. Each host must have a unique address, called an *IP address*. (IP stands for Internet Protocol.) An IP address identifies the host on the network so that IP data packets can be properly routed to the host. IP data packets are simply data encapsulated in IP format for transmission using TCP/IP. Every IP address on the network must be unique; conflicting (identical) IP addresses on two or more computers prevent those computers from correctly accessing and using the network.

An IP address is a 32-bit value usually represented in *dotted-decimal notation*, in which four octets (eight bits each) are separated by decimals, as in 198.87.118.1. The IP address actually contains two items of information: the address of the network and the address of the host on the network. How the network and address are defined within the address depends on the class of the IP address.

IP addresses are grouped into three classes: A, B, and C. These classes are designed to accommodate networks of varying sizes. Table 22.1 describes the IP address classes, where the variables w.x.y.z designate the octets in the address structure.

Table 22.1   IP Address Classes

Class	w	Network ID	Host ID	Available Networks	Available HOSTS Per Network
A	1–126	w	x.y.z	126	16,777,214
B	128–191	w.x	y.z	16,384	65,534
C	192–223	w.x.y	z	2,097,151	254

 TIP   The address 127 is reserved on the local computer for loopback testing and interprocess communication, and it therefore is not a valid network address. Addresses of 224 and higher are reserved for special protocols and can't be used as host addresses. Host addresses 0 and 255 are used as broadcast addresses and should not be assigned to computers.

As Table 22.1 shows, class A networks are potentially quite large, encompassing as many as 16,777,214 hosts. If you set up your own TCP/IP network, yours most likely falls into the class C network category, which is limited to 254 hosts.

You might wonder what's so important about an IP address. Routing data packets between computers is impossible without an IP address. By referencing the network portion of your IP address, a sending computer can route packets (with the help of intermediate routers and networks) to your network. The host portion of your IP address then routes the packet to your computer when the packet finally reaches the network.

Using Subnet Masks

A *subnet mask* is a 32-bit value expressed as a series of four octets separated by periods, just like an IP address. The subnet mask enables the recipient of an IP data packet to strip (*mask*) the IP address to which the IP packet is being sent into the network ID and host ID—in essence, breaking the IP address into its two component parts. Table 22.2 shows the default subnet masks for standard class A, B, and C networks, with each subnet mask shown in binary and dotted-decimal forms.

Table 22.2   Default Subnet Masks

Class	Bit Value	Subnet Mask
A	11111111 00000000 00000000 00000000	255.0.0.0
B	11111111 11111111 00000000 00000000	255.255.0.0
C	11111111 11111111 11111111 00000000	255.255.255.0

In addition to enabling an IP address to be resolved into its network and host components, subnet masks also serve to segment a single network ID into multiple local networks. Assume that your large company has been assigned a class B IP network address of 191.100. The corporate network comprises 10 different local networks with 200 hosts on each. By applying a subnet mask of 255.255.0.0, the network is divided into 254 separate subnetworks, 191.100.1 through 191.100.254. Each of the 254 subnetworks can contain 254 hosts.

TIP The subnet masks described in Table 22.2 are not the only masks you can use. Sometimes you have to mask only some of the bits in an octet. The network address and subnet mask must match, however, for every host on a local network.

Acquiring an IP Address

Although you could theoretically arbitrarily assign your own IP network address for your network, any address you might choose would probably already be assigned to someone else's network. If your network is self-contained and not connected to the Internet, duplicate addressing shouldn't cause any problems. If your network is connected to the Internet or you decide to connect it in the future, however, duplicate addressing causes serious routing problems for both networks. The Internet Service Provider (ISP) you choose to provide Internet network services will provide IP addresses to you.

N O T E Unused IP addresses are becoming scarce, so your ISP might require you to use a proxy server to reduce the number of public IP addresses your organization needs. Using a proxy server enables the ISP to assign you relatively few IP addresses while you use nonpublic addresses behind the proxy server. ■

Understanding Gateways and Routing

TCP/IP subnetworks that are interconnected with one another or connected to the Internet use gateways (routers) to interconnect and route data packets. A *default gateway* generally is a computer or router that maintains IP address information of remote networks (networks outside its own network). Default gateways are required only on interconnected networks; standalone TCP/IP subnets do not require default gateways.

Before a host transmits an IP packet, IP inserts the originating and destination IP addresses into the packet. It then checks the destination address to determine whether the packet is destined for the same local network as the originating host. If the network addresses match (based on the subnet mask), the packet is routed directly to the destination host on the same subnet. If the network addresses don't match, the packet is sent to the subnet's default gateway, which then handles routing of the packet. The default gateway maintains a list of other gateways and network addresses, and it routes the packet accordingly. Although the packet might pass through many gateways, it eventually reaches its destination.

If yours is a standalone subnet, you don't need a default gateway. Otherwise, you need at least one functioning default gateway to communicate outside of your subnet. If for some reason your default gateway becomes inoperative (a router fails, for example), you can't communicate outside your subnet, but you still can work within your subnet. If you need to ensure a connection, you might want to consider using multiple gateways.

 TIP You can use the route utility from the command prompt to specify a static route and override the default gateway. Note that static routes are subnet-specific; they cause traffic destined for a specific subnet to use a specific route. The default gateway handles all other traffic for which there is no static route defined.

Using Dynamic Host Configuration Protocol (DHCP) for Dynamic Address Assignment

In TCP/IP networks that comprise relatively few nodes or in which the network configuration is static (computers do not access the network remotely and the number of hosts don't fluctuate), IP address administration is relatively easy. The network administrator simply assigns specific IP addresses to each host.

On large or dynamic networks, however, administering IP addresses can be difficult and time-consuming. To help overcome this problem, Windows 2000 supports *Dynamic Host Configuration Protocol*, or *DHCP*, which enables a host to automatically obtain an IP address from a DHCP server when the host logs on to the network. When you move a host from one subnet to another on your network, the host automatically receives a new IP address, and its original IP address is released, making it available for other connecting hosts.

By providing dynamic addressing, DHCP enables you to manage a pool of IP addresses for a group of hosts. Assume that your company has 100 employees who often dial into your subnet from remote locations, but not at the same time. At any one time, 25 to 30 remote users might be connected to the network, but your subnet has only 50 available subnet host addresses. If you assign IP addresses manually, you can accommodate only 50 of the remote users. You can't assign the same IP address to two users, because if they both connect to the network at the same time, routing problems prevent them from using the network.

Through DHCP, you can allocate a pool of 50 IP addresses to be assigned automatically to the dial-in users. When a user dials in and connects, DHCP assigns the host a unique IP address from the pool. As long as no more than 50 users attempt to log on to the network remotely and acquire IP addresses, you can accommodate all 50 with unique addresses. If the number of users who need to connect exceeds the number of available addresses, the only solution is to expand your pool of available addresses or modify the subnet mask to accommodate more than 50 addresses.

DHCP in Windows 2000 Professional relies on a Windows 2000 DHCP server that can assign IP addresses to hosts on the local subnet when the hosts start Windows 2000, and can assign IP addresses to hosts that connect to the network remotely.

In addition to using DHCP, Windows 2000 can request an IP address from a PPP (Point-to-Point Protocol) dialup router. Whether you use DHCP or connect to a PPP dialup router, you use the same configuration option to configure dynamic address assignment.

Understanding the Domain Name System (DNS)

Computers have no problems using IP addresses to locate other networks and hosts. The average user, however, can have trouble remembering those dotted-decimal addresses. Domain names and computer names make specifying the addresses of other networks or hosts much easier.

A *domain name* is a unique name formatted much like an IP address, except that the domain name uses words rather than numbers. The domain name identifies your network and is associated with your network's IP address. If your company is Foo Fang Foods, Inc., for example, your departmental subnet might be known as `sales.foofang.com`. The first portion, `sales`, identifies your subnet. The second portion, `foofang`, identifies your corporate network. The last portion, `com`, specifies the type of organization, and in this example, indicates a commercial network.

 TIP As with your IP address, your domain must be unique. If you connect your network to other networks or to the Internet, contact Network Solutions at `http://www.networksolutions.com` or one of the other domain registration entities to apply for a unique domain name.

A *computer name* specifies a host on the subnet. Your host computer name is combined with your domain to derive your Internet address. The combination of hostname and domain name represents a *fully qualified domain name*, or *FQDN*. If your computer's name is `jimb` and the domain is `que.mcp.com`, the FQDN would be `jimb.que.mcp.com`. Partial domain names (such as the hostname only) are called *unqualified* domain names.

No direct translation or correlation exists between IP addresses and domain names and hostnames. Some method, therefore, is required to enable computers to look up the correct IP address when a user specifies a name rather than an IP address. Your Windows 2000 host can use one of two methods: DNS or WINS. In this chapter, I focus on using DNS.

DNS stands for Domain Name System. DNS is a distributed database system that enables a computer to look up a computer name and resolve the name to an IP address. A DNS name server maintains the database of domain names and their corresponding IP addresses. The DNS name server stores records that describe all hosts in the name server's zone.

If you use DNS for your Windows 2000 Professional workstation, you specify the IP address of one or more DNS servers in your TCP/IP configuration. When your workstation needs to resolve a name into an IP address, it queries the DNS servers. If the server doesn't have an entry for the specified name, the name server returns a list of other name servers that might contain the entry you need. The workstation then can query these additional name servers to resolve the name.

Besides a DNS server, you can use the HOSTS file to resolve host.domain-formatted names to IP addresses.

Installing and Configuring TCP/IP

Before you can begin taking advantage of TCP/IP, you naturally have to install it. Of all network protocols, TCP/IP is the most complex to install and configure owing to its many settings and options. This section explains those settings and options, beginning with the installation process.

Pre-Installation Checklist

As you install and configure TCP/IP, you will need to supply specific information about your system. Therefore, the first step in the installation process is to gather this information:

- ❏ *Network Address and Domain.* Acquire valid network address and domain through ISP (for public Internet connection) or assign your own for private network.
- ❏ *IP Address.* Acquire IP address from your system administrator or ISP if you're not using DHCP for IP address assignment.
- ❏ *Subnet Mask.* Determine the correct subnet mask for your system's subnet.
- ❏ *Default Gateway(s).* Acquire the IP address of default gateway (router) if your computer is connected to other networks or the Internet. No gateway is required for single-subnet network with no external connections.
- ❏ *DNS.* Requires hostname for your computer, domain name, and IP addresses of DNS servers for your network.
- ❏ *WINS.* Obtain IP addresses of primary and secondary WINS servers, if they're used on your network.
- ❏ *Bindings.* Determine which services will be bound to TCP/IP protocol (such as File and Printer Sharing, Client for Microsoft Networks, etc.). Bind TCP/IP only to services requiring it to improve security.

Installing Windows 2000 TCP/IP

TCP/IP installs through the network connection properties like any other network transport protocol. To install TCP/IP, follow these steps:

1. Right-click My Network Places and choose Properties.
2. Right-click the network connection for which you want to install TCP/IP and choose Properties.

3. Click Install and then click Protocol, **A**dd.

4. Select Internet Protocol (TCP/IP) from the protocol list, click OK, and then click Close.

 TIP Adding TCP/IP installs it for all network connections, so you'll need to unbind TCP/IP from those connections not requiring it. See the section "Changing Bindings" later in this chapter to learn how.

Next, you need to specify a number of settings to properly configure TCP/IP, beginning with the IP address. Following sections explain each setting. To access TCP/IP settings for a connection, right-click the connection and choose P**r**operties. Select TCP/IP and click Properties.

 TIP You can configure and use multiple sets of TCP/IP settings. You can use one configuration for your LAN TCP/IP connection, for example, and specify different settings for each dialup connection you use.

General Settings

The General tab of the TCP/IP properties sheet enables you to set IP address and subnet, default gateway, and DNS addresses. Figure 22.1 explains options on the General tab.

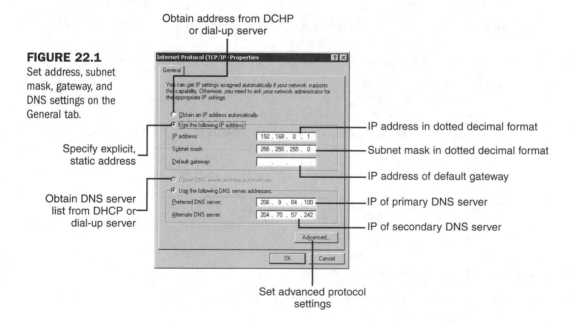

FIGURE 22.1
Set address, subnet mask, gateway, and DNS settings on the General tab.

Advanced Settings

You can set several advanced settings for the TCP/IP protocol by clicking Advanced on the General tab of the protocol's properties. The following sections explain these advanced options.

IP Settings   The IP Settings tab of the Advanced TCP/IP Settings properties enables you to assign multiple addresses to a single computer and multiple default gateways. Multiple IP addresses are common on Web servers to enable hosting of multiple Web sites. Multiple default gateways are common to provide backup routes to other networks or the Internet in the event a router or connection fails.

The IP addresses area on the IP Settings tab enables you to assign one or more IP addresses to the computer, but only if the computer is not configured to retrieve an address through DHCP. Click Add to add a new address and then specify the address and subnet for the new address. To change an existing address, click the address and then click Edit to change the address or subnet.

The Default gateways area lists assigned default gateways. Click Add to add an IP address and metric for the gateway. The metric specifies the cost of using the selected gateway and provides a means of prioritizing gateway use. When multiple routes exist in the routing table, the default route with the lowest metric is used. The default value is 1.

DNS   Use the DNS tab of the Advanced TCP/IP Settings sheet (see Figure 22.2) to specify DNS servers and the order in which they are used, along with other options that determine how DNS queries are performed. The following list summarizes the options on the DNS tab:

FIGURE 22.2

Specify how DNS searches are accomplished through the DNS tab.

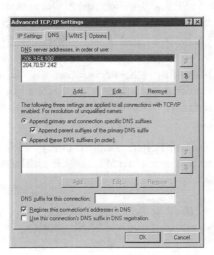

- *DNS Server Addresses, in Order of Use.* Click **A**dd to add other DNS server IP addresses. Click up or down arrows to change priority order of DNS servers (highest used first). Use **E**dit and Remo**v**e to edit and remove entries, respectively. Use to direct DNS queries to a specific server, reducing traffic to others. Secondaries are used only if primary doesn't respond.

- *Append **P**rimary and Connection-Specific DNS Suffixes.* Restrict searches for unqualified domain names to parent domains. Windows 2000 appends domain name of computer to specified host to perform name resolution. For example, if specified host is fred and computer's domain is que.com, DNS will search for fred.que.com. Simplifies DNS queries for user to hosts in own domain (doesn't require user to specify FQDN of host).

- *Append Parent Suffi**x**es of the Primary DNS Suffix.* Causes all parent domains in name space to be appended to unqualified domain names to perform search, starting with domain of local computer and working up through the name space. Simplifies searching through domain tree by allowing full upward search without specifying FQDN.

- *Append T**h**ese DNS Suffixes (in Order).* Specify list of domain suffixes to append, in order, to unqualified domain names for search. Use A**d**d, Edi**t** and Re**m**ove to modify list. Use when you want to search a specific list of domains other than parent domain(s).

- *DNS **S**uffix for This Connection.* Specify domain suffix to use for this connection only, overriding global domain suffix specified in network properties (right-click My Computer, **P**roperties, Network Identification, P**r**operties, **M**ore). If no suffix specified, global domain suffix is used. When computer configured to retrieve DNS settings from server through DHCP, the DHCP server can provide the domain suffix. Use where connection is in different domain from others.

- *R**e**gister This Connection's Address in DNS.* Register IP address with DNS server for this connection under computer's FQDN. Provides dynamic DNS registration by client to DNS server; useful for registering client IP addresses when DCHP is used to assign IP address. Enabled by default.

- *U*se This Connection's DNS Suffix in DNS Registration. Register IP address with DNS server for this connection under domain name of connection in addition to FQDN. Provides additional dynamic client DNS registration; useful when DHCP assigns IP address. Disabled by default.

WINS The WINS tab of the Advanced TCP/IP Settings sheet enables you to define addresses of WINS server(s) and configure other WINS settings. The following list summarizes the options on the WINS tab:

- *W*INS Addresses, in Order of Use. Use **A**dd, **E**dit, Remo**v**e, and up/down arrows to create and modify list of WINS servers to use for WINS queries.

- *Enable **L**MHOSTS Lookup*. Use the LMHOSTS file to resolve NetBIOS names. WINS servers queried only if query not resolved by LMHOSTS lookup. This setting applies to all TCP/IP connections.

▶ For a closer look at LMHOSTS, **see** "Using HOSTS and LMHOSTS Files," **p. 408**

- *Im**p**ort LMHOSTS*. Click to specify location of LMHOSTS file to use.
- *En**a**ble NetBIOS over TCP/IP*. Use NetBIOS-over-TCP/IP (NetBT) and WINS. Required if computer communicates by name with other computers running earlier versions of Windows 9x/NT. Not required in a homogenous Windows 2000 environment or when connecting to computers on the Internet through DNS.
- *Di**s**able NetBIOS over TCP/IP*. Disable use of NetBT and WINS. Use when computer is in homogenous Windows 2000 environment or communicates only with computers on the Internet using DNS.
- *Use Net**B**IOS Setting from DHCP Server*. Retrieve NetBT and WINS settings from DHCP server. Allows automatic configuration and lets DHCP server assign settings as needed.

IPSec and IP Filtering Options   The Options tab of the advanced TCP/IP settings enables you to configure IP security settings. Optional settings provided with Windows 2000 by default are IPSec (IP Security) and IP filtering. IPSec enables you to apply a security policy to IP traffic, and IP filtering enables you to define which TCP ports, UDP ports, and IP protocols are allowed or denied on the computer.

Use the IP security option on the Options tab to specify which IPSec policy to use for this connection. Click IP security in the **O**ptional settings list and click **P**roperties. Choose **D**o not use IPSEC to prevent IPSec from being applied to the connection. Or, choose **U**se this IP security policy and select an existing IPSec policy to apply the IPSec policy to the connection.

▶ **See** "Configuring IPSec," **p. 412**

With IP filtering you can allow all TCP ports, UDP ports, and IP protocols through the connection or permit only specific ones. While this feature certainly isn't the same as a firewall, it does let you restrict IP traffic through the computer.

Click IP Filtering in the **O**ptional Settings list and click **P**roperties to access the TCP/IP Filtering dialog. Figure 22.3 defines the options on the dialog. These settings apply to all network adapters in the computer.

Turn on IP filtering (applies to all network
adapters in computer)

FIGURE 22.3
Apply an IP filter to TCP
ports, UDP ports, and
IP protocols for the
computer.

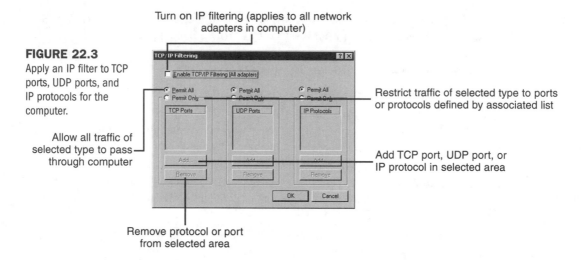

Restrict traffic of selected type to ports
or protocols defined by associated list

Allow all traffic of
selected type to pass
through computer

Add TCP port, UDP port, or
IP protocol in selected area

Remove protocol or port
from selected area

Using HOSTS and LMHOSTS Files

DNS name servers resolve FQDN names provided in the host.domain format to IP addresses. A WINS server can resolve IP host.domain names to IP addresses and also resolve a computer's NetBIOS name into its address name. Sometimes, however, being able to resolve names locally without relying on a DNS or WINS name server comes in handy. You might not have a DNS or WINS name server available to you, for example, or the server might be temporarily unavailable.

Windows 2000 Professional provides two methods for resolving names to IP addresses locally, which you can use in conjunction with or in place of DNS and WINS name resolution. Both methods rely on simple ASCII files to store database entries for names and corresponding IP addresses. The first of these files, HOSTS, resolves DNS-formatted names, and works with or in place of DNS. The second file, LMHOSTS, resolves NetBIOS names into IP addresses, and works with or in place of WINS.

The following sections explain the HOSTS file and the LMHOSTS file, respectively.

Using the HOSTS File for Name Resolution

If you can't access a DNS server, or you want to supplement a DNS server with your own entries, you can use the HOSTS file to maintain a database of hostnames and their corresponding IP addresses. The HOSTS file is called a *host table* because it contains a table of hostnames and their IP addresses. Windows 2000 can look up entries in the HOSTS file to resolve names.

When you install Windows 2000 TCP/IP, Windows 2000 creates a file named HOSTS in *systemroot*\system32\drivers\etc. The HOSTS is an ASCII file that you can edit using Notepad,

WordPad, or any other ASCII editor. You should copy HOSTS to HOSTS.bak to retain the base file for future reference in case your HOSTS file becomes corrupted or is accidentally deleted. Then, edit the HOSTS file as needed to incorporate additional entries.

The Windows 2000 HOSTS file uses the same format as the HOSTS file used on 4.3 BSD UNIX, stored in the /etc/HOSTS file. HOSTS contains comments identified by a leading # character and a single address entry for localhost. The localhost entry is always 127.0.0.1 and is used for loopback testing. You should not change the IP address for localhost or remove it from the HOSTS file.

To add an entry to the HOSTS file, enter the IP address and then tab to the second column and enter the hostname. You can specify more than one hostname for an IP address, but you must use multiple entries for the different domains, each with the same IP address, as in the following example:

```
102.54.94.97      tools.acme.com
102.54.94.97      TOOLS.ACME.COM
102.54.94.97      fooyang.gruel.com
```

Entries in the HOSTS file are case-sensitive. The two entries for tools.acme.com and TOOLS.ACME.COM would enable the correct hostname resolution if you specified the hostname in lowercase or uppercase.

You can include a single hostname for each entry or specify multiple hostnames for a single IP address. The following, for example, are valid entries:

```
198.87.118.72    me           theboss       bozo.que.mcp.com
198.87.118.50    TheServer    theserver     THESERVER
```

Each of the entries in this example specify three hostnames for each IP address.

Windows 2000 parses the entries in the HOSTS file in sequential order until it finds a match. If you have a large HOSTS file, you can speed up lookup time by placing the most often-used hostname entries at the top of the file.

Using the LMHOSTS File for Name Resolution

If you want Windows 2000 Professional to be able to resolve NetBIOS computer names to IP addresses, you need to use a WINS or LMHOSTS file. NetBIOS names are the computer names assigned to computers on Microsoft-based networks, such as the name you assigned to your computer during setup. As explained previously, your computer's NetBIOS name is not equivalent to your TCP/IP hostname, although the two can use the same name.

Windows 2000 automatically resolves NetBIOS names for computers running TCP/IP on a local network. To resolve IP addresses of computers on other networks to which yours is connected by a gateway (when a WINS server is not available), you need to use LMHOSTS.

TIP Like HOSTS, LMHOSTS is an ASCII file, and the format of an entry is similar to entries in a HOSTS file. The LMHOSTS file, however, supports special keywords, which are explained later in this section. Windows 2000 includes a sample LMHOSTS file named LMHOSTS.sam, located in *systemroot*\system32 \drivers\etc folder. To use LMHOSTS, copy LMHOSTS.sam to LMHOSTS without a file extension and then modify LMHOSTS to add entries.

Windows 2000 TCP/IP reads the LMHOSTS file when you start the computer. As it does the HOSTS file, Windows 2000 parses each line sequentially, which means you should place often-accessed names at the top of the file for best performance. You also need to place entries that contain special keywords at specific locations in the file (these placement rules are explained later in the section). First, here are a few rules for structuring an LMHOSTS file:

- Each entry must begin with the IP address in the first column, followed by its computer name in the second column. Any additional keywords appear in subsequent columns. Columns must be separated by at least one space or tab character. Some LMHOSTS keywords follow entries, while others appear on their own lines (explained later).

- Place each entry on a separate line.

- Comments must begin with the pound (#) character, but special LMHOSTS keywords also begin with the # character. Keeping comments to a minimum improves parsing performance. Place often-accessed entries near the top of the file for best performance.

- The LMHOSTS file is static, so you must manually update the file to create new entries or modify existing entries.

 TIP Although Windows 2000 TCP/IP reads the LMHOSTS file at system startup, only entries designated as pre-loaded by the #PRE keyword are read into the name cache at startup. Other entries are read only after broadcast name resolution queries fail. Because the entire file is parsed at each query, including comments, you should keep comments to a minimum and place often-used names near the top of the file to improve performance.

You can use any or all of six special keywords (described in the following list) in an LMHOSTS file:

- **#PRE.** Causes associated entry to be preloaded into name cache, rather than loaded only after broadcast resolution queries fail. If you want names stored in a remote LMHOSTS file to be added to the name cache at startup, use the #INCLUDE and #PRE statements in combination, such as the following:

```
#INCLUDE    \\server\pub\lmhosts    #PRE
```

- **#DOM:<domain>.** Designates remote domain controller and enables you to identify Windows 2000 domain controllers located across one or more routers. Entries that use the #DOM keyword are added to a special Internet workgroup name cache that causes Windows 2000 TCP/IP to forward requests for domain controllers to remote domain controllers as well as local domain controllers. The following example identifies a domain controller named appserver in a domain named thedomain, and also causes the entry to be preloaded into the name cache at startup:

```
184.121.214.2  appserver  #PRE  #DOM:thedomain
```

■ #INCLUDE<filename>. Includes entries from separate LMHOSTS file. You can use #INCLUDE to include your own set of entries stored on your own computer, but you most commonly would use #INCLUDE to enable use of a centralized, shared LMHOSTS file for multiple users. The following example includes an LMHOSTS file from a local drive and directory:

```
#INCLUDE  c:\mystuff\Lmhosts      #Includes local file
```

NOTE If you reference a remote LMHOSTS file on a server outside of your network in an #INCLUDE statement, you must include an entry for the IP address of the remote server in the LMHOSTS file. The server's entry must be inserted in the LMHOSTS file before the #INCLUDE statement that references it. You also should not use #INCLUDE to reference an LMHOSTS file on a redirected network drive, because your drive mappings might be different from one session to another. Use the UNC path for the file instead. Centralized LMHOSTS files should never use drive-referenced entries, because the drive mappings in the file probably will not apply to all users who might use the file. ■

■ #BEGIN_ALTERNATE. Signals the beginning of a block of multiple #INCLUDE statements (called a *block inclusion*). The statements within the block designate primary and alternate locations for the included file. The alternate locations are checked if the primary file is unavailable. The successful loading of any one entry in the block causes the block to succeed, and any subsequent entries in the block are not parsed. You can include multiple block inclusions within an LMHOSTS file. The following is an example of a block inclusion:

```
#BEGIN_ALTERNATE
#INCLUDE         \\server\pub\lmhosts        #Primary source
#INCLUDE         \\othersrvr\pub\lmhosts      #Alternate source
#INCLUDE         \\somewhere\pub\lmhosts      #Alternate source
#END_ALTERNATE
```

■ #END_ALTERNATE. Signals the end of a block of multiple #INCLUDE statements.

■ \0xnn. This keyword enables you to specify nonprinting characters in NetBIOS names. You must enclose the NetBIOS name in quotation marks and use the \0xnn keyword to specify the hexadecimal value of the nonprinting character. The hexadecimal notation applies to only one character in the name. The name must be padded to a total of 16 characters, with the hexadecimal notation as the 16th character.

Example:

```
109.88.120.45    "thename   \0x14"       #Uses special character
```

Adding an Entry to LMHOSTS

NetBIOS computer names of computers on your LAN are resolved automatically. To resolve remote names when a WINS server is not available, add the NetBIOS names and their corresponding IP addresses to the LMHOSTS file. To add an entry, use Notepad, WordPad, Edit, or any other text editor that enables you to edit and save ASCII files.

Each line consists of the IP address and NetBIOS name, and also can contain optional keywords and comments as explained previously. The following are examples of LMHOSTS entries:

```
192.214.240.2        me                                #Alias for my
➥computer
198.87.118.72        tower                             #Fred's computer
198.87.118.50        rli-server     #PRE               #Application
➥server
120.89.101.70        server         #PRE   #DOM:tigers #Some comment
➥here
182.212.242.2        sourcesrvr     #PRE               #Source for
➥shared Lmhosts
182.212.242.3        source2        #PRE               #Source for
➥shared Lmhosts
182.212.242.4        source3        #PRE               #Source for
➥shared Lmhosts
187.52.122.188       images                            #Imaging server

#INCLUDE             c:\mystuff\lmhosts                #My private
➥Lmhosts file

#BEGIN_ALTERNATE
#INCLUDE             \\sourcesrvr\pub\Lmhosts          #Primary central
➥Lmhosts
#INCLUDE             \\source2\pub\Lmhosts             #Alternate source
#INCLUDE             \\source3\pub\Lmhosts             #Alternate source
#END_ALTERNATE
```

In the preceding example, only the rli-server, server, sourcesrvr, source2, and source3 entries are preloaded into the name cache at system startup, because only they include the #PRE keyword. Other entries are parsed only after broadcast name resolution requests fail.

 TIP The addresses of servers you specify in a block inclusion must be preloaded through entries earlier in the file. Any entries not preloaded are ignored.

Configuring IPSec

IPSec provides a mechanism for securing IP traffic between two computers through authentication, encryption, and filtering. With IPSec you can ensure against unauthorized interception of data and prevent network attacks by users both inside and outside your network. IPSec is

Microsoft's implementation of the Internet Engineering Task Force's (IETF) IP Security Protocol. IPSec itself provides a framework of mechanisms that provide encryption, authentication, secure transmission and receipt, and filtering of IP traffic. You define how these features are applied through the IP security policies, either at a domain level group policy or local policy.

Understanding IPSec in depth requires an understanding of authentication and encryption methods use by IPSec—a topic which would require several chapters of its own. This chapter assumes that you are familiar with authentication mechanisms used by IPSec and need to know how to configure it within Windows 2000 as a local policy.

N O T E You also can configure IPSec as a group policy at the domain level. Because this book is specific to Windows 2000 Professional, this chapter focuses solely on defining the IPSec policy at the local computer. ■

Overview of Preconfigured Policies

When you install TCP/IP, Windows 2000 copies all the files necessary to implement an IPSec policy to the computer. Windows 2000 also defines three standard IPSec policies that you can use as-is to quickly configure IPSec policy. Rather than take the time to define a new one, you can simply select an existing policy. These three predefined policies are:

- *Server (Request Security)*. Typically for a server, this policy requests security using Kerberos trust for all IP traffic; it allows unsecured communication with clients that do not respond to secure request.

- *Secure Server (Require Security)*. Typically for a secure server, this policy requests security using Kerberos trust for all IP traffic; it does not allow any communication with untrusted clients.

- *Client (Respond Only)*. Typically for a client, this policy normally uses unsecured communication. It also uses a default response rule to negotiate with servers requesting security. Only the protocol and port requested by the server are secured.

You can use these predefined policies as-is, modify them, or create a new IPSec policy. You manage IPSec policies through the IP Security Policies snap-in for the MMC. To use the snap-in, open an MMC console and then add the IP Security Policies snap-in to the console through Console, Add/Remove Snap-In.

▶ To learn more about Kerberos security, **see** "Working with Kerberos Security," **p. 208**

Modifying an Existing IPSec Policy

To open the IPSec policy properties sheet, double-click the IPSec policy (or, right-click the policy and choose Properties). The Properties sheet for an IPSec policy contains two tabs, Rules and General.

The Rules tab enables you to define the rules that apply to the policy, such as requiring security on all IP traffic, permitting or denying specific IP addresses or ports, requiring specific types of authentication, etc. You can edit an existing rule or add a new rule. Click a rule then click **E**dit to modify the rule. Click A**d**d to create a new rule. Select a rule's check box to apply the rule to the policy. Deselect the rule to turn it off.

TIP Select Use Add **W**izard before clicking A**d**d if you want Windows 2000 to step you through the process of creating a rule, rather than specifying settings manually through individual dialogs.

A rule's properties sheet contains three-tabs (double-click the rule to view/modify its properties). Figure 22.4 describes options on the Security Methods tab, which enables you to define the type of security applied to the IP traffic.

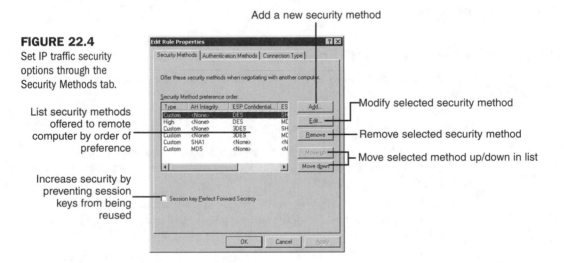

FIGURE 22.4

Set IP traffic security options through the Security Methods tab.

When you define or modify a security method you can choose between **H**igh (ESP), **M**edium (AH), and **C**ustom. **H**igh uses authentication, encryption, and ensures that the data is unmodified. **M**edium provides the same without encryption.

Custom enables you to fully define the security method, choosing not only between AH and ESP, but also selecting the integrity and security algorithms used. You also can specify how often session security keys are generated. Figure 22.5 describes options on the Custom Security Method Settings dialog.

Use AH security

FIGURE 22.5
Specifying custom settings is recommended only for experts.

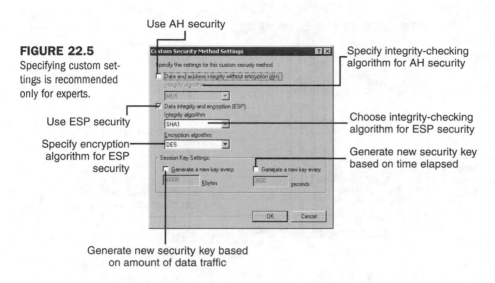

Specify integrity-checking algorithm for AH security

Use ESP security

Specify encryption algorithm for ESP security

Choose integrity-checking algorithm for ESP security

Generate new security key based on time elapsed

Generate new security key based on amount of data traffic

The Authentication Methods tab of a rule's properties enables you to define the types of authentication used by the rule and order their preference. You can choose from three authentication methods—use native Windows 2000 Kerberos, use a certificate issued by a Certificate Authority (CA), or use a pre-shared key and protect the key with a string you specify. You select from these three options on the Authentication Method tab. The last rule property tab, Connection Type, enables you to specify which types of network traffic are subject to the rule:

- *All Network Connections.* Apply rule to local traffic (LAN) and remote traffic (RAS/dial-up traffic).
- *Local Area Network (LAN).* Apply rule only to LAN traffic.
- *Remote Access.* Apply rule only to RAS/dial-up traffic.

The General tab enables you to control general settings and options that control the way the policy is applied, such as policy name and description, authentication methods, key generation times, and so on. Figure 22.6 describes its options.

You can click Advanced to access the Key Exchange Settings dialog where you can specify options that determine how often security keys are generated and type of security methods applied. Figure 22.7 describes the options.

Creating a New IPSec Policy

You can create a new IPSec policy if you prefer to leave the predefined policies as-is. To create a new IPSec policy, open the IP Security Policy console in the MMC as described previously, right-click IP Security Policies in the right half of the window and then choose Create IP Security Policy. Windows 2000 Professional starts a wizard that prompts you for basic policy information. After the wizard creates the policy you can view and modify its settings as described in the previous section.

FIGURE 22.6
Click Advanced to set
key generation and
authentication options

Name to appear in IP
Security Policy snap-in

How often to poll AD
for policy changes;
applicable in domain
only

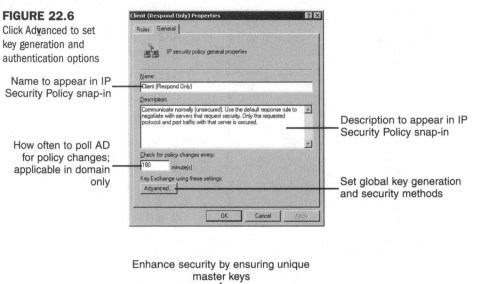

Description to appear in IP
Security Policy snap-in

Set global key generation
and security methods

Enhance security by ensuring unique
master keys

FIGURE 22.7
Click Methods to spec-
ify security methods
and integrity/encryp-
tion algorithms.

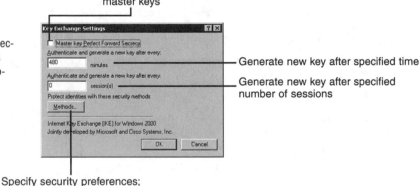

Generate new key after specified time

Generate new key after specified
number of sessions

Specify security preferences;
recommended for expert users

Assigning an IPSec Policy

The previous two sections explained how to create and modify policies, but not apply them. In order for a policy to be imposed you must apply the policy within the IP Security Policy. In the IP Security Policy snap-in, right-click the policy you want to apply and choose **A**ssign. You can assign only one policy; assigning a given policy unassigns the currently assigned policy (if any). To unassign a policy right-click the policy and choose **U**n-Assign.

Defining and Managing Global Filters

You can create and edit the list of filters that are available when you define a policy. You might want to create several filters for use in specific situations and have them available ahead of time, rather than create them on the fly when needed.

To manage the filter list, editing existing filters and creating new ones, right-click IP Security Policies or right-click anywhere in the right half of the window and then choose **M**anage IP Filter List and Filter Actions. Windows 2000 opens a two-tab dialog you can use to define filter settings. Note that defining the settings simply stores the settings by name; it doesn't actually apply them to a policy or assign them as active.

N O T E For more detailed information about IPSec, refer to the Windows 2000 Server Help file or Windows 2000 Professional Resource Kit. ■

Configuring and Using Dial-Up Connections

Like previous versions of Windows NT, Windows 2000 Professional provides excellent dial-up networking capability, enabling you to connect to other networks (including the Internet) through a modem. You also can configure Windows 2000 Professional as a dial-up server, allowing one user at a time to dial into the computer to gain access to the resources on the computer or the LAN, as defined by the connection properties.

N O T E Because dial-up networking has been such an integral feature of Windows 9x and Windows NT, this chapter assumes you have some background in using dial-up connections on those systems. This chapter primarily serves as a guide to show you where to go in Windows 2000 Professional to configure dial-up connections. New features such as Internet Connection Sharing are covered in detail. ■

Creating and Managing Connections

Dial-up connections reside in the Network and Dial-Up Connections folder with local network connections. You can use the Make New Connection icon to create a new dial-up connection or set properties of existing connections. Choose Start, **S**ettings, **N**etwork and Dial-Up Connections to open the folder.

 Choose Start, **S**ettings, right-click **N**etwork and Dial-Up Connections, and then choose Open if you have configured the Start menu to automatically expand the Network and Dial-Up Connections folder on the menu. This opens the folder rather than displaying its contents on the menu.

Double-click the Make New Connection icon in the Network and Dial-Up Connections folder to create a new dial-up connection. Windows 2000 starts the Network Connection Wizard to step you through the process. You can create three dial-out connection types: Dial-up to private network, dial-up to the Internet, and Connect to a private network through the Internet. The first two provide essentially the same thing and by default create the same type of connection. The third enables you to create a tunneled connection through the Internet using PPTP (Point-to-Point Tunneling Protocol) or L2TP (Layer 2 Tunneling Protocol).

To create a connection, run the Make New Connection wizard. In the wizard you'll specify phone number and dialing rules, whether you want to restrict the connection to yourself or make it available to all users, and a name for the connection.

Right-click a connection and choose Properties to modify the dial-up connection's settings. Windows 2000 provides a tabbed dialog for configuring settings, most of which are self-explanatory. If you have experience with Windows 9x or Windows NT dial-up connections, you'll have no problem with the Windows 2000 settings. If not, simply click the question mark button at the upper-right corner of the dialog and then click an option to learn more about it.

Of particular note is the Networking tab. Use the settings on this tab to choose the type of connection protocol (PPP or SLIP) and which protocols, clients, and services are bound to the dial-up connection. Simply select and deselect protocols, services, and clients as desired.

Earlier in this chapter you learned how to configure TCP/IP. You use the Networking tab to define TCP/IP settings for the dial-up connection. In most cases, you'll want to configure the dial-up connection to obtain IP address, DNS server, and gateway settings from the remote server. Select the TCP/IP protocol and click Properties if you need to change IP properties for the dial-up connection.

N O T E   See the section "Internet Connection Sharing" later in this chapter for information on using a single computer to handle dial-up Internet access for multiple computers. ▪

▶   To learn more about working with dial-up connections through the Control Panel, **see** "Setting Network and Dial-Up Connections Options," **p. 180**

Setting Advanced Dial-Up Preferences

You can configure a handful of advanced settings that affect dial-up connections globally rather than individually. In the Network and Dial-Up Connections folder, choose Advanced, Dial-up Preferences. Windows 2000 provides a tabbed dialog that controls certain security and autodial features.

The Autodial tab enables you to control how autodial works for specific dialing locations. Autodial enables Windows 2000 to automatically dial to connect to a remote network when you attempt to access a resource not available on the local LAN (such as an Internet Web page, remote share, and so on). The available options are self-explanatory.

Use the Callback tab to define how to handle callback, which is a mechanism that enables you to reverse dialing charges by having the server dial you back. The options are self-explanatory.

TIP You can use callback at the server end to apply additional security to the connection. You can configure each user for callback at a specific phone number, preventing unauthorized users from gaining access with a stolen account from another location. See the section "Configuring a Dial-Up Server" for detailed information.

Virtual Private Networking

Like Windows 9x and Windows NT, Windows 2000 includes support for Virtual Private Network (VPN) connections. A VPN connection creates a secure, *tunneled* connection from the local computer to a remote host. In effect, VPN enables you to create a secure, private network connection through a public network—the Internet.

For example, assume you want to create a connection from your hotel to your office LAN to work on a report or presentation, or even print to a printer in your office. VPN enables you to dial up an ISP to establish a connection to the Internet and then use a VPN connection to create the secure connection to office LAN (assuming the office LAN is connected to the Internet).

Windows 2000 Professional supports two VPN protocols—Point-to-Point Tunneling Protocol (PPTP) and Layer-2 Tunneling Protocol (L2TP). You can choose either one explicitly for the connection or use Automatic, which attempts PPTP first and then L2TP.

TIP To use L2TP, your computer's Trusted Root Certification Authorities certificate store must contain certificates for the root authority for the CA that issued your machine certificate and the L2TP server. See Chapter 15, "Certificate Manager," for more information on working with certificates.

You can use multiple protocols for a VPN connection, if necessary, just as you can for other types of connections. For example, you can use NetBEUI—a non-routable protocol in itself—to connect to and use resources on the remote LAN. Windows 2000 encapsulates the NetBEUI protocol in the IP traffic, in effect making NetBEUI routable.

To create a VPN connection, run the Make New Connection wizard and choose the Connect to a Private Network through the Internet option. The wizard gives you the option of configuring the VPN connection to automatically dial a dial-up connection first. Choose this option if you use the VPN from the same location most of the time. Windows 2000 will first dial the modem connection and then dial the VPN connection. You also provide the IP address or DNS name of the remote VPN server.

N O T E See the section "Configuring a Dial-Up Server" later in this chapter for information on configuring a Windows 2000 Professional computer to act as a VPN server. ▪

A VPN's connection settings are, for the most part, the same as settings for any dial-up connection. The primary differences are that you specify an IP address or DNS name instead of a phone number, and can direct Windows 2000 to automatically dial the Internet through a dial-up connection before dialing the VPN connection.

 TIP A VPN connection doesn't actually *dial*, per se. Instead, the connection establishes a session between your computer and the remote VPN server. In effect, you're *dialing* the server through the Internet.

You might also have to adjust the security settings for the VPN connection to match the requirements of the server. Figure 22.8 explains options on the VPN connection's Security tab in its properties.

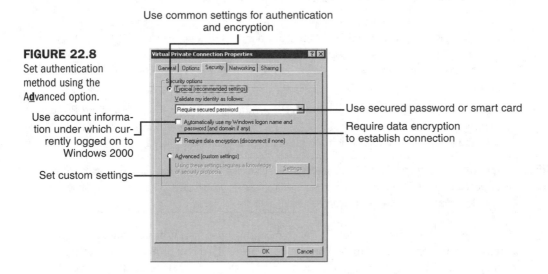

FIGURE 22.8
Set authentication method using the Advanced option.

Use common settings for authentication and encryption

Use account information under which currently logged on to Windows 2000

Set custom settings

Use secured password or smart card

Require data encryption to establish connection

If you click Advanced you can specify options for data encryption, logon security, and authentication protocols. You can use the default settings for dialing most Internet service providers, but might need to modify advanced security settings when dialing other types of servers. Set security settings as required by the remote server.

Internet Connection Sharing

You can configure a Windows 2000 Professional computer for Internet Connection Sharing (ICS), enabling other users to connect across the LAN through your computer to the Internet. The number of users that can effectively access the Internet at one time depends on the bandwidth of the connection and types of tasks the users are performing. Several users retrieving text-based email through a single 56K dial-up connection is practical; the same users uploading and downloading via ftp is not. In the same situation with a T1 or fractional T1 connection to the Internet instead of a dial-up connection, the latter scenario becomes more feasible.

N O T E You shouldn't think of ICS as an effective means of securing internal systems from outside attack. ICS provides very limited ability to restrict applications and services or filter and monitor traffic. Consider a Windows 2000 Server proxy server or other server-based proxy solution, in addition to a firewall, if you need positive security. ■

While ICS offers the useful benefit of sharing an Internet connection, it also offers little flexibility of configuration. Enabling ICS assigns the static IP address 192.168.0.1 with a Class C subnet mask of 255.255.255.0 to the LAN adapter for the local network where the other clients are located. You can't change that assignment.

Because of this automatic assignment, network connections could be disrupted between your computer (the ICS server) and the rest of the network when ICS is enabled if your network uses a different subnet. Other users would be able to get on the Internet, but you wouldn't be able to browse their shared resources or vice-versa. You won't lose connectivity between your computer and the other clients, however, if they share the 192.168.0.0 subnet.

The secret to maintaining connectivity all the time is to allow the Windows 2000 ICS computer to function as a DHCP server, assigning addresses to the other clients on the LAN. The other clients will automatically be assigned an IP address in the same subnet.

 ICS is included with both Windows 2000 Professional and Server and is intended primarily as an easy-to-use means of connecting a home or small office network to the Internet. If you require greater flexibility and have the technical background to configure and manage a routing service, consider using the Network Address Translation (NAT) protocol through the Routing and Remote Access service under Windows 2000 Server.

ICS requires that the host computer be a multi-homed system, which means it must have two network connections. One is the connection to the local area network where the other clients reside, and the second is the connection to the Internet. This second connection can be a dial-up connection (modem, cable-modem, ISDN, etc.) or a network adapter for a direct Internet connection.

Enabling ICS and On-Demand Dialing

After you create the connection on the computer to the Internet, you can configure it for sharing with other users on the LAN. Follow these steps to enable ICS:

1. Open the Network and Dial-Up Connections folder and then open the properties of the Internet connection you want to share. This is the connection that connects the ICS host computer to the Internet, not the local LAN connection.

2. Click the Sharing tab.

3. Select **E**nable Internet Connection Sharing for This Connection.

4. Select the connection where the clients are located via the **F**or Local Network drop-down list.

5. Select Enab**l**e On-Demand Dialing if you want the proxy computer to automatically dial the Internet when a client requests a connection.

6. Click Settin**g**s if you want to restrict applications and services, or click OK to allow all traffic.

As explained previously, the LAN IP address for the ICS server computer is set to 192.168.0.1 when ICS is enabled. The ICS computer will function as a DHCP server, assigning IP addresses, DNS settings, etc., to client computers on the network.

 TIP   To ensure that your dial-up connection isn't connected when not being used, open the Options tab for the Internet connection and configure the setting Idle Ti**m**e before Hanging Up for an appropriate length of time (such as 15 minutes). Note that many ISPs configure the connection to be dropped at their end when a certain idle time has passed. Many ISPs use settings between 15 and 20 minutes.

Configuring the Clients

The clients that connect through the ICS server don't need any special software or support for ICS, nor do you have to configure applications (such as Internet Explorer) to connect through a proxy server. You simply ensure that the clients reside on the same subnet as the ICS host and use it as their default gateway. The easiest way to accomplish this is to configure the clients to retrieve their TCP/IP settings automatically (use DHCP).

> **N O T E**   If you prefer, you can configure the client computer settings manually, assigning each a static IP address in the Class C range 192.168.0.2 through 192.168.0.254, with a subnet mask of 255.255.255.0. Assign 192.168.0.1 as the default gateway for the client computers. ■

Configuring Applications and Services

You can configure remote applications for use by clients on your network, as well as local services for access by remote clients. You configure these through the ICS settings for the shared connection. Open the properties for the shared Internet connection and click the Sharing tab. Click Settin**g**s to access the Internet Connection Sharing Settings dialog. The following sections explain the options on this dialog.

Configuring Remote Applications   The Applications tab enables you to configure remote applications for access by clients on your LAN. Click A**d**d to define an application. Figure 22.9 explains the available options.

FIGURE 22.9
Configure settings for a remote application for access by local clients.

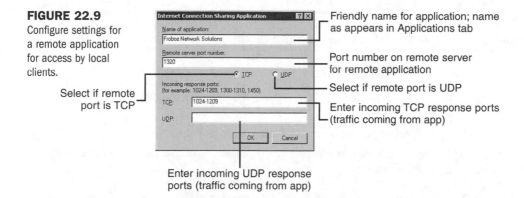

Friendly name for application; name as appears in Applications tab

Port number on remote server for remote application

Select if remote port is TCP

Select if remote port is UDP

Enter incoming TCP response ports (traffic coming from app)

Enter incoming UDP response ports (traffic coming from app)

Configuring Local Services The Services tab enables you to define local services that can be accessed by remote clients. Select existing services from the **S**ervices list to enable those services to be provided to the remote network. Click A**d**d on the Services tab to add a new service. Figure 22.10 explains the available options.

FIGURE 22.10
Configure a local service for access by remote clients.

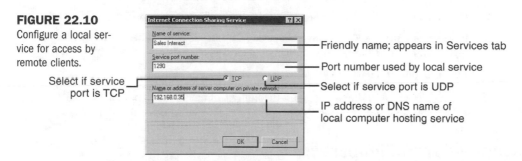

Friendly name; appears in Services tab

Port number used by local service

Select if service port is TCP

Select if service port is UDP

IP address or DNS name of local computer hosting service

VPN Connections Through ICS

Because ICS extends your LAN and doesn't require any special support for ICS on the client computers, you don't have to do anything special to enable a VPN connection from a client through an ICS host to another computer on the Internet. Simply configure the client computer to acquire addresses through DHCP. When you dial the VPN connection it will attempt to connect through the local LAN, which ultimately will take it through the ICS server to the remote VPN server.

Configuring a Dial-Up Server

You can use a Windows 2000 Professional computer as a dial-up server, allowing other computers to connect to it via modem. The dial-up server can provide access only to its local files or to the LAN. Windows 2000 Professional supports a single connection; Windows 2000 Server is limited only by the capabilities of the hardware.

TIP You must be logged on as a member of the Administrators group to enable and configure incoming connections.

To set up a dial-up server, follow these steps:

1. Open the Network and Dial-Up Connections folder and then run the Make New Connection wizard.

2. In the wizard, select **A**ccept Incoming Connections and click Ne**x**t.

3. Select the connection device through which you want to allow connections (typically, a modem) and then click Ne**x**t.

N O T E You can enable incoming connections on multiple devices. ▨

4. Choose **A**llow Virtual Private Connections if you want to support VPN on the dial-up server. Choose **D**o Not Allow Virtual Private Connections to prevent VPN connections to the server. Click Ne**x**t.

5. Select which users are allowed to connect through the dial-up connection.

6. Select a user and click P**r**operties to specify callback options, if desired.

7. Specify which protocols, clients, and services are used by the dial-up server connection, and then click Ne**x**t.

8. Click **F**inish to create the connection.

Windows 2000 creates a connection named Incoming Connections to contain the dial-up server settings. Modify this connection's properties as needed to control dial-up access.

Configuring General Properties

The General tab for Incoming Connections enables you to specify settings for the modem or other device(s) servicing the incoming connections. You also can enable/disable VPN connections through the General tab.

Configuring User Properties

Use the Users tab to define which users can dial in, security for the connection, callback options, and general account properties. Select/deselect user accounts in the **U**sers list to enable/disable dial-in access. The option Re**q**uire All Users to Secure Their Passwords and Data specifies (when selected) that remote users must use encryption for passwords and data.

 TIP Select the option Requi**r**e Data Encryption (Security tab of connection properties, Windows 2000 client) at the remote client to enable password and data encryption.

Select a user and click Properties to specify account properties for full name, password, and callback options. The options are self-explanatory.

Configuring Dial-In Protocols

You might need to configure the network protocol settings used by the incoming connections. You do this through the Networking tab of the Incoming Connections properties. The following sections explain the options available for TCP/IP and NetBEUI.

TCP/IP   Open the Networking tab of the Incoming Connections properties and double-click the TCP/IP protocol to set its properties. Figure 22.11 explains the options you can set.

FIGURE 22.11
Configure how TCP/IP settings are applied to incoming connections.

Selected: clients can access shared resources on LAN. Deselected: clients can access only shared resources on your computer

Dial-up server will assign IP address dynamically

Specify range of IP addresses using From and To; server will assign one IP from range to client

Let remote client use pre-assigned IP

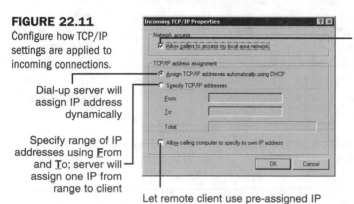

As you can see in Figure 22.11, you can grant access to the LAN through the dial-up server or restrict access to the local computer. If you configure the connection to allow LAN access, remote clients can access shared resources on the LAN if their accounts have the necessary privileges. Deselecting this option restricts access to only resources shared on the dial-up server, subject to the remote user's account restrictions as they apply to the local shares.

Also, if you select Assign TCP/IP addresses automatically using DHCP, the workstation assigns an IP address to the remote client in the Class B 169.254 subnet (255.255.0.0 subnet mask).

You can configure Incoming Connections to allow the remote client to use a predefined IP address (one they assign at their computer), for situations in which a predefined IP address is reserved for a specific user. This isn't a good option in most cases, however, since there is nothing to prevent the remote user from specifying an IP that's already in use on the LAN (or on your machine). This would result in an IP conflict, routing problems, and potential network disruption. The only situation in which this should be used is where the remote client must have a specific IP address for application or security reasons.

NetBEUI   Open the Networking tab of the Incoming Connections properties and double-click the NetBEUI protocol to configure it for incoming connections. The only option available is Allow <u>c</u>allers to access my local area network. When selected, remote users can access other computers on your local LAN through the dial-up connection, subject to privileges of their user account at each shared resource. When deselected, remote users can only access resources shared on your local computer.

Configuring a Telnet Server

Windows 2000 Professional includes a Telnet Server service that allows remote users to connect to the computer via telnet to run a remote console. Users can connect to the telnet server through the Internet and run essentially any Windows 2000 console commands, subject to the privileges of their accounts. For example, you might connect from home to your office PC through telnet and then use a remote ftp session to download files from the Internet to your office PC. The files would be waiting on your system when you got to work, and you'd save yourself a trip to the office or the download time you'd otherwise spend downloading the files to your home computer.

N O T E   Windows 2000 includes two telnet client applications. Telnet.exe is a command-line version of telnet, and telnetc.exe is a Windows-based version. Because they aren't specific to Windows 2000 installation or configuration, the telnet clients are not covered in this book. Use `telnet /?` to view command-line options for the telnet.exe application. ■

Configuring the Telnet Service

The Telnet service by default is set to manual startup. To allow remote clients to connect to a computer through telnet, you need to start the Telnet service. To do so, open the Services snap-in (Start, <u>P</u>rograms, Administrative Tools, Services). Right-click the Telnet service and choose <u>S</u>tart.

Although you can start the Telnet service manually whenever you need it active, you might prefer to configure the service for Automatic startup so it starts when the system starts. Open the properties for the Telnet service in the Services snap-in and set Startup typ<u>e</u> to Automatic.

Using Manual startup adds an additional layer of security because the Telnet service is active only when you manually start it. If you apply tight security procedures and privileges to local and LAN resources, however, Automatic startup is certainly more convenient.

Managing a Telnet Server

Windows 2000 provides a console-based utility to manage the Telnet service and connections. To manage Telnet on a computer, open a console session and enter **tlntadmn**. The tlntadmn.exe program provides a menu-based utility for starting and stopping the Telnet service, viewing current connections, terminating user connections, and displaying/changing registry settings that affect the Telnet service.

Most of the commands in the tlntadmn utility are self-explanatory. Table 22.3 describes the registry settings you can modify with tlntadmn.

Table 22.3   Telnet Registry Settings

Value	Purpose	Default
AllowTrustedDomain	Allow Telnet access to trusted domain accounts	1
AltKeyMapping	Enable/disable alternate key mapping	1
DefaultDomain	Default domain name	null
DefaultShell .exe /q /k	Path to command shell *systemroot*\\System32\\Cmd	
LoginScript in.cmd	Path to login script *systemroot*\\System32\\Log	
MaxFailedLogins	Maximum failed login attempts before disconnect	3
NTLM	Enable/disable NTLM authentication	1
TelnetPort	Telnet server port	23

N O T E   You must be logged on as a member of the Administrators group to use tlntadmn. ▦

## CHAPTER 23

Internet and TCP/IP Tools

In this chapter

Overview

Windows 2000 includes several TCP/IP utilities you can use to troubleshoot TCP/IP connectivity problems. These tools help you troubleshoot not only problems with your local computer but also with remote computers and the connections between them. This chapter focuses on the core set of TCP/IP configuration and troubleshooting tools in Windows 2000, all of which are command-line tools that you run from a console prompt.

TCP/IP Troubleshooting

TCP/IP can be a real source of problems because there can be so much manual configuration required with the protocol. Windows 2000 includes several console-based tools you can use to view your local TCP/IP configuration and troubleshoot connectivity problems locally and across the LAN or Internet.

Troubleshooting is a fine art, and doing it well requires attention to detail as well as a good set of troubleshooting tools. Your goal is to identify and eliminate the source of the communication problem. For example, if an FTP session fails, you can use several tools to determine where the problem lies in the connection between your computer and the remote FTP server.

 TIP In a newly installed system where TCP/IP is not functioning correctly, the most common cause of problems is an incorrect IP address, subnet mask, or default gateway setting in the TCP/IP properties. When a working system suddenly stops working and you haven't made any configuration changes, the problem typically lies with the hardware—the NIC, cable, router, or other downstream device.

The first step in troubleshooting a connectivity problem is to try to reproduce and localize the problem. If you can't connect to one FTP site, see if you can connect to another. If both fail, you have a connectivity problem. If only one fails, the problem probably lies with the unresponsive FTP server.

When you have a problem connecting to a website, first verify that you can connect to other websites. As with FTP, all connections failing points to a local problem, but a single connection failing points to a remote problem. If you can connect to other computers on the LAN but not the Internet, for example, the problem probably lies in your LAN link to the Internet.

In environments where you have multiple segments (router between you and other computers in your organization), see if you can connect to computers past the router. If not, try connecting to a computer on your side of the router. If you can connect, the problem lies with the gateway settings, subnet mask, or the router itself. Inability to connect to any other computers points to a problem with your computer.

Above all, be methodical. Start your testing from your local computer and work outward. For example, make sure you can ping your own workstation. When that is successful, try pinging other computers on the network, and then the router. Move outward until you locate the point at which the connection fails. Then begin troubleshooting based on that knowledge.

Table 23.1 lists common problems and their sources.

Table 23.1   Common TCP/IP Problems

Source	Problem Characteristics
Configuration	Host won't initialize, or one or more services won't start.
IP addressing	Can't communicate with other hosts; other hosts stop responding.
Subnet	You can ping your computer but can't access local or remote hosts.
Address resolution	You can ping your computer but not other hosts.
NetBIOS name resolution	Access a host by IP address but can't connect using NET command from console.
Host name resolution (DNS problem)	Access host by IP address not by host name.

Using *ping*

ping (which stands for Packet InterNet Groper) is a TCP/IP diagnostic utility that made its way from the UNIX world to Windows 2000. As its name implies, ping is like TCP/IP sonar—you send a packet to a remote host and it bounces the packet back to you. If the packet doesn't come back, the host is not available, is configured to ignore ping traffic, or there is something wrong with the connection. ping is a very useful tool for troubleshooting TCP/IP connections.

ping transmits Internet Control Message Protocol (ICMP) packets to a remote host and then waits for response packets to be received from the host. The version of ping included with Windows 2000 waits for as long as one second for the packets to be returned and prints the results of each packet transmission. ping sends four packets by default, but you can use ping to transmit any number of packets or transmit continuously until you terminate the command. The following shows a sample ping command and its output:

```
C:\WINDOWS>ping 198.87.118.1

Pinging 198.87.118.1 with 32 bytes of data:

Reply from 198.87.118.1: bytes=32 time=261ms TTL=118
Reply from 198.87.118.1: bytes=32 time=250ms TTL=118
Reply from 198.87.118.1: bytes=32 time=231ms TTL=118
Reply from 198.87.118.1: bytes=32 time=320ms TTL=118

Ping statistics for 198.87.118.1:
        Packets: Sent = 4, Received = 4, Lost = 0 (0% loss),
Approximate round trip times in milliseconds:
        Minimum = 231ms, Maximum = 320ms, Average = 265ms
```

In addition to helping test connections and determining when a host or router is not available, ping enables you to test for routing and name resolution problems. If you can ping a host using its IP address but ping fails to reach the host when you use the host name, the host probably is not listed in your DNS server or in your local Hosts file, you have specified an invalid DNS server, or the DNS server is unavailable. Add the remote host's name and IP address to the Hosts file to alleviate the problem.

Before you begin troubleshooting connection or routing problems, you should ping your own computer to verify that its network interface is working properly. To ping your own machine, use any of the following commands (for the third example, substitute your computer's IP address in place of *yourIPaddress*):

```
ping localhost
ping 127.0.0.1
ping yourIPaddress
```

The following is the syntax of the ping command:

```
ping [-t] [-a] [-n count] [-l length] [-f] [-i ttl] [-v tos] [-r count]
➥[-s count] [[-j host-list] ¦ [-k host-list]] [-w timeout] destination-list
```

The parameters you can use with the ping command are described in Table 23.2.

Table 23.2   *ping* Command Switches

Switch	Usage
-t	Continue pinging remote host until you interrupt by pressing Ctrl+C. Use for extended testing to check for intermittent connection problems.
-a	Resolve IP addresses to host names; useful for troubleshooting DNS and Hosts file problems.
-n count	Specify number of ICMP packets to be sent to remote host (default is four). Specify greater number to perform extended test.
-l length	Specify length of ICMP packets that ping transmits to remote host (default is 64 bytes). Specify up to a maximum of 8,192 bytes to test for packet fragmentation and response time.
-f	Include Do Not Fragment flag in each packet; prevents gateways through which packet passes from fragmenting the packet.
-i ttl	Set Time To Live (TTL) field to value specified by ttl. Modify to overcome slow connections.

Switch	Usage
-v tos	Set Type of Service field to value specified by tos.
-r count	Record route of outgoing packet and return packet. Specify from 1 to 9 hosts using the count value.
-s count	Specify time stamp for number of hops specified by count.
-j host-list	Use a route list to route the packets. You can separate consecutive hosts by intermediate gateways. Maximum number of hosts supported by IP is 9.
-k host-list	Route packets by means of the list of hosts specified by host-list. You cannot separate consecutive hosts by intermediate gateways.
-w timeout	Specify the time-out value in milliseconds for packet transmission.
Destination-list	Specify host to ping.

Part

V

Ch

23

Using *ipconfig*

The ipconfig command displays all current TCP/IP network configuration values. ipconfig is particularly helpful on computers using DHCP for TCP/IP configuration because it lets you determine which values have been set by the DHCP server for your workstation. Knowing your own IP information is the first step in any troubleshooting situation.

Using the ipconfig command without any parameters causes it to list all current TCP/IP configuration values, as shown in the following example:

```
Windows NT IP Configuration
Ethernet adapter Local Area Connection:

        Adapter Domain Name . . . . :
        DNS Servers . . . . . . . . :
        IP Address. . . . . . . . . : 205.219.128.87
        Subnet Mask . . . . . . . . : 255.255.255.0
        Default Gateway . . . . . . : 205.219.128.65
```

Following is the syntax for the ipconfig command:

```
Ipconfig [/all ¦ /renew [adapter] ¦ /release [adapter]
```

Table 23.3 explains the options you can include with the ipconfig command.

Table 23.3 *ipconfig* **Command Switches**

Switch	Usage	Notes
/all	Display all configuration information (DHCP status and server, physical MAC address, etc.).	If omitted, ipconfig displays only the IP address, subnet mask, and default gateway for each network card.
/renew [adapter]	Renew DHCP configuration parameters; applicable only on DHCP clients.	Include adapter name to renew only a specific adapter's configuration; issue ipconfig command without any parameters to determine adapter names.
/release [adapter]	Release current DHCP configuration; specify optional adapter name to release only specific adapter.	Releasing values disables TCP/IP for selected adapter(s); renew configuration to re-enable TCP/IP.
/flushdns	Purge DNS resolver cache.	Purging cache clears some resolution problems but slows resolver response until cache is rebuilt.
/registerdns	Refresh all leases and register host record with DNS.	Requires Windows DNS Server.
/displaydns	Show contents of local resolver cache.	
/showclassid	Show all class IDs allowed for the specified adaptor.	
/setclassid	Set class ID to specified string.	Only one class ID active at a time.

Using *netstat*

The netstat program lets you monitor your connections to remote hosts and view protocol statistics for the connections. The netstat program also is useful for extracting the IP addresses of hosts to which you have connected using domain names. The syntax of the netstat command is as follows:

```
netstat [-a] [-ens] [-p protocol] [-r] [interval]
```

Table 23.4 describes the parameters you can use with the netstat command.

Table 23.4 *netstat* **Command Switches**

Switch	Usage
-a.	Display all connections. Normally, server connections are not displayed.
-e.	Display Ethernet statistics. Use -e in conjunction with -s parameter.
-n.	Display addresses and port numbers in numerical format instead of listing names in host.domain format.
-s.	Display statistics on a per-protocol basis. By default, netstat displays statistics for the TCP, UDP, ICMP, and IP protocols.
-p protocol.	Display connections for protocol specified by the protocol parameter.
-r.	Display contents of the routing table.
interval.	Specify interval, in seconds, at which netstat will display the requested information. Terminate with Ctrl+C. Display only once if omitted.

If you want to determine the IP address of a remote host to which you're connected, use the netstat -n command. The following example uses netstat without any parameters to list the connected hosts, and then issues netstat again with the -n parameter to derive the IP addresses. You can tell from the second output that the IP address of the connected Microsoft FTP server is 207.46.133.140.

```
C:\WINNT>netstat

Active Connections

        Proto  Local Address        Foreign Address          State
        TCP    bart:1025            localhost:1026           ESTABLISHED
        TCP    bart:1026            localhost:1025           ESTABLISHED
        TCP    bart:1337            207.46.133.140:ftp       ESTABLISHED

C:\WINNT>netstat -n

Active Connections

        Proto  Local Address        Foreign Address          State
        TCP    127.0.0.1:1025       127.0.0.1:1026           ESTABLISHED
        TCP    127.0.0.1:1026       127.0.0.1:1025           ESTABLISHED
        TCP    206.9.83.19:1337     207.46.133.140:21        ESTABLISHED
```

In addition to using netstat for deriving an IP address from a host.domain name, you also can do the reverse: Derive the host.domain name of a host to which you have connected using its IP address.

Using *hostname*

hostname displays the IP host name of the local machine as registered by the DNS specified in the TCP/IP properties. There are no optional command switches for hostname. Use hostname to save the trouble of opening the TCP/IP properties to hunt for the computer's host name. The machine name specified in the network properties is used for a host name if no other is specified.

Using *tracert*

While ping is useful for determining if a connection to a remote system is working, it can't tell you how the connection is established. When you're troubleshooting routing and connection problems, it's often as important to know how the packets get to their destination or whether they get there at all. For example, you might need to know exactly where in the loop the problem is occurring. If the problem happens at your ISP (Internet service provider), for example, you know you need to contact its technical support staff for assistance.

Tracert displays the route taken by IP packets from source to destination. Tracert sends a series of ICMP packets to the destination with steadily incrementing Time-to-Live values. The TTL values are decremented by each gateway the packet passes through. The first packet has a TTL of 1. The first gateway changes the TTL to 0, expiring the packet. The gateway sends an ICMP Time Exceeded packet back to the sender along with the transpired time in milliseconds. The second packet goes out with a TTL of 2, so it makes it to the second gateway before being expired. Each subsequent packet gets one step farther until one reaches the destination. The result is a list of hops and time delay values:

```
C:\>tracert support.baynetworks.com
Tracing route to support.baynetworks.com [134.177.3.25]
over a maximum of 30 hops:

  1    141 ms    125 ms    141 ms   Rothsay-TS.dialup.means.net [206.9.83.3]
  2    140 ms    141 ms    125 ms   206.9.83.1
  3    172 ms    172 ms    187 ms   border1-h4-0.ply.mr.net [207.229.192.1]
  4    171 ms    172 ms    172 ms   core1-fe4-0-0.ply.mr.net [206.8.12.254]
  5    172 ms    187 ms    188 ms   Core1-S1-1-0.msc.mr.net [198.174.42.29]
  6    188 ms    203 ms    453 ms   h3-0.minneapol1-cr1.bbnplanet.net [4.0.246.249]
  7    203 ms    203 ms    204 ms   h2-1-0.chicago1-br1.bbnplanet.net [4.0.5.237]
  8    187 ms    188 ms    203 ms   p2-0.chicago1-nbr1.bbnplanet.net [4.0.5.90]
  9    203 ms    203 ms    203 ms   p2-0.nyc4-nbr3.bbnplanet.net [4.0.3.122]
 10    219 ms    219 ms    219 ms   p4-1.bstnma1-ba2.bbnplanet.net [4.24.4.237]
 11    235 ms    234 ms    219 ms   p4-0.washdc3-br1.bbnplanet.net [4.0.1.245]
 12    203 ms    235 ms    218 ms   p7-0.washdc3-ba1.bbnplanet.net [4.24.4.121]
 13    219 ms    234 ms    235 ms   p0-0-0.washdc3-bp1.bbnplanet.net [4.24.4.169]
 14    219 ms    219 ms    218 ms   s0.xwashdc17-level3.bbnplanet.net [4.24.4.182]
 15    281 ms    297 ms    359 ms   core1.SanJose1.Level3.net [209.244.2.21]
 16    297 ms    281 ms    609 ms   hsipaccess1.SanJose1.Level3.net [209.244.2.226]
 17    297 ms    296 ms    282 ms   209.0.252.134
 18    281 ms    296 ms    297 ms   new-support.BayNetworks.COM [134.177.3.25]

Trace complete.
```

N O T E A *hop* is the connection between two nodes, such as from your computer to your router. ▪

The syntax of the `tracert` command is:

`Tracert [-d] [-h max_hops] [-w timeout] hostname`

Table 23.5 explains the `tracert` options:

Table 23.5 *tracert* **Command Switches**

Switch	Usage
-d	Prevent display of resolved names of interim systems.
-h*max_hops*	Specify maximum number of hops to be traced.
-w *timeout*	Specify maximum period in milliseconds to wait for a reply.
hostname	Specify full host name or IP address of destination system.

Using *arp*

Address Resolution Protocol (ARP) lets you view and modify the ARP table on your computer. The ARP table associates physical MAC addresses with IP addresses for other workstations on the network. The ARP table serves as a cache to speed up connectivity, eliminating the need to constantly look up MAC addresses. Being able to view and modify the ARP table helps you overcome connection problems with specific computers.

The syntax of the `arp` command is

`Arp [-a] [-d ipaddress] [-s ipaddress macaddress] [hostaddress]`

Table 23.6 explains the `arp` options.

Table 23.6 *arp* **Command Switches**

Switch	Usage
-a	Display all ARP table information for all hosts.
-d *ipaddress*	Remove entry for specified IP address from ARP table.
-s *ipaddress macaddress*	Create new permanent ARP table entry associating specified IP address with specified MAC address.
Hostaddress	IP address of host adapter whose table should be modified.

Using *route*

route lets you view, modify, add, or delete entries in the workstation's static routing table. You can add an entry to the routing table to override the default gateway when transmitting to a particular network, and also review the contents of the routing table to troubleshoot connections. Use route print to view the contents of the routing table.

The syntax for the route command is:

Route [-f] [print] [add] [delete] [change] [*destination*] [MASK *netmask*]
➥[*gateway*] [METRIC *costmetric*]

Table 23.7 explains these options.

Table 23.7 *route* Command Switches

Switch	Usage
-f	Clear all gateway entries from the routing table before any other commands are executed.
Print	Display a routing table entry; with no parameters, display all entries.
Add	Create new routing table entry.
Delete	Delete routing table entry.
Change	Modify existing routing table entry.
Destination	Specify host to which command should be addressed.
MASK netmask	Subnet mask value for routing table entry.
Gateway	Gateway for routing table entry.
METRIC costmetric	Integer cost metric from 1–9999 used to calculate best route to specific network.

Using *nbtstat*

Nbtstat displays statistics and connections for NetBIOS over TCP communications. It's also useful for making changes to the lmhosts file immediately active by purging the name cache and reloading it from the lmhosts file. The syntax for nbtstat is

Nbtstat [-a *remotename*] [-A *remoteaddress*] [-c] [-n] [-R] [-r] [-S] [-s]
interval

Table 23.8 explains these options.

Table 23.8 *nbtstat* **Command Switches**

Switch	Usage
-a remotename	Display NetBIOS name table for specified machine name.
-A remoteaddress	Display NetBIOS name table for specified IP address.
-c	Display contents of NetBIOS name cache.
-n	Display NetBIOS names for local machine.
-R	Purge NetBIOS name and reload lmhosts file.
-RR	Send Name Release packets to WINS then refresh.
-r	Display NetBIOS name resolution statistics.
-S	Display current NetBIOS workstation and server sessions, listing remote hosts by IP address.
-s	Display current NetBIOS workstation and server sessions, listing remote hosts by name.
Interval	Specify number of seconds between displaying protocol statistics. Use to provide continuous output until you cancel with Ctrl+C.

Installing and Configuring Internet Information Services

In this chapter

A Quick Review of IIS Features

Internet Information Server (IIS) is Microsoft's offering of a Web publishing and Web server application that allows users of Windows NT/2000 to serve Web pages on the Internet. You can also set up an FTP server for the purposes of making files available on the Internet or an intranet, and use the SMTP service to create a virtual SMTP e-mail server, as well.

N O T E   IIS in Windows 2000 Server also includes an NNTP service for creating a news server. ▦

Users of Windows NT 4.0 Workstation did not have the luxury of Internet Information Server (IIS). They had to deal with the Personal Web Server (PWS). Although PWS provides a platform for running an intranet site or even a small Web site, it isn't suited to the large amounts of traffic that can be generated on a Web site connected to the Internet.

N O T E   IIS is available in both the Professional and Server versions of Windows 2000. In Windows 2000 Professional, IIS is designed to work with intranets rather than the Internet, although you can use it for a small, low-traffic, noncommercial Web site on the Internet. ▦

N O T E   If you do not have PWS installed on an NT 4.0 Workstation when you upgrade to Windows 2000 or if this is a new installation, IIS is not installed by default. See "Installing IIS," later in this chapter, for more details. ▦

IIS 5.0 offers some very nice features and enhancements to help you in establishing a powerful and effective intranet. These features of IIS break down into four categories:

- ▦ Security
- ▦ Administration
- ▦ Programmability
- ▦ Internet standards

IIS Security Features

IIS 5.0 uses *Secure Sockets Layer* (*SSL*) 3.0 and *Transport Layer Security* (*TLS*) to provide secure connections between the client and server. By using this feature in IIS 5.0, a Web programmer can actually track a user as he travels through the site. Another advantage of using SSL and TLS is that the server is able to verify the client computer's identity before the user even logs on.

IIS 5.0 includes these new security features:

- ▦ *Digest Authentication.* Provides for authentication through proxies and firewalls. Although this has been implemented, for backward compatibility, IIS 5.0 is still capable of anonymous and Windows NT Challenge/Response Authentication (NT CHAP).
- ▦ *Fortezza.* IIS 5.0 supports this U.S. Government security standard.

- *Kerberos V5 Authentication*. This protocol is integrated in Windows 2000 and allows IIS 5.0 or any other application to pass authentication credentials among computers running Windows 2000.

- *Server-Gated Cryptography (SGC)*. By using a special SGC certificate, financial and other institutions can use SGC with the 128-bit strong encryption versions of IIS for secure transactions. SGC is actually an extension of SSL.

- *Certificate Storage*. IIS 5.0 has integrated its certificate storage with the Windows CryptoAPI storage. The Windows Certificate Manager enables you to store and configure site certificates.

IIS Administration Features

Administration is central to almost any program or system, and IIS is no exception. The administrator has the ability to perform security administration, information backup and retrieval, and overall control of IIS from a central program. The IIS administration features include the following:

Part

V

Ch

24

- *Centralized Administration*. IIS 5.0 uses the Microsoft Management Console (MMC) as the platform for its administrative tools. If you are not familiar with MMC, it is a tool that hosts snap-ins for the purpose of administering the computer and/or network. This also allows administrative access to other IIS servers on the network.

- *Configuration*. You can set the security permissions such as Read, Write, and so on, and even FrontPage Web operations. These options are customizable at the site, directory, or file level.

- *Backup and Restore IIS*. This feature enables you to back up your configuration and sites so that you can quickly return to an operational state in the event of a server or hardware failure.

- *Restarting IIS*. You can start and stop IIS services without requiring a reboot of the server.

- *Personal Web Manager (PWM)*. PWM is an administrative tool for administering and monitoring your site. You will look at this tool in more depth later in the chapter.

IIS Programmability Features

IIS 5.0 supports server-side scripting to aid in developing browser-independent Web sites. This capability is provided in the form of *Active Server Pages* (*ASP*). ASP is an equivalent of CGI scripting, and ISAPI and provides for dynamic content on your Web pages.

IIS 5.0 also offers greater protection for your Web applications. IIS achieves this increased protection by running your applications separately from the IIS processes.

 TIP If you are a power user and/or Web applications programmer and you like to have control over how your applications execute, you can run your Web-based applications outside IIS and in total isolation from other application processes.

IIS Internet Standards Features

IIS 5.0 still complies with the HTTP 1.1 standard. IIS offers a few new features to aid in standard compliance:

- *FTP Resume.* This feature provides for the restarting or resuming of a file download that was interrupted. This prevents the need to download the whole file all over again. How many times have you been "slightly upset" when that 650MB download crapped out at the 649.8MB stage?

- *WebDAV.* Another new feature, Web Distributed Authoring and Versioning enables remote authoring, searching, and configuring of documents on the Web. This feature is an extension to the HTTP 1.1 protocol.

- *PICS Ratings.* If you ever wanted to publish adult content or any other material that is intended for a mature audience, you can use the Platform for Internet Content Selection (PICS) feature of IIS 5.0.

Installing IIS

If you are upgrading from NT 4.0 Workstation and you had Personal Web Server installed in that version, the upgrade process installs IIS 5.0 for you. However, IIS is not automatically installed with new installations of Windows 2000. The information in this section walks through the procedure for a manual installation of IIS.

The installation procedure is really simple; follow these steps to install IIS:

1. Insert the Windows 2000 Professional CD into your CD-ROM drive or connect to the network share if you installed Windows 2000 over the network.

2. Click the Start button, select Settings, Control Panel.

3. Click the Add/Remove Windows Components icon in the left pane; the Windows Component Wizard opens.

4. In the Components list, click the Internet Information Services (IIS) check box to select that component.

5. With IIS selected, click the Details button. A list of the subcomponents of IIS appears, from which you can select and deselect these individual subcomponents:

   Common Files. These are necessary for the operation of IIS and must be installed.

   Documentation. This includes documentation to help you learn to use IIS and also includes some sample sites.

   FTP Server. This enables you to use your computer as an FTP server to provide file download and upload capabilities.

FrontPage 2000 Server Extensions. Install this if you want to be able to administer your Web site using FrontPage or Visual InterDev.

Internet Information Services Snap-In. This feature is required for you to interact with the administration tool in the MMC.

Personal Web Manager. A GUI-based administration tool for IIS.

SMTP Service. Install this if you want to use the SMTP service on your server to create a mail-forwarding server. (SMTP Service is described later in this chapter.)

Visual InterDev RAD Remote Deployment Service. This is useful if you are performing remote installs of applications on your IIS server.

World Wide Web Server. Offers support for connecting to Web sites.

6. Click to select or deselect the subcomponents to be installed with IIS and then click <u>N</u>ext; the wizard configures and installs IIS.

Part
V

Ch
24

Opening IIS and Viewing the Web Server Contents

Windows NT Server 4.0 provided access to IIS through the Internet Information Services entry on the Start menu. In Windows 2000, you access IIS through the Control Panel and Administrative Tools applet.

To open IIS, double-click the Administrative Tools icon in the Control Panel Window, and then double-click the Internet Services Manager icon in the Administrative Tools window. The Internet Information Services window opens. Click the + before the server name to expand the contents list, as shown in Figure 24.1.

FIGURE 24.1
The Tree pane of the Internet Information Services window shows the default contents of IIS on your system, with the Server contents expanded.

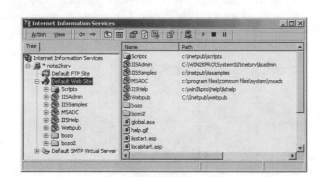

The default server contents include a default Web site, a default FTP site, and—if you chose to install it—a default SMTP server. Note that the server name you gave to this computer during the installation of Windows 2000 Professional appears in the Tree pane of this window.

Configuring the Web Server

Essentially, you can use the IIS Web server by simply placing your Web page files into the default directory of \InetPub\wwwroot and naming the home page Default.htm or Default.asp; IIS will serve the pages up for you as easily as that. Most site administrators, however, want to configure their Web site to provide a more functional and customized interface. With your Web page files in the previously mentioned directory, you are ready to begin the configuration process.

 TIP It's a good idea to stop the Web server while you make configuration changes. To stop the server, click the Stop button in the server's toolbar.

Failing to stop the server while you make changes will make pages unavailable to users or could corrupt data if you use ASP scripts.

When you configure IIS, you are actually setting up directory structure for your Web site or sites. When you configure these directory structures, you also need to be aware of security and permissions. You might or might not want visitors to be able to administer or otherwise make changes to your Web site files and folders. IIS also offers you the ability to tune the performance of the server. This tuning allows you to determine the approximate hits per day that you expect the entire server to experience. This allows IIS to utilize resources accordingly.

You also have the ability to set expiration dates on pages as well as rating the content. Content ratings allow browsers that support it to filter out pages based on certain ratings criteria.

The Web server configuration tools are available within the Properties sheet. You can open the Web Site Properties sheet by right-clicking the Default Web Site listing in the Tree pane of the IIS window and then choosing Properties from the context menu. Alternatively, click to select Default Web Site and then choose Action, Properties from the menu. This brings up the Web Site Properties sheet as shown in Figure 24.2.

FIGURE 24.2

The tabs in the Web Site Properties sheet contain all the configuration options you'll use to customize your site. Here, you configure the home directory, security settings, content ratings, and other critical server settings.

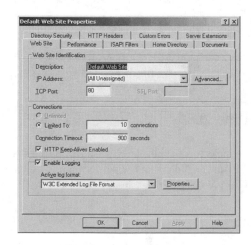

Configuring Web Site Properties

The Web Site tab contains options to control the Web Site Identification settings, connection parameters, and logging functions. In the Description text box in the Identification area, type the name or description that you want IIS to assign to this Web site. This name is for your use; it's not the name that will be seen in the Web browser title bar. If this site is your default Web site, leave the IP Address as the default (All Unassigned). If you already have a Default Web site on your network, you can click the arrow and choose the IP address of this computer from the dropdown list.

N O T E Configuring a Web site for all unassigned IP addresses means that the site will be served to clients who request a site on any IP address that doesn't already have a site explicitly assigned to it or when a requested site on the server is unavailable. If you're hosting multiple sites on a server, design the default site to accommodate situations in which the client is redirected to the site even though he requested a different site (the requested site is stopped, for example.) So, think of the default site in these situations as a sort of error handler for Web services. ▪

In most cases, you should leave the TCP port setting at 80 because that is the default port for HTTP traffic. You can change this port number to another if you prefer, but you must be careful not to use one that is already assigned, such as port 21, which is used for FTP. You must also ensure that you let your users know what port you are using so they can connect to your Web site.

Click the Advanced button to display the Advanced Multiple Web Site Configuration dialog box. As indicated in the dialog, each site has three properties: IP address, port, and host header. On a given server, sites can share any two of these properties, but one must be unique. So, several sites can share the same IP address as long as they have unique port assignments or host headers. Among other things, this means that you don't need multiple IP addresses to host multiple sites on the same server.

The host header is the site address minus the `http://` prefix. The client's browser passes the host header to the server with the HTTP request, and server decides which site to serve based on the host header. Internet Explorer 3.0 and Netscape 2.0 and later support the use of host headers.

N O T E Hosting multiple sites on a server is more applicable to Windows 2000 Server than to Windows 2000 Professional. Hosting multiple sites is therefore not covered in detail in this chapter. ▪

In the Connections area, the Unlimited option is grayed out; this option is unavailable because Windows 2000 Professional is limited to 10 simultaneous connections. (Windows 2000 Server allows unlimited Web connections.) You can set any number in the Limit To box, up to 10. If you try a higher number and click the Apply button, you are given a connection limit error message.

Part
V

Ch
24

This connection limit will prevent any more than that specified from connecting to the Web server at any one time. Because you are using the Professional version of Windows 2000 and there is a hard-coded 10-connection limit, it is recommended that you leave this number at 10. However, if you are using this computer as a personal workstation and find that performance is suffering due to these Web server connections, you can reduce this to a lower number. This can help to prevent a resource drain by having fewer computers connected to the Web server at one time.

With a 10-connection limit, it's important that idle connections be terminated as quickly as possible, to enable maximum user access. The Connection Timeout option enables you to set a timeout value, in seconds, that the server will wait before disconnecting an inactive user. If your site is frequently inaccessible to new users, you might want to adjust this setting to more quickly disconnect an inactive user.

In most situations, you should leave checked the HTTP Keep-Alive Enabled check box (which is checked by default). This option helps to reduce the load on your server by allowing clients to maintain open connections, rather than requiring them to reopen a new connection with each new request.

By default, the Enable Logging check box in the Logging area of the Web Site Properties sheet is checked, and IIS logs user activity on your Web server. The Active Log Format drop-down list enables you to choose one of three formats for your log file:

- *Microsoft IIS Log Format*. This log is generated in ASCII format.
- *NCSA Common Log Format*. This format is compatible with the original NCSA log format.
- *W3C Extended Log File Format*. This is in ASCII format, but it is completely customizable.

Your choice of which log to use should be based on your requirements. If you need to see more information about who was connected and their activities, you might want to choose the W3C Extended Log Format. If you only need to see general information, the standard Microsoft IIS Log Format can be read by any text editor.

Clicking the Properties button enables you to set the frequency of the log time period as well the location of the logfile for the selected format. W3C Extended Format has an extra tab for the Extended properties that include things such as Client IP address, Bytes Sent, and Bytes Received, along with Process Accounting options.

Configuring Web Site Performance and ISAPI Filters

The only area of the Performance tab that is available to Windows 2000 Professional is the Performance Tuning section. By using the slider control, you can adjust IIS performance based on the number of hits per day that you expect your Web site to receive.

With a 10-connection limit, the default setting of Fewer Than 100,000 is a good starting point. If you select the higher setting, IIS will use more system memory to ensure that each Web request is satisfied in the least amount of time. This will reduce the amount of memory available to other applications, which will affect overall computer performance.

You need to balance this setting based on the quantity of hits to the Web site that you expect and the actual computer usage your system normally experiences. If this is a computer that is sitting in a back room of the office and is only being used for the office intranet, the higher settings are more appropriate because IIS will use more RAM and serve pages faster.

ISAPI filters respond to events during processing of HTTP requests and can provide background processing for site traffic. Use the settings in the ISAPI Filters tab to add or remove ISAPI filters, set their order of preference, and edit them. Click the Add button on this tab to indicate the filter name and the executable file.

Configuring the Home Directory

The Home Directory tab offers three options for specifying where content should come from when it is requested from your site:

- *A Directory Located on This Computer*. This is a self-explanatory option.
- *A Share Located on Another Computer*. An option that enables you to specify that part or all of the content is on a different computer.
- *A Redirection to a URL*. Choosing this option forwards requests to another URL for processing.

The remaining options in this tab are determined by your selection of one of the three options described above. For example, if you select A Directory Located on This Computer, you see the Local Path options, as shown in Figure 24.3.

FIGURE 24.3

These are the options that you need to set when you have determined that the home directory will reside on the local computer.

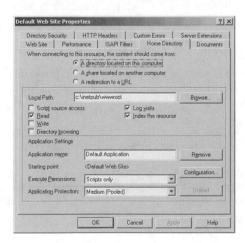

In this area, you can set the following options:

- *Local Path.* This is the directory where the Web pages reside. You can use the Browse button to navigate the hard drive and locate the directory you want.
- *Script Source Access.* Enables users to see and access the source code of the Web page, provided that the necessary Read and Write permissions are set.
- *Read.* Enables users to read or view the directories and to download files.
- *Write.* Enables users to change the contents of the directory and to upload files into it.
- *Directory Browsing.* Enables users to see a directory listing of this directory in HTML format.

> **CAUTION**
>
> You might not want to activate the Directory Browsing option because it could create a security risk. If hackers can see the directory structure and contents of your Web site, they can exploit these to gain access to your server or create havoc.

- *Log Visits.* Creates an entry for each user visit in log file.
- *Index This Resource.* Creates a full-text index of the entire Web site; enabling this option is important if you are using the Microsoft Indexing Service.

The Application Settings area provides options with which you can configure IIS Web-based applications.

Use the Execute Permissions text field to determine the level of execution for the application. Use the drop-down list to select one of these choices:

- *None.* Only static HTML files or images can be accessed.
- *Scripts Only.* Only scripts, such as ASP scripts, can run.
- *Scripts and Executables.* All files can be accessed, or all applications can execute.

The Application Protection option is where you select the area in which the application runs:

- *Low (IIS Process).* This allows the application to run in the same process as the Web services.
- *Medium (Pooled).* This runs the application in an isolated pool process along with other applications.
- *High (Isolated).* The application runs in a separate isolated process from any other process.

Choosing the Remove button removes an application; choosing the Configuration button opens the Application Configuration dialog box, with controls that enable you to configure applications on your server.

Configuring Web Site Documents

You use the Documents tab to choose the documents that will be displayed by default on your Web site and to determine the order in which they are displayed.

In the Enable Default Document area, enter the name of the document you want to be displayed when a user accesses your Web site without requesting a specific page on that site. If you don't enter the name of an HTML page here, users who don't specify a page name will receive an error message, or if directory browsing is enabled on the Home Directory tab, will see a directory of your site. Most default documents on an IIS server are either Default.htm or default.asp but you can use any name you wish. Click the Add button and enter a document name.

The Enable Document Footer section enables you to specify a footer that is displayed on each Web page.

Configuring Directory Security

Use the settings in the Anonymous Access and Authentication Control area of the Directory Security tab to determine whether your Web site is open to the public with anonymous access or is restricted to specific users.

To set your access options, click the Edit button, and the Authentication Methods dialog box opens.

To permit anonymous access to your Web site, select the Anonymous Access check box. By clicking the Edit button here, you can choose the account to be used for anonymous access. This account is very important; by setting the appropriate restrictions on this account, you can limit anonymous users' access to specified files and directories on your site.

If you don't allow anonymous access, you must specify the necessary authentication methods for accessing your site. You can do so in the Authenticated Access area of the Authentication Methods dialog box, using these options:

■ *Basic Authentication* is set for valid user accounts, but it has the serious drawback of transmitting passwords in clear text with no encryption. Unencrypted passwords are less secure than are encrypted passwords. When you select this option, you are also given the option to select a default domain.

■ *Integrated Windows Authentication* offers higher security. Formerly known as Windows NT Challenge/Response, this authentication method does not send the username or password across the network; the browser only must prove that it knows what the password is. This is done using a *cryptographic hashing routine* (a complex mathematical calculation used to encrypt information).

N O T E Note that the IP Address and Domain Name Restriction area of the Directory Security tab is grayed out and unavailable. These options are available only to a Windows 2000 Server. ■

Part

V

Ch

24

The Secure Communications area of the Directory Security tab enables you to configure and create *server certificates*. Server certificates provide your users with a means of authenticating the server before transmitting any personal information. If you are hosting a site using SSL, you must install and configure a certificate for that purpose.

IIS provides a Web Server Certificate Wizard you can use to request and install a certificate on the computer. You can request a certificate from an enterprise Certificate Authority (CA) on your network (a Windows 2000 Server running Certificate Services) or from an outside CA located on the Internet such as Thawte, VeriSign, and so forth. Use the following steps to request and install a certificate, and enable SSL for a Web site:

1. Obtain a certificate for the Web server from a Certificate Authority (CA). You can obtain a certificate from a local CA if you have Certificate Services installed on a Windows 2000 Server in your enterprise. Otherwise, you'll need to obtain a certificate from another CA such as Thawte, VeriSign, and so forth. The remaining steps assume you're using a Windows 2000 Server running Certificate Services on a computer in your enterprise to generate certificates for you, but the installation process is very similar for a third-party certificate.

2. Open the IIS console, then open the properties for the site for which you want to obtain a certificate to enable SSL. Open the Directory Security page.

3. Click Server Certificate to start the Web Server Certificate Wizard. Select the option to create a new certificate. (You have the option of assigning an existing certificate and importing a certificate from a Key Manager backup file, but this procedure assumes you're requesting a new certificate.)

4. Complete the wizard to create the request using the following list as a guide. You can submit the request immediately if an Enterprise CA is available on the network. IIS will not detect a standalone CA server on the network. In this situation, you need to create the request using the wizard, which creates an encrypted text file. Then run the wizard again to submit the encrypted request to the CA.

   - **Prepare the request now, but send it later:** Use this option if you have no enterprise CA in your enterprise, or to submit to a standalone CA.

   - **Send the request immediately to an online certification authority:** Use this option to submit the request immediately to an enterprise CA (dimmed if IIS doesn't detect an available CA).

   - **Name:** This is a friendly name for the certificate.

   - **Bit length:** A longer bit length increases security but can decrease performance. The default is 512.

   - **Server Gated Cryptography certificate:** Request an SGC certificate, which uses stronger encryption.

   - **Organization:** The name of your organization (typically, the business name).

- **Organizational Unit:** Department or other OU to further define the certificate.

- **Common name:** Specify the domain name (such as www.foofang.com) for a site hosted on the Internet. You can specify a DNS name or NetBIOS name for a site hosted on your Intranet.

- **Regional information:** Specify country, state, city, or other regional information for your organization.

- **Filename:** Specify a filename under which the certificate request will be saved.

5. Connect to the CA using http://*ServerCA*/CertSrv, where *ServerCA* is the DNS name or IP address of the certification server. Choose Request a certificate and click Next.

6. Select Advanced Request and click Next.

7. Choose Submit a certificate request using a base 64 encoded PKCS #10 file then click Next.

8. Click Browse and browse for the file created in Step 4, then click Read to read the file into the form. Or, open Notepad and then open the certificate request created in Step 4. Copy the text from the file and paste the text into the Saved Request text box on the form. Make sure to select Web Server from the Certificate Template drop-down list. Then click Submit.

9. Follow the prompts provided by the CA to complete the request. Depending on how the certificate server is configured, you'll either be granted the certificate immediately or will have to return to the page after an Administrator has issued the certificate. In either case, you'll have the option of downloading the certificate in DER or base 64 encoded formats. Either format is acceptable.

10. Open the IIS console and open the property sheet for the site, then open the Directory Security page. Click Server Certificate to run the wizard again, which will recognize that a certificate request is pending for the site. Through the wizard, specify the location of the certificate file provided by the CA in Step 9 then complete the wizard to install the certificate.

11. On the Directory Security page, click Edit to display the Secure Communications page. Configure options based on the following list and then close the property sheet and stop / start the site in preparation for testing the site:

- **Require Secure Channel:** Select this option to require the client to use SSL to connect to the site. Deselect the option to allow unencrypted access to the site.

- **Require 128-bit encryption:** Select this option to require the client to use 128-bit encryption.

- **Client certificates:** Specify how client certificates are treated. For a public Web site, choose Ignore client certificates. Select Accept client certificates to allow clients to optionally use client-side certificates to authenticate on the site. Select Require client certificates to force clients to use a certificate.

Part

V

Ch

24

- **Enable client certificate mapping:** Use this option to allow clients to use their client-side certificates to authenticate against user accounts on the server. This enables you to integrate client logon with your Windows 2000 user accounts and groups.
- **Enable certificate trust list:** Select this option and use the associated controls to define a list of CAs that are trusted for the site.

Test the site to make sure it functions properly. Open a browser on another system and connect to https://*site name*, where *site name* is the Web site's DNS name or the NetBIOS server name (applicable for Intranet server). If you receive an error that the site can't be displayed, open the Directory Security properties for the site and view the certificate. Make sure the Issued To field for the certificate matches the name of the site (www.foofang.com, for example) or the NetBIOS name of the server (for an Intranet site). If not, remove the certificate and request a new certificate with the correct name.

▶ **See** Chapter 12, "Managing User Accounts and Groups," **p. 217**

▶ **See** Chapter 11 "Understanding Security Issues," **p. 193**

Configuring HTTP Headers

The HTTP Headers tab contains options with which you can set content expiration dates and ratings as well as any custom HTTP headers that you need to add to the pages on your server.

The Enable Content Expiration area of the tab holds options that enable you to determine the expiration parameters for any date-sensitive pages or content. For example, you might want to set expiration dates for information related to a staff Christmas party or limited-time-only sale prices. With an expiration option selected, the browser compares the current date to the expiration date and decides whether it should load cached pages or obtain an updated page from the server.

There are three expiration options:

- *Expire Immediately*. Content won't be cached.
- *Expire After*. Enables you to set the date after which the content will expire.
- *Expire On*. Enables you to be a little more precise by setting the date and time that the content will expire.

N O T E If you choose the Expire Immediately option, your server will experience more traffic as a result of pages not being cached on the client. If a page has not expired, the local client will not need to download the page from the server. ■

You use the settings in the Custom HTTP Headers area to specify any custom headers necessary to support the various Web browser versions that you anticipate will be connecting to your server. Custom headers are used to provide instructions to browsers that might not be supported in the current HTML specification.

Click the **A**dd button and enter the header name and the header value. To edit existing custom headers, select one and choose the **E**dit button to edit it or choose **D**elete to stop sending the header.

The Content Rating section of the HTTP Headers tab contains settings that enable you to embed labels into the headers of your Web pages that provide to the user's browser the content ratings for the material on your Web site. To edit content ratings, click the Edit Ratings button. The Content Ratings sheet opens, as shown in Figure 24.5.

FIGURE 24.4

To find out more about the ratings services and what their ratings mean, use the options on the Rating Service tab of the Content Ratings sheet.

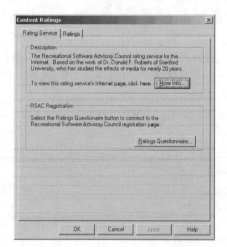

Use the options in the Ratings tab, shown in Figure 24.5, to set the ratings for your Web site.

Select the Enable Ratings for This Resource check box to set the content ratings. You can enter the email address of the individual who set the current ratings and an expiration date when the ratings should be renewed.

N O T E   In most circumstances, the Content Ratings options are used for servers connected to the Internet, rather than an intranet. If you are using your computer to serve the pages on the Internet, it is your responsibility to familiarize yourself with the requirements of these ratings by visiting the Web sites that the Rating Service tab buttons take you to. ■

FIGURE 24.5

Click a content category and then use the slider to indicate the level of that content on your site.

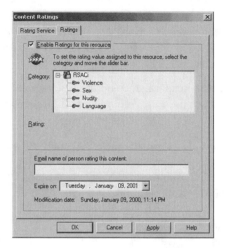

The final area on the HTTP Headers tab is MIME Map. MIME stands for *Multi-purpose Internet Mail Extensions*. This option configures the different file types that are returned to browsers by your Web server.

Click the File Types button to add or edit MIME mappings. For more information on MIME mappings, see the online help.

Configuring Custom Errors

You use the Custom Errors tab of the Directory Security dialog box to create and edit error messages that will appear on your site. Error messages display when your Web server encounters an error while processing a client request. Most Web surfers have encountered the familiar 404 "File Not Found" error message, which displays when a client requests an HTML file that no longer exists at the current Web site. You can use the default error messages or define your own here.

Configuring Server Extensions

You use the settings in the Server Extensions tab to configure FrontPage Server Extensions. If you select the Enable Authoring check box, you allow the Web site to be authored remotely from the Microsoft FrontPage Web authoring tool.

The Version Control options (None or Built-in) determine whether the system uses its built-in programs or another source-code control program (such as Visual Source Safe) to track and maintain code or page changes. The Visual Source Safe program offers more security, but it isn't packaged with Windows 2000 Professional. You need only concern yourself with this issue if you're using Windows 2000 Professional as a development test platform. In most situations where that is the case, source control will already have been factored into your environment.

Use the Performance option to set the amount of pages that the Web site contains. This setting enables IIS to adjust its caching accordingly.

Use the Client Scripting drop-down list to indicate what scripting language (either JScript or VBScript) will be used to generate scripts contained in the pages.

N O T E Be aware that using VBScript can limit your available audience to those using Internet Explorer. JScript is more widely accepted among browsers.

In the Options area of this tab, you can choose how email should be sent. Click the Settings button to display the Email Settings dialog box.

Use these settings to configure how email is delivered to Web site visitors:

- *Web Server's Mail Address.* This is the sender's address the user will see in received email, and it is the address to which replies will be routed. Your Web site administrator's email address would be the best choice here.

- *Contact Address.* The address to which users should report problems with your site; enter your tech support address here.

- *SMTP Mail Server.* The SMTP server that routes your email messages.

- *Mail Encoding.* Use the drop-down box to choose an encoding method for email on your site; as a rule, you should leave this setting at the default of 8-bit encoding, which is the most commonly used encoding for email, to enable the majority of supported platforms to read your mail.

- *Character Set.* Choose a character set from the available options for the email. The character sets determine what regional or local characters are available for the email text. Once again, the default encoding here allows for the broadest support.

By default, the root Web inherits the global settings of the Web server. You can override this default with the options in the Inherit Security Settings area of the Configuring Server Extensions tab. If you disable the Don't Inherit Security Settings option, you are given three options:

- *Log Authoring Actions.* This option will log the various details resulting from authoring being performed on the Web site. It details such items as time, author's username, Web site authored, and other information pertaining to the actions. If you are going to allow authoring of your Web site, you should select this option because it will provide you with details as to what changes were made to the site and who made those changes.

- *Manage Permissions Manually.* This prevents the server security settings from being modified by the FrontPage Server Extensions. In most situations, leave this option unselected so you can administer security using the FrontPage Server Extensions snap-in under the Microsoft Management Console.

Part
V

Ch
24

■ *Require SSL for Authoring.* If you have decided to allow Web authoring, this option requires that the author be authenticated using SSL. For intranet usage, this option is not a concern. On the other hand, if you are authoring the server over the Internet, you would want to enable this option to ensure that information such as the Web author's username and password are encrypted before being sent over the Internet.

Applying Web Server Configuration Settings

After you have made all the necessary changes to tabs in the Web site Properties dialog box, your Web server is configured and ready to run. Click either the Apply or the OK button to apply the changes.

When you are returned to the Internet Information Services window, remember to restart the Default Web Site by clicking the Run button on the toolbar. You can now serve Web pages on your intranet or the Internet.

Configuring an FTP Server

IIS is not just for Web servers. You can also set up an FTP server to make files available for download on your intranet or the Internet. In this section, you learn how to configure an FTP server.

With the Internet Information Services window open, right-click the Default FTP Site entry to display the Default FTP Site Properties sheet, shown in Figure 24.6.

FIGURE 24.6
The Default FTP Site properties sheet provides settings with which you configure your FTP server site. Many of the settings on these tabs are identical to those you worked with in the tabs of the Web Site Properties sheet.

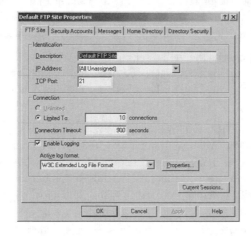

Configuring Site Settings

The settings in the FTP Site tab control your site identification, connection, and logging parameters. In the Identification area of the tab, enter your site's name (typically, your company's name) in the Description text box, and then fill in the IP Address text box. This IP address can be the same as that of the server, or it can be left at the default of (All Unassigned) to allow this FTP site to be the default site. Leaving this setting at its default is recommended if you are on a network that assigns dynamic IPs. The default setting prevents your system from locking the FTP server into an IP that is not accessible to users.

FTP servers default to a TCP Port setting of 21, and you should leave this value as is if you intend to offer this FTP on the Internet. If you change the port number, you must inform all users of the new port to attach to so they can configure their client programs accordingly.

In the Connection area of the FTP site tab, the Limited To setting should be no higher than 10; your site must be limited to 10 simultaneous connections or fewer due to Windows 2000 Professional's limitation. The Connection Timeout setting enables you to set a time limit that a user can remain connected while idle. It is a good idea to set a limit on the Professional version because one idle user could tie up a connection and prevent someone else from connecting to your FTP site. In most circumstances, the default setting here is adequate.

The Enable Logging area options are identical to those used in the Web Site Properties dialog box described in the "Configuring Web Site Properties" section earlier in this chapter. Set the appropriate logging option to satisfy your requirements for security auditing.

Configuring Security Accounts

The settings in the Security Accounts tab control Anonymous connections and Administration permissions for your FTP site. Enable the Allow Anonymous Connections to make your site available to anonymous users. Next, you must specify the username and password for the account that you want to use for anonymous access. The account must exist on your computer.

> **CAUTION**
>
> It's very important that you configure the Anonymous Users account restrictions and permissions correctly; these settings determine what anonymous users are able to gain access to on your computer.

Click the **A**dd button to add another user account or choose the **R**emove button to remove a user. Added users must be actual valid user accounts on the system.

▶ **See** "Understanding User Rights," **p. 222**

Configuring Messages

In the Messages tab of the FTP Site Properties sheet, you can create messages that your site will display automatically to users as they access the site, leave the site, or attempt to enter your site while it already has the maximum connections open. The first and last of these three messages are really essential. The connection closing message isn't critical, but many FTP site operators create a simple "Thanks, Come Again" message for display when people close the connection.

In each of the three sections of this tab, create and apply the appropriate messages. In the first area of the tab, you can enter any Welcoming message you want them to see, such as legal copyright notices, information about the FTP site, or perhaps the rules regarding uploading files. Use the same technique to enter an exiting message in the Exit area.

The Maximum Connections message is especially useful on Windows 2000 Professional with its 10-user connection limit. Using this field, you can enter a message that is displayed to users attempting to connect when your FTP site already has the maximum allowable connections. One such message might be the following:

Sorry, but the maximum number of sessions has been reached. Please try again later. Thank you for choosing our FTP site.

Configuring Home Directories

Use the settings in the Home Directories tab to configure the directory structure for your FTP site along with the security and permission settings for uploading files and creating directories. You can also determine the style of directory listing here as well.

The first option to set is whether this or another computer on your network contains the FTP site contents. Simply select the appropriate radio button.

Settings in the FTP Site Directory enable you to specify the home directory for the FTP site. The local path can be a directory on this computer, or it can reside on another computer as a network share. In this case, you would enter the share name using the UNC conventions. Alternatively, you could use the Browse button to locate the share or directory.

You will notice three option check boxes here as well. These are explained as follows:

- *Read*. Allows the users to view the directory contents and to download the files.
- *Write*. This option, when enabled, allows users to upload files to the specified directory. This is important information that should be placed in your welcome message as discussed earlier.
- *Log Visits*. If logging is enabled for this FTP site, enabling this option writes information to a log file for each site visit.

The Directory Listing Style area of this tab offers two options:

■ *UNIX*. If you select this option, visitors to your FTP site will see the file and directory listings displayed in the standard UNIX style that the ls command uses.

■ *MS-DOS*. This option will cause the FTP server to return a standard DOS file listing to the user.

The choice is yours, but take a small bit of advice here. With all the security issues that have plagued Microsoft and IIS, it might be wise to use the UNIX listing style.

The reason I say this is that in the past, hackers used any information available to break into computers. One piece of information that was displayed on early UNIX computers was the brand and version number. The hackers used this to their advantage by exploiting known cracks that existed for that particular OS.

In much the same way here, if a hacker connects to your FTP site and gets a listing in MS-DOS format, he will know that you are using IIS right off. By using the standard UNIX style, you can mask the fact that you are using IIS. Of course, most good hackers would follow up anyway, but it's better than nothing at all.

Configuring Directory Security

The Directory Security tab contains an area with options controlling TCP/IP Access Restrictions. You use this feature to grant or deny access to your FTP site by specific IP address or Subnet Mask. Use the **A**dd, **R**emove, or **E**dit buttons to configure the IP addresses that will be allowed or denied access to the FTP site.

N O T E When you select the Directory Security tab, the Granted Access and Denied Access radio buttons are grayed and not available. IIS under Windows 2000 Professional does not allow you to configure this option.

Creating the FTP Server Directory

When you have configured the FTP server, you are ready to decide on a directory structure and copy the files you want to make available to those directories.

By default, the root directory of the FTP server is \inetpub\ftproot. You can copy all your files into the root directory or create an elaborate directory structure. The choice is yours, but you should keep your users in mind when setting up the directories. Having too many subdirectories results in users becoming frustrated and leaving the site, never to return again.

In addition to the subdirectories under the physical root for the ftp site, you can also add *virtual directories*. These directories don't show up in the listing when a remote client browses the site, but clients can use the **cd** command to change to these "hidden" directories. What's more, virtual directories can be located on a different volume or even a network share.

TIP Users who connect to a site with a user name that matches a virtual directory alias name are auto-matically directed to that virtual directory at logon. For example, if the site contains a virtual directory named **jeff** and a user connects with the user name **jeff**, his session starts in the **jeff** folder rather than the ftp root. This offers an easy means of directing users to their own ftp folders.

In the IIS console, right-click the ftp site and choose <u>N</u>ew, Virtual Directory, then follow the wizard's prompts to create the virtual directory. The options are self-explanatory.

Configuring SMTP Services

If you installed the SMTP service for IIS you'll find a Default SMTP Virtual Server branch in the IIS console. The SMTP service enables you to use a Windows 2000 Professional computer as a virtual SMTP e-mail server. An SMTP branch in the IIS console shows Domain and Current Sessions items. You use the Domain item to create local or remote domains. When you right-click this entry and choose <u>N</u>ew, <u>D</u>omain, the New Domain Wizard walks you through the process of creating a new domain.

Clicking the Current Sessions item will list any current users by displaying the username, where they are from, and the connected time.

To configure the SMTP services on your Windows 2000 Professional computer, you invoke the same procedure you used for the Web and FTP sites. Right-click Default SMTP Virtual Server and choose <u>P</u>roperties from the pop-up menu. This displays the Default SMTP Virtual Server Properties Window as shown in Figure 24.7.

FIGURE 24.7
The Default SMTP Virtual Server Properties Window is where you configure the delivery and rout-ing options for the SMTP Virtual Server. You set up access con-trol and security set-tings here as well.

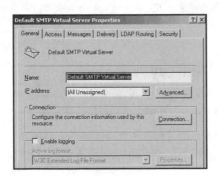

Configuring the General SMTP Server Settings

Use the settings in the General tab to identify your SMTP Virtual Server. Enter a descriptive name for your server in the Name text box. In most cases, you should leave the IP Address at the default setting of (All Unassigned) to have this site configured as the default.

To configure connection options, choose the Connection button to open the Connections dialog box. In the Incoming area of this dialog box, you can set the timeout value and the maximum number of connections for incoming connections. Unlike the Web Site connections limit, you can set a higher limit on the number of incoming connections your site will accept. If your server performance is suffering, you might be able to improve it by setting a lower incoming connection limit or by reducing the default timeout setting.

Use the settings in the Outgoing area to set the timeout values as well as the port that is used for outgoing connections (port 25 is the default SMTP port). You can also set the maximum amount of connections here for the site and for domains.

As mentioned earlier, the 10-connection limit does not apply to the SMTP virtual server. By clearing the limit check boxes, you can have unlimited outgoing and incoming connections. Be aware that unlimited connections will cause performance issues. You must enable the Incoming and Outgoing limit check boxes to enforce limits. The maximum allowable limit is 1,000.

When you have finished making your selections, click OK to close the Connections dialog box.

Part

V

Ch

24

 TIP Take notice of the Limit Number of Connections per Domain To option. This is used to set a limit on the number of outgoing connections to a remote domain. Ensure that this number is less than or equal to the limit specified in the Limit Connections To setting above it.

Back on the General Tab, use the properties button in the Logging area of the tab to configure logging properties, as you did for the Web Site and FTP Site Properties sheets.

Configuring the SMTP Operators

The options on the Security tab enable you to add or remove user accounts for the purpose of administering the SMTP site. Once again, the user accounts must exist on the computer. If you are connected to a domain, click the Add button to display the Select Administrator Account window.

Select the groups or users to whom you want to give the administration privileges for the SMTP Virtual Server. Only select those users or groups who are qualified to administer this service.

Configuring SMTP Messages

Use the settings in the Messages tab to configure message transmission limits and requirements. The Messages tab is shown in Figure 24.8.

FIGURE 24.8

The settings you choose in the Messages tab can help determine your server's performance.

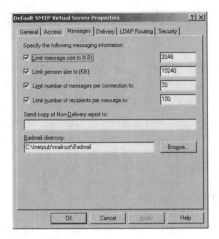

The Limit Message Size To option enables you to set the maximum message size. This is expressed in kilobytes and determines the maximum size of an email message that this server will accept. If the remote server supports EHLO, it will pick up on the maximum size limit that is advertised by your server. If you are receiving messages from other servers that your mail is being bounced because the message size is too large or if people are telling you that messages are not getting delivered, choose a smaller size to try to rectify these problems.

You use the Limit Session Size To setting to limit the amount of data accepted per session. This figure is also expressed in kilobytes and should be set to a value larger than the maximum message size.

You can set the Limit Number of Messages per Connection To on this tab as well. This setting limits the number of messages sent in a single connection; it doesn't limit messages to the server as a whole. Adjust this setting to prevent one session from hogging the entire server bandwidth for mail purposes. This setting also can be used to increase your system performance because it can send messages using more than one connection to a single domain. If you do reach a set limit, the server will open a new connection and continue to send the messages until that limit is reached.

The Limit Number of Recipients per Message To setting enables you to limit the number of email recipients you will serve. The default here is 100, which is actually the minimum specified in Request For Comments (RFC) 821. This RFC describes the SMTP protocol and can be found on the Internet at various locations.

TIP The Limit Number of Recipients per Message To setting can also be a way to prevent your computer from being used as a mail-forwarding gateway if you have it connected to the Internet.

Enter your site administrator's address in the Send Copy of Non-Delivery Report To text box to have all nondelivery reports (NDRs) sent to that person. The most common reason for an NDR report to be generated is that an email address doesn't exist any longer on a remote server.

The last setting enables you to specify a directory to store *badmail* in. Badmail is actually any undeliverable mail and its accompanying NDR.

Configuring SMTP Directory Security

The Access tab contains all the options necessary to secure your SMTP Virtual Server. By setting options here, you can deny or permit computers, networks, or users access to this server. There is also an option that can be set to block users trying to relay mail through your server; to do so, choose the Relay Restrictions button to open the Relay Restrictions dialog box shown in Figure 24.9.

FIGURE 24.9
In the Computers area of the Relay Restrictions dialog box, enter the IP addresses or domain names of computers that you want to deny or enable to relay mail through your server. Choose the appropriate radio button, add the names/addresses, and then choose OK to return to the Access tab.

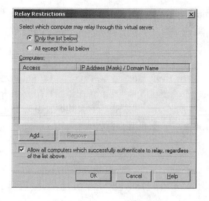

N O T E *Relaying mail* refers to the practice of connecting to and routing email messages through an unsuspecting party's server. If someone relays mail through your server, you'll suffer heavy usage on your server, and because mail relay masks the original sender's identity, you'll be considered an email spammer by the recipients of the routed messages. ■

Click the Authentication button in the Access control area of the Access tab to display the Authentication Methods dialog.

If you don't want to perform authentication on the server, click to disable the Anonymous Access check box (you also must clear the remaining two check boxes).

Selecting the Basic Authentication check box enables you to authenticate users using standard username and password authentication methods. Enabling basic authentication sends passwords using clear text. You can provide somewhat higher security by clicking to enable the TLS Encryption check box and specifying a domain to use for authentication.

The Windows Security Package option, when activated, requires the server and client to use the Windows Security Provider Interface for authentication.

The Secure communication area of the Directory Security tab enables you to run the Certificate Wizard by clicking the Get Certificate button. The wizard walks you through the process of acquiring a certificate.

When you have a certificate and it is installed, you can click the Communication button to open the Secure Communications dialog box and set the security requirements for your communications channel. You can require a secure channel and set the encryption level to 128-bit here.

N O T E At this time, 128-bit encryption is the highest encryption level available for use in North America; it provides the best security that you can get for encrypting data. ■

The IP Address and Domain Name Restrictions options are identical to that for the Web and FTP sites. They enable you to grant or deny access to the SMTP server, based on IP address or domain. Click Relay in the Relay Restrictions area of this tab to configure settings that can prevent the SMTP server from being used as an SMTP relay agent. You can choose to grant or deny this permission by IP address or domain name.

Configuring SMTP Delivery

You set delivery and routing options in the Delivery tab of the SMTP Virtual Server Properties dialog box, such as the retry intervals for undeliverable mail. You can also set the expiration timeouts and delay notifications.

If you have requirements to authenticate your server to a remote server, click Outbound Security to display the Outbound Security dialog box shown in Figure 24.10.

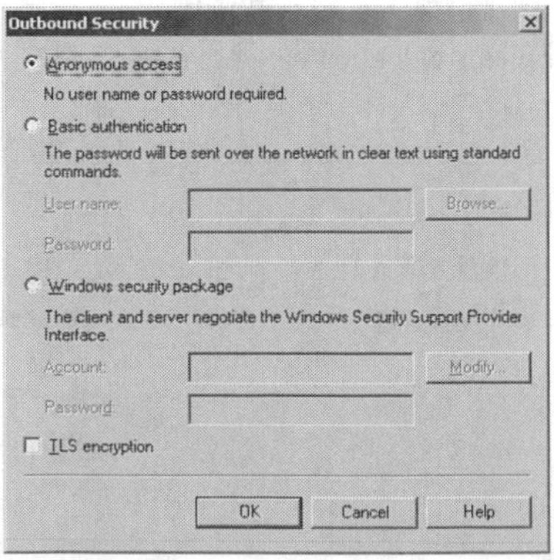

FIGURE 24.10
The Outbound Security dialog offers you the capability to set authentication, security, and encryption for outbound email.

Adjust your outbound security settings using these options:

- *Anonymous Access*. No authentication required.
- *Basic Authentication*. Password sent in unencrypted text.
- *Windows Security Package*. Client and server use Windows Security Support Provider interface.
- *TLS Encryption*. The highest possible security is applied.

As you can see, the level of security progresses as you move from the first to the last item on this list.

You can set the following additional settings by clicking Advanced on the Delivery tab:

- *Maximum Hop Count*. As your messages travel over the network or the Internet, they go through routers on the way to their destination. You can use this option to limit the amount of routers that the messages are allowed to travel over before they are determined undeliverable. The default is 15.
- *Masquerade Domain*. This entry is used to replace the local domain name that is displayed in the Mail From header information in the SMTP protocol.
- *Fully Qualified Domain Name*. This entry lists the name that your computer is known by in terms of the name assigned to the computer and the domain that it resides in.
- *Smart Host*. Use this option to route your outgoing messages through a smart host instead of sending them directly to the domain. Routing through a smart host will be less expensive or faster for some messages.
- *Attempt Direct Delivery before Sending to Smart Host*. This tells the SMTP server to attempt sending the message itself directly to the remote domain. If it determines that the route is too costly, it will forward it to the indicated smart host.
- *Perform Reverse DNS Lookup on Incoming Message*. You can use this option to verify that the message is coming from the indicated sender. The SMTP server does this by verifying that the IP address indicated in the From field is the same as the originating IP address that is contained in the header.

Configuring LDAP Routing

LDAP stands for Lightweight Directory Access Protocol and is used by the SMTP Virtual Server to communicate with directory services. If you are using a directory services server on your network, you can use the settings in this tab to specify that server so that it can provide LDAP services to your SMTP server.

The available options are listed as follows:

- *Server Name*. Enter the name of the computer that is running the LDAP services.
- *Schema Type*. Choose one of these options:
  - *Exchange LDAP Service*. Use this when you have Microsoft Exchange Server installed on a Windows 2000 Server using Active Directory.

- *Active Directory.* Use this if a Windows 2000 computer is running as the LDAP server without Exchange Server.

- *Site Server Membership Directory.* Use this for computers running the Site Server 3.0 or later software to manage LDAP mailboxes.

■ *Binding.* This is used to indicate how your SMTP server will be authenticated by the directory service.

■ *User name.* If you are using the plain text or Windows SSPI bindings you can specify the distinguished name (DN) of the account that you want to use for binding to the LDAP directory.

■ *Domain.* Specify the domain of the account specified by User name.

■ *Password.* Type in the password that is used to connect to the directory service.

■ *Naming Context.* Used to indicate the container name of the directory that you are accessing.

Using the Personal Web Manager

The Personal Web Manager (PWM) is a GUI-based administration tool for managing your Web site. Most of the configuration options available in the Personal Web Manager are available in the Web Site properties sheet that was discussed earlier in the chapter. PWM just makes administering the site a little easier. You can use this tool to create and customize your Web site, to add new directories, and for publishing, advanced configuration, and maintenance, which I will go into a little later.

You can access the Personal Web Manager from within the Administrative Tools Window under Control Panel. The Personal Web Manager Window is shown in Figure 24.11.

FIGURE 24.11
Click the Tour icon in the left band of this window to take a virtual tour of IIS. The tour images appear in the right pane.

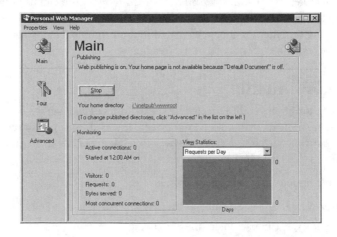

The Main Window in the Personal Web Manager

Essentially, you can use the Main page for quick and dirty control and statistics viewing of your Web server rather than going into the full-fledged IIS Manger.

Looking at the Main screen, you can see some information and statistics regarding your Web site. For example, the first section, Web Publishing, tells you that Web publishing is on and that your home page is located at the address listed.

Note the $\underline{S}$top button on the form. You can use this to stop the IIS Web server and prevent any connections from being made to the Web server. Once again, ensure that you stop the service prior to making changes to Web pages or configuration issues.

The bottom section displays some of your Web site's statistics:

- *Active Connections*. This will display the number of connections that are currently in progress for this Web site. After a certain time frame, this value will indicate 0 again until another connection is requested.

- *Started At*. This value indicates the last time that the server was started. Every time you stop and restart the Web site, this value will indicate that start value.

- *Visitors*. This indicates how many visitors have connected to this site.

- *Requests*. This value tells you how many requests were sent to the Web site. This value will differ from the amount of visits as a result of the way HTML pages are served (for example, if you have graphics on your pages, each of those requires a separate request).

- *Bytes Served*. This value tells you the amount of bytes that have been transmitted since the last server start.

- *Most Concurrent Connection*. This indicates the most connections that took place simultaneously on the site. You can use this value to troubleshoot any complaints of users not being able to get pages or experiencing delays.

In the lower right corner of the PWM Main page, you will see a graph. This graph provides a visual representation of four site statistics: Requests per Day, Requests per Hour, Visitors per Day, and Visitors per Hour. Use the drop-down list to choose one of these options.

Setting Advanced Options in Personal Web Manager

Again, rather than use the IIS manager, you will find it easier to use the PWM interface to set some advanced options for your Web server. The Advanced Options window of Personal Web manager contains three areas of options; the first of these deals with Virtual Directories.

A *virtual directory* is one that actually resides elsewhere on your hard drive and not in the wwwroot directory of your Web site. Virtual directories thus help reserve disk space on your computer by having the Web files reside on another computer's hard drive. To any visitors who are on your Web site, it appears as though that directory is in fact a part of the Web site.

You can add, remove, and configure virtual directories in the Advanced Options window. To add a virtual directory, first select a directory in the list of available directories that you want to create a subdirectory under. This can include the root directory, which is indicated as <Home>. Select the **A**dd button and the Add Directory dialog box appears.

Enter the path and directory name that you want to add as a virtual directory or root directory in the Directory text box.

In the Alias text box, enter the name that you want to call your virtual directory.

N O T E Note that you cannot change the home directory alias. ▦

Use options in the Access Permissions area to determine the access level for visitors:

- *Read*. This only allows the visitors to view or download pages and files.
- *Write*. This allows visitors to upload files to the enabled directory. They can also change the contents of any write-enabled files.
- *Script Source Access*. This allows access to the source code of scripts on the site and the execution of those scripts.

 TIP If you have any directories that contain CGI scripts or ISAPI DLLs, you should disable Read access on them. If you don't, visitors would be able to download your scripts and application files. Be aware that Write access is only possible with browsers that support the PUT feature from the HTTP 1.1 standard.

By setting the appropriate option in the Application Permissions area, you can choose to prevent applications and scripts from running in the directory, to allow scripts only, or to allow the visitor to run applications in the directory. Click the OK button to close the Add Directory dialog box and return to the Advanced Options window.

By clicking the Edit **P**roperties button, you can change existing configurations for the selected directory.

The options in the Enable Default Document area are used to display a default document to any visitor who does not append a filename to the end of the URL. Enter the name of the default document here such as Default.htm. If you are using multiple default documents, you can enter the names of each separated by commas.

At the bottom of the Advanced Options page, you will notice two check boxes. The first one, Allow Directory Bro**w**sing, allows any visitor to see a list of documents and files that reside on your Web site. This list is displayed only if the user does not specify a document name at the end of the URL and you did not specify Enable Default Document as indicated previously.

The last option is the Save Web Site Activity Log. This option, when enabled, logs the traffic activity for the Web site. A new log is started each month and they are stored in the `\System\LogFile\W3spc1` directory.

Using FrontPage Extensions

Microsoft provides the FrontPage Server Extensions for use on various computing platforms, including Windows NT/2000, Digital UNIX, and SunOS. These extensions provide cross-platform compatibility, and they enable users of the FrontPage Web Authoring tool to publish and administer Web sites installed on a computer other than a Windows NT/2000 server.

The FrontPage Web Authoring tool enables the Web author to view the Web using a graphical layout. If the server has the FrontPage Server Extensions installed, you can even use FrontPage to remotely author and administer the Web site. FrontPage Extensions also offer these advantages:

■ The capability to author a Web site while it resides on another computer altogether, even over the Internet. This feature saves a lot of downloading and uploading of changes to the Web pages.

■ Web authors can collaborate on Web sites and maintain them remotely.

■ Support for full-text searches. (Microsoft Index Server makes an excellent addition for the purposes of indexing documents on the server and making your searches more precise.)

■ Supports hit counters and forms handling so that you don't need CGI programs.

■ As mentioned previously, the capability to work on different OS platforms.

■ If you move or delete pages within the Web, the server extensions can update the necessary links accordingly.

■ For those of you running Microsoft Office or Visual Source Safe, the extensions provide integration capabilities with these products.

The FrontPage Server Extensions are administered using the FrontPage MMC Snap-in. There are several tools available for working with the FrontPage Extensions, and the MMC snap-in is just one of them. Microsoft makes available a FrontPage 2000 Resource Kit on its Web site at `http://www.microsoft.com/frontpage/wpp/serk`.

The FrontPage Extensions snap-in is shown in Figure 24.12. You gain access to this snap-in through the Control Panel. Open Control Panel, double-click the Administration Tools icon to open that window, and choose the Server Extensions Administrator program. You can use the snap-in to perform most of the administration tasks for the FrontPage Extensions, as described in the sections that follow.

FIGURE 24.12
You use the FrontPage Extensions snap-in to configure the extensions on your server that allow the Microsoft FrontPage published Web pages to display as they were intended.

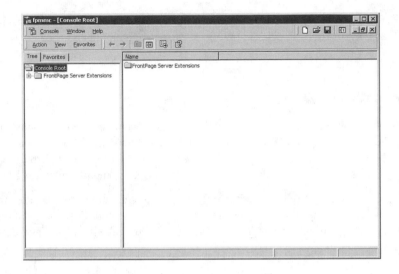

Creating a SubWeb

Sometimes, you might want to create a subWeb under your root Web. A *subWeb* is just another folder or Web that resides under your root Web and is a part of the whole Web site. You might want to use subWebs, for example, to assign authoring permissions to certain authors based on a particular page or set of pages. You can create the subWeb and set the necessary permissions for that author or group of authors only.

Follow these steps to create a subWeb:

1. In the left pane of the MMC console, right-click the Web or folder under which you want to create the subWeb.
2. Select New from the pop-up menu.
3. Choose Server Extensions Web; the New SubWeb Wizard opens.
4. Follow the steps and instructions that the wizard walks you through to create the subWeb.

Add an Administrator

Most companies require more than one Administrator so that the site will be covered during the regular Administrator's vacations and sick days. Follow these steps to add an Administrator:

1. In the left pane of MMC, right-click the listing for the Web to which you want to add the Administrator.

2. Choose New from the pop-up menu and the select Server Extensions Administrator.

3. Enter a valid Windows account name into the Username box.

4. Choose the OK button.

You can also remove the server extensions, check and update them, and even delete FrontPage Extended Webs all from the snap-in and MMC.

Index Server and Message Queuing Service

Installing and Configuring Index Server

Index Server is a service that you use to maintain an index of the documents on your computer. Index Server does this by extracting information from the documents you specify and organizing it for quick and easy access through the Search function of Windows 2000 (using either the Indexing Service query form or accessing the function from a Web browser).

The search process is typical of those used in other programs, applications, and systems. The Index Server extracts information such as a document's text, creation date, or author name. Users can construct searches based on words, phrases, or document properties. The Indexing Service then returns documents based on the search criteria. Most Web sites that run on IIS use the Index Server feature to allow users to search the Web site and all documents contained in the Web. This service helps minimize the time visitors to the site must spend searching for a specific page. They can rely on the Indexing Service to do the search and return the results.

Understanding the Indexing Process

The Indexing Service uses indexing to filter the text in a document and pass the results to a Web or System catalog. The service then searches the catalog for the requested text or phrase instead of searching all the drives on the computer or an entire Web site.

N O T E Most people use indexes regularly and understand what a powerful tool they can be for locating items and information. Think of the department store catalog that you receive from time to time. It is much easier for you to look in the index for the item you want than it is to search through page after page of items in the catalog. A well-constructed index always simplifies the process of finding specific information within a large collection of data. ■

Here is the process Index Server uses to index documents:

1. Index Server uses a filter to read through the document and extract the contents and property values. The property values are stored in a path to the document in the index.
2. It then determines the language of the document and breaks the contents into individual words.
3. The Index Service then checks the exception list and removes any words from the document that are on this list. To see the exception list, see the online help for Index Server; this list varies with each language.
4. The Remaining words are then stored in the index.
5. Selected property values are stored in the property cache. This is simply a file that stores document property values.

N O T E *Document filters* are software components that are familiar with the structure of a particular document type such as HTML or a word processor. Index Server comes with the following filters (provided by Microsoft):

- Microsoft Office Application documents
- HTML documents
- Text documents
- Internet Mail and News documents

Third-party software vendors might provide filters for their document types. ■

Installing and Running Index Server

Before you install Indexing Service, you should be aware of the Service's memory requirements. Although the hardware requirements for the service are the same as those for
Windows 2000, the performance can be affected by the size and quantity of documents that
you are indexing. Index Server has the capability to index the following documents:

- HTML Documents
- ASCII text documents
- Documents created in Microsoft Office 95 and later versions
- Microsoft Internet Mail and News documents
- Other documents that have filters available

Table 25.1 lists recommended memory configurations based on the total number of indexed
documents.

Table 25.1   Recommended Memory Configuration

# of Documents	Recommended Memory
Less than 100,000	64MB
100,000 to 250,000	64MB to 128MB
250,000 to 500,000	128MB to 256MB
500,000 or more	256MB or higher

When you have determined that your system's memory is adequate for running the service,
you are ready for installation. To install Microsoft Index Server, follow these steps:

1. Open Control Panel and double-click the Add/Remove Programs icon; the
   Add/Remove Programs dialog box opens.
2. Select the Add/Remove Windows Components icon; the Windows Components Wizard
   opens.

Part
V

Ch
25

3. In the Components window, select the Indexing Service Component check box and then choose the **N**ext button. The wizard will go through the process of installing the service.

4. Choose the **F**inish button when the Wizard displays the Completing the Windows Components Wizard screen. The wizard closes, and the Indexing Service installation is complete.

As with any Windows 2000 component, Index Service has security issues that deserve consideration:

- If you have deployed your Windows 2000 system using the NTFS file system, any documents that are indexed still maintain the permissions set on them for user access.

- If a user does not have access to a particular file, he will not be given access through Indexing Service either.

- If the documents exist on a UNC share, users will be able to see them in the document list but might not be able to access them, depending on the permissions.

N O T E A UNC (Universal Naming Convention) share is a directory or disk drive that is shared over the network from another computer. UNC is used to indicate the computer name and directory name on the remote computer, such as the following:

`\\server\sharename`

- If you place the catalog on a FAT partition, there are no security settings. (The FAT file system, used for years on DOS and non-Windows NT systems, doesn't have the capability to use file permissions.) Users can see all documents.

- Indexing Service must have permission to access the files that you want indexed, so you must set the correct permissions for the System account (the account used by Indexing Service).

- Index Service is not able to decrypt information stored in files and therefore cannot index it correctly. If you have any encrypted documents, they will not be indexed. If you encrypt a document after it has been indexed, it will be removed from the catalog.

▶ **See** "The NT File System (NTFS)," **p. 74**

▶ **See** "Managing Group Policies," **p. 225**

▶ **See** "The FAT and FAT32 File Systems," **p. 72**

Finally, keep in mind these do's and don'ts when running Indexing Service:

- Don't store your catalog on a Web site. IIS might lock the files and prevent Index Server from accessing them.

- Do store catalogs in a catalog folder and create subfolders for multiple catalogs.

■ Don't run antivirus software while the Indexing Service is running. Antivirus utilities can lock files, preventing them from being accessed and indexed.

■ Do shut down the Indexing Service before running backup utilities. These programs lock files as well and could cause the Indexing Service to time out if it were accessing these files.

Setting General Properties

Indexing Service extracts the information from the document types listed previously and creates an index that is easily searchable. You need to configure the service first to tell it what you want to index and how to do it. For example, Indexing Service can generate abstracts—short previews of the documents that contain the word or words that you searched for—and by using options in the properties sheet, you can assign a maximum number of characters for these abstracts.

N O T E   Indexing Service comes with filters for various document types. It uses the file extensions to determine the correct filter to use. For example, the extension .htm would indicate an HTML document, and the .doc extension is used for Microsoft Word documents. ■

To configure the properties of Indexing Service, follow these steps:

1. From Control Panel, open the Administrative Tools window and then double-click the Computer Management icon. The Computer Management window opens.

2. In the console Tree, expand the Services and Applications contents and then click to highlight the Indexing Service entry.

3. Open the Action menu and choose Properties. The Indexing Service Properties sheet appears with the Generation tab open, as shown in Figure 25.1.

Part
V

Ch
25

FIGURE 25.1
By default, Indexing Services indexes files with unknown extensions and generates abstracts. You can deselect those settings in the Generation tab of the Indexing Services Properties sheet.

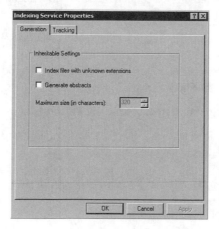

4. Select the Index Files with Unknown Extensions check box to tell Indexing Service to index files with missing or unknown extensions and extract what information it can from them. (This option might be selected by default.)

5. Make sure the Generate Abstracts check box is selected if you want Index Server to Generate Abstracts of the documents that contain the searched-for words or phrases. If you don't want IS to generate abstracts, deselect this option and move to step 7.

6. Choose the maximum number of characters to be displayed in the list that will be generated and displayed when you perform a search.

 TIP When you choose to have Index Server generate abstracts, set a maximum size of 100–150 characters to prevent your users from having to scroll to see all the text.

7. Click to open the Tracking Tab. The Add Network Share Alias Automatically option, when selected, allows Indexing Service to use the share name as an alias for that directory (rather than referring to a full UNC pathname).

8. Click the OK button to close the properties sheet and apply the settings. You will also have to stop and restart the Indexing Service for the changes to take effect.

Managing Directories

Indexing Service stores the information that it indexes in catalogs. When you install Indexing Service, it automatically creates a catalog called the System catalog. This catalog contains the contents of all nonremovable drives on your system.

If you have IIS installed, Indexing Service also creates a Web catalog that contains indexed documents on the Web sites that IIS contains.

You can tell Indexing Service to index all or only certain directories on your computer's disk drives, based on whether those directories contain sensitive information. Those that do contain sensitive information are unlikely candidates for indexing.

To view the directories contained in the Systems catalog of Indexing Service, double-click the System catalog icon in the console Tree of the Computer Management window and then click the Directories folder. This action opens a Computer Management window with Indexing Services displayed, similar to the window shown in Figure 25.2.

To create a new directory within the System catalog, follow these steps:

1. With the System catalog icon selected, open the **A**ction menu and choose **N**ew, **D**irectory; the Add Directory dialog box opens.

2. Enter a path in the **P**ath text box or use the **B**rowse button to locate a directory on the local hard drive or a network share that you want to add to the list.

3. If the directory is a network share, enter the Alias if required in the <u>A</u>lias (UNC) field, and choose a radio button in the Include in Index area to indicate whether to index the directory.

4. Click the OK button, and Indexing Service adds the directory to the list of indexed directories.

FIGURE 25.2
The contents of the Indexing Service System Directories folder, shown in the right pane of this window, will be unique to each installation. The right-pane columns can be modified by customizing View settings.

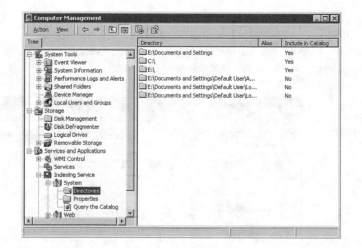

To verify that your new directory has been added, click the System catalog icon and then click the Directories folder. The right pane displays all available directories and includes three columns that describe the directories:

- *Directory*. This column displays the directory name as it exists on the computer or network.

- *Alias*. This column indicates the alias name for network shares if you billed in that information.

- *Include in Catalog*. This column has two possible choices, Yes or No, to indicate whether the directory has been included in the indexed catalog.

You can customize the view by selecting the <u>V</u>iew menu and then choosing Co<u>l</u>umns. In the Modify Columns dialog box that appears, you can hide or display columns as you want.

By selecting the Properties folder in the console Tree, MMC displays these System catalog properties in the right pane:

- *Property Set*. This is the property number given to a group of properties.

- *Property*. The string or hex ID of the property.

- *Friendly Name*. The property label that is used in sort specifications or query restrictions.

- *Data Type.* The data type used for storing the property in the cache.
- *Cached Size.* The amount of space allocated in the cache for the property measured in bytes.
- *Storage Level.* The level of the cache (primary or secondary) that the property is stored in.

The System catalog also contains an HTML-page icon labeled Query the Catalog. When you select this icon, an HTML page containing the Indexing Service Query Form appears in the right pane of MMC. You use the options on this page to enter queries and set search parameters for a search of the System catalog (see Figure 25.3).

FIGURE 25.3
Enter a word or phrase in this search to query the System catalog.

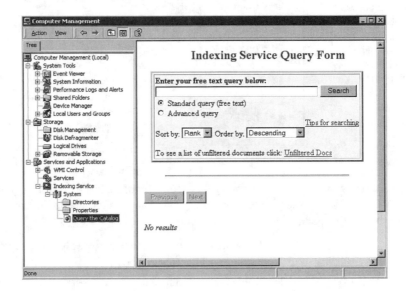

Enter the text or phrase that you want to search for and the results are displayed in Internet Explorer with hyperlinks that will take you to the document containing the search criteria.

Figure 25.4 shows a partial search result of documents within the catalog on my computer that contains the characters `inf`.

Managing Web Properties

As stated earlier, the Web catalog is created and added by default if you have IIS installed on your system. To index a Web site, you need to open the Web catalog in the console Tree pane of Computer Manager and then choose Properties from the Action menu to open the Web Properties sheet.

FIGURE 25.4

The search results contain the filename, file size, modified date, and the file path. If you click the file-name, Indexing Service attempts to open the file using a program associated with the extension.

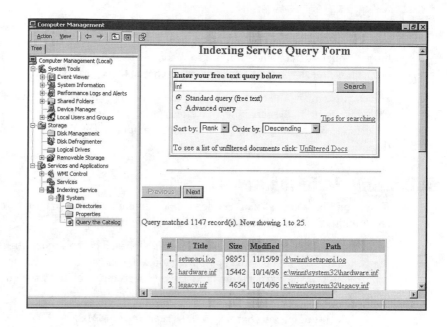

Part

V

Ch

25

Much of the Web Properties sheet is identical to the System catalog properties sheet. You will note differences, however, on the Tracking tab, where you must select the WWW Server that contains the Web site that you will index (see Figure 25.5). Most of the settings in this sheet are self-explanatory, and in most situations, the default settings should be left in place.

FIGURE 25.5

From the Tracking tab, you can select the drop-down arrow next to WWW Server to select from the list of available Web servers.

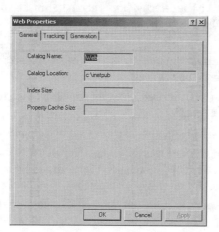

If you open the Properties folder of the Web catalog by selecting it in the Tree pane and then you double-click a property to edit, you will notice a slight difference in the options you are presented for configuring Web catalog properties. For instance, the only option that you can select is whether to cache the property. You cannot set the data type, size, or storage level.

Again, you are wise to leave the defaults in place, unless you have a specific reason for needing to cache the documents (for example, if you intend to access certain documents much more frequently than others). It is also recommended that you do not attempt to alter these properties unless you have a full understanding of their purpose.

You can also query the catalog by using the Query option. When you enter a search query, Indexing service will search the Web sites and directories listed and return the results as hyperlinks. By clicking the hyperlink, your default browser is started and displays the HTML document.

Optimizing Performance

If you find that your Indexing Service is not running as fast as you want, you can perform some optimizing tasks to gain better performance from the service.

Indexing Service performance can be fine-tuned, based on how much the service is used on the computer. By selecting the appropriate option, you can allow Indexing Service to configure itself to provide the optimum indexing and search capabilities based on this selection. To optimize the performance of Indexing Service, follow these steps:

1. Select the Indexing Service in the Tree pane of MMC.
2. From the **A**ction menu, choose the Stop option to stop the Indexing Service.
3. Select the **A**ction menu again, and then choose All Tas**k**s and then Tune Performance; the Indexing Service Usage dialog box opens.
4. Select one of the four available options based on how the computer is used. Used Often is the default and should be left selected if this computer makes heavy use of the Indexing Service. Note that this will exact a toll on the computer's performance for other applications. If you keep this default setting, move to step 6.

   If you select the **Customize** radio button, choose the **Customize** command button; the Desired Performance dialog box appears.
5. Use the two sliders to set your desired Indexing and Querying performance:
   - Move the Indexing slider closer to the Lazy option to slow the indexing of documents; move it toward Instant to give more immediate indexing results.
   - Move the Querying slider toward Low Load if you only expect to service a few requests at a time. To speed up the processing of a greater number of requests, move this slider toward the High Load position.
6. Close the properties sheet by clicking the **OK** buttons and then stop and restart the Indexing Service.

N O T E The higher that you set the performance on the Indexing and Querying sliders, the better the service works; *however*, you will exact a toll on the server running the services. Monitor the performance of both the service and the server, and make these adjustments accordingly. ■

When you have configured the Indexing Service using the procedures outlined here, it will run continuously and maintain itself with no intervention at all. All operations are automatic.

Installing and Configuring Message Queuing Service

In a networking environment that might include different types of host computers or where there is no guarantee that the network will always be up, the administrator must make provisions to determine that all messages are, in fact, delivered. This is where message queuing comes into play.

The Message Queuing Service is designed as a communication infrastructure for the purposes of ensuring message delivery. It is also a tool for developers writing network applications that need to communicate across heterogeneous networks.

Message Queuing Service provides this functionality by sending the messages to a message queue, or temporary storage space, for later transmission. By doing so, it can provide guaranteed message delivery, security, support for transactions and efficient routing.

Users can communicate across the network even if a host is offline because Message Queuing will ensure delivery of the messages when the host comes back online.

The major features of Microsoft Message Queue (MSMQ) include the following:

- *Active Directory Integration*. Integrates with Active Directory for the purposes of storing status and configuration information.
- *Mixed-mode Operation*. MSMQ is capable of working in Windows NT and Windows 2000 mixed environments.
- *Integration with Windows 2000 Security*. Uses all Windows 2000 security features.
- *Workgroup Support*. MSMQ can be installed in a workgroup environment as well as the usual domain environment.
- *Active/Active Cluster Support*. Allows MSMQ to run on all nodes in a server cluster.
- *Support for CE*. Windows CE contains a special version of the MSMQ client for handheld PCs.
- *Message Backup and Restore*. Storage, transaction log, and log files as well as registry settings can now be backed up.
- *MMC Support*. MSMQ now runs in the Microsoft Management Console as a snap-in.
- *Message Prioritization*. Allows for message to be sent base on priority level.
- *Cross Platform Support*. With the acquisition of the FalconMQ Bridge software product from Level8 Systems, MSMQ can now connect seamlessly to IBM MQSeries versions 2 and 5. With the set of APIs provided, MSMQ can also connect to other OS software such as UNIX, AS400, Digital VMS, and Unisys ClearPath HMP.

Part

V

Ch

25

Installing Message Queuing Service

To install the Message Queuing Service, you need to open the <u>C</u>ontrol Panel. Select the Add/Remove Programs applet and then select the Add/Remove Windows Components.

When the wizard screen displays, check the box next to the Message Queuing Service and then click <u>N</u>ext button and follow the wizard's prompts to install the service. When the wizard has installed the service, click the <u>F</u>inish button.

MSMQ is now installed and can be accessed through the Computer Management applet.

Configuring Message Queuing Service

You configure the Message Queuing service by double-clicking the Message Queuing icon in <u>C</u>ontrol Panel. This will display the Message Queuing Properties sheet shown in Figure 25.6.

FIGURE 25.6
The Message Queuing Properties sheet contains options with which you can specify the location of message files and log files as well as set security parameters of MSMQ. It also enables you to configure a new computer or site to which to transfer your files if you are being relocated within the network to a different workstation.

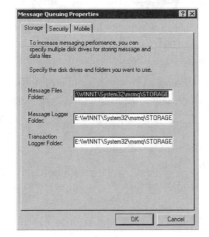

The Message Queuing Properties sheet contains three tabs:

- Choose settings in the Storage tab to specify the locations for storing messaging information. In the first field, indicate where to store the message file folders. Use the second to indicate the path for storing the message log files; in the third field, indicate the path that will contain the transaction log files.

TIP As the Storage tab text tells you, it is a good idea to store message files on multiple drives if they are available to increase the speed of MSMQ.

- Use the Security tab to set security options. In the Certificates area, select the Register button to select a certificate from a list of available certificates on the computer. This certificate will be registered for use with the Messaging Service on this computer.

Click the **V**iew button to see a list of all registered certificates in the Active Directory or click the **R**emove button to delete unwanted certificates.

Enable the Windows NT Server 4.0 MSMQ Controllers option if the network is using an NT 4.0 server for the certificate authority. Click the Certification Authorities button to view, select, and delete the certificate authorities setup on the computer. If you don't want to use a certificate that is in the list, clear its check box.

N O T E Windows 2000 Server uses Active Directory for the organizational structure of the network and uses certificates for security purposes. You can create or obtain a user certificate from a Certificate server. ■

Use the options in the Internal Certificate area to renew your internal certificate for MSMQ should it become corrupt or if your private key becomes compromised. (You must have an internal certificate already to use this feature.)

You will only need to use the last section, Cryptographic Keys, if your keys have been compromised. It is also a good idea to renew them once a year. Simply click the button to perform the renewal.

CAUTION

If you renew your cryptographic key, any messages that were encrypted with the old key cannot be read until the new public key is replicated.

■ Use the options in the Mobile tab if your users have notebook computers or are moving to another network site. Use the options, as instructed in the tab, to indicate a new site where messages will be waiting. *You must do this before you disconnect from the current network!*

View, Add, or Remove Queue Folders   Queue folders are merely directories on the MSMQ computer that are used for temporary storage of messages. These folders can contain messages or log files as mentioned previously in the configuration procedure.

You can also view, add, or remove queue folders from within the MMC application.

To view the queue folders, start the Computer Management program and then expand the Message Queuing entry in the left pane. Message Queuing contains four folders: Outgoing, Public, Private, and System Queues.

The Outgoing Queue folder lists any messages that are waiting to be transmitted. The columns available here display the status of the messages—the message name, quantity of messages, messages not acknowledged or processed, the current state of the message, and the next hop it will take on the network.

N O T E The Public Queue folder is not available on computers that only participate in workgroups. You will need to be connected to a domain to use this folder. Public Queues are published in Active Directory and replicate throughout the Windows 2000 forest. ■

Part
V

Ch
25

The Public Queue uses the following columns to display information about the messages in this queue:

- Name
- Messages
- Format Name
- Journal Messages
- Journal Message Size
- Messages Size
- Transacted

You can add new Public Queues by right-clicking the Public Queue folder and choosing **N**ew, Public Queue from the pop-up menu. In the New Public Queue dialog box that appears, you can give the queue a name and determine whether it will be transactional.

N O T E Private Queues are not published in Active Directory like the Public Queues; they reside on the local computer. They can only be accessed by MSMQ applications that know the exact path or format name of the queue. ■

The Private Queue folder contains, in addition to the same columns as the Public Queue folder, these columns:

- Authenticated
- Journal Quota
- Privacy Level
- Quota
- Transactional
- Type GUID
- Label

The Private Queue folder contains four queues:

- admin_queue$ is used to store administrative messages.
- mqis_queue$ stores returned MQPing messages.

N O T E MQPing is a utility similar to the PING utility that TCP/IP uses to verify computer connections. When an MSMQ computer sends an MQPing to another MSMQ computer, that destination will return a response message. This is the message that is stored in the mqis_queue$ directory. ■

- notify_queue$ stores notification messages relating to the creation and deletion of queues and any property changes.
- order_queue$ tracks any transactional messages that require in-order delivery. (In-order delivery messages are those that must be delivered in a specific order.)

The System Queue displays messages relating to Journals, Dead-letters, and Transactional Dead-letter messages. System Queues are also Private Queues and are not published in the Active Directory. Also, you cannot delete System Queues.

N O T E The queues that reside in the System Queue do not serve any function in a workgroup environment. To need or use queues within this folder, you must be connected to a Windows 2000 Active Directory forest. ■

The Journal Messages queue stores messages for source and target journaling. Dead-letter messages are those that have expired or were undeliverable. Expired transactional messages are stored in the Transactional Dead-letter messages queue.

You can right-click any of these queues and choose the Purge option from the All Tasks menu. You might want to do this after you have deemed that the messages are no longer needed or to clear up some storage space.

Configuring Queues within Folders   By right-clicking on the queue of your choice, you can set the properties for that queue. Although I only show the admin_queue$ properties here, the other queues contain the same properties.

To configure the admin_queue$ queue properties, open the Public Queue, right-click the admin_queue$, and choose Properties. Figure 25.7 shows what the admin_queue$ properties sheet looks like.

Part

V

Ch

25

FIGURE 25.7
The admin_queue$
Properties Sheet
enables you to set a
limit on the storage of
messages in this
folder, and it provides
a number of journaling
and security options.

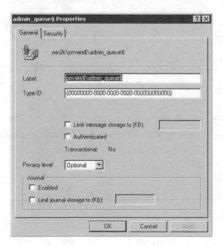

In the admin_queue$ Properties sheet, you can change the label and Type ID of this queue. You also can activate a message queue quota by selecting the Limit Message Storage To (KB) check box and specifying a limit. You might want to use this option if disk space is a concern on the computer.

If you select the Authenticated check box, this queue will only accept authenticated messages. Note that the Transactional property is set to No, and you cannot change that.

Use the Privacy Level drop-down list to select what level of privacy you want for the messages in this queue:

- *None*. The queue will only accept unencrypted messages.
- *Optional*. The queue will accept both unencrypted and encrypted messages.
- *Body*. The queue will only accept encrypted messages.

Use the options in the Journal area to enable and configure a journal of activities for this queue and to limit the amount of disk space that it will take up. You can enable target journaling by selecting the check box labeled Enabled and set the total size of all journal messages stored in the queue by selecting the Limit Journal Storage To (KB) check box and entering a value in the text box. Set this number to a reasonable amount to allow for the collection of journals without taking up too much disk space. You can best determine the amount of space to use based on the amount of messages transferred, which you'll note when you check your journals and delete them.

Click the Security tab to set the permissions for this queue. You can assign permissions based on user account. Click the **A**dd button to add valid user accounts to the list, or select an account from the list and click the **R**emove button to delete the account from the list.

In the Permissions area, you can either allow or deny the specific permission by choosing the appropriate check box.

N O T E If you do not select Deny or Allow in the Permissions area of the Security tab, the user might have permissions granted based on group membership. If the user is not a member of any group that has permissions assigned here and no permission is selected, the user has no access to the queue. ▪

If you click the Advanced button at the bottom of the form, you are given another window that displays additional access control settings. These additional settings enable you to set auditing and ownership for the queue based on user or group permissions.

Optimizing Performance

The recommended approach to optimizing performance under Messaging Service is to place the storage of the files on separate drives. As a rule, you should place the storage files on one drive, the message log files on another, and the transaction log files on a third.

If you do not have three drives available, place the storage files on one drive and the log files on a second.

> **N O T E** You really need to read through the online help files and documentation to fully implement the Message Queuing Service because it relies heavily on a networked environment using Windows 2000 Server and Active Directory Forests.

Part

V

Ch

25

## CHAPTER 26

Installing and Configuring Optional Networking

In this chapter

Routing Services in Windows 2000 Professional

Windows 2000 Professional comes with some extra networking components that provide various services for the operating system. These extra components provide functionality that makes your computer work better and smarter on the network.

Microsoft has made a commitment to implementing the TCP/IP set of protocols on all its operating systems, and Windows 2000 is no exception. One of the issues that are of prime importance in this protocol is routing. No traffic can travel over a TCP/IP network without proper routing among IP addresses. Because users tend to reference computers by name, whereas computers identify other computers with numbers, the routing table was established to satisfy both sides of the coin. This table is used to map the IP addresses to computer names and make it easy for people to locate computers on a TCP/IP network. Route Listening is a service that helps make this process much easier to deal with.

TCP/IP also enables different computing platforms to communicate with each other for the purposes of file and print sharing. If you are in an environment where there is a mixture of Windows 2000 and UNIX computers, the TCP/IP Print Services for UNIX are a great help.

The SNMP (Simple Network Management Protocol) Service in Windows 2000 Professional manages the TCP/IP network and checks the status of hosts on that network. These and other features and services within Windows 2000 Professional make networking easier and more efficient. Though many users feel that TCP/IP is overly complex and that configuring it is beyond their means, the information and procedures in this chapter will help you manage this aspect of your Windows 2000 Professional networking functions.

Installing and Configuring Route Listening Service

TCP/IP relies on routing information to transfer files and requests to other hosts on the network. System users refer to these hosts by their names; TCP/IP knows them by their IP addresses.

In order to synchronize these two forms of identification, TCP/IP uses a *routing information table*. In this table, computer names are mapped to their corresponding IP addresses.

For smaller networks, the task of maintaining this table is relatively easy. The routing table takes its information from the hosts.sam file on a Windows 9x machine or the lmhosts.sam file on NT and Windows 2000 computers. These are text-based files that take on the format shown in the excerpt included in Listing 26.1.

Listing 26.1   Routing Table Sample

```
# Copyright (c) 1993-1999 Microsoft Corp.
#
# This is a sample LMHOSTS file used by the Microsoft TCP/IP for
# Windows.
#
# This file contains the mappings of IP addresses to computernames
# (NetBIOS) names.  Each entry should be kept on an individual line.
# The IP address should be placed in the first column followed by the
# corresponding computername. The address and the computername
# should be separated by at least one space or tab. The "#" character
# is generally used to denote the start of a comment (see the exceptions
# below).
#
#
# 102.54.94.97      rhino         #PRE #DOM:networking  #net group's DC
# 102.54.94.102     "appname  \0x14"           #special app server
# 102.54.94.123     popular       #PRE        #source server
# 102.54.94.117     localsrv      #PRE        #needed for the include
```

For the sake of room, I have not included the complete file because most of the entries are comments aimed at someone who will be editing the file directly. Here, you need only note how the information is stored in the file.

As you can see, if you had a large network or one that changed a fair bit, such as the Internet, maintaining this file could be quite time-consuming.

The Internet has Domain Name Servers (DNS) that perform automated updates of this information. Windows 2000 provides the Route Listening Service otherwise known as RIP Listening. RIP stands for Routing Information Protocol and is used for the purpose of discovering routing information. It acts on its own behalf, listening for the necessary RIP messages that might be broadcast on the network and modifying the routing table if necessary. The RIP Listening service can help to increase your network efficiency by identifying new and shorter routes to destinations.

Installing RIP Listening

RIP Listening is installed through the Control Panel by using the Add/Remove Programs applet. Place the Windows 2000 Professional CD in the CD-ROM drive and then follow these steps to install the service:

1. With Control Panel open, double-click the Add/Remove Programs icon; the Add/Remove Programs window opens.

2. Choose the Add/Remove Windows Components icon in the left Tree pane. Windows 2000 responds with a *please wait* message while it starts the Windows Component Wizard.

3. On the first wizard screen, scroll through the list of components that is displayed and choose the Networking Services component by clicking the name and not the check box.

4. Click the Details button to see the available subcomponents. There are actually only two, RIP Listener and Simple TCP/IP Services.

5. Select the check box next to RIP Listener and click OK. (You will install the other option later in the chapter.)

6. When you return to the Windows Component Wizard, you will notice that the check box for Networking Services now displays a check mark and is gray in color. This indicates that not all the options were chosen. Click the Next button.

7. If you haven't already done so, the wizard will prompt you to place the Windows 2000 Professional CD into the drive. The wizard configures the necessary files and copies them onto your computer. When the wizard completes the installation process, it will tell you that you have successfully installed the component and request that you click the Finish button to complete the install. Click that button.

When you have completed these steps, you have the RIP Listening service installed and are ready to configure it.

Configuring RIP Listening

To configure the RIP Listening Service, you need to access its properties from within the Computer Management Window. Open Control Panel, and double-click the Administrative Tools icon.

Double-click the Computer Management icon to open the MMC console. Click the plus (+) sign next to the Services and Applications entry in the left pane, and highlight the Services entry as shown in Figure 26.1.

FIGURE 26.1

You configure the RIP Listener for Windows 2000 Professional by either double-clicking the RIP Listener entry in the right pane or by highlighting it and choosing Properties from the Action menu.

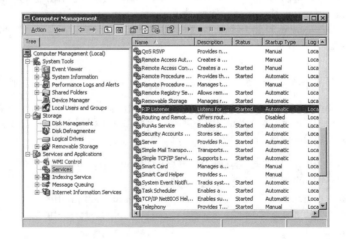

Scroll through the list of services in the right pane and locate the RIP Listener service. Right-click the entry and choose Properties from the pop-up menu. This will display the RIP Listener Properties (Local Computer) sheet, shown in Figure 26.2.

FIGURE 26.2

Using the RIP Listener Properties (Local Computer) sheet, you configure the service's user account informa-tion, recovery options in the event of failures, and application dependencies.

This property sheet has four tabs that contain settings for RIP Listener: General, Log-On, Recovery, and Dependencies options.

Configuring the General Tab Settings The General tab provides some basic information about the RIP Listener Service such as the following:

- Service Name. As it implies, it is the name of the service. You cannot change this name, but you can use it for reference when trying to locate it in the list of services in task manager.

- *Display Name.* This is the name you see displayed in the Services applet. In most cir-cumstances, you should leave this at its default setting.

- *Description.* This entry fills in the description field in the Services applet. This setting also should be left at the default, unless you want to provide a different description for your own purposes.

- *Path to Executable.* This entry displays the full pathname and filename of the executable file for the service. You cannot change this entry because the service pulls this location information from the registry.

- *Startup Type.* This is actually another way of configuring the type of startup that the RIP Listening Service uses. All services under Windows 2000 can be accessed under the Services applet and have three possible startup options: Automatic, Manual, and Disabled. Automatic means that the service starts up every time the computer is rebooted. Manual doesn't start the service until you start it yourself, and Disabled means that the service is not running and cannot be started automatically.

Part

V

Ch

26

If you use the RIP service on a regular basis, you should have it start automatically to make the service available and running after each reboot of the computer.

If you find that RIP is causing a fair bit of network traffic and is impacting the performance of your computer, you can set the startup type to manual. This prevents the service from starting automatically but still enables you to start it when needed.

If you have no use for the service, you can choose the disable option. This prevents the service from operating at all. You might not want to use the service at all but are prohibited by company policy from removing it. In this case, disable the service to prevent it from consuming system resources unnecessarily.

- *Service Status.* This section enables you to start or stop the service and set any command-line arguments that it might need.

Configuring the Log On Tab Settings   When a service is running, it normally needs to be running under an account name. Most operating system services operate under the Administrator or the Local System account.

You can use the options in the Log On tab to determine the account that this service will use for logging on to the computer when it starts. The account must be a valid user account on the computer.

At the bottom of the Log On tab is a listing of hardware profiles; you can enable or disable this service for each hardware profile in the list box. Simply select the hardware profile you desire and click either the Enable or the Disable button.

 You might want to disable this service for a hardware profile that resides on a laptop computer when it is not docked or connected to a network. If you have no network connection, RIP listener is not really required and serves no purpose. You can free resources by disabling it in the hardware profiles where it is not needed.

▶ **See** "Managing Hardware Profiles," **p. 125**

Configuring the Recovery Tab Settings   The Recovery tab, shown in Figure 26.3, contains options that enable you to set the computer's response action should this service fail to start. You can choose individual response options for the first, second, and subsequent failures.

You can choose between these options when configuring the failure response:

- *Take No Action.* If the service is not critical to the operation of the computer, this is sometimes the best choice.
- *Restart the Service.* This response is useful if you have set the RIP service to start automatically when the computer boots up. This option can avoid the need for your immediate involvement if the service doesn't start the first time (which might be due to a dependency service not starting first).

FIGURE 26.3
The Recovery tab of the RIP Listener properties sheet enables you to determine how your system will respond if the service fails.

■ *Run a File.* You can use this option to run an executable program or batch file that can contain commands to send an administrative alert to someone. If you choose this option, you must fill in the bottom section, *Run File.* The information required here is the filename and pathname (you can use the Browse button to locate that information), and any command-line parameters that are needed to customize the program's startup action. You also need to specify whether you want to append the fail count to the end of the command line.

■ *Reboot the Computer.* Be careful with this option if you have a tendency to leave your computer running unattended for long periods of time. If the service fails and you have this option turned on, your computer could continually reboot itself over and over. When you have selected this option, click the Restart Computer Options button to set the reboot options. You set the number of minutes delay between failure and rebooting, and you specify a reboot notification message to send to users that are connected to your computer.

Configuring the Dependencies Tab Settings   The Dependencies tab contains options that enable you to view any services that RIP Listener relies on to function or any service that relies on RIP Listener. Using this tab, you can troubleshoot RIP startup problems by determining what services to check when RIP problems occur. The tab contains two principal areas: RIP Listener Depends on These Services and These Services Depend on RIP Listener.

The first of these areas lists any programs or services that RIP Listening relies on to operate correctly. On your computer, the only listing you should see in this area is the Remote Procedure Call (RPC) service.

The second area lists any services or applications that rely on RIP Listening to maintain service performance. Unless you have a nonstandard installation of RIP Listening Service, you

Part

V

Ch

26

are unlikely to find any listings in this area. Users of Windows 2000 Server might see the Routing and Remote Access Server (RAS) service listed here if they have the RIP protocol installed for use with RAS.

Installing and Configuring Simple TCP/IP Services

The Simple TCP/IP Services are installed using the same procedure as that for the Route Listening Service. As a matter of fact, these services are the other option that you did not install along with RIP Listening previously. You will install them now.

Place the Windows 2000 Professional CD in the CD-ROM drive and then follow these steps to install the Simple TCP/IP Services:

1. With Control Panel open, double-click the Add/Remove Programs icon; the Add/Remove Programs window opens.

2. Choose the Add/Remove Windows Components icon in the left Tree pane. Windows 2000 responds with a *please wait* message while it starts the Windows Component Wizard.

3. On the first wizard screen, scroll through the list of components that is displayed and choose the Networking Services component by clicking the name and not the check box.

4. Click the Details button to see the available subcomponents. Select the check box next to Simple TCP/IP Services, and click OK. The Windows Components Wizard sets off on its trek of installing the necessary components and files.

The simple TCP/IP services consist of various tools and utilities—known as *protocol services*— to help you use and troubleshoot TCP/IP. These protocol services are the following:

- CHARGEN (Character Generator)
- Daytime
- Discard
- Echo
- QUOTE (Quote of the day)

CAUTION

Microsoft recommends that you don't install these Simple TCP/IP services on a computer if you do not specifically need them. They can cause excessive network traffic and congestion.

The CHARGEN Protocol Service

This tool is useful for testing line printers that are connected to a network. The CHARGEN tool will send a set of characters to the printer as data made up of the standard 95 ASCII printable characters.

This protocol follows the RFC864 standard that indicates that the protocol is used to send data to any terminal on a TCP/IP network. It can do this using either TCP or UDP.

Here's an example of some data that would be sent using the ASCII character set:

```
!"#$%&'()*+,-./0123456789:;<=>?@ABCDEFGHIJKLMNOPQRSTUVWXYZ[\]^_`abcdefgh
"#$%&'()*+,-./0123456789:;<=>?@ABCDEFGHIJKLMNOPQRSTUVWXYZ[\]^_`abcdefghi
#$%&'()*+,-./0123456789:;<=>?@ABCDEFGHIJKLMNOPQRSTUVWXYZ[\]^_`abcdefghij
$%&'()*+,-./0123456789:;<=>?@ABCDEFGHIJKLMNOPQRSTUVWXYZ[\]^_`abcdefghijk
%&'()*+,-./0123456789:;<=>?@ABCDEFGHIJKLMNOPQRSTUVWXYZ[\]^_`abcdefghijkl
&'()*+,-./0123456789:;<=>?@ABCDEFGHIJKLMNOPQRSTUVWXYZ[\]^_`abcdefghijklm
'()*+,-./0123456789:;<=>?@ABCDEFGHIJKLMNOPQRSTUVWXYZ[\]^_`abcdefghijklmn
()*+,-./0123456789:;<=>?@ABCDEFGHIJKLMNOPQRSTUVWXYZ[\]^_`abcdefghijklmno
)*+,-./0123456789:;<=>?@ABCDEFGHIJKLMNOPQRSTUVWXYZ[\]^_`abcdefghijklmnop
*+,-./0123456789:;<=>?@ABCDEFGHIJKLMNOPQRSTUVWXYZ[\]^_`abcdefghijklmnopq
+,-./0123456789:;<=>?@ABCDEFGHIJKLMNOPQRSTUVWXYZ[\]^_`abcdefghijklmnopqr
,-./0123456789:;<=>?@ABCDEFGHIJKLMNOPQRSTUVWXYZ[\]^_`abcdefghijklmnopqrs
-./0123456789:;<=>?@ABCDEFGHIJKLMNOPQRSTUVWXYZ[\]^_`abcdefghijklmnopqrst
./0123456789:;<=>?@ABCDEFGHIJKLMNOPQRSTUVWXYZ[\]^_`abcdefghijklmnopqrstu
/0123456789:;<=>?@ABCDEFGHIJKLMNOPQRSTUVWXYZ[\]^_`abcdefghijklmnopqrstuv
0123456789:;<=>?@ABCDEFGHIJKLMNOPQRSTUVWXYZ[\]^_`abcdefghijklmnopqrstuvw
123456789:;<=>?@ABCDEFGHIJKLMNOPQRSTUVWXYZ[\]^_`abcdefghijklmnopqrstuvwx
23456789:;<=>?@ABCDEFGHIJKLMNOPQRSTUVWXYZ[\]^_`abcdefghijklmnopqrstuvwxy
3456789:;<=>?@ABCDEFGHIJKLMNOPQRSTUVWXYZ[\]^_`abcdefghijklmnopqrstuvwxyz
456789:;<=>?@ABCDEFGHIJKLMNOPQRSTUVWXYZ[\]^_`abcdefghijklmnopqrstuvwxyz{
56789:;<=>?@ABCDEFGHIJKLMNOPQRSTUVWXYZ[\]^_`abcdefghijklmnopqrstuvwxyz{|
6789:;<=>?@ABCDEFGHIJKLMNOPQRSTUVWXYZ[\]^_`abcdefghijklmnopqrstuvwxyz{|}
```

This sample is a greatly abbreviated example of the type of data that is sent over the wire.

▶ **See** "Installing SNMP Service," **p. 504**

The Daytime Protocol Service

This protocol can be used for a variety of time-related chores on the network. It will return a message containing the following information:

- Year
- Month
- Day
- Day of the week
- Current time format (hh:mm:ss)
- Time zone information

Part

V

Ch

26

If you have any talented programmers around, they can use this protocol to write an application that will check each computer on the network for this information and report on any that are not synchronized with a server. You can then have an application adjust the date and time information on those that need it.

For more information on this protocol, look up RFC867. Although you can search the Internet for RFCs, I have found a good starting point that categorizes them for you at this URL:

```
http://www.uwaterloo.ca/uw_infoserv/rfc.html
```

The Discard Protocol Service

This protocol has a couple of uses. First, you can use it in conjunction with the CHARGEN protocol to verify computer connectivity. That protocol sends out meaningless data to a computer to check for connectivity, but the information is unimportant and need not be saved. The Discard protocol deletes the meaningless test data so that it doesn't take up hard drive space.

Further, you can set up the listening port for Discard, and anything that comes in that port is thrown away. In this configuration, the listening port is considered a NULL port.

The Discard protocol follows the RFC863 specification and should be set up using TCP or UDP port 9.

The ECHO Protocol Service

The ECHO tool can be used for network troubleshooting and debugging. You can use this tool to echo back any data that is received to the sending computer.

This tool works on port 7 as either TCP or UDP.

The QUOTE Protocol Service

Anyone familiar with UNIX knows that some systems provide a Quote of The Day when you log into the system. This tool provides that same functionality on the Windows 2000 platform.

This protocol follows RFC865 and uses port 17 to send and receive the data. Any data that is received is basically thrown away.

 TIP Some use the QUOTE tool for debugging the network. Although it is not a network analyzer in any sense of the word, QUOTE is a cheap and quick way to verify that a computer is connected to the network and receiving data.

QUOTE will randomly select from the available quotes that it finds in the %systemroot%\System32\Drivers\Etc\Quotes directory. If there are no quotes in this directory to send, the service fails. Here is a short clipping from the default quote file that is installed with the Simple TCP/IP Services:

> "My spelling is Wobbly. It's good spelling but it Wobbles, and the letters get in the wrong places." —A. A. Milne (1882–1958)

> "Man can climb to the highest summits, but he cannot dwell there long." —George Bernard Shaw (1856–1950)

> "In Heaven an angel is nobody in particular." —George Bernard Shaw (1856–1950)

> "Assassination is the extreme form of censorship." —George Bernard Shaw (1856–1950)

> "When a stupid man is doing something he is ashamed of, he always declares that it is his duty." —George Bernard Shaw (1856–1950)

The Quote file from which the preceding excerpt comes is an ASCII file. Therefore, you can add your own quotes or edit those in the file using NotePad or any other text editor. To edit the Quote file, use only the standard ASCII character set and follow the conventions present in the existing file.

Simple TCP/IP Services

Simple TCP/IP Services offers a handful of settings you can configure that are nearly identical to the RIP Listener. See the section, "Configuring RIP Listening," earlier in this chapter for details.

Installing and Configuring SNMP Service

As mentioned before, the SNMP service is used to provide management capabilities and status information on TCP/IP hosts on the network. This service is capable of configuring remote devices such as host computers, monitoring network performance, detecting faults in the network, dealing with inappropriate access, and auditing groups and users for their network usage.

The SNMP service uses messages to send requests to agents for information. The agent uses a set of messages to retrieve the information from its Management Information Base (MIB) and then sends the information back to the requesting SNMP management system. These messages include the following:

- *Get*. A basic request message that is used to get information about a single item such as hard drive space.
- *Get-next*. Used a lot on dynamic tables, this message can be used to browse the object tree within the MIB. Using this message, the agent returns the requested object but also sends the identity and value of the next logical object.
- *Set*. If the requesting SNMP management computer has write permissions, this causes the agent to write or change an updated value to an object.
- *Getbulk*. If the management computer has made a request for a large amount of data to be transmitted, the agent can use this option to send more than one item at a time. This

Part
V
Ch
26

can be useful in preventing multiple packets from being sent over the network. The agent will send the maximum allowable packet size based on the MTU setting for the network.

■ *Notify.* If an agent has been configured to detect certain events, the agent will send a notify message to the SNMP management computer informing it of the event. These messages are known as *trap* messages, and they are sent to *trap destinations*. You will see more on traps later in this section.

 If you need more information on the details of SNMP and its implementation in networks, you can download and read the RFCs available from the Internet at http://www.uwaterloo.ca/uw_infoserv/rfc.html.

 In particular, read RFC1155, which deals with the structure and identification of management information, RFC1157 for information on SNMP itself, and RFC1213, which deals with the MIB-II structure for the database.

To implement SNMP, you must complete the following major tasks:

■ Gather the necessary information required, such as contact names, computer locations, SNMP community names, IP addresses, and names of the SNMP management computers.

■ Install the SNMP service onto the computer.

■ Configure the SNMP agent properties.

■ Configure trap destinations.

■ Configure SNMP security.

The following sections offer more details about the SNMP installation process.

Installing SNMP Service

When you have gathered all the necessary information (as indicated in the preceding checklist), you are ready to install the service. Insert the Windows 2000 Professional CD-ROM into the CD and then follow these steps to install SNMP:

1. Open the Control Panel and choose the Add/Remove Programs icon in the Tree pane to open the Add/Remove Programs Wizard.

2. With the Windows Components Wizard window displayed, select the check box next to the Management and Monitoring Tools listing and then click the Next button. The Windows Components Wizard configures and installs the necessary files for the selected services.

3. When the wizard completes its tasks, choose the Finish button to complete the installation.

To use the SNMP software, you must have two components in place: an SNMP management system and an SNMP Agent. By installing the SNMP Service on each computer that is to participate or use the service, you put these two components into place.

The SNMP Management System component is responsible for sending requests to an SNMP agent. By communicating with the SNMP agent on another computer, the management system can get information such as hard drive space or any active connections that the computer might have to shared resources.

The SNMP Agent is responsible for responding to requests made by the SNMP management system. You can configure the Agent to track only those system statistics that you decide on that computer. You can also select which management systems are authorized to make requests from this agent.

The SNMP Management System and Agent work together in what is known as a *community*. An SNMP community is an assembly of hosts that are grouped for administrative purposes.

The SNMP systems transfer the community messages using the User Datagram Protocol (UDP). UDP is a connectionless protocol that consumes much less connection overhead than does TCP/IP. UDP is unlike TCP/IP in that it does not require a confirmation of delivery. The two protocols can be compared to regular mail delivery and registered mail delivery. The registered letter, like TCP/IP, results in more work on behalf of the post office. Regular mail, like UDP, requires less effort and cost but presents no confirmation that the message has reached its destination.

The information used by SNMP is stored in what is known as the *Management Information Base (MIB)*. The MIB is actually a database that keeps track of the various information required by the SNMP service for monitoring the network.

Configuring the Agent Properties

Many of the properties and settings for the SNMP Service are like those of the RIP Listener Service. In the SNMP Properties sheet, the General, Log On, Recovery, and Dependencies tabs all contain the settings and information previously described for tabs of the same name in the RIP Listener Properties sheet. However, you need to configure the agent portion of SNMP to determine which statistics will be monitored and to designate which systems are authorized to make requests to the agent.

Follow these steps to configure Agent properties of the SNMP Service:

1. Open Control Panel and double-click the Administrative Tools icon.
2. Double-click the Computer Management icon; the MMC opens.
3. Click to highlight the Services entry in the console Tree. (To find this entry, you might have to expand the Services and Applications entry; the available services are displayed in the right pane.)
4. Click the SNMP Service entry to highlight it. You should see a window identical to the one shown in Figure 26.4.

FIGURE 26.4

The SNMP Service Under MMC is shown in the details pane. You can determine the status of the service from here, or you can access the properties sheet by double-clicking the entry or by opening the **A**ction menu.

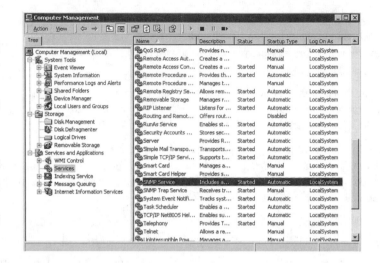

5. Choose the P**r**operties option from the **A**ction menu; the SNMP Service Properties (Local Computer) properties sheet appears.

6. Select the Agent tab. In the Contact field, enter the name of the Administrator or user of this computer. The Network Administrator uses this information to determine who uses the computer and who he should see to resolve issues with it.

7. In the Location field, enter the physical location of this computer. An example of a typical entry here might be the name of a building that the computer is located in or a room number within a building. This helps the Administrator locate the computer within the building.

8. Choose Service options, based on the computer's installed components and configuration:

   - *Physical.* This is used to indicate whether this computer deals with physical devices such as hard drive partitions.

   - *Applications.* This specifies if the computer contains applications that use the TCP/IP protocol.

   - *Datalink and Subnetwork.* This tells the SNMP service whether this computer is being used to manage a bridge on the network.

   - *Internet.* If checked off, this would indicate that this computer is an IP router or gateway.

   - *End-to-end.* This indicates whether this computer is an IP host.

9. Click the Traps tab. In the Community Name field, enter the name of the community to which you want to add this computer; choose one from the drop-down list, or type in a new name if you are creating a new community. After you enter the name, click the Add to List button.

N O T E A *trap* is a host on the network that has the SNMP management software installed; the trap acts sort of like a security guard. Essentially, the trap monitors the SNMP messages and reports to trap destinations specific events, such as an authentication request from another SNMP host on a different community. ■

10. Click the **A**dd button under the Trap Destinations list box; the SNMP Service Configuration dialog pops up, prompting you for a host name, IP address, or IPX address. Fill in the appropriate information for the host that will be a trap destination and click the **A**dd button. Your entry is added to the list.

    You can add more destinations by following the same procedure. You also have the opportunity to edit or remove destinations that exist in the list by choosing the **E**dit or **R**emove buttons.

11. Click the Security tab. Here, you designate the communities to whom a trap message will be sent, should authentication fail. To send the message, select the Send Authentication Trap check box.

12. In the Accepted Community Names list box, enter the names of the communities that have the appropriate rights necessary to send and receive messages to or from this computer, and then click the Add button. The SNMP Service Configuration dialog box opens.

13. From this dialog box, you choose one of the available rights from the Community Rights drop-down box and enter the Community name that will be assigned this right. The rights are the following:

    - *None*. This right will prevent the host from processing any SNMP requests.
    - *Notify*. This will allow the host to send traps only to the community.
    - *Read Only*. Use this to prevent the host from processing the SET request.
    - *Read Write*. This will allow the host to process the SET requests.
    - Read Create. The host will be allowed to create new entries in the SNMP table.

    You should leave the default setting or Read Only unless you have reasons to allow the host to process SET requests or create new entries. You can also edit or remove the entries in this list by first selecting the desired entry and then clicking the Edit or Remove button.

14. By default, security is set at Accept SNMP Packets from Any Host. To raise this setting, choose the Accept SNMP Packets from These Hosts option, and then click the Add button to specify those hosts. You can enter the name, IP address, or IPX address for each host, and they will be added to the list. You can Edit or Remove entries from the list.

15. Click the OK or Apply button at the bottom of the Properties window to apply the changes you have just made.

Any changes that you make to these settings will take effect immediately. You do not have to stop and restart the SNMP service.

Part
V

Ch
26

Now, you have installed and configured the SNMP service on your computer. If you are running into any problems with this service, you can perform some troubleshooting by looking at the Event Viewer to determine what events took place specific to SNMP.

Follow this procedure to start the Event Viewer:

1. Open Control Panel.
2. Open the Administrative Tools window.
3. Double-click the Event Viewer icon.
4. Select the System Log entry in the left pane of Event Viewer.

Installing and Configuring Print Services for UNIX

Print Services for UNIX enables the local computer to print to TCP/IP printers on the network (either connected directly or by a UNIX host). You install it using the same procedures for adding programs that you have followed throughout this chapter. You will find this service under the Other Network File and Print Services option in the Windows Components Wizard. Simply check off the box next to it because there is only one service under that category for the time being.

Click the Next button and wait while the wizard performs the install. When the wizard completes the installation, click the Finish button.

This service provides the computer with the ability to print to TCP/IP-based printers either connected directly to the network or on a UNIX host computer. A printer that is directly connected to the network through a TCP/IP interface must support LPD for TCP/IP printing to work. LPD stands for Line Printer Daemon and is the service on a host computer that accepts print jobs submitted by the LPR (Line Printer Remote) utilities.

To use the TCP/IP print services, you must install the LPR port. To install this port, follow these steps:

1. Click the Start button, point to Settings, and choose Printers.
2. Double-click the Add Printer icon and choose Next from the Add Printer Wizard dialog that appears.
3. Select the Local Printer option and clear the Automatically Detect and Install My Plug and Play Printer check box and click the Next button.
4. Select Create a New Port at the bottom of the dialog, choose the LPR option from the drop-down list, and click Next.
5. In the Name or Address of Server Providing LPD field, enter the DNS name or IP address of the server or host that the printer is on.

6. In the Name of Printer or Print Queue on That Server field, enter the name of the printer that the host computer has identified or of the directly connected printer and click the <u>N</u>ext button.

7. You are presented with the Add Printer Wizard, which walks you through the process of choosing a printer and installing the necessary drivers.

N O T E The printer must exist on the host computer already, or you will receive an error when setting up the port. ■

This service is the same as any other service in that it can be configured by selecting it from the list of services and choosing the properties option from the pop-up menu.

You can set the Name and Description along with the start-up options on the General tab. In the Log On tab, specify the account to be used and the hardware profiles.

You use the Recovery tab to identify the actions the system is to perform when the service fails. The Dependencies tab displays the files or services that this service depends on as well as those services that depend on this one.

Appendixes

The Registry and Registry Editors

Understanding the Registry Function and Structure

The Registry is a database that is an integral component of all Windows 2000 systems. The Registry provides a central point for system settings and configuration information.

The following list describes a typical example of how Windows 2000 uses the Registry in the boot process (don't worry if you don't understand the significance of the Registry keys as you read this list; the keys' significance will be explained later in the chapter):

1. In the hardware detection phase of the boot process, NTDETECT.COM detects the installed hardware on the system. This information will be stored in the HKEY_LOCAL_MACHINE\HARDWARE key in the Registry.

2. NTLDR then loads the information in HKEY_LOCAL_MACHINE\SYSTEM, which contains information about all device drivers and services that will be loaded. This information is called a *Control Set*.

3. NTLDR then creates the HKEY_LOCAL_MACHINE\HARDWARE key and a *Clone Control Set*. The Clone Control Set is a read-only copy of the control set created in step 2. It is used as a backup if changes are made to the control set during the boot process.

4. The process then initializes the drivers and services loaded earlier and records any errors in the Registry.

Applications also store data in the Registry. Most applications keep a history of the last few files opened in the Registry and display this information in the file menu for quick access. Application defaults and preferences are also stored. Other examples of information stored in the Registry are installed network protocols and services, hardware profiles, and user profiles.

Registry Structure

There are a few terms regarding the Registry that you need to understand in order to understand the Registry structure. A *subtree* is the root level of the Registry. There are five subtrees in the Registry (more about subtrees later in this chapter).

Keys and *subkeys* are like folders in the file system. They can contain values and other subkeys.

Values are the main components of the Registry. The keys define the structure of the Registry, but values contain the data. Values can be of one of five types and are contained in subkeys.

Hives are the files that contain the Registry database. Hives exist for most keys in the Registry except those that are volatile (that change frequently.) Hives consist of a data file and a log file. The log files track changes to the Registry and are used to ensure the integrity of the Registry database files. These files are contained in %systemroot%\System32\Config.

The Registry is structured in a hierarchical layout. The layout of the Registry is similar to the layout of files and folders on a disk. Subtrees are the root objects in the Registry. There are actually only two physical subtrees in the Registry, HKEY_LOCAL_MACHINE and HKEY_USERS. However, the Registry is split up logically to enable easier use, and there are five logical subtrees that are shown in the Registry editor:

- HKEY_LOCAL_MACHINE contains all information pertaining to the local system. Hardware information, device drivers, service information, and machine-specific application data are stored in this subtree.

- HKEY_USERS contains two subkeys. DEFAULT stores the default user profile information used before a user logs on. HKEY_CURRENT_USER is also a subkey of HKEY_USERS.

- HKEY_CURRENT_USER contains the profile information for the currently logged on user, such as desktop settings. If settings are stored in both HKEY_LOCAL_MACHINE and HKEY_CURRENT_USER, the settings in HKEY_CURRENT_USER take precedence.

- HKEY_CLASSES_ROOT contains software configuration information such as file associations. HKEY_CLASSES_ROOT actually points to HKEY_LOCAL_MACHINE\ SOFTWARE\Classes.

- HKEY_CURRENT_CONFIG contains a combination of hardware information pertaining to the hardware profile currently in use. The HKEY_CURRENT_CONFIG subtree data is extracted from the SOFTWARE and SYSTEM keys of the HKEY_LOCAL_MACHINE subtree after startup.

The layout of the Registry keys is fairly logical. Most names of keys and values are quite descriptive. The structures of the five subtrees are all quite similar. For example, the subtree HKEY_CURRENT_USER contains several subkeys. Some of those keys are listed below with a description of their function. Figure A.1 shows the layout of the HKEY_CURRENT_USER subtree.

FIGURE A.1
The layout of the HKEY_CURRENT_USER Layout Registry subtree is just like that of a folder or disk.

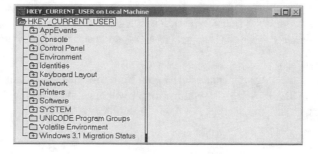

Within this subtree are the following elements:

- *Console* contains settings pertaining to the MS-DOS command prompt.
- *Control Panel* stores settings that are set using control panel applets such as desktop appearance, screen savers, accessibility, and mouse settings.
- *Environment* contains user-defined environment variables.
- *Identities* contains the name of the last logged on user, default user, and some email settings.
- *Network* contains network drive mappings.
- *Printers* contains local and network installed printers.
- *Software* stores settings and preferences for applications installed on the system.
- *Volatile Environment* contains settings that change frequently, such as the name of the domain logon server (which can change if there are multiple domain controllers).

Using the Registry Editors

Windows 2000 is supplied with two Registry editors, REGEDT32.EXE and REGEDIT.EXE. It is recommended that you only use REGEDT32.EXE because REGEDIT.EXE does not support read-only mode, does not have a security menu, and does not support adding the REG_EXPAND_SZ or REG_MULTI_SZ value types. REGEDIT.EXE, however, can be useful and so is discussed below.

When the Registry is edited, it is done in real time, so it is unnecessary to save your changes as you do when editing a document. As soon as a change is made in the Registry editor, it is reflected in the Registry database.

> **CAUTION**
>
> Editing the Registry can be harmful! Changing or deleting the wrong values can permanently and irreversibly damage your system. Only make changes to the Registry if you have a backup copy of the Registry and repair disks. Before you perform any actual edits to the Registry, read and follow the procedures outlined in the section "Creating an Emergency Repair Disk Containing the Registry" later in this chapter.

To begin using the Registry editor, select **R**un from the Start menu and enter **REGEDT32.EXE**. The Registry editor window will open showing the five subtrees as seen in Figure A.2.

FIGURE A.2
Each of the five sub-
trees is contained in
its own window in the
REGEDT32.EXE
Registry editor. To
switch to a new win-
dow, click its title bar
or select it from the
Window menu.

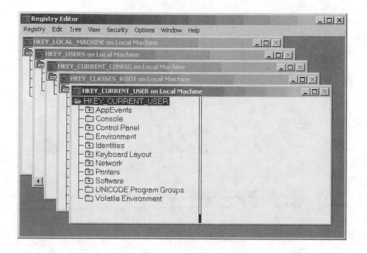

 TIP If you use the Registry editor a lot, add a shortcut to the desktop or the start menu pointing to
REGEDT32.EXE to save time. A shortcut is not added during a default installation to avoid untrained people
modifying the Registry.

To add a key, select the subtree in which you want to add the key. Select the key in the left
pane of the window under which you want to create the new key. Values are shown in the
right pane. To add a key, click Add Key from the **E**dit menu. The Add Key window will appear
(see Figure A.3), and you can type the name of the new key and the class of the key. The
class parameter is optional.

FIGURE A.3
Use the Add Key dialog
box to add a key to
any subtree.

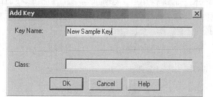

Click OK to add the key. The selected key is shown before and after adding the new key in
Figures A.4 and A.5.

To add a new value, click Add Value from the **E**dit menu to display the Add Value window.
You must specify a name for the value and a data type. Table A.1 shows the available data
types.

FIGURE A.4
The subtree contents before adding the new key...

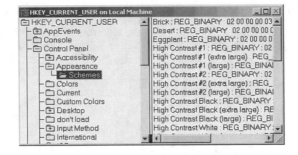

FIGURE A.5
...and after adding the new key.

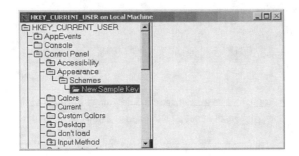

Table A.1   Registry Data Types

Data Type	Description
REG_BINARY	Binary Value.
REG_DWORD	Doubleword value. Double word values can be a maximum of four bytes long (32 bits binary, 4294967295 decimal, or FFFFFFFF hexadecimal)
REG_SZ	Single line string value.
REG_MULTI_SZ	Multiple line string value.
REG_EXPAND_SZ	Expandable string value.

After you specify a name and a data type and click OK, the data editor specific to each type of value will appear as shown in the figures that follow. The REG_BINARY type uses the binary editor, the REG_DWORD type uses the DWORD editor, the REG_SZ and REG_EXPAND_SZ types use the string editor, and the REG_MULTI_SZ uses the multiple line string editor. Figure A.6 shows the new Registry key with the newly added values in the right pane.

FIGURE A.6
When you add new values to a key, the newly created values appear in the right pane when you highlight the key.

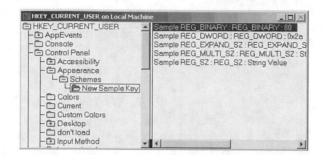

The process for modifying an existing value uses the same data editors as discussed previously. To modify a value, highlight the appropriate key in the left pane and select the value in the right pane. Select the proper editor that corresponds to the value data type from the **E**dit menu or double-click the value to modify it.

One other useful feature in the Registry editor is the Find Key feature. To find a key, click Find Key from the **V**iew menu. Enter the name or part of the name of the key to locate. If only part of the name is specified, the Match Whole Word Only box must not be checked. The direction control specifies whether you want to search up or down in the tree from the selected key. The one caveat with the Find Key feature is that you must be in the same subtree as the key you want to find.

It is possible to put REGEDT32 into read-only mode. Select Read Only Mode from the **O**ptions menu. When the read-only mode option is selected, changes cannot be made to the Registry. This prevents the accidental modification or deletion of data. If you attempt to modify the Registry while the Registry editor is in read-only mode, you will be prompted with an error stating "Registry Editor is operating in Read Only Mode. Changes made to this value entry will not be saved in the Registry." Modifying data from the data editors does not save the changes to the Registry.

To begin using the REGEDIT Registry editor, select **R**un from the Start menu and enter **REGEDIT.EXE**. The Registry editor window opens into the key that was open when REGEDIT was last closed. The REGEDIT display is laid out in a tree form like Windows Explorer with My Computer at the top of the list and the five subtrees under that. The REGEDIT utility is shown in Figure A.7.

To add a new key or value, select a key under which to add it and then choose **E**dit, **N**ew. You can also add a new key or value by right-clicking a blank space in the right pane and selecting **N**ew and then **K**ey or the type of value from the context menu. Use the options that appear to add Keys, and REG_BINARY, REG_DWORD, and REG_SZ values. To modify a value, select that value in the right pane and then choose **E**dit, **M**odify. Right-clicking a value in the right pane also enables you to modify, delete, or rename the value. Unlike REGEDIT32, the find feature of REGEDIT can find a key regardless of which subtree it is contained in.

FIGURE A.7
The REGEDIT.EXE utility uses a different layout than REGEDT32.EXE. All Registry subtrees are shown under a single root instead of in separate windows.

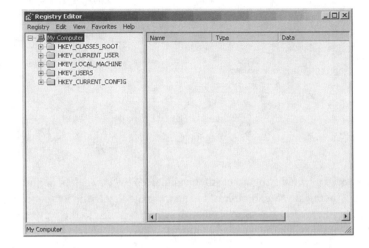

Setting and Maintaining Registry Security

Security can be set on Registry keys directly from the REGEDT32.EXE program. It is possible to set security on any individual key including the top-level subtrees. By default, only members of the local administrators group and the system have full access to the Registry. It is possible to assign read-only access, full access, and special permissions to the keys. Inheritance behavior can also be controlled. Access to the Registry can be audited in the security event log.

Setting Registry Permissions

To begin setting permissions in REGEDT32, select the key on which you want to set permissions. You can set permissions on any key, including the root subtree. Inheritance behavior can also be set to determine whether permissions are inherited to child keys. When you have selected the key on which to set permissions, choose Permissions from the Security menu. This will open the Permissions sheet shown in Figure A.8. The Permissions sheet contains one tab, labeled Security.

By default, only the System and administrators have permissions to edit the Registry. To add permissions to enable a user to read or edit the Registry, click Add; select the user from the Name list and click Add or type the username including the domain (DOMAIN\USER). Click OK to add the user to the permissions list. Select the user and click the Allow box to enable either Read access or Full Control. If a user is a member of a group that has permissions to the Registry, it is also possible to deny the user access by selecting the Deny box. The Allow Inheritable Permissions from Parent to Propagate to This Object check box controls how the selected key behaves when permissions are propagated from parent objects. When checked (the default setting), permissions inherited from parent objects are applied to the selected key. When unchecked, permissions are blocked from propagating to the selected key.

FIGURE A.8

From the Security tab in the Permissions sheet, you can add and remove users and change permissions assigned to them.

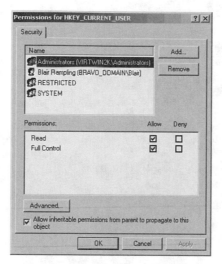

You can also set advanced permissions by clicking the Advanced button in the permissions window to open the Access Control Settings sheet (see Figure A.9).

FIGURE A.9

The tabs in the Access Control Settings sheet enable you to set more granular permissions, set the owner of a particular key, and set auditing events.

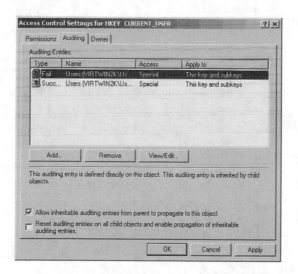

The Permissions tab enables you to allow or deny permissions to specified users. A list of currently assigned permissions is shown in the window. Click Add to add permissions for a user. You will be prompted to select a user or group; then click OK. The Permission Entry sheet opens, as shown in Figure A.10, listing the permission types with Allow and Deny check boxes.

FIGURE A.10
By allowing and deny-
ing access to users
and groups, you can
configure a secure sys-
tem but still allow
access where neces-
sary.

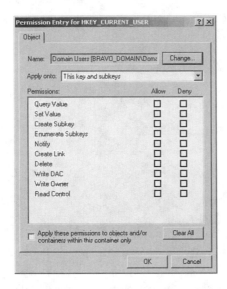

Permission types and their descriptions are listed in Table A.2.

Table A.2 Registry Permission Objects

Object Name	Description
Query Value	Audits attempts to read values from selected Registry key
Set Value	Audits attempts to add or change values in selected key
Create Subkey	Audits attempts to add subkeys under the selected key
Enumerate Subkeys	Audits attempts to view the subkeys of selected key
Notify	Any notification events from a key in the Registry
Create Link	Audits attempts to create symbolic links in selected key
Delete	Audits attempts to delete any object from selected key
Write DAC	Audits attempts to write a discretionary access control list on the selected key
Write Owner	Audits attempts to change the owner of the selected key
Read Control	Any attempts to open the discretionary access control list on the selected key

After you choose to allow or deny the relevant permissions and click OK on each of the permissions sheets, the permissions become effective. There are also two check boxes in the
Access Control Settings sheet that affect the inheritance behavior of permissions. By default,
propagation of inheritable permissions, from parent to child, is allowed. To block that propagation on the selected key, uncheck the Allow Inheritable Permissions from Parent to

Propagate to This Object box. Checking the Reset Permissions on All Child Objects and Enable Propagation of Inheritable Permissions check box causes the permissions set on the selected object to propagate to all existing child objects. By default, inheritable permissions are applied to all new child objects but not to existing ones.

The Owner tab provides for the configuration of the owner of the selected key. By default, the local administrators group is the owner of all keys. Only users with permissions to the selected key can be owners. The Replace Owner on Subcontainers and Objects check box causes the owner change to propagate to all child objects.

Auditing Registry Access

Several different types of Registry access can be audited for any specified user or group. Auditing can be set on any key and inheritance of auditing objects can be controlled. You must be a member of the administrators group to set auditing configuration. To access the auditing properties for any key, select the key and click Permissions in the Security menu. Click the Advanced button and then select the Auditing tab. You should see an Access Control Settings sheet similar to that in Figure A.11.

FIGURE A.11
The Auditing tab of the Access Control Settings sheet shows the auditing entries currently defined on the selected Registry object.

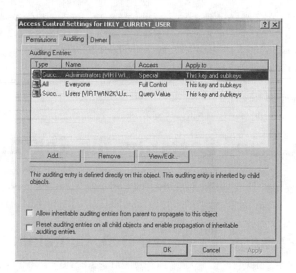

The first step is to add a user or group to audit. Click the Add button and select a user or group, and then click OK. The Auditing Entry sheet opens with the Object tab displayed. Table A.2 in the previous section shows the available auditing objects and their meaning. Figure A.12 shows the Auditing Entry sheet.

FIGURE A.12
In this view of the Auditing Entry Window, the local Users group is being audited.

You can choose to audit success or failure events for each of the auditing objects, or both successes and failures. The Apply Onto drop-down box selects what key the selected auditing events are applied to. The selections are This Key and Subkeys, which applies the auditing events to the selected key and all subkeys; This Key Only, which applies the settings to the selected key and not its subkeys; and Subkeys Only, which applies the events to only subkeys of the selected key and not the key itself.

Backing Up and Restoring the Registry

There are two main methods of backing up and restoring the Registry. The first is by creating an Emergency Repair Disk from the Backup utility and the second is by saving individual keys to file from the Registry editor (REGEDT32.EXE or REGEDIT.EXE).

Creating an Emergency Repair Disk Containing the Registry

To create an emergency repair disk containing Registry information, first start the backup utility. The backup utility is located in the Start menu under Programs, Accessories, System Tools. When the Backup utility loads, click the Emergency Repair Disk button. You will be prompted to insert a blank formatted disk in the disk drive. Select the Also Backup the Registry to the Repair Directory check box. An example of the backup utility and the prompt is shown in Figure A.13. Click OK to create the disk. When this process is completed, a copy of the Registry is saved in %systemroot%\repair. This copy of the Registry is restored when performing a system repair using the Emergency Repair Disk.

To learn more about performing system repairs, see "Emergency Repair Disk," **p. 536**

FIGURE A.13
Don't add or edit anything in the Registry until you've made an Emergency Repair Disk. In this figure, the Backup Utility is creating a Repair Disk.

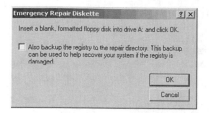

Saving and Restoring Keys in REGEDT32.EXE

Saving and restoring keys in REGEDT32.EXE is a method of backing up the Registry and is also very useful when making changes to the Registry. Saving a key makes an image of the key in a file. If you then change values within that key or its subkeys and suffer adverse effects, you can simply restore the key from the file. Any key can be saved, including top-level subtrees. To save a key, highlight the key you want to save. Click Save Key in the Registry menu. Choose a location to save the key and give the key a descriptive name. A descriptive name is important for when you need to restore the file back into the key later. Click Save.

To restore saved keys back into the Registry, select the key in the Registry editor that you want to restore and click Restore from the Registry menu. Locate the saved key you want to restore and click Open. If the Registry key already exists, you will be prompted with a warning that the saved key will overwrite the currently selected key. Ensure that the selected key and the key stored in the file are the same; otherwise, the data in the selected key will be lost.

Saving and Restoring Keys in REGEDIT.EXE

Saving keys in REGEDIT.EXE is different from saving in REGEDT32.EXE. Saved keys in REGEDIT can be merged into the Registry by double-clicking (assuming that you have permissions to the key). To save the entire Registry to a file, click **E**xport Registry File from the **R**egistry menu. Select **A**ll in the Export Range section (see Figure A.14), then specify a location and a name for the file, and click Save.

To save individual keys in REGEDIT, select the key you want to save. Click **E**xport Registry File from the **R**egistry menu. Choose a location and name for the Registry file. The Registry file will be given an extension of .REG by default. From the Export Registry File window, you can also verify the key to export in the Export Range section. Click Save to save the key. The exported Registry file can be edited in any text editor. A Registry file can be edited by right-clicking the file and selecting **E**dit. This will open the file into Notepad by default. Below is an example of a REDEDIT Registry file:

```
Windows Registry Editor Version 5.00

[HKEY_LOCAL_MACHINE\SOFTWARE\Microsoft\SchedulingAgent]
"TasksFolder"=hex(2):25,00,53,00,79,00,73,00,74,00,65,00,6d,00,52,00,6f,00,
➥6f,00,74,00,25,00,5c,00,54,00,61,00,73,00,6b,00,73,00,00,00
```

```
"LogPath"=hex(2):25,00,53,00,79,00,73,00,74,00,65,00,6d,00,52,00,6f,00,6f,
➥00,74,00,25,00,5c,00,53,00,63,00,68,00,65,00,64,00,4c,00,67,00,55,
➥00,2e,00,54,00,78,00,74,00,00,00
"MinutesBeforeIdle"=dword:0000000f
"MaxLogSizeKB"=dword:00000020
"OldName"="VIRTWIN2K"
```

The first line of the .REG file identifies the file as a REGEDIT export file. The next line contains the name of the key followed by the values contained in the key. Values are identified by their names in quotation marks, then an equal sign, and then the type of value, followed by a colon and the value itself. Multiple keys can coexist in one .REG file.

There are two methods of importing a REGEDIT .REG file into the Registry. The first method is to simply double-click the .REG file or right-click the file and select **M**erge. This will append the Registry entries contained in the file into the Registry. If the entries in the file already exist, they will be overwritten.

The second method of importing the .REG file is from within REGEDIT.EXE. Click **I**mport Registry File from the Registry menu. Select the .REG file and click Open. This performs the same append operation as the first method.

FIGURE A.14

The Export Registry File Window allows selected keys or the entire Registry to be exported to a man readable .REG file.

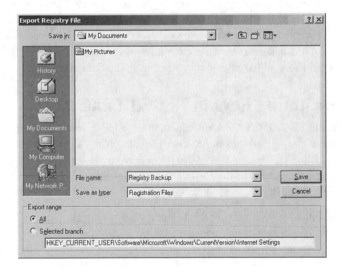

Editing .REG Files

Editing Registry files is a useful ability. It is possible to change settings in one system, export the relevant Registry keys, merge the .REG files into one, edit the files to leave only the relevant entries as all values in a key are exported by default, and merge the new .REG file into each computer that you want to change. For example, I want to set a group of users to enable command-line completion and set the Internet Explorer proxy settings. I know that the user-based command-line completion settings are stored in HKEY_CURRENT_USER\Software \Microsoft\Command Processor, so I can open REGEDIT.EXE and edit the relevant settings. I will add a DWORD value called CompletionChar equal to 0x6h and a DWORD value called PathCompletionChar cqual to 0x4h. I can export the HKEY_CURRENT_USER\Software \Microsoft\Command Processor key to a file. I now have a .REG file containing the following:

```
Windows Registry Editor Version 5.00

[HKEY_CURRENT_USER\Software\Microsoft\Command Processor]
"CompletionChar"=dword:00000006
"DefaultColor"=dword:00000000
"EnableExtensions"=dword:00000001
"PathCompletionChar"=dword:00000004
```

I don't know where the Internet Explorer proxy settings are stored, so I will attempt to find them. I will change the Internet Explorer proxy server to a string that is not likely to be found elsewhere in the Registry, such as looking.for.proxy, and click Apply. I will then open REGEDIT.EXE and open the find box (shown in Figure A.15) by choosing Find from the Edit menu. I'll then enter looking.for.proxy in the Find What text box and click Find Next.

FIGURE A.15

When you enter a string in the Find What text box of the Find dialog box, REGEDIT will search the Registry for that entry.

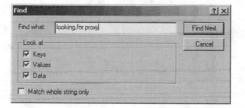

REGEDIT searches the Registry for that entry and finds it in the following location:

```
HKEY_CURRENT_USER\Software\Microsoft\Windows\CurrentVersion\Internet Settings
```

I can change the proxy settings, all stored in the same key, to whatever values I like and then export the key to a file. The file looks like this (there is more in the file than just this key because subkeys are exported as well, but this is the important part):

```
Windows Registry Editor Version 5.00

[HKEY_CURRENT_USER\Software\Microsoft\Windows\CurrentVersion\Internet
➥Settings]
"User Agent"="Mozilla/4.0 (compatible; MSIE 5.0; Win32)"
"IE5_UA_Backup_Flag"="5.0"
"NoNetAutodial"=hex:00,00,00,00
"MigrateProxy"=dword:00000001
"EmailName"="IEUser@"
"AutoConfigProxy"="wininet.dll"
"MimeExclusionListForCache"="multipart/mixed multipart/x-mixed-replace
➥multipart/x-byteranges "
"WarnOnPost"=hex:01,00,00,00
"UseSchannelDirectly"=hex:01,00,00,00
```

```
"EnableHttp1_1"=dword:00000001
"ProxyEnable"=dword:00000001
"ProxyServer"="192.168.124.107:80"
"EnableAutodial"=hex:00,00,00,00
```

I now have two files, each containing some values I want to merge. The first step is to open one of the .REG files and select the entries I want from that file and copy them to the clipboard using the Copy option from the Edit menu or Ctrl+C. I can now open the second .REG file and paste the Registry entries in. The new file should look like this:

```
Windows Registry Editor Version 5.00

[HKEY_CURRENT_USER\Software\Microsoft\Command Processor]
"CompletionChar"=dword:00000006
"PathCompletionChar"=dword:00000004

[HKEY_CURRENT_USER\Software\Microsoft\Windows\CurrentVersion\Internet
➥Settings]
"ProxyEnable"=dword:00000001
"ProxyServer"="192.168.124.107:80"
```

The important parts I cut out of the two Registry files are the key names and the values that I want to merge.

I can save this file with a new name and test it out by changing the entries manually on my computer and double-clicking the file. I can check the settings again to make sure the merge was successful. If so, I can distribute the .REG files to each user and have them merge the file.

Windows 2000 Professional Troubleshooting Guide

In this appendix

Using the Windows 2000 Troubleshooting Tools

Windows 2000 includes several tools to aid in troubleshooting hardware devices and software applications. Most devices have interactive troubleshooters that walk you through the troubleshooting process. You also can make use of a number of diagnostic utilities that help you identify disk errors, hardware errors and conflicts, and system repair. Most error messages have help files associated with them to assist you in repairing the error.

Interactive Troubleshooters

The interactive troubleshooters are useful when a hardware device is not functioning. Table B.1 lists and describes the available troubleshooters.

Table B.1   Interactive Troubleshooters

Troubleshooter Name	Description
Client Service for NetWare	Troubleshoots problems connecting to Novell NetWare servers
Display	Fixes problems with video drivers and display settings
Hardware	Troubleshoots problems with hardware devices such as add-on cards and peripherals
Internet Connections (ISP)	Troubleshoots problems connecting to the Internet through an ISP
Modem	Troubleshoots modem connection
MS-DOS Programs	Identifies and fixes problems with running MS-DOS programs under Windows 2000
Multimedia and Games	Troubleshoots DirectX and multimedia problems
Networking (TCP/IP)	Identifies and repairs problems connecting to systems on a TCP/IP network
Print	Troubleshoots problems printing and connecting to network printers
Remote Access	Troubleshoots problems connecting to remote access servers through a modem
Sound	Identifies and repairs problems with sound devices
System Setup	Assists with the installation and setup of Windows 2000
Windows 3.x Programs	Troubleshoots the use of older 16-bit Windows 3.x software on Windows 2000

The interactive troubleshooters are available through several methods. To get to a list of all the troubleshooters, open Windows 2000 Help and click the Index tab. Type the word **Troubleshooters** and choose (list) in the left pane of the window. The list of interactive troubleshooters will appear in the right pane. Click the name of the troubleshooter you want to use, and it will open in a new window.

Another way to access the troubleshooters is from the Device Manager. The Device Manager is accessed by right-clicking the My Computer icon on the desktop and selecting **M**anage. Alternatively, you can select Computer Management from the Administrative Tools folder in the Control Panel. From the Computer Management console, select Device Manager in the left pane. Open the properties sheet for the device you want to troubleshoot and click the Troubleshooter button. The troubleshooter will appear in a new window.

Whenever you experience a problem with a device for which a troubleshooter is available, Windows 2000 Professional prompts you to indicate whether you want to troubleshoot the problem. When using the interactive troubleshooters, it is important to follow all instructions exactly. When you have completed the tasks presented to you in the Troubleshooter window, click the appropriate statement of the problem in the What Problem Are You Having? area of the window and then click Next. The troubleshooter walks you through the steps of repairing the problem. A sample of an interactive troubleshooter is shown in Figure B.1.

Part

VI

App

B

FIGURE B.1
This TCP/IP Troubleshooter asks you to open a command prompt window and then choose the appropriate "problem" from the list.

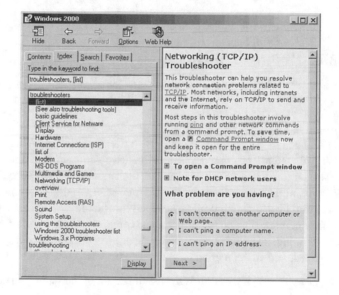

The System Information Utility is a Microsoft Management Console (MMC)–based utility that provides an outline of the hardware and software in the system to aid in diagnostics as well as shortcuts to several of the diagnostic and repair utilities listed in the next section. The System Information Utility can be started by opening the Run command from the Start menu and typing **MSINFO32**. The objects under the Console Root in the left pane all open to show status and information on system resources. The System Information Utility is shown in Figure B.2.

FIGURE B.2
The tools menu in the
System Information
Utility provides access
to the utilities.

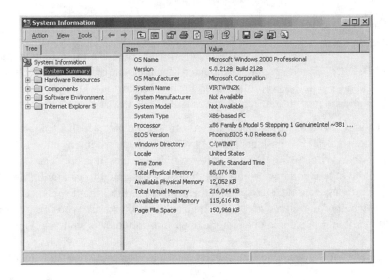

Diagnostic and Repair Utilities

There are several diagnostic and repair utilities available in Windows 2000 Professional, the first of which is the Disk Cleanup Wizard. This utility cleans old unnecessary files from the hard drive to create more disk space. The Disk Cleanup Wizard is accessed by selecting Disk Cleanup from the Programs, Accessories, System Tools menu. Also, when you are low on disk space, you will be prompted to run the Disk Cleanup Wizard. When you start the Disk Cleanup Wizard, you are prompted to select the drive you want to clean. Select a drive and click OK. The Disk Cleanup Wizard calculates the amount of disk space that can be freed by its cleanup routine. The Disk Cleanup Wizard then offers to delete temporary downloaded Internet program files, delete temporary cached Internet files, empty the recycle bin, delete automatically and manually cached offline files, compress old files, and delete catalog files from the content indexer. The amount of disk space freed by performing each of these operations is displayed, and you can choose whether to perform each one.

Figure B.3 shows the Disk Cleanup Wizard and the list of file types you can choose to delete.

Another utility that is useful is the Disk Error Checking utility. If you notice problems copying files or notice file corruption, there might be errors on the hard disk. To run the error-checking utility, open My Computer and right-click the hard disk you want to check for errors. Click Properties and select the Tools tab. Click the Check Now button in the Error Checking area to start the utility. There are two options in the Error Checking utility, both of which are disabled by default. The first is Automatically Fix File System Errors. By default, the error-checking utility only checks for errors and reports them. Selecting this option instructs the utility to repair any errors it finds. The second option is Scan for and Attempt Recovery of Bad Sectors, which instructs the utility to do a thorough check of the disk surface for bad sectors. Any data in bad sectors are moved if possible, and the sector is marked unusable. Clicking the Start button starts the error check. When the check completes, the utility reports that it is complete and closes. If there are errors, they are reported.

FIGURE B.3
When you run the Disk Cleanup Wizard, select the file types you want to delete and click OK. You are prompted to verify that you want to delete the files. The wizard then performs the selected operations and exits.

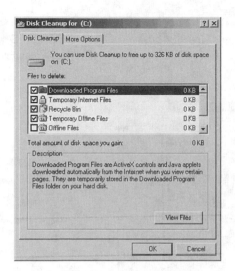

Another disk-related tool is the Disk Defragmenter. When files are written to a disk, they are written to the first available sector, regardless of whether all the required sectors are contiguous. The Disk Defragmenter places all the data for a file in contiguous sectors, which increases file access speed. To run the defragmenter, open My Computer and right-click the hard disk you want to check. Click Properties and select the Tools tab. Click the Defragment Now button to start the Disk Defragmenter.

When the defragment utility opens, click the disk you want to defragment and then click the Analyze button. Disk Defragmenter analyzes the drive and reports the results of the analysis. If you choose to defragment, the process begins, and you are notified when it completes. The Disk Defragmenter is shown in Figure B.4 during a defragment operation.

FIGURE B.4
The Disk Defragment Utility lets you know whether the drive requires defragmentation. You can choose to defragment the drive, close the status window, or view a report on fragmentation.

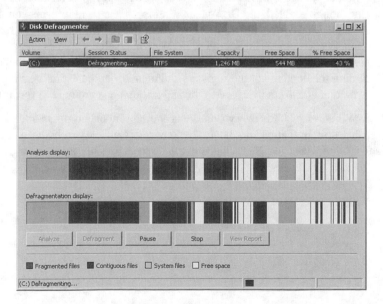

Windows 2000 also contains the Dr. Watson tool, which is very useful for troubleshooting application errors. Dr. Watson properties can be configured. To start Dr. Watson, type **drwtsn32** from the **R**un command in the Start menu. The Dr. Watson configuration opens as seen in Figure B.5.

FIGURE B.5

The Dr. Watson Utility can be configured in a number of ways to give you the application troubleshooting actions and report that you choose.

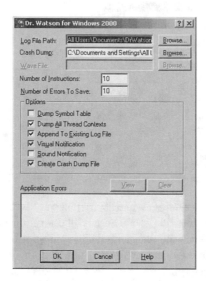

From here, you can define where the utility will create log files and crash dump files, and you can select the number of errors and number of instructions to save. You can also choose what actions to take on a crash, including visual and sound notifications, whether to create a crash dump file, and what information to include such as the symbol table and thread contexts. The Dr. Watson utility is activated automatically when a program terminates abnormally. If visual notification is enabled, the Dr. Watson window appears and informs you that a report is being generated. These reports can be viewed from the Dr. Watson utility in the Application Errors section by clicking the View button. Dr. Watson crash dump files contain a step-by-step assembly language version of the process that was happening when the application crashed, including the contents of the registers and memory and a list of the running processes. This information is extremely useful to the application programmers in repairing the problem.

The Windows 2000 Recovery Console is another important utility and is designed to help repair a system that will not boot. The Recovery Console can be used to fix services and disks and to copy files to an NTFS file system if system files become lost or corrupted.

Safe Mode

Windows 2000 can boot into Safe Mode if there are device driver problems that are preventing it from starting. Safe Mode starts the system with only the drivers necessary to operate. From Safe Mode, you can remove any drivers that are causing conflicts and causing Windows 2000 to fail to boot. To start the system in Safe Mode, hold the F8 key during boot. The Safe Mode boot menu appears, showing the Safe Mode options. The system will not start in Safe Mode if any system files are damaged, including NTOSKRNL.EXE or HAL.DLL, or if there is a problem with a storage driver for the disk controller. The Safe Mode options are shown in Figure B.6.

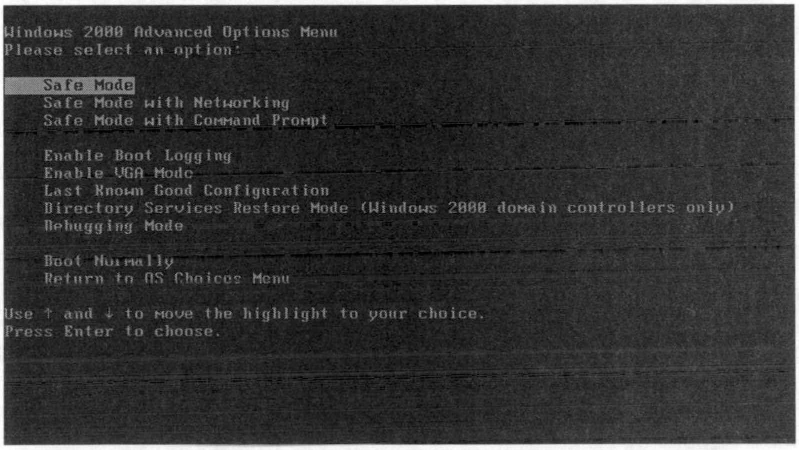

FIGURE B.6
Safe Mode Boot Options enable you to start your system with a limited set of drivers and services to recover from system problems that stop the system from booting normally.

The first Safe Mode boot option is Safe Mode. This starts the system with only basic display, keyboard, and mouse drivers. Serial mouse drivers are not loaded in Safe Mode. Using this mode you should be able to remove any device drivers or applications causing conflicts, including network drivers.

Safe Mode with Networking boots the system with the basic Safe Mode drivers but includes network support. If the network drivers are causing problems on the system, this mode will not boot.

Safe Mode with Command Prompt boots the system with only the basic Safe Mode drivers, but instead of the desktop, the command prompt is displayed after logging on. This is useful for moving or replacing files.

Enable Boot Logging causes the Windows 2000 boot process to log the startup of all drivers and services to a file called ntbtlog.txt in the %windir% directory. This file lists the success or failure of each driver and service's startup. Using the boot log, you can identify drivers and services that are conflicting or otherwise not functioning.

Enable VGA Mode causes Windows 2000 to boot with only the default VGA video drivers. All other drivers and services are unaffected. VGA mode is used when a video driver is installed that does not function with the installed video card or when an unsupported video mode is selected.

Last Known Good Configuration boots Windows 2000 with the Registry settings saved at the last shutdown. If the last shutdown was successful, this mode has no effect. Last Known Good Configuration is used when changes are made to the Registry that cause the system to cease functioning. This mode loads all services and drivers that would normally be loaded.

Directory Service Restore Mode is used only on Windows 2000 Server systems but is included in the Safe Mode list for Windows 2000 professional systems. It is used to restore the Active Directory service on a domain controller.

Debugging Mode causes Windows 2000 to send debugging information through a serial port while it is booting. This information can be used to identify problems on a system that will not start in Safe Mode or that has problems that are unidentifiable through other means.

Emergency Repair Disk

The emergency repair disk can be used to repair the system in the event that system files are damaged or that there are problems with the boot partition tqhat cause the system to not start. It is important to only run the repair disk in the case that the system will not start and other options have been exhausted because running an emergency repair can cause the loss of some settings and application data.

Use the Backup utility to create an emergency repair disk. From the Start menu, click Programs, Accessories, System Tools, Backup. Click the Emergency Repair Disk button. You are prompted to insert a blank formatted floppy disk. From this prompt you can also choose to make a backup of the Registry. Insert a disk and click OK to begin the process. Repair information is stored in the %systemroot%\repair directory.

To repair a damaged system using the Windows 2000 installation media and an Emergency Repair Disk, follow these steps:

1. Place the Windows 2000 Installation CD or boot disk in the Drive.
2. The Setup program asks if you want to **S**et up Windows 2000 or **R**epair a Windows 2000 installation. Choose **R** to Repair a Windows 2000 installation.
3. In the next screen, choose **R** again to use the Emergency Repair Process.
4. Another screen appears, asking whether you want to do a **M**anual Repair or a **F**ast Repair. Press **M**; a list of available repair options appears.

N O T E A Fast Repair from the setup program will perform all three of the repair operations listed under Manual Repair as well as repairing the Registry. The backup utility restores the Registry from the last copy of the Registry saved by the Emergency Repair Disk process. If that does not exist, the Registry is restored from the copy of the Registry made when Windows 2000 was first installed. All Registry settings changed since that time will be lost. The Registry is not repaired if the manual repair option Is used. ▪

5. Choose one or more of these options:

- *Inspect Startup Environment* checks the boot loader and related files that allow multiple operating systems to boot.

- *Verify Windows 2000 System Files* checks all base files, such as HAL.DLL and NTOSKRNL.EXE, which are necessary for Windows 2000 to operate.

- *Inspect Boot Sector* checks the boot sector of the hard disk. (The boot sector contains file system information and the software to begin the Windows 2000 boot process.)

6. Select **C**ontinue (perform selected tasks).

7. At the next screen, press Enter if you have a current Emergency Repair Disk.

 If you do not have a current Emergency Repair Disk, press **L** to have the system search the hard drive for the repair directory.

8. If you pressed Enter at the last screen, you are prompted to insert the emergency repair disk and press Enter.

 If you pressed **L** at the last screen, the repair process finds a Windows 2000 installation and asks whether you want to repair that installation. Press Enter to continue.

9. The repair process proceeds and the system reboots.

Troubleshooting Techniques

There are some important steps to troubleshooting a Windows 2000 system. One of the most important things to always keep in mind is to take small steps and only change one factor at a time. The process for troubleshooting the system is to first examine the symptoms and history to isolate the problem and then to try to determine a method of repairing the problem. Here's a short checklist of troubleshooting techniques that might help you find and fix your problem efficiently:

- *Look at the problem and try to determine what area of the system is causing it.* If the network connection is not functioning, it could be with the network card drivers, the card itself, or the Windows 2000 network protocol drivers. If the problem is having no sound, it could be with the sound card or its drivers. After you isolate the problem to a certain area, you can look at the symptoms more specifically.

- *Try to recall whether anything has been altered in the system configuration around the time when the problem started.* If so, reverse those changes and see if the problem is repaired. It is always a good idea to write down any changes you make to the system so you have documentation to aid you in case the changes must be reversed. Write down each change you make in the steps to repairing the problem.

- *Try to determine whether the problem is repeatable or it happens at random.* Try to find the conditions that cause the error. From those conditions, it might be possible to determine the cause of the problem.

■ *Look for help from the experts.* Check the online help and any other help resources such as the Microsoft Knowledge Base (http://support.microsoft.com) because many problems have occurred with other systems and been reported. These reported problems are written up with solutions in articles in the Knowledge Base.

■ *Check to see that all device drivers have been installed for the hardware in question and that the services related to the problem have started.* If the services have not started, it is likely that an error has been logged in the event log with a reason why they have failed to start. Try disabling the failed services one at a time to try to isolate the problem.

Don't forget to use the Enable Boot Logging option on startup as discussed in the previous section. This will log the startup of each device driver and indicate whether any have failed to start.

Getting the Most from the System Monitor Tool

System Monitor is a Microsoft Management Console (MMC)–based tool used for monitoring system performance. Performance can be monitored in the form of graphs, logs, reports, and alerts. System Monitor is an excellent tool for determining precisely what load is on each of the system components and what components are performance bottlenecks.

To begin using the System Monitor tool, open the Control Panel, then open the Administrative Tools folder. Double-click Performance to start System Monitor. The System Monitor console should open as seen in Figure B.7.

FIGURE B.7
The System Monitor Tool allows the performance counters of system components to be monitored. Use the toolbar to access the System Monitor functions.

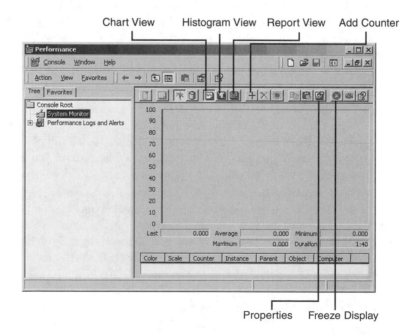

Chart View   Histogram View   Report View   Add Counter

Properties   Freeze Display

Many system components have performance objects associated with them. A *performance object* is a collection of performance data (called *counters*) that is generated by the system component. Aside from the performance objects included with the system components, many add-on products also have their own performance objects that contain counters that can be monitored by the System Monitor.

The counters contained within Performance Objects are individual pieces of performance data respective to the system components. An example of a performance object is the Memory object. The Memory object contains all performance data that relates to system memory. One example of a counter within the Memory object is Pages/sec, which tracks a specific aspect of memory performance. Only counters can be monitored.

Using the System Monitor

The first step to using System Monitor is to add a counter. To add a counter, follow these steps:

1. Click the Add Counters button in the right-pane toolbar of the Performance window. The Add Counters window appears, as shown in Figure B.8.

2. Select the performance object to monitor from the Performance Object drop-down box.

FIGURE B.8

In this Add Counters Window, the %Processor Time counter is selected; this counter measures the total activity of the processor relative to the maximum activity of the processor and gives an indication of the load on the processor.

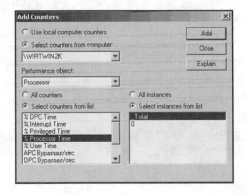

3. Select a counter from those in the Select Counters from List box.

4. Select an instance from the Select Instances from List box.

N O T E *Instances* are used when there is more than one of the system components defined by the Performance Object. For example, on a multiprocessor machine, there is an instance for each processor. The Total instance option shows the performance for all instances. For a single-processor machine, Total and the instance 0 will generate the same data. ∎

5. Click the Add button to add the counter to the System Monitor. When you are finished adding counters, click the Close button.

Now, there should be a counter defined in System Monitor. There are three ways to view the counter. The default view is the Chart View, shown in Figure B.9. Chart View is accessed by clicking the Chart button. The Chart View displays a line graph of the defined counters. The values are shown on the Y axis. The Chart View is good for viewing the activity of the defined counters over time. An example of the Chart View is shown in Figure B.9.

FIGURE B.9

In the System Monitor Chart View, you can select each of the counters from the list of defined counters and view the Last, Minimum, Maximum, and Average values, and the duration that the counter has been active.

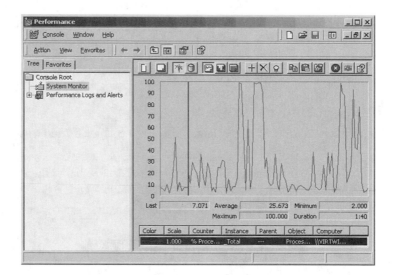

Click the Histogram View button to access that view, shown in Figure B.10. The Histogram View is a bar graph view of the defined counters, and it displays the Last, Minimum, Maximum, Average, and Duration information, as shown in Chart View.

FIGURE B.10

The Histogram View is useful for viewing the instantaneous values for the defined counters in a graphical format.

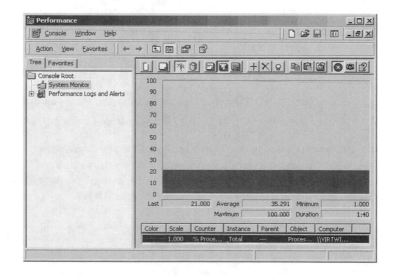

The Report View shows the instantaneous values for the defined counters in a text format. The Report View is helpful for getting a numerical representation of counter data that does not change frequently, such as hard drive space. Figure B.11 is a sample of the Report View.

FIGURE B.11

The System Monitor Report View is good for viewing performance data in a numerical format for accurate representation.

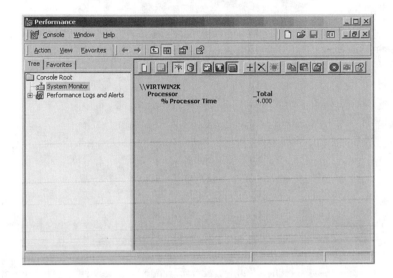

Several options are useful when using the System Monitor. The first of these options is the Freeze Display button. This button will stop data collection so a capture of the data can be made. To access the Properties sheet for the System Monitor, click the Properties button. From the General tab of the System Monitor Properties sheet (see Figure B.12), the view can be changed to Graph (Chart View), Histogram, or Report, which has the same effect as clicking the respective buttons in the main System Monitor window.

Display elements can also be toggled on or off, including the Legend (which shows the counters at the bottom of the window), the Value bar (which shows Last, Minimum, Maximum, Average, and Duration), and the Tool bar at the top of the window. Report and Histogram data can be defined to display the Default, Current, Average, Minimum, or Maximum values, with the default being the current value. Appearance and borders can be customized from this tab. There is also a check box and value that define whether and how often the data should be updated (1 second is the default value). Data that changes less frequently can warrant a higher value. The final check box instructs the System Monitor whether to allow duplicate counters to be defined.

FIGURE B.12

The General tab of the System Monitor Properties window contains options with which you can configure nearly every aspect of the System Monitor report display.

The Source tab of the properties sheet enables you to view either the current performance data or performance data from a previously recorded log file. If performance data is viewed from a log file, the name and location of that file must be specified. The time range of the log file can also be specified if only a certain range is to be viewed. Defining the time range is accomplished by clicking the Time Range button and then sliding the bars at each end of the time range. The far left of the time range bar represents the time of 0:00 in the log file. The far right of the bar represents the final moment of the log file. By sliding the left bar, you change the time at which the playback of the log file begins (relative to the beginning), and the right bar controls the relative time at which the playback of the log file ends.

The Data tab shows the counters that are currently defined and allows counters to be added and removed. The line color, width, and style can be changed, as well as the scale for the counter. Counter scales can be adjusted in the case that multiple counters are displayed but one or more have a value that is significantly higher or lower than the others.

The Graph tab enables you to change the title for the graph and the vertical axis as well as toggle horizontal and vertical grid lines and vertical axis numbers. You can also define minimum and maximum values for the vertical axis to define the scale.

From the Color tab, colors can be selected for the various parts of the System Monitor from the property name drop-down box such as the time bar, background, foreground, and grid lines.

The Fonts tab enables you to change the font used for the System Monitor display.

▶ For an in-depth discussion of log files and their use, **see** "Viewing Events Log," **p. 376**

Configuring System Monitor Logging and Alerts

System Monitor counters can be logged and alerts generated when threshold values are exceeded. Logging and alerts are accessed by clicking the Performance Logs and Alerts object under the Console Root in the System Monitor console. Logs and alert definitions are created and can be used repeatedly. The three available options are Counter Logs, Trace Logs, and Alerts. Counter logs record counter data over time, much like the regular System Monitor, except counter logs are stored in a file. Counter logs can be viewed from the System Monitor using the Source tab of the Properties window. To access counter logs, click the Counter Logs object in the left pane of the console. By default, the System Overview log definition is created. The properties for the System Overview log are shown in Figure B.13.

FIGURE B.13

This System Overview Properties sheet shows the Memory\Pages/sec, Physical Disk(_Total) \Avg. Disk Queue Length and Processor (_Total)\% Processor Time counters defined with data sampled every 15 seconds (the default for a log file).

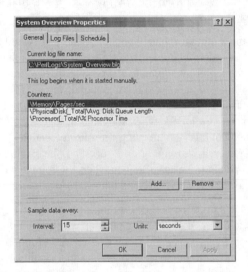

To start the log file capturing data, click the Start the Selected Log button. The log file will continue until the Stop the Selected Log button is clicked.

To create a new log file, follow these steps:

1. Right-click the Counter Logs object in the right pane of the Performance Logs and Alerts window and then click **N**ew Log Settings or select **N**ew Log Settings from the **A**ctions menu; you are prompted to enter a name for the new log.

2. Enter a name and click OK. The Properties sheet for the new log appears.

3. Click the Add button to add counters to the log. Adding counters to a log works the same as adding counters to the System Monitor. The added counters will appear in the Counters box. You can change the sample interval depending on the frequency of updates of the counters.

TIP You also can use the **N**ew Log Settings command of the Counter Logs object to copy an existing log file and modify its contents.

From the Log Files tab of the System Overview Properties sheet, you can define the name and location of the actual log file. By default, logs are stored in C:\PerfLogs, and the name of the file is the log name followed by a six digit number starting at 1 and incrementing with each capture. Log file types can be binary files (default), binary circular files (which overwrite themselves when the file size exceeds the maximum), comma-delimited text files (CSV), and tab-delimited text files (TSV) . Only the CSV and TSV files can be read without the System Monitor tool. They can be opened with any spreadsheet that can open CSV and TSV files. The maximum log file size can also be set from the Log Files tab. If Maximum Limit is selected, the log will fill the drive before it stops.

The Schedule tab allows the log to be started and stopped at a specified time. For example, the log could be activated during a scheduled system event such as a backup or database maintenance. By default, the log is scheduled to start immediately (after the OK button is pressed) and stop manually. If a log file size limit is defined, the log file can be scheduled to stop when the log file is full. This prevents the log file from being overwritten when it fills. You can also choose to start a new log file when the current log stops if the log file is scheduled to stop after a specified amount of time using the After selection. This makes the System Monitor create a new log for every amount of time specified; for example, every day if After is set to 1 day. You can also specify a command to run when the log file stops, such as a MAPI email program to email the log to yourself if need be.

After you click OK in the log's properties sheet, assuming you haven't changed the scheduled start time, the log begins to collect data. The log file stops at the scheduled time or when you click the Stop button. The log can be opened using the System Monitor. Open the System Monitor Properties sheet and click the Source tab. Select the log file as the data source, and the log file will replay. The log file can be replayed in the Chart, Histogram, or Report View.

Trace logs monitor system activity that isn't monitored by counters or other means. Trace logs can monitor data from the System Provider or Nonsystem Providers. To create a new trace log, follow these steps:

1. Right-click the Trace Log object in the right pane of the console and click New Log Settings; you are prompted for a name for the new trace log.

2. Enter a name and click OK. The properties sheet for the trace log will appear.

3. Select the events you want to monitor. By default, the Nonsystem Provider is specified. (An example of a nonsystem provider event is an Active Directory Netlogon event.) Click the Provider Status button to view a list of all providers that have events defined. To add an event from a nonsystem provider, click the Add button.

4. To monitor System Provider events, select the System Provider radio button and select the events from the list. The events are as follows:

- Process Creations/Deletions monitors the creation and deletion of system processes.
- Thread Creations/Deletions monitors the creation and deletion of processor threads by the system.
- Disk Input/Output monitors the disk I/O activity.
- Network TCP/IP monitors TCP/IP network activity.
- Page Faults monitors faults accessing the page file.
- File Details monitors file I/O data details.

5. Click OK.

The Log Files tab provides the same function as in the Counter Logs object, enabling you to change filenames, locations, and maximum sizes. The difference is in the file types. The valid file types for trace logs are Sequential Trace File or Circular Trace File. A *circular* trace file overwrites itself when it fills, whereas a *sequential* trace file does not. The Schedule tab also functions identically to that tab in the Counter Logs properties.

The Advanced tab enables you to set buffering information for the trace logs. You can specify the buffer size as well as the number of buffers used. The larger the buffers and the higher their number, the more system memory is used. The data stored in the buffers is written to the log file only when the buffers are full by default. From this tab you can instruct the Trace Log to write the buffered data to file every specified number of seconds by selecting the check box.

After you click OK in the log's properties sheet, the log will begin to collect data (assuming that you haven't changed the scheduled start time). The log file will stop at the scheduled time or when you click the Stop button. Trace Logs can be viewed using the System Monitor display.

Alerts generate notifications when specified counters go over specified thresholds. A sample alert is shown in Figure B.14.

FIGURE B.14
This Sample Performance Alert notifies the user that the counter has gone over its threshold, and it reports the value of the overflow.

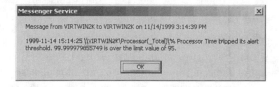

Part
VI

App

B

To create a new alert, follow these steps:

1. Right-click the Alerts object in the right pane of the console and choose **N**ew Alert Settings from the context menu. You are prompted to name the alert.

2. Give the alert a name and click OK. The properties sheet for the new alert is displayed.

3. If you choose to do so, add a comment to the alert that will be displayed in the console.

4. Add the counters that will be monitored and assign thresholds to them. Add the counter just as you would for a Counter Log or the System Monitor, then select Under or Over from the drop-down box, and enter a threshold in the Limit text box. You can also change the sample interval time.

From the Action tab, you can select from four actions to be taken when the threshold is reached:

- *Log an Entry in the Application Event Log.* The default setting.

- *Send a Network Message To.* Sends a network message to a computer that you specify by typing its name in the text box.

- *Start Performance Data Log.* You define it by selecting a log from the drop-down box.

- *Run This Program.* Can be used to send an email message if you have a command-line mailer. There are several MAPI mail utilities available. If you use this option, specify the command-line arguments for the program to customize the data that the program uses; for example, you can configure it to mail the alert data.

The Schedule tab enables you to schedule when the alert is running and when it stops. By default, the alert starts immediately and stops when you click the Stop button. If the alert scan is scheduled to stop after a specified amount of time (one day, for example), the Start a New Scan check box can be selected to start a scan every day. When you click OK on the properties sheet, the alert scan starts, assuming no changes were made to the alert start schedule. When the specified counters exceed their thresholds, alerts will be sent.

Putting the System Monitor to Work

The System Monitor is an excellent tool for detecting bottlenecks in system performance. Here are some specific uses of the System Monitor for finding performance problems.

The first step to determining performance problems is to establish a *baseline*. A baseline is an indication of how the system performs under a smaller load, before there are any problems. By monitoring the counters listed in the following text with low load levels and without all applications and processes running, you can get an idea of where the load values should be because Interrupts/Sec isn't a value for which very many people can determine an ideal value.

The first performance bottleneck to be addressed is the system processor, or processors if applicable. The system processors can become a bottleneck when the applications being run are highly processor-intensive such as databases, graphics rendering software, and even many games that use lots of 3D graphics. The processor can also be a problem when there are many processes running at once. To determine the overall load on the processor, view the % Processor Time counter for the Processor object. The % Processor Time counter gives an overall view of the total processor load. This value should be fairly low on average with higher spikes. Specific values for processor time are debatable, but a % Processor Time value consistently over 85 percent indicates a processor bottleneck. The system either needs a processor upgrade (to a faster or second processor) or needs some processes offloaded to another system.

Another counter to view for processor performance is the Interrupts/Sec counter for the Processor object. This gives an indication of the I/O load faced by the processor. Interrupts are caused by system devices vying for processor time to have their data processed.

The last processor counter to monitor is the Processor Queue Length counter for the System object. This counter shows the number of instructions queued and waiting to be processed.

To find memory-related bottlenecks, view the Pages/Sec Available Bytes counters for the Memory object. Available Bytes shows the amount of free memory available to processes that might need it. Pages/Sec represents the number of writes to the page file on the hard disk that are made every second. A large value for Pages/Sec (over 20) or a low value for Available Bytes (under 4MB) reveals a memory bottleneck. More memory needs to be added to the system.

The page file can also be monitored for activity. The % Usage counter for the Paging File object represents the total usage of the page file. This value should not be consistently over 99%. If so, the size of the page file might need to be increased.

Disk bottlenecks are also common. The % Disk Time counter for the Physical Disk object represents the total time that the system is reading or writing to the hard disks. This value should be low on average with some spikes of activity. A value that is consistently over 90% represents a performance problem. Another disk counter is Average Disk Queue Length for the Physical Disk object. This value represents the read or write operations queued and waiting to be processed. This number should be less than the number of physical disks plus two.

The last counters to monitor are Disk Reads/Sec and Disk Writes/Sec for the Physical Disk object. The threshold for these values is defined by the type of disk drive interface (for example: IDE, UDMA, SCSI) and by the disk drive manufacturer's specifications. Faster drives and faster interfaces can handle more reads and writes per second than slower drives and interfaces. If these values exceed their threshold values or increase substantially over their baseline values, the number of physical disks or the type of drive interface might need to be increased.

Part

VI

App

B

Third-Party Tools and Resources

There are several third-party utilities available for troubleshooting and repairing Windows 2000. One large collection of such software can be found at Systems Internals (http://www.sysinternals.com). There are many system-level diagnostic, repair, and debugging tools listed.

One set of tools located at Systems Internals includes Diskmon, Filemon, Pmon, Portmon, and Regmon, which monitor activity on the disk, file system, processes and threads, serial and parallel ports, and Registry, respectively. These are known as spying utilities because they watch what the system is doing with the monitored components. These utilities can give you a better idea of how the system functions in the background.

Another set of related tools includes Handle, HandleEx, and ListDLLs. Handle lists what files are open and by which processes. HandleEx is a more extensive version that shows what files, Registry keys, and DLLs are open by which processes. The ListDLLs utility shows a list of all currently loaded DLLs.

The NTFSInfo utility gives detailed information on NTFS volumes, including information about the Master File Table and MFT-Zones. It also shows the sizes of NTFS metadata files.

Another utility that can be useful is Logcaster by Rippletech (http://www.rippletech.com). Logcaster provides a central place to monitor services, performance monitor counters, event logs, text-based logs, and network information. Logcaster is useful for monitoring large numbers of systems on the network.

One Internet Site that has a large amount of software and information about Windows 2000 is BHS.com (http://www.bhs.com). BHS has listings of software organized by name as well as search features. BHS also has a tech support section with technical information.

What's on the CD?

The Windows 2000 Professional Installation and Configuration Handbook CD contains a host of powerful tools. Here's a rundown of the CD's contents.

Advanced Security Control Shareware

from SmartLine, Inc.

Advanced Security Control (ASC) enables administrators to set up rules for the local computer, defining when any program can be executed and by whom. You can control access to any 32-bit software, such as games, Internet browsers, or anything else depending on the time of day and day of the week. Configuration is as simple as setting up login hour restrictions. Just choose a program, define users who should be affected by the rules, and choose when to enable and disable access on a one-week grid. If users try to access the program outside of the allowed hours, they're given an access-denied message. ASC enhances access control for Windows NT users and helps to maintain a more protected environment.

BugTrapper™ Trial Version

from MuTek Solutions Ltd.

BugTrapper™, MuTek's flagship product, is a software quality tool akin to a "black box" aircraft flight recorder. It significantly reduces troubleshooting and debug time by completely eliminating the tedious and difficult task of reproducing the user's actions, data, and environment. As a result, BugTrapper users are able to improve quality and deliver more reliable code while reducing support and upgrade costs.

CDLock Shareware

from SmartLine, Inc.

CDLock enables you to set up rules for the local computer, defining when any removable disks that support the auto-eject feature can be used and by whom. You can control access to any removable disks, such as CD-ROMS, optical disks, or anything else depending on the time of day and day of the week. CDLock enhances access control for Windows users and helps you to control the removable disks usage.

DeviceLock Shareware

from SmartLine, Inc.

DeviceLock enables network administrators to specify which users can access which devices (ports, floppies, Mos, and so on) on the local computer. After DeviceLock is installed, administrators can assign permissions to LPT ports, CD-ROMS, COM ports, or any other device as they would to any share on the hard disk. Network Administrators can use DeviceLock to flush unsaved files' buffers (it's very useful for a removable media) and to get extended information about devices and NTFS partitions. Remote control is also available.

Eraser

from Sami Tolvanen

Eraser is an advanced security tool that enables you to completely remove sensitive data from your hard drive by overwriting it several times with carefully selected patterns. You can drag and drop files and folders to the on-demand eraser, use the convenient Explorer shell extension, or use the integrated scheduler to program overwriting of unused disk space or, for example, browse cache files to happen regularly, at night, during your lunch break, at weekends, or whenever you want.

FTP Voyager Demo Version

from Deerfield.com

FTP Voyager is the most powerful FTP client program for Windows 9x/NT on the market today. With an intuitive drag-and-drop interface, FTP Voyager enables you to update a Web site with a single click, transfer files directly between FTP servers, and resume interrupted downloads. A perfect tool for Web developers or anyone who moves files on the Internet.

GimmIP Evaluation Version

from Idyle Software

Idyle GimmIP always has your current IP a click away. It will monitor your connection to see whether you are connected and give you output through the color of its tray icon. Furthermore, it can save you much time in finding problems with your network. Your DNS server is down? You'll see that. Your mail server doesn't answer? You'll know why.

GkSetup Free Edition Version

Gero Huehn–GkWare.com

GkSetup is a setup toolkit that will display your license and README texts, collect user information, add icons to the Start menu, and create a full, automatic uninstall for your application. It supports disk spanning and shared DLL and OCX registration. The Professional Edition includes several new features, such as support for silent setups, customization dialog logos, and setup variables.

Part
VI

App
C

Install Manager Evaluation

from Wise Solutions

This enables System Administrators to create install packages and identify file conflicts.

Macro Magic Evaluation Version

from Iolo Technologies

You can create macros that represent all your frequent tasks and then run them instantly with the press of a key.

Macro Scheduler Demo Version

from MJT Net Ltd.

A powerful scheduling and macro scripting tool for Windows 95, 98, and 2000. Scripts can be built to control any program or command that accepts keyboard and mouse input. You can even edit recorded macros. Any number of macros can be scheduled to take place at a specified time on any day or days of week. It can, for example, fetch your email, run your virus checker, automate backups, or check your hard drive. It can control file transfers, create financial reports, upload and download content from the Web, and more.

Multi-Remote Registry Change Demo Version

from Eytcheson Software

Windows NT Registry management tool available supporting every value type as well as Registry security management.

NeoSpace Shareware

from NeoWorks, Inc.

NeoSpace makes use of Neolite technology to provide an easy, automated solution for individual users. NeoSpace compresses existing programs installed on your computer, enabling you to recover needed disk space.

NeoTrace Shareware

from NeoWorks, Inc.

NeoTrace Internet Trace Route software is the world's leading Internet Tracer software for diagnostic and investigative purposes used by network professionals worldwide, as well as government investigative agencies, Internet sales representatives, Telecom Engineers, and home users. With over two million downloads to date, Neotrace has proven to be the world's leading high-speed Internet tracer tool.

NTFSDOS Professional Evaluation

from Winternals Software LP

Boot off an MS-DOS diskette and have full access to your NTFS drives. Unlike previous NTFSDOS releases, this tool provides full read/write capability, including CHKDSK support. MS-DOS programs can run on and access NTFS drives just as they do FAT drives. You can use it as a system repair tool to add, update, or delete files that prevent your NT system from booting. It is also useful for automating your NT rollouts.

Ostrosoft Internet Tools Evaluation Version

from Ostrosoft

Ostrosoft Internet Tools is an integrated set of network information utilities. It is intended for use by network, domain, and systems administrators, network security professionals, Internet users, and everyone who wants to know more about networks and the Internet. It helps to find hidden resources on networks. It reveals security holes and helps to fix them. It is fast, reliable, and user-friendly.

Process View

from Spytech Software and Design

Spytech Process View 2.0 is ideal for active file management. Process View 2.0 is, at its heart, a fired-up Windows task window. Process 2.0 enables you to view all the currently running applications (tasks/processes) on the machine and gives you the option of terminating those tasks. This is ideal for hung applications that are frozen on your screen and are not responding. The Process View 2.0 task killer responds and works instantly.

Remote Recover Evaluation

from Winternals Software LP

Remote Recover enables you to access NTFS (and FAT) drives across your network, without needing to run NT or even have it installed on the machines you want to access. It enables you to salvage critical data from dead machines or restore systems from backup with ease.

Remote Task Manager Shareware

from SmartLine, Inc.

An easy-to-use tool with a handy interface that enables you to manage tasks, processes, services, and events on remote computers. RTM is a perfect tool for network administrators who want to control tasks, processes, services, and events on user workstations from their own computer.

RippleTech LogCaster Trial Version

from Ripple Technologies, Inc.

RippleTech LogCaster® is an NT Systems Management software that monitors events, services, network devices, performance counters, ASCII logs, applications, and security parameters.

Rosenthal Utilities

from Rosenthal Engineering

A collection of system utilities such as System Support, Diagnostic, Maintenance, Uninstall, and Security Audits. A "must have" collection of software that has won top honors!

Spynet Firewall

from Spytech Software and Design

Spynet Firewall 2.0 is an easy-to-use, configurable IP firewall. The firewall keeps outside users from connecting to the protected ports on your PC. It is useful against outside attacks from users of malicious Trojans.

Spynet NetAdmin

from Spytech Software and Design

Spynet NetAdmin 2.0 is an easy-to-use, extremely powerful remote administration software suite. With NetAdmin servers installed on your local area network, the administrator can easily monitor each individual remote machine. Among monitoring options available are real-time keystroke logging, process viewing and killing, open window manager, remote file navigation, remote user idle time, two-way chat with the remote machine, remote system and drive information, mouse freeze/unfreeze, system shutdown/restart/logoff/lockup, and much, much more!

Spytech SpyEncrypt

from Spytech Software and Design

Spytech SpyEncrypt 2.0 enables you to quickly and easily encrypt and decrypt personal files to prevent outside users from viewing them. SypEncrypt works on all file types: application, document, images, and so on. SpyEncrypt is the perfect solution for quick file encryption and security.

System Mechanic Evaluation Version

from Iolo Technologies

Keep your PC running faster, cleaner, and error-free with System Mechanic's full suite of 10 powerful tools. Hunt down and remove junk and obsolete files and drivers.

VMWare for Windows NT and Windows 2000 Evaluation Version

from Vmware, Inc.

VMWare is software that runs multiple virtual computers on a single PC at the same time without partitioning or rebooting. VMWare features undoable virtual disks, full networking, sound, and multimedia support. It's like having another computer (or computers) inside your PC, and more.

WinZip

from Nico Mak Computing, Inc.

WinZip brings the convenience of Windows to the use of Zip files and other archive and compression formats. The optional wizard interface makes unzipping easier than ever. WinZip features built-in support CAB files and for popular Internet file formats such as TAR, gzip, UUencode, BinHex, and MIME. ARJ, LZH, and ARC files are supported via external programs. WinZip interfaces to most virus scanners.

Yes2K NT Evaluation Version

from SafetyNet, Inc.

It installs as a device driver and pierces the HAL, enabling it to view and detect hardware date problems on Windows and DOS. Automatically fixes noncompliant hardware.

Part

VI

App

C

Index

X-Z

Other Related Titles

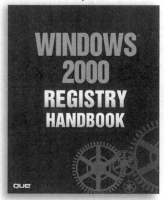

Exam Guide

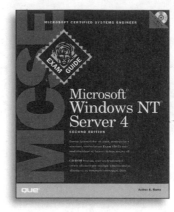

Windows NT 4.0 Server Exam Guide
Emmett Dulaney
0-7897-2264-x
$39.99 US/
$57.95 CAN

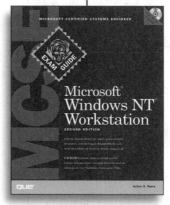

Windows NT 4.0 Workstation Exam Guide
Emmett Dulaney
0-7897-2262-3
$39.99 US/
$57.95 CAN

LPIC Linux Level 1 Test 1 Exam Guide
Theresa Hadden
0-7897-2292-5
$39.99 US/
$57.95 CAN

All prices are subject to change.